Stop

YOU'RE READING
THE WRONG WAY!

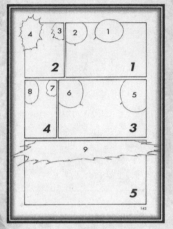

BLACK CLOVER
reads from right to left, starting
in the upper-right corner. Japanese
is read from right to left, meaning
that action, sound effects, and
word-balloon order are completely
reversed from English order.

THE ACTION-PACKED SUPERHERO COMEDY ABOUT ONE MAN'S AMBITION TO BE A HERO FOR FUN!

ONE-PUNCH MAN

STORY BY
ONE | ART BY
YUSUKE MURATA

Nothing about Saitama passes the eyeball test when it comes to superheroes, from his lifeless expression to his bald head to his unimpressive physique. However, this average-looking guy has a not-so-average problem—he just can't seem to find an opponent strong enough to take on!

Can he finally find an opponent who can go toe-to-toe with him and give his life some meaning? Or is he doomed to a life of superpowered boredom?

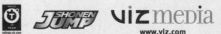

www.viz.com

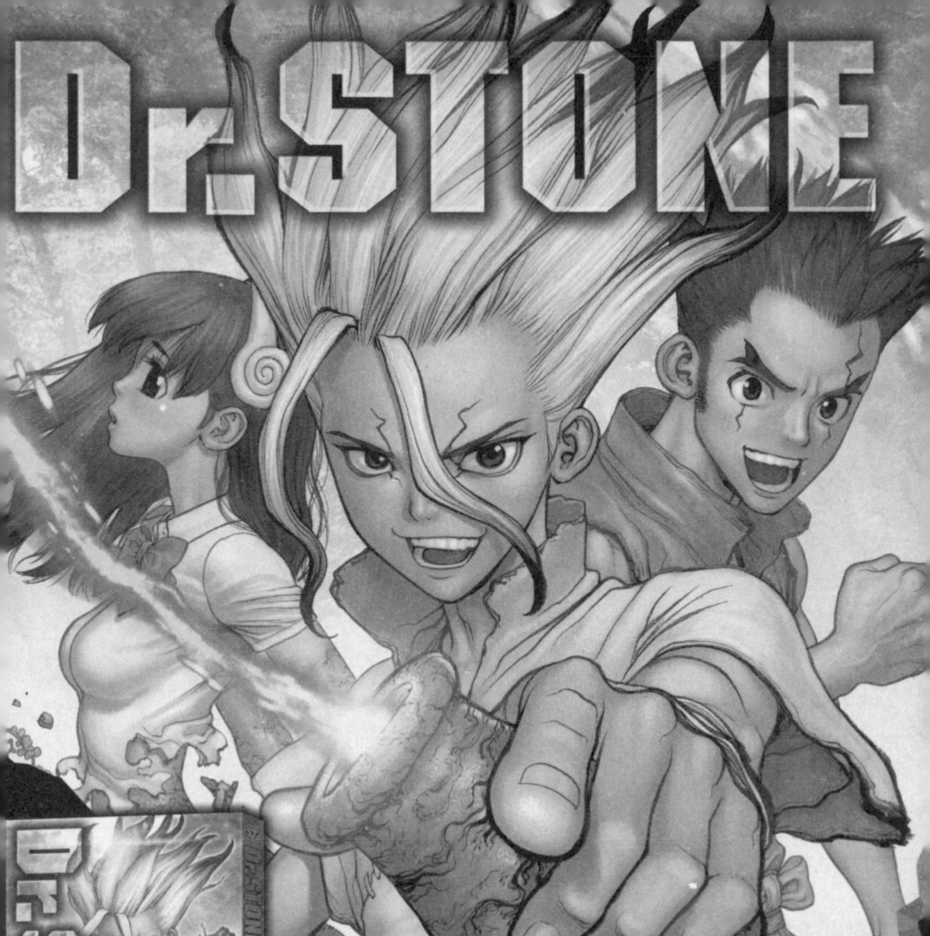

Dr. STONE

STORY BY
RIICHIRO INAGAKI

ART BY
BOICHI

One fateful day, all of humanity turned to stone. Many millennia later, Taiju frees himself from petrification and finds himself surrounded by statues. The situation looks grim—until he runs into his science-loving friend Senku! Together they plan to restart civilization with the power of science!

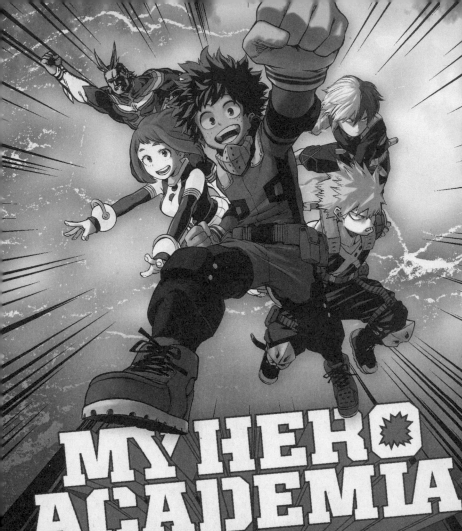

MY HERO ACADEMIA

IZUKU MIDORIYA WANTS TO BE A HERO MORE THAN ANYTHING, BUT HE HASN'T GOT AN OUNCE OF POWER IN HIM. WITH NO CHANCE OF GETTING INTO THE U.A. HIGH SCHOOL FOR HEROES, HIS LIFE IS LOOKING LIKE A DEAD END. THEN AN ENCOUNTER WITH ALL MIGHT, THE GREATEST HERO OF ALL, GIVES HIM A CHANCE TO CHANGE HIS DESTINY...

viz media

www.viz.com

ASTRA
LOST IN SPACE

CAN EIGHT TEENAGERS FIND THEIR WAY HOME FROM 5,000 LIGHT-YEARS AWAY?

It's the year 2063, and interstellar space travel has become the norm. Eight students from Caird High School and one child set out on a routine planet camp excursion. While there, the students are mysteriously transported 5,000 light-years away to the middle of nowhere! Will they ever make it back home?!

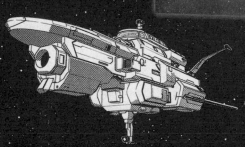

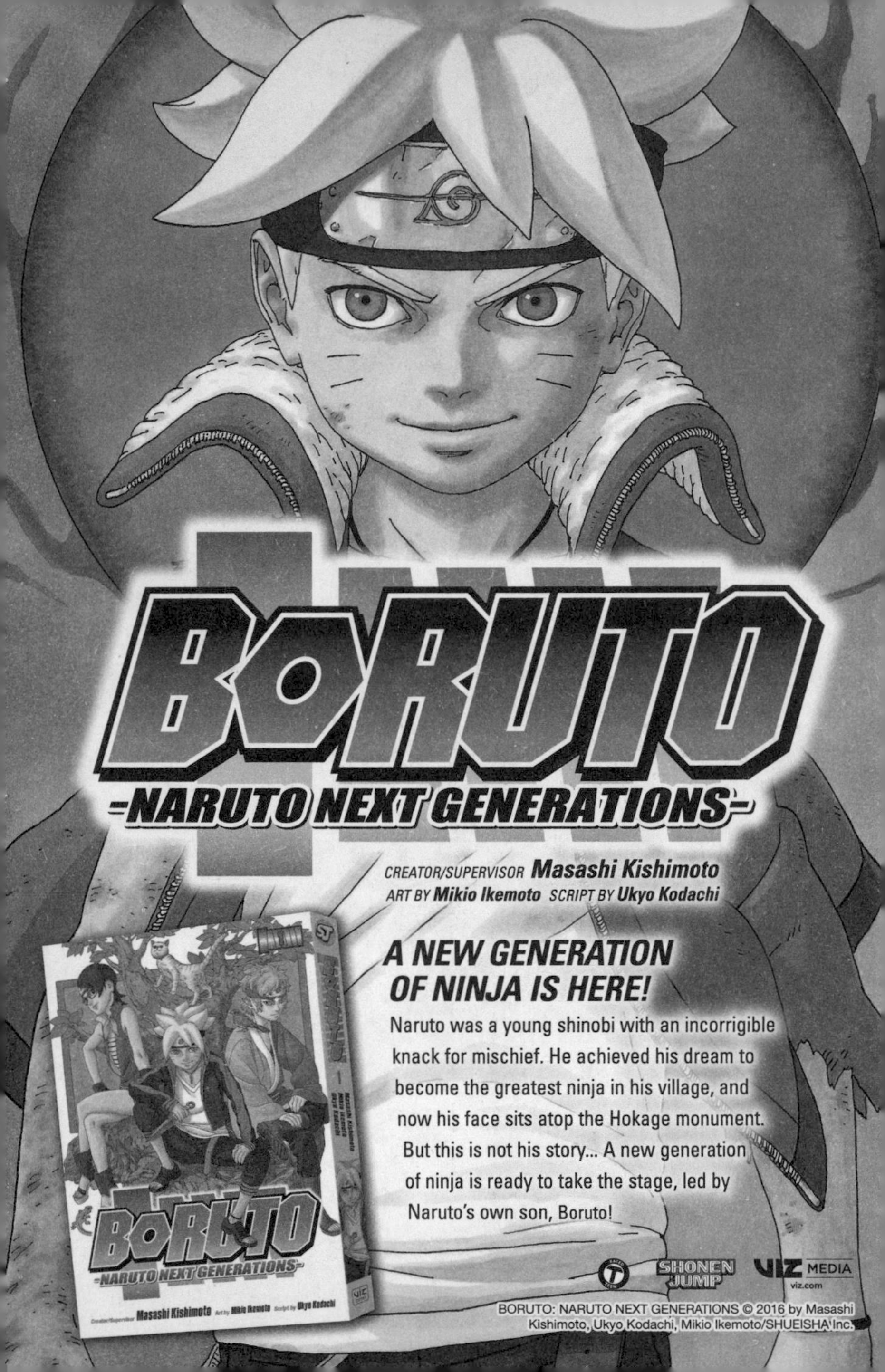

BORUTO
-NARUTO NEXT GENERATIONS-
CREATOR/SUPERVISOR Masashi Kishimoto
ART BY Mikio Ikemoto SCRIPT BY Ukyo Kodachi
A NEW GENERATION OF NINJA IS HERE!
Naruto was a young shinobi with an incorrigible knack for mischief. He achieved his dream to become the greatest ninja in his village, and now his face sits atop the Hokage monument. But this is not his story... A new generation of ninja is ready to take the stage, led by Naruto's own son, Boruto!
BORUTO
-NARUTO NEXT GENERATIONS-
Masashi Kishimoto
SHONEN JUMP
VIZ MEDIA
viz.com
BORUTO: NARUTO NEXT GENERATIONS © 2016 by Masashi Kishimoto, Ukyo Kodachi, Mikio Ikemoto/SHUEISHA Inc.

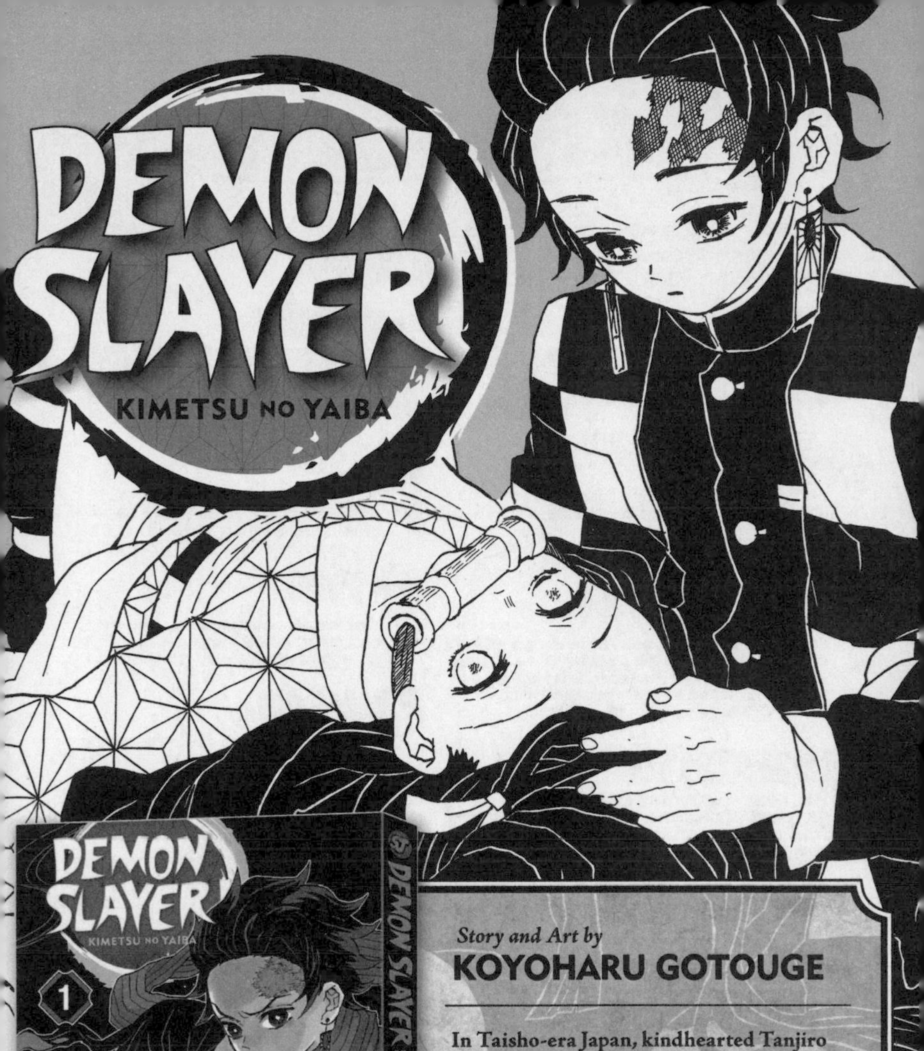

DEMON SLAYER

KIMETSU NO YAIBA

Story and Art by
KOYOHARU GOTOUGE

In Taisho-era Japan, kindhearted Tanjiro Kamado makes a living selling charcoal. But his peaceful life is shattered when a demon slaughters his entire family. His little sister Nezuko is the only survivor, but she has been transformed into a demon herself! Tanjiro sets out on a dangerous journey to find a way to return his sister to normal and destroy the demon who ruined his life.

DEMON SLAYER
KIMETSU NO YAIBA
1
Story and Art by
KOYOHARU GOTOUGE

RATED TEEN

VIZ

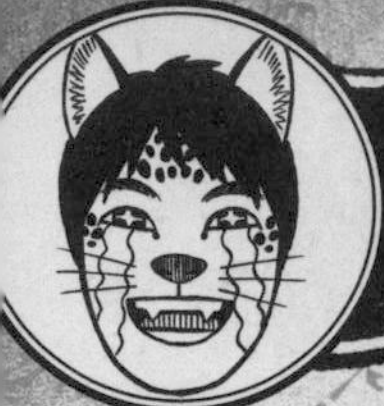

Editor Iwasaki's Tearful Graduation Brigade

An editor switch was conducted behind the scenes during volume 25's production! We've condensed Editor Iwasaki's thoughts on *Black Clover* into this one page!!

With Tabata Sensei! Top Three Unforgettable Memories

1 The days we spent watching his daughter's angelic sleeping face together

Even now, I remember how Tabata Sensei and I forgot about our work meeting and just gazed at his daughter's face, smiling, as she slept peacefully. (Three minutes later, we realized "We have to actually work!!")

2 The pizza I ate with Tabata Sensei and his wife after the chapter was done

While working on a chapter, we're always chasing deadlines and the days are hectic. After the pages were turned in, I had pizza with Tabata Sensei and his wife and happily thought, "What a peaceful place this is."

3 Deadlines and days spent fighting the sandman

With weekly serials, every week is a battle against deadlines. What's the most interesting thing we can produce for the readers during that limited time? It was Tabata Sensei's warm personality that made it possible for me to give it my best too.

Editor Iwasaki's Top Three Characters

1 Asta

No matter what, Asta's in first place!! No matter how hard things get, he never gives up. As both a reader and an editor, he's given me courage again and again.

2 Yami

Yami is funny and way too cool!! When he was in a scene, I'd always get really hyped up, wondering what he'd do next!

3 Zenon

He's a character who started appearing after I'd taken over as editor, and my feelings about him are pretty intense! Even though he's an enemy, I was charmed by that cool flair of his!

Black Clover was the first manga I got to be in charge of! It was a manga I'd read all along and really loved, and I remember being incredibly happy. Since it was my first time, there was way too much I didn't know, but Tabata Sensei and the *Black Clover* family welcomed me warmly! I'm no longer the supervising editor, but from now on I'll look forward to what happens in *Black Clover* as a reader!! In closing...thank you for everything, Tabata Sensei!!!

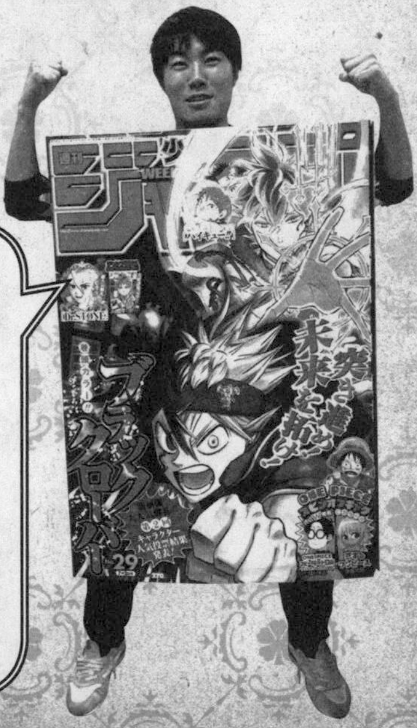

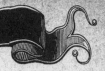

The Blank

This volume's topic:
Your three favorite
TV dramas.

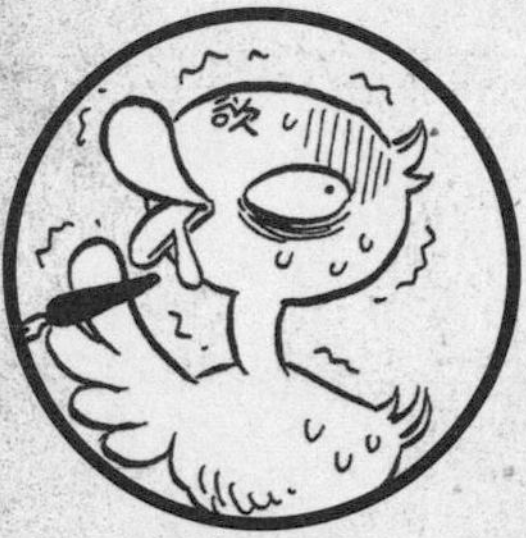

1. Ikebukuro West Gate Park
2. Kisarazu Cats-Eye
3. Lovely

Captain Tabata

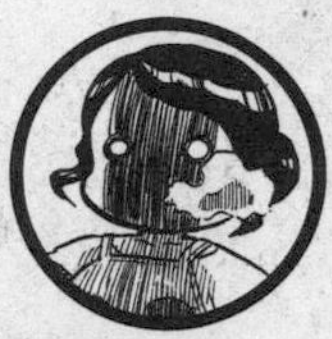

1. Watermelon
2. Thanks for the Food
3. What Did You Eat Yesterday?

©

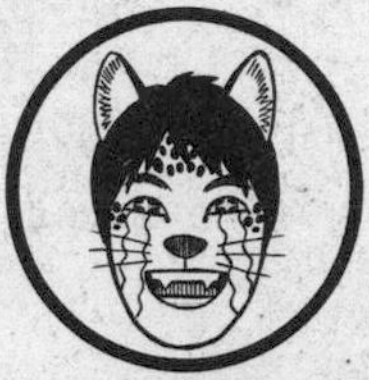

1. Operation: Proposal
2. Pride
3. Rich Man, Poor Woman

Editor Iwasaki

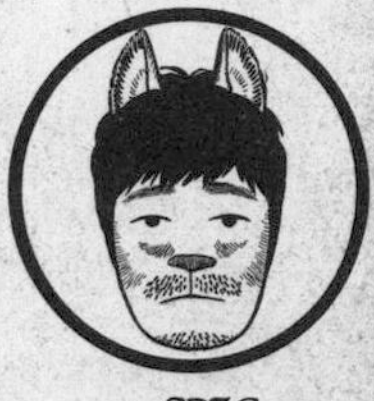

1. SPEC
2. JIN-Humanity
3. Hanzawa Naoki

Comics editor Fujiwara

AFTERWORD

Farewell, Editor Iwasaki!!!

Iwasaki is the sort of agreeable young guy you just don't see these days. He's such an extremely good person, so this lightning-fast editor change makes me sad and kinda lonely...

He watched over my baby daughter's growth every week, and "If this keeps up, he might end up being her first love" was a thought that concerned me.

Hang on... Looking back, I realize I forgot to write a comment here when my previous editor Toide left...

Both Toide and Iwasaki, thank you very much!!!

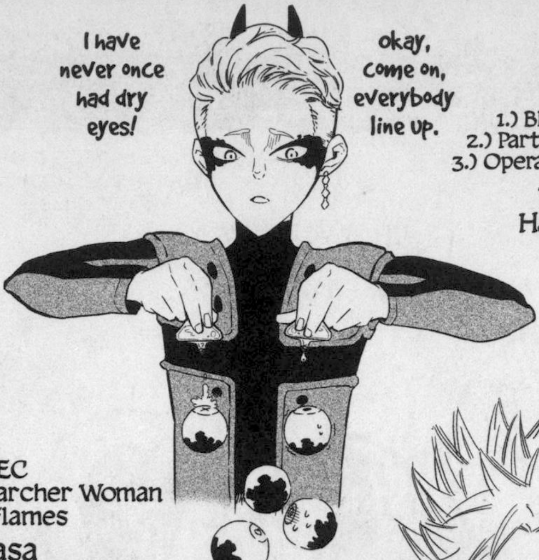
okay, come on, everybody line up.
I have never once had dry eyes!

1.) Blue Flames
2.) Partner Season 4
3.) Operation: Proposal

Yōtarō Hayakawa

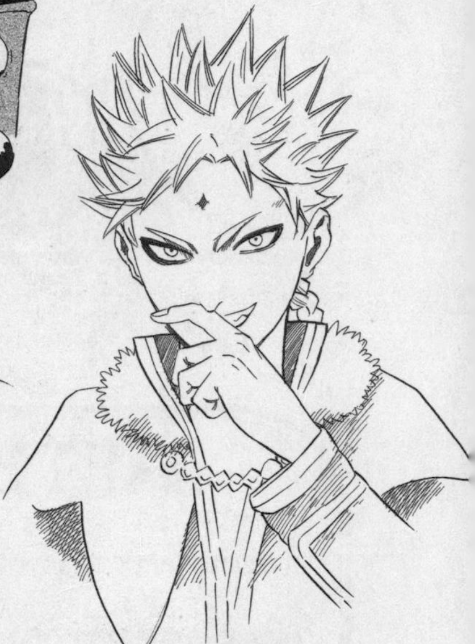

1. Water Boys
2. Galileo
3. For You in Full Blossom ~ Handsome Guy Paradise ~

Kazuhiro Wakao

1. SPEC
2. Forensic Researcher Woman
3. Blue Flames

Yagasa

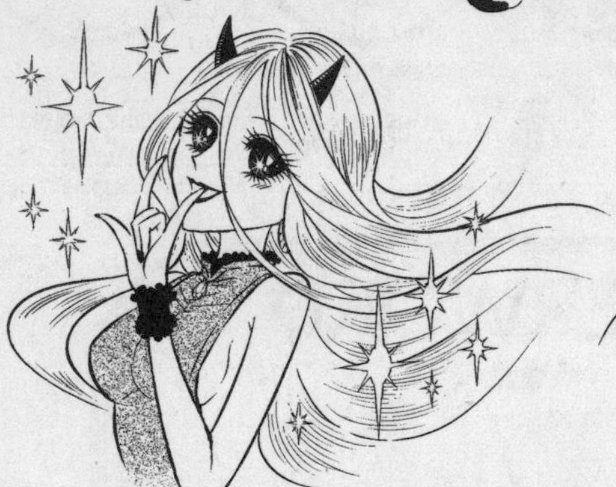

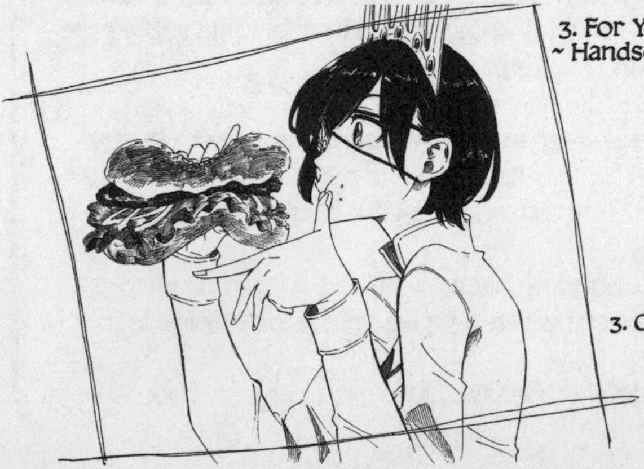

1. Legal High
2. Gokusen
3. Operation: Proposal

Hayato Gotō

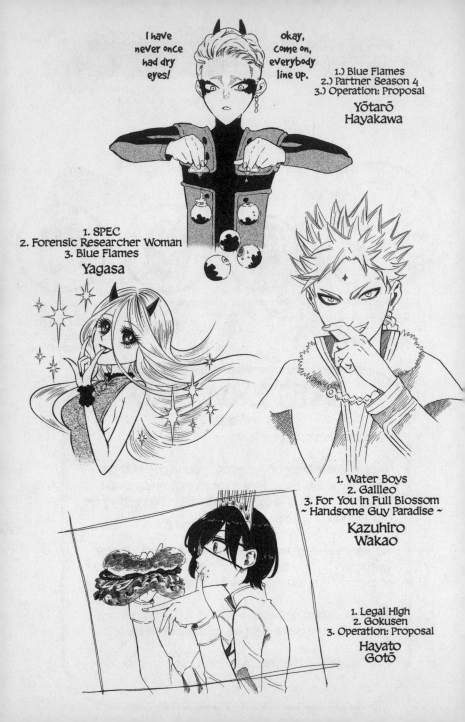

The Blank Page Brigade

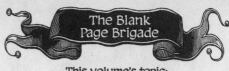

This volume's topic:
Your three favorite
TV dramas.

1. Legal High
2. My☆Boss, My☆Hero
3. Kyoko Okitegami's Notes

Masayoshi
Satoshō

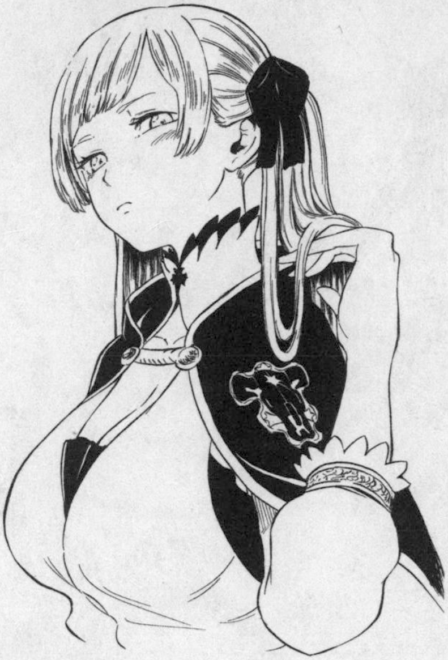

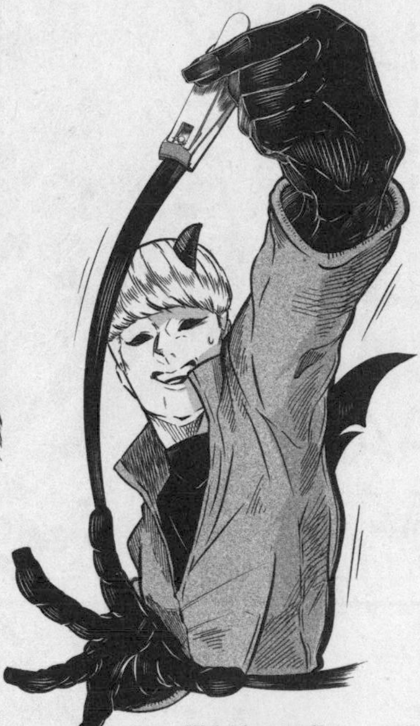

1. JIN-Humanity
2. Nodame Cantabile
3. Legal High

Sōta
Hishikawa

IF BIG BRO DANTE HAD AN ARTISTIC SIDE

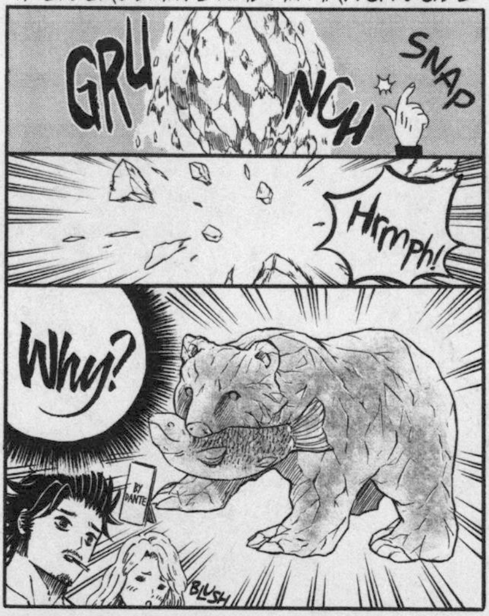
SNAP
GRUNCH
Hrmph!
Why?
BY DANTE
BLUSH

1.) Blue Flames
2.) Masked Rider Den-O
3.) Legendary Teacher

Seiya
Miyamoto

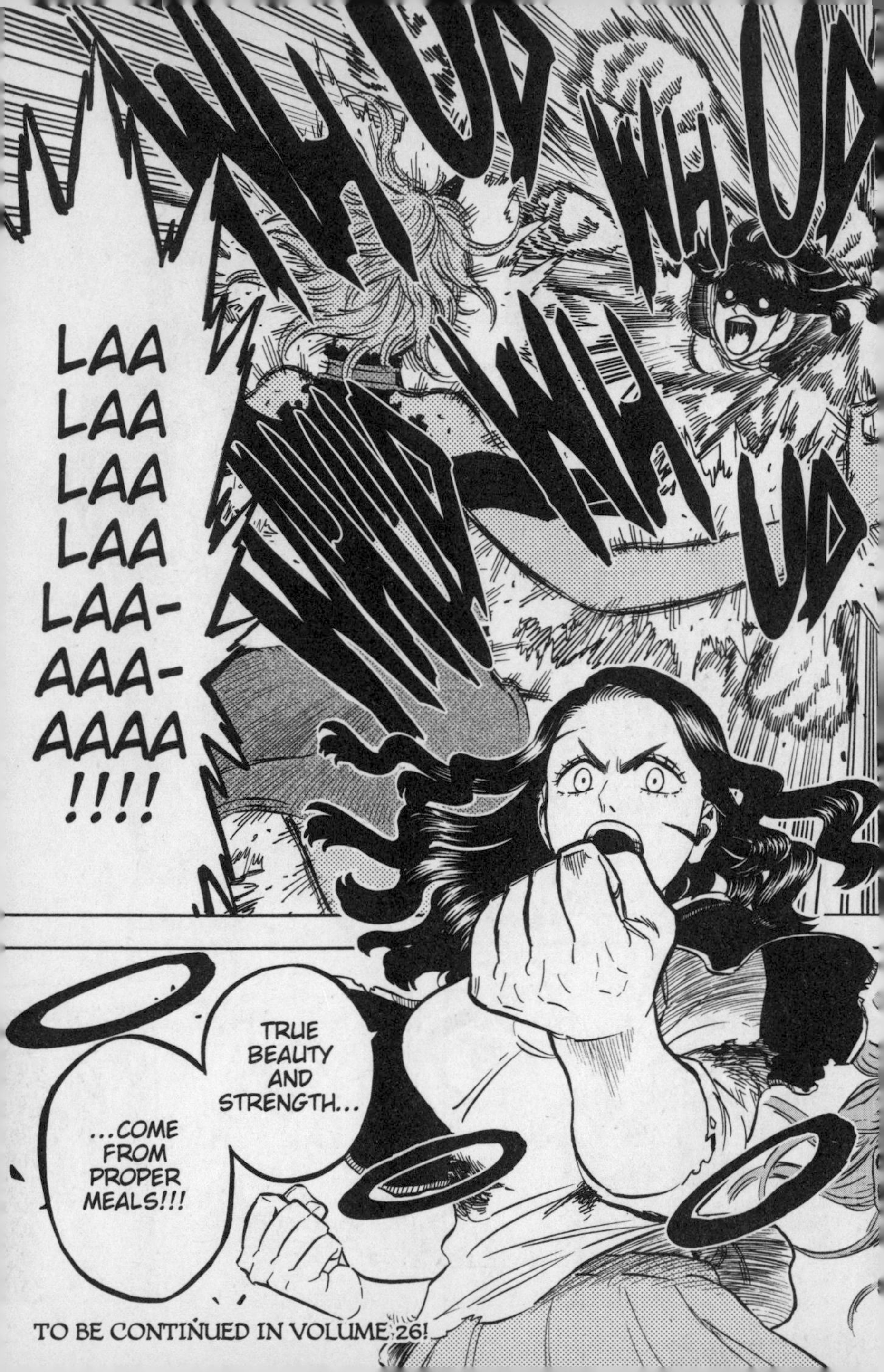
LAA LAA LAA LAA LAA-AAA-AAAA!!!!
TRUE BEAUTY AND STRENGTH... ...COME FROM PROPER MEALS!!!
TO BE CONTINUED IN VOLUME 26!

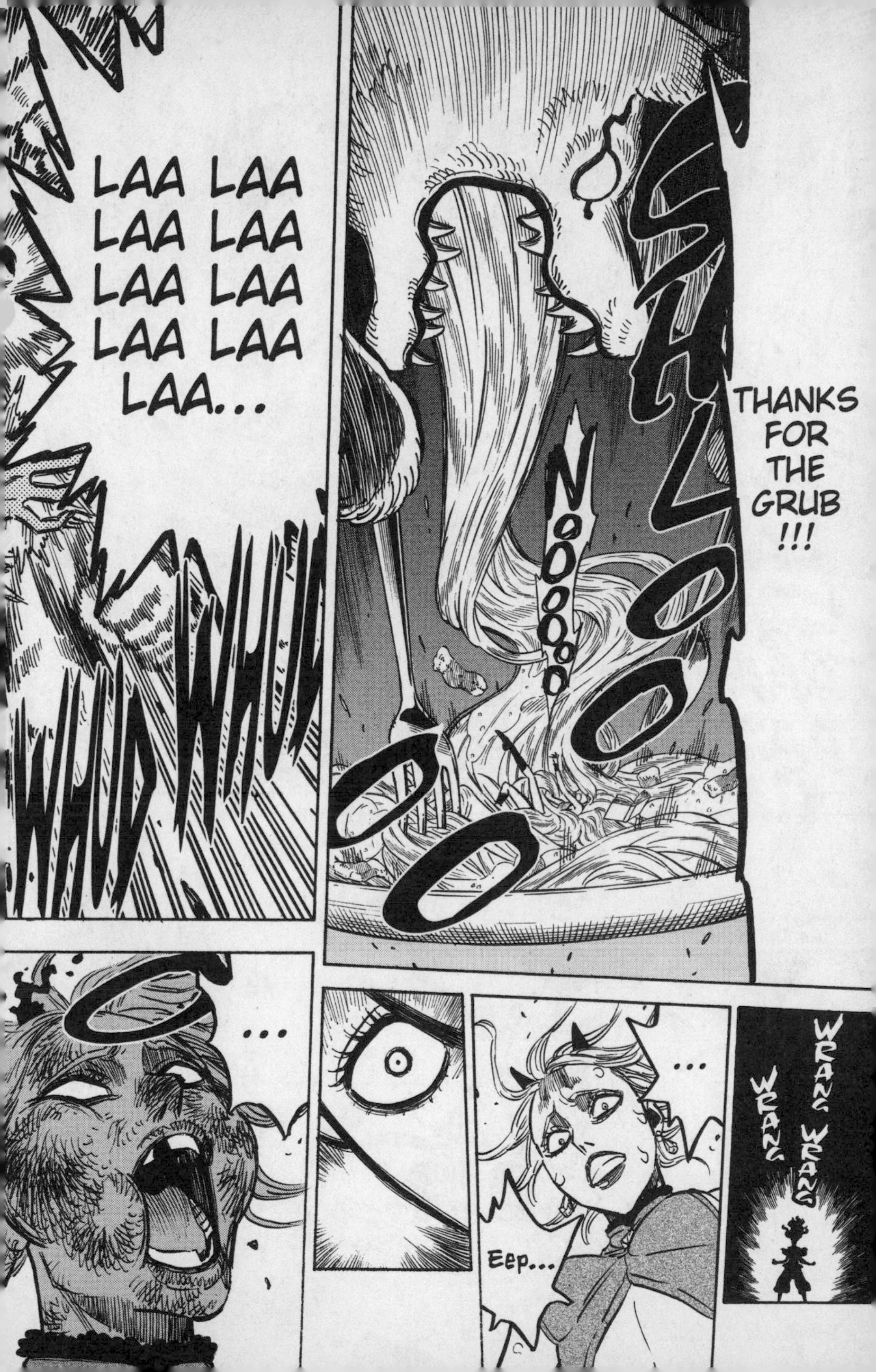
THANKS FOR THE GRUB!!!
NOOOOOOO
LAA LAA LAA LAA LAA LAA LAA LAA LAA...
WRANG WRANG
WRANG WRANG
...
Eep...
...

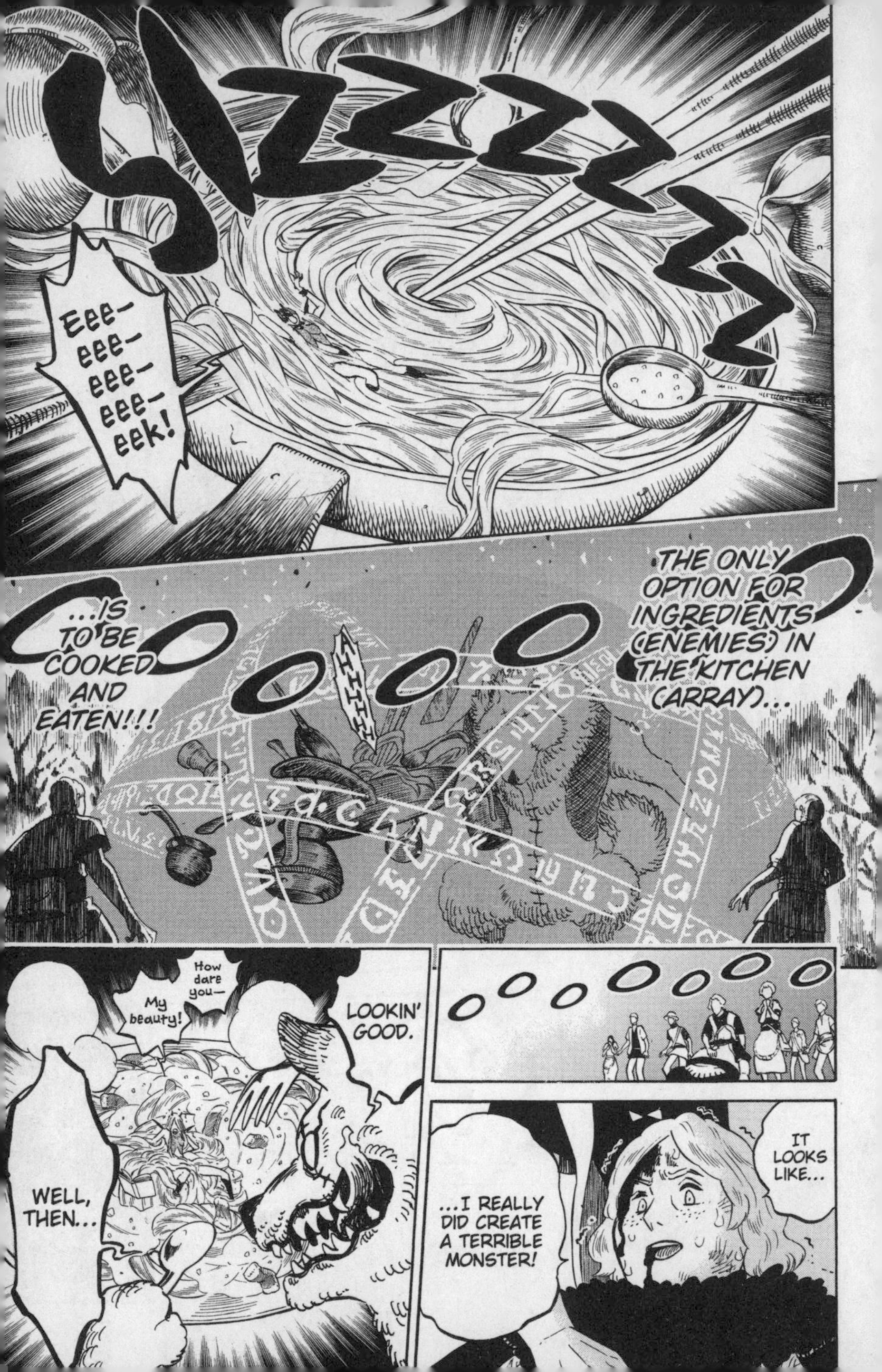
Eee-eee-eee-eee-eek!
THE ONLY OPTION FOR INGREDIENTS (ENEMIES) IN THE KITCHEN (ARRAY)...
...IS TO BE COOKED AND EATEN!!!
AHHHHH
IT LOOKS LIKE...
...I REALLY DID CREATE A TERRIBLE MONSTER!
LOOKIN' GOOD.
How dare you—
My beauty!
WELL, THEN...

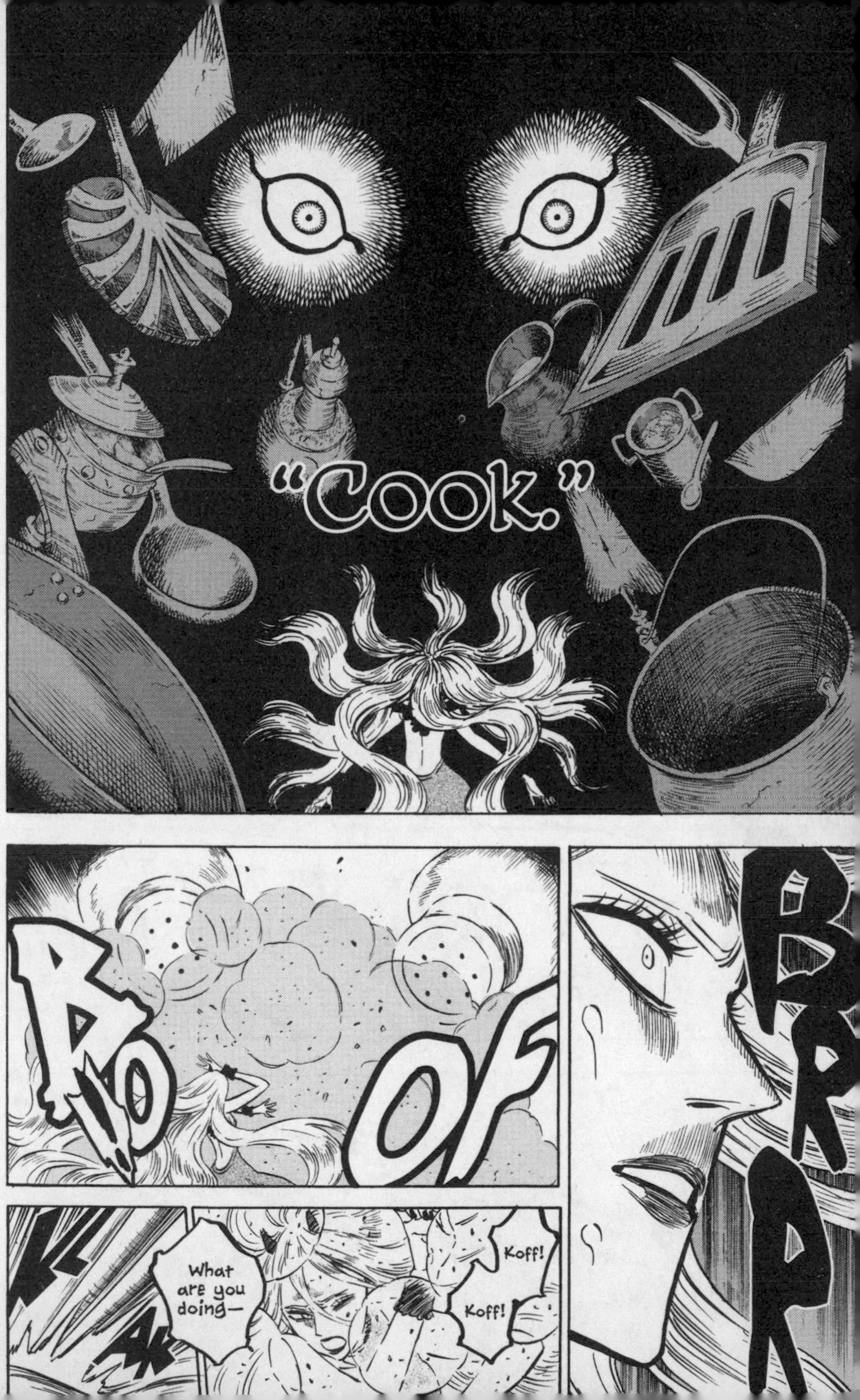
"Cook."
Koff!
What are you doing—
Koff!

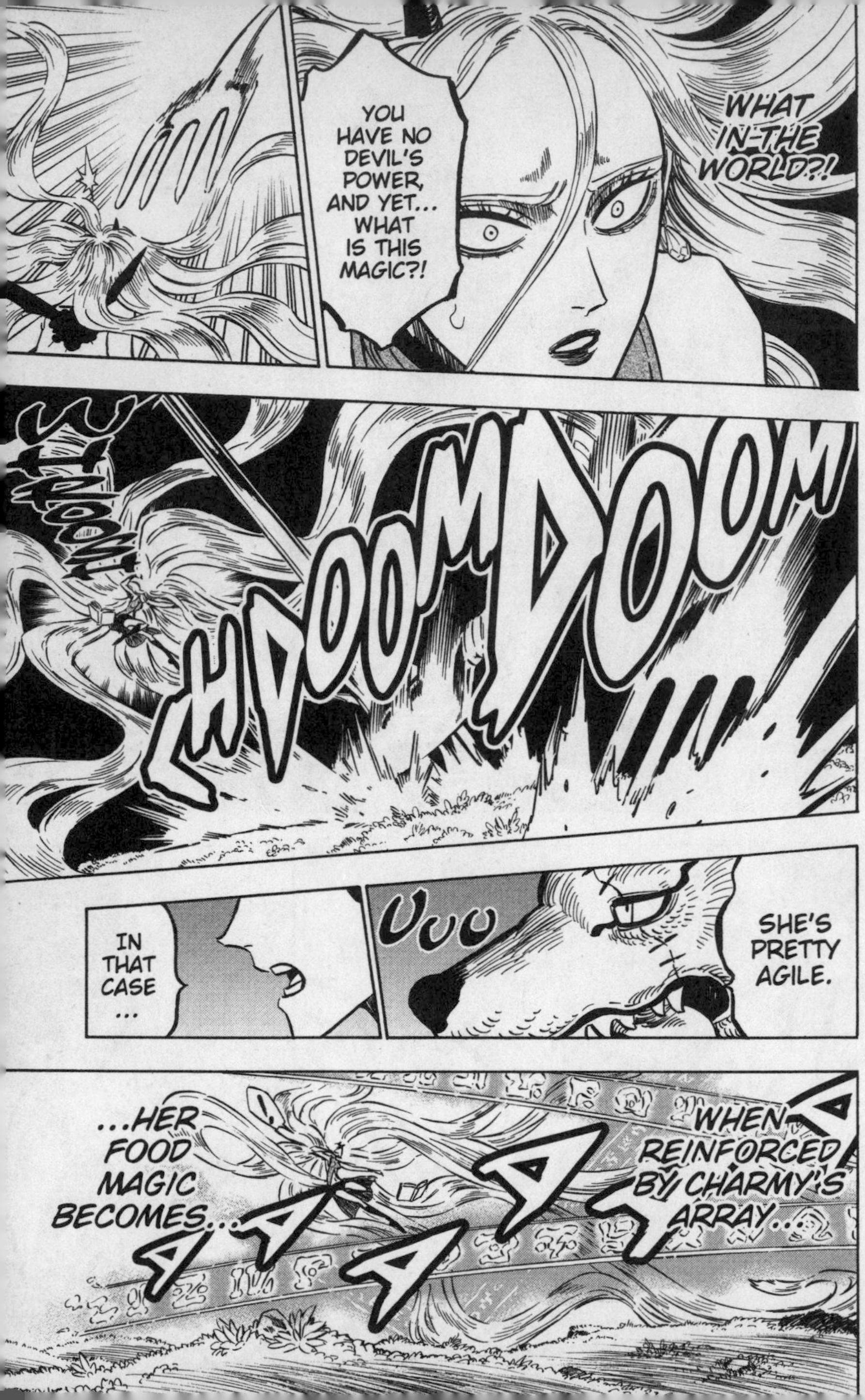
WHAT IN THE WORLD?!
YOU HAVE NO DEVIL'S POWER, AND YET... WHAT IS THIS MAGIC?!
THDOOM
DOOM
FWOOSH
SHE'S PRETTY AGILE.
IN THAT CASE...
WHEN REINFORCED BY CHARMY'S ARRAY...
...HER FOOD MAGIC BECOMES...
AAAAAAA

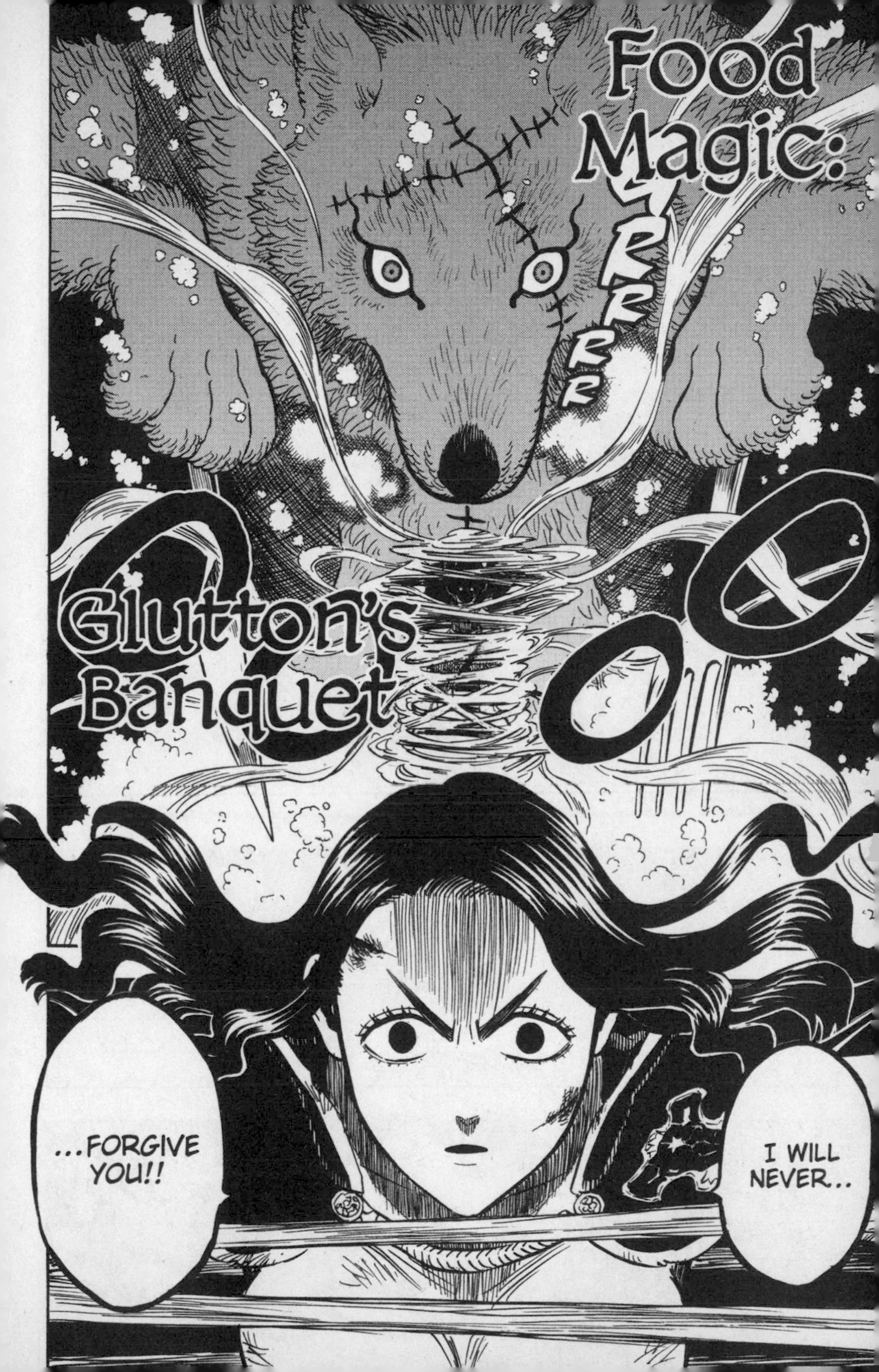
Food Magic:
Glutton's Banquet
I WILL NEVER...
...FORGIVE YOU!!

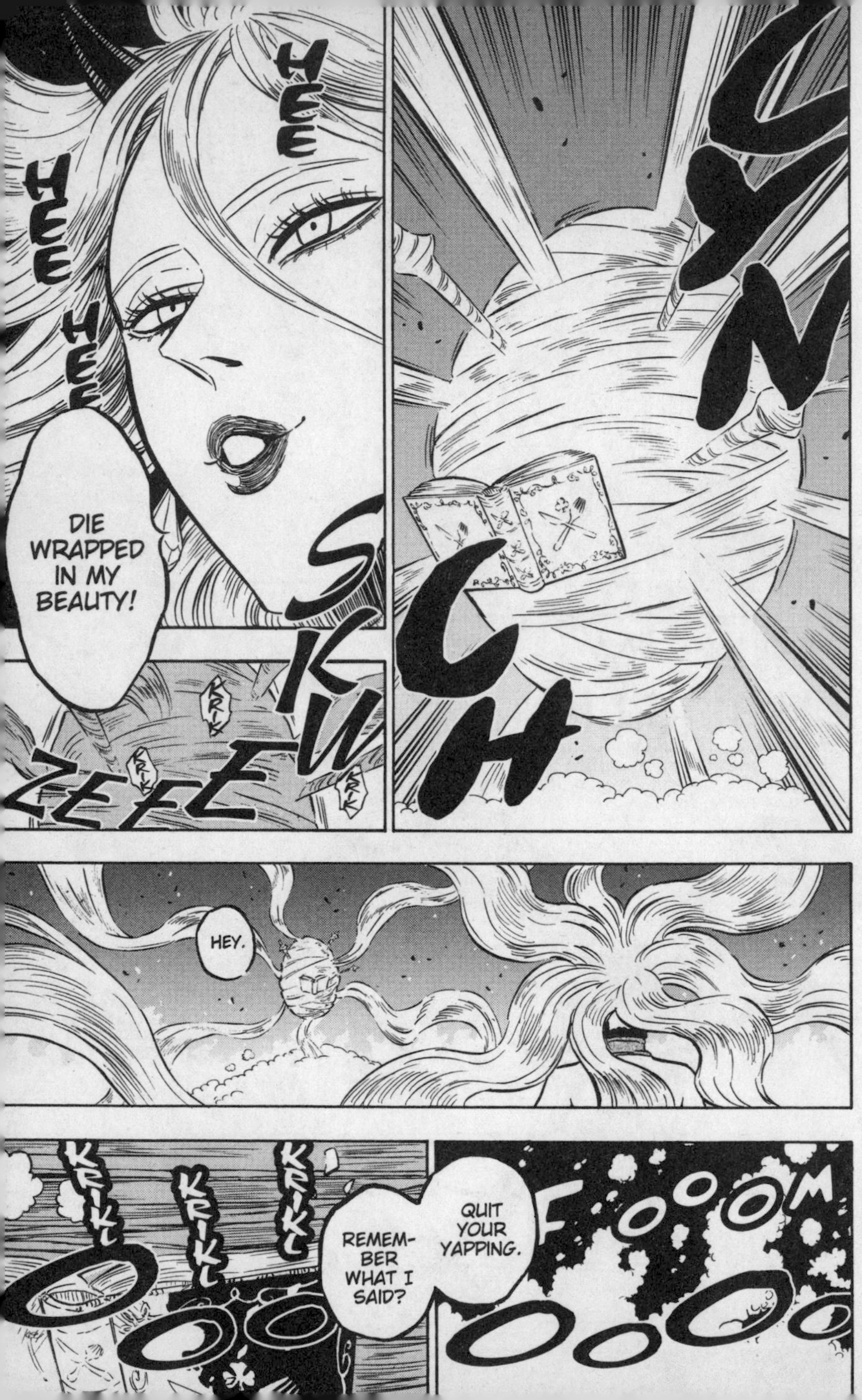
HEE HEE
HEE HEE
DIE WRAPPED IN MY BEAUTY!
SKWEEZE
KRIK
KRIK
KRIK
HEY.
FOOOOM
QUIT YOUR YAPPING.
REMEMBER WHAT I SAID?
KRIKL
KRIKL
KRIKL

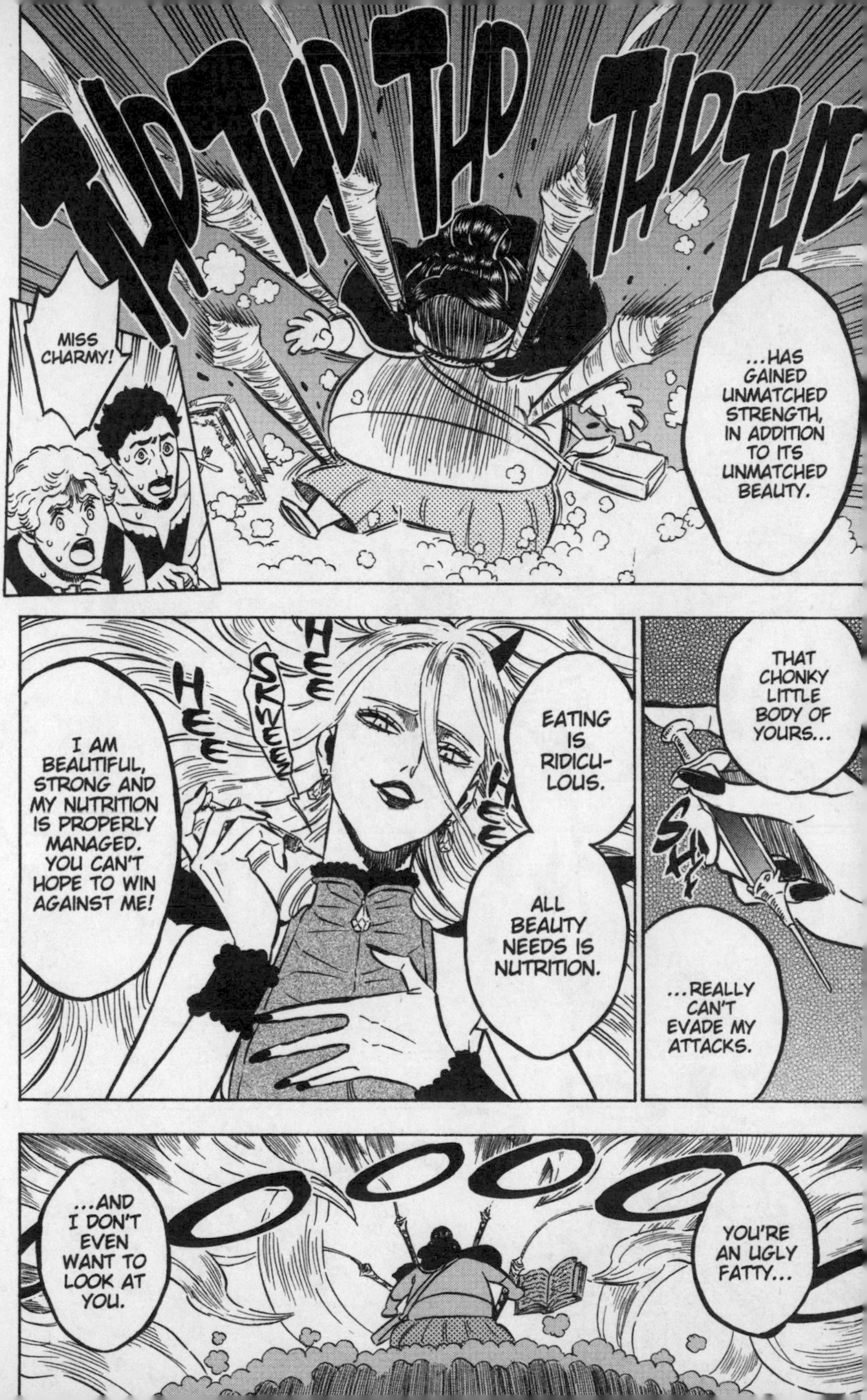
THD THD THD THD THD
...HAS GAINED UNMATCHED STRENGTH, IN ADDITION TO ITS UNMATCHED BEAUTY.
MISS CHARMY!
THAT CHONKY LITTLE BODY OF YOURS...
...REALLY CAN'T EVADE MY ATTACKS.
EATING IS RIDICULOUS.
HEE
SKWEE
HEE
HEE
ALL BEAUTY NEEDS IS NUTRITION.
I AM BEAUTIFUL, STRONG AND MY NUTRITION IS PROPERLY MANAGED. YOU CAN'T HOPE TO WIN AGAINST ME!
YOU'RE AN UGLY FATTY...
...AND I DON'T EVEN WANT TO LOOK AT YOU.

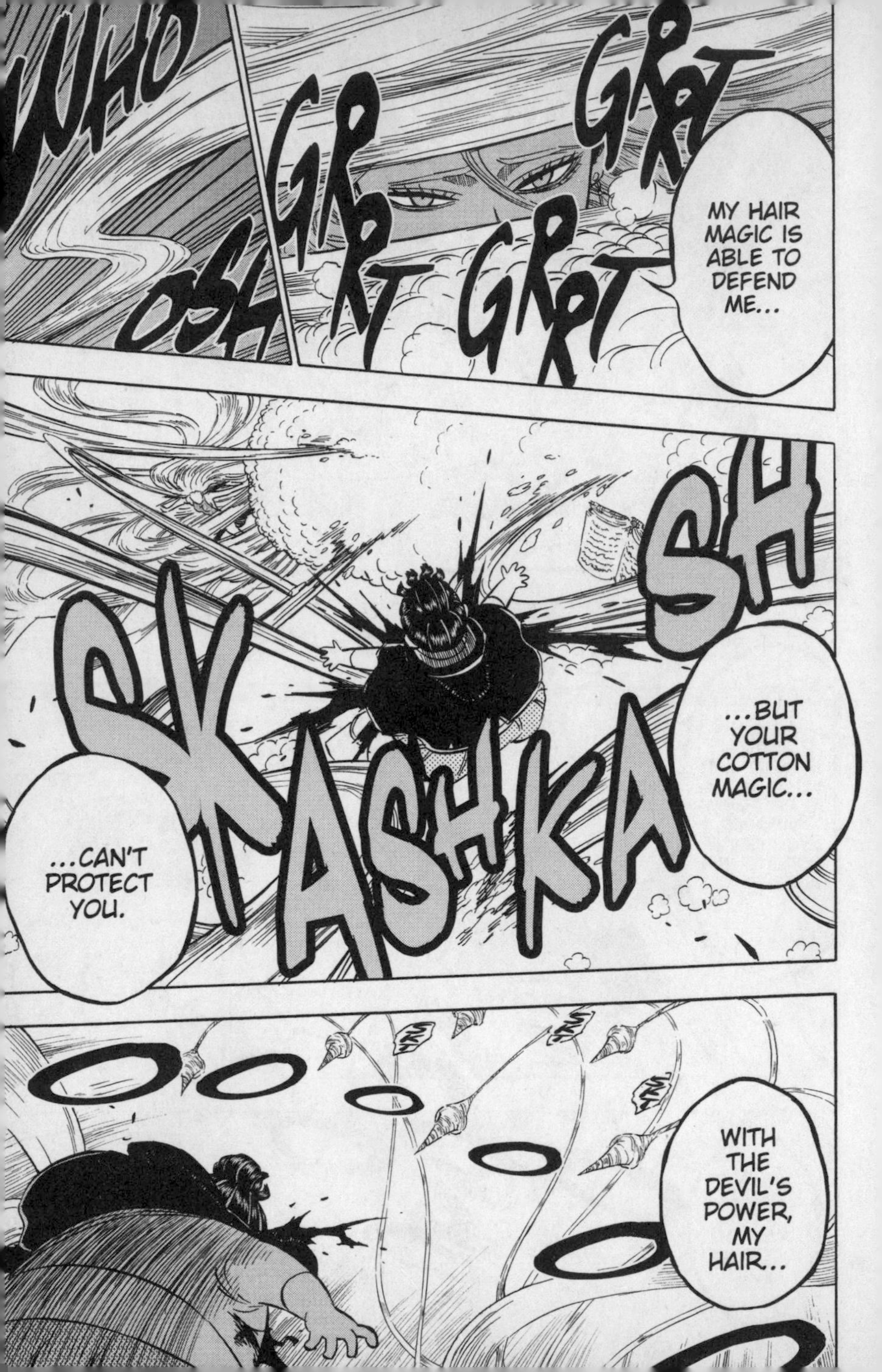
GRRT GRRT
GRRT GRRT
MY HAIR MAGIC IS ABLE TO DEFEND ME...
WHOOSH
...BUT YOUR COTTON MAGIC...
SKASHKASH
...CAN'T PROTECT YOU.
WITH THE DEVIL'S POWER, MY HAIR...

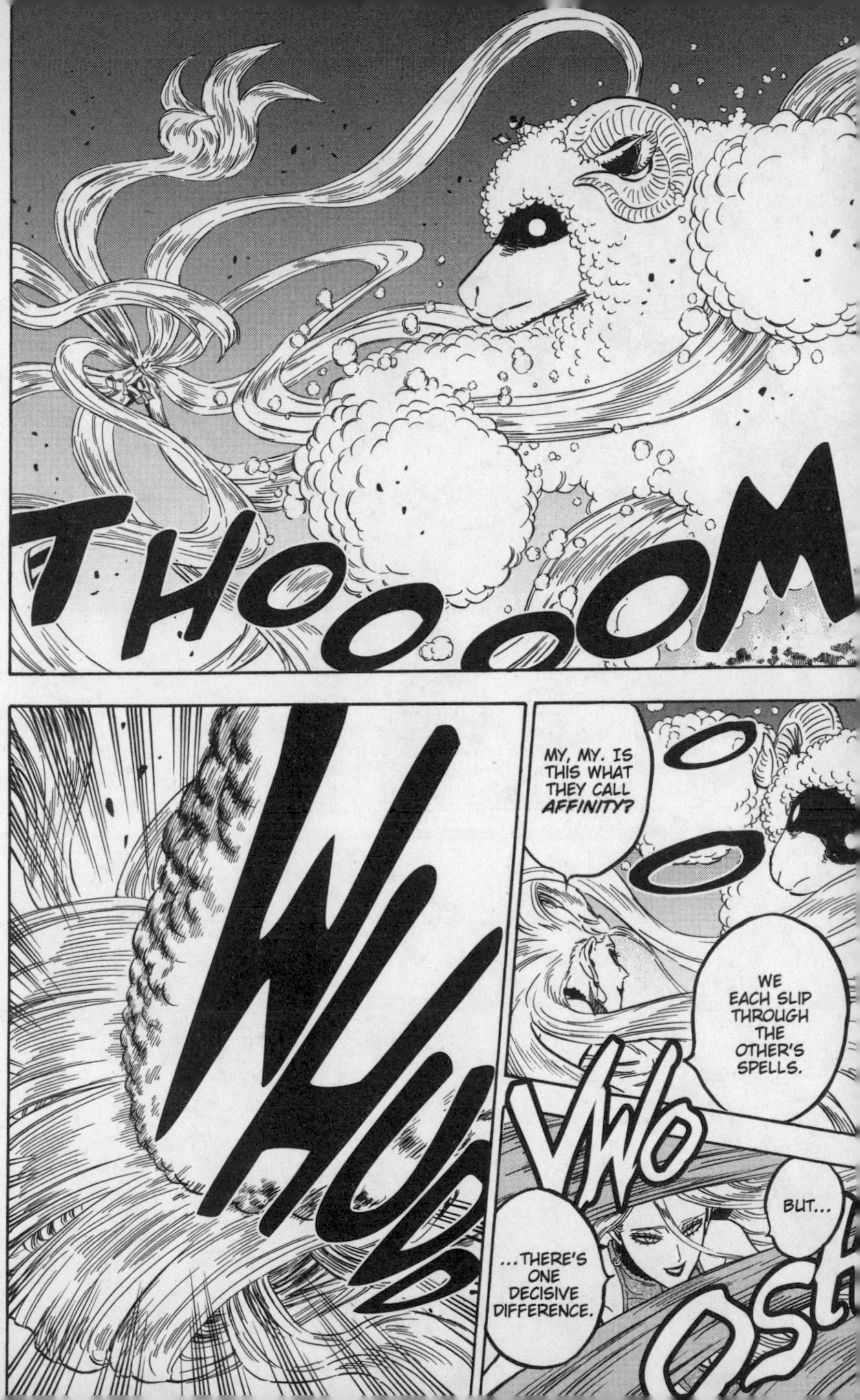
THOOOOOM
MY, MY. IS THIS WHAT THEY CALL *AFFINITY?*
WE EACH SLIP THROUGH THE OTHER'S SPELLS.
BUT...
...THERE'S ONE DECISIVE DIFFERENCE.

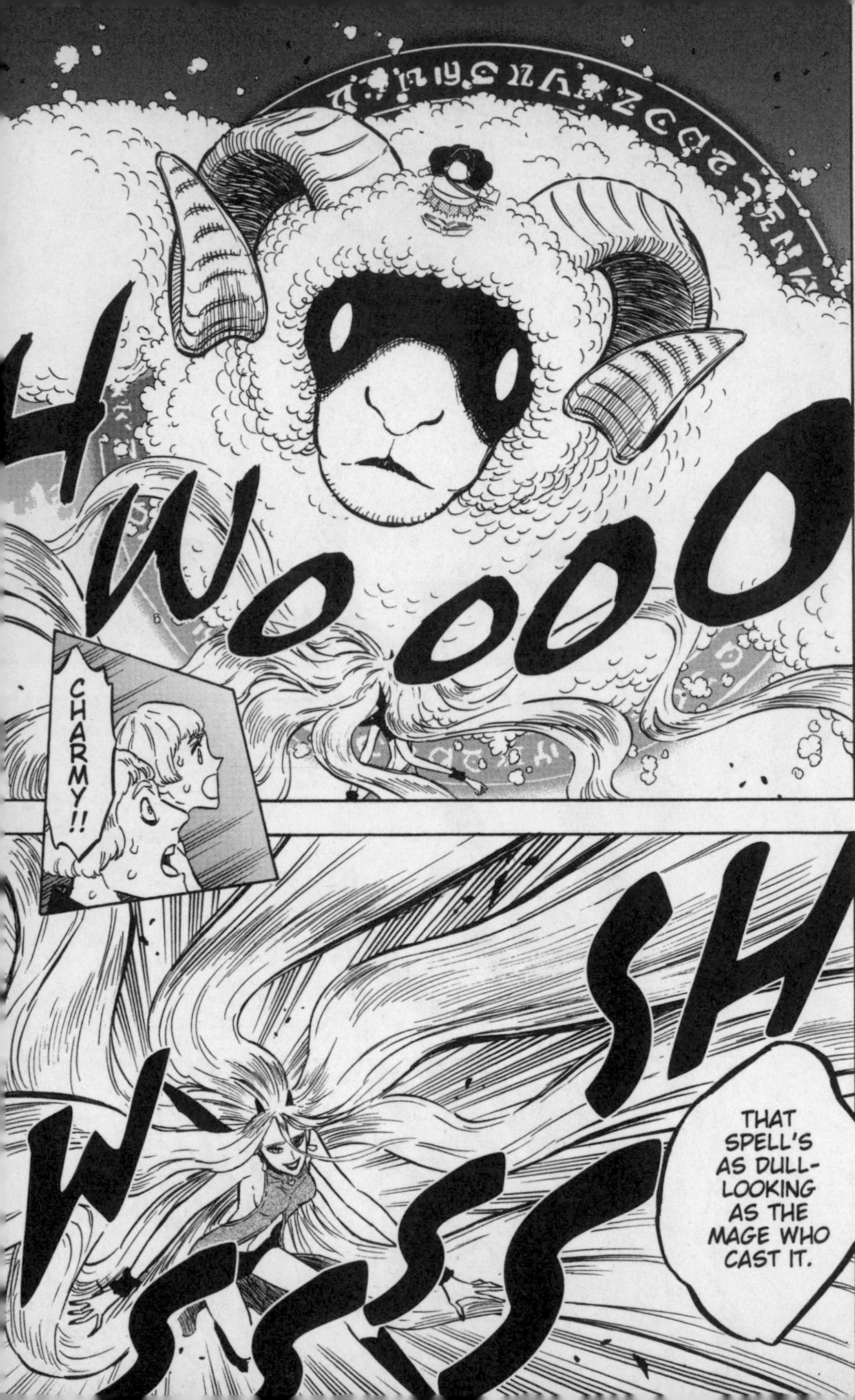
WHOOOO
CHARMY!!
WHSSSSH
THAT SPELL'S AS DULL-LOOKING AS THE MAGE WHO CAST IT.

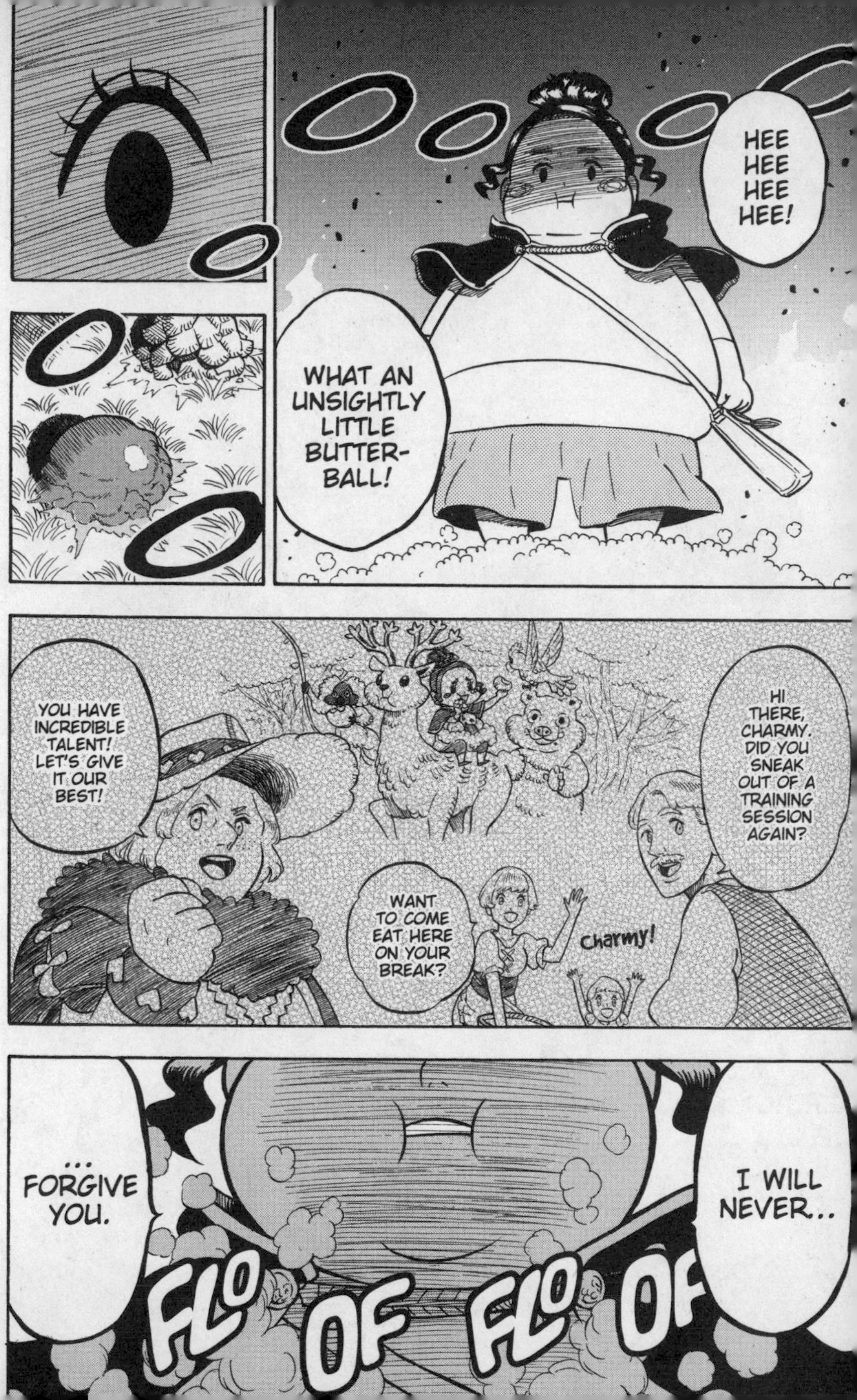
HEE HEE HEE HEE!
WHAT AN UNSIGHTLY LITTLE BUTTER-BALL!
HI THERE, CHARMY. DID YOU SNEAK OUT OF A TRAINING SESSION AGAIN?
Charmy!
WANT TO COME EAT HERE ON YOUR BREAK?
YOU HAVE INCREDIBLE TALENT! LET'S GIVE IT OUR BEST!
I WILL NEVER...
...FORGIVE YOU.
FLO OF FLO OF

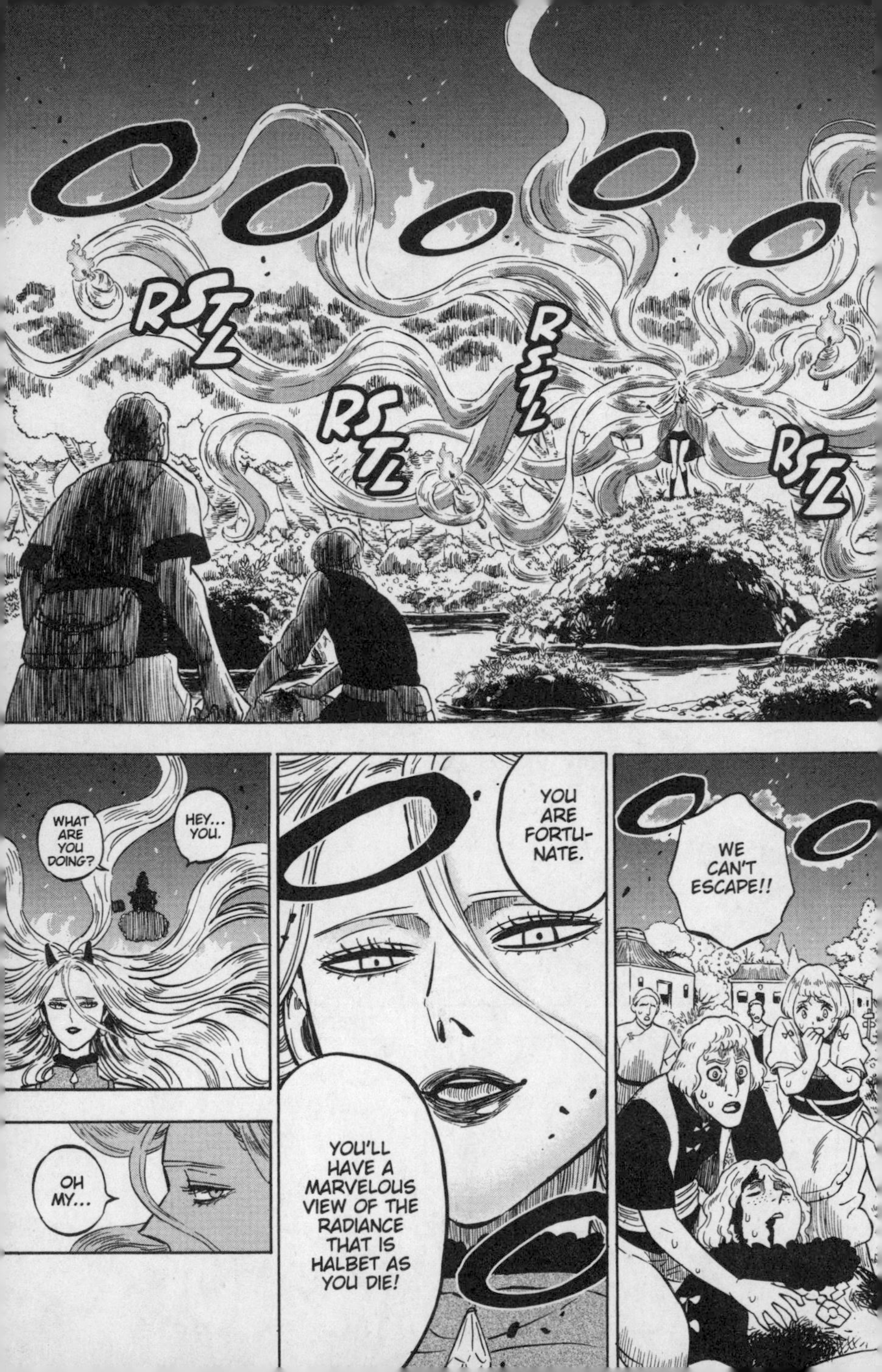
RSTL
RSTL
RSTL
RSTL
WE CAN'T ESCAPE!!
YOU ARE FORTU-NATE.
YOU'LL HAVE A MARVELOUS VIEW OF THE RADIANCE THAT IS HALBET AS YOU DIE!
HEY... YOU.
WHAT ARE YOU DOING?
OH MY...

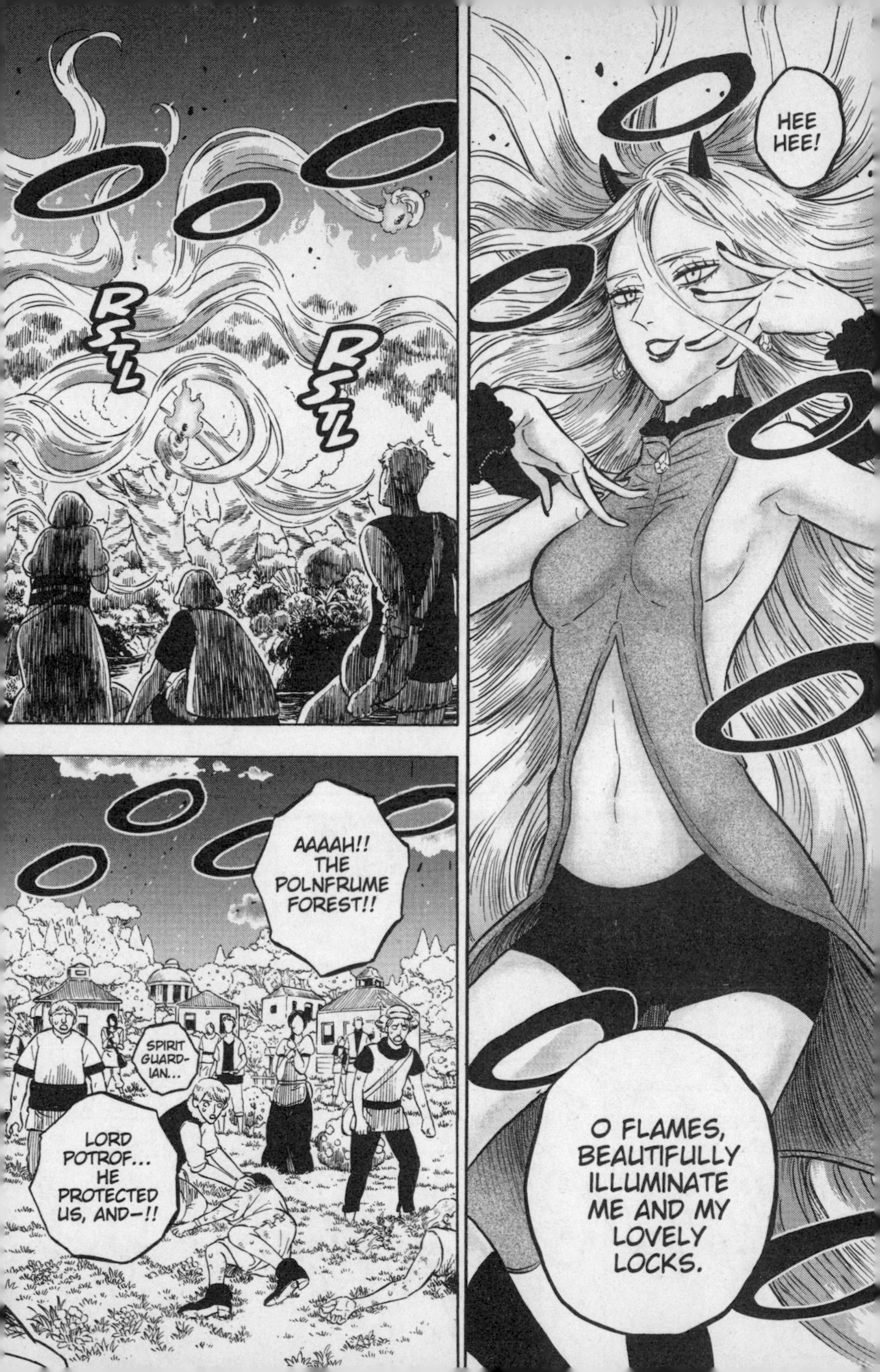
HEE HEE!
O FLAMES, BEAUTIFULLY ILLUMINATE ME AND MY LOVELY LOCKS.
RSTL
RSTL
AAAAH!! THE POLNFRUME FOREST!!
SPIRIT GUARD-IAN...
LORD POTROF... HE PROTECTED US, AND—!!

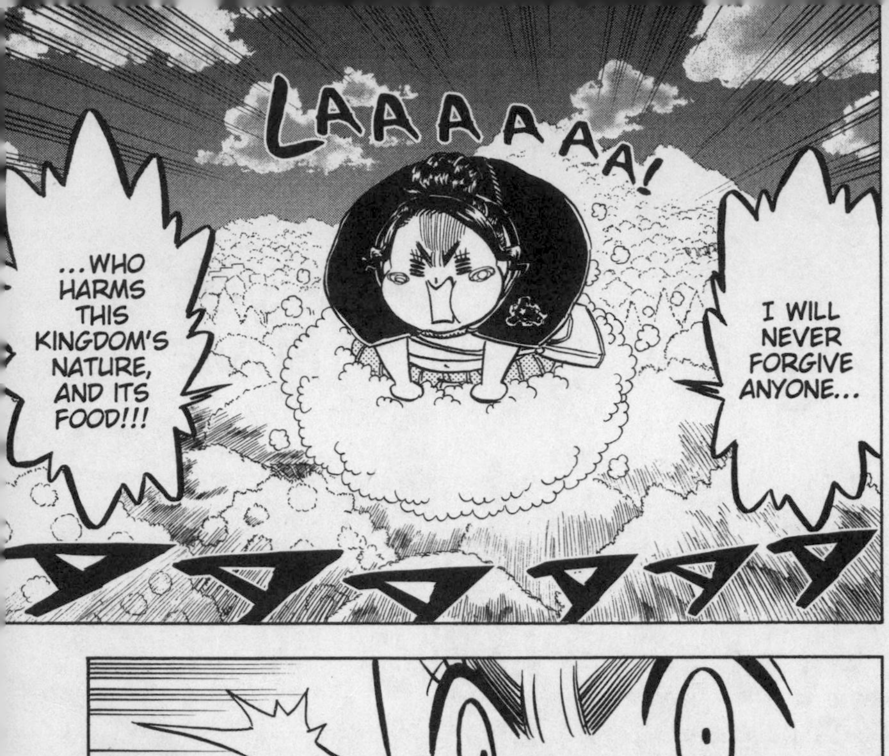
LAAAAAAA!
I WILL NEVER FORGIVE ANYONE...
...WHO HARMS THIS KINGDOM'S NATURE, AND ITS FOOD!!!
AAAAAA

Page 250: Charmy Vs. Halbet

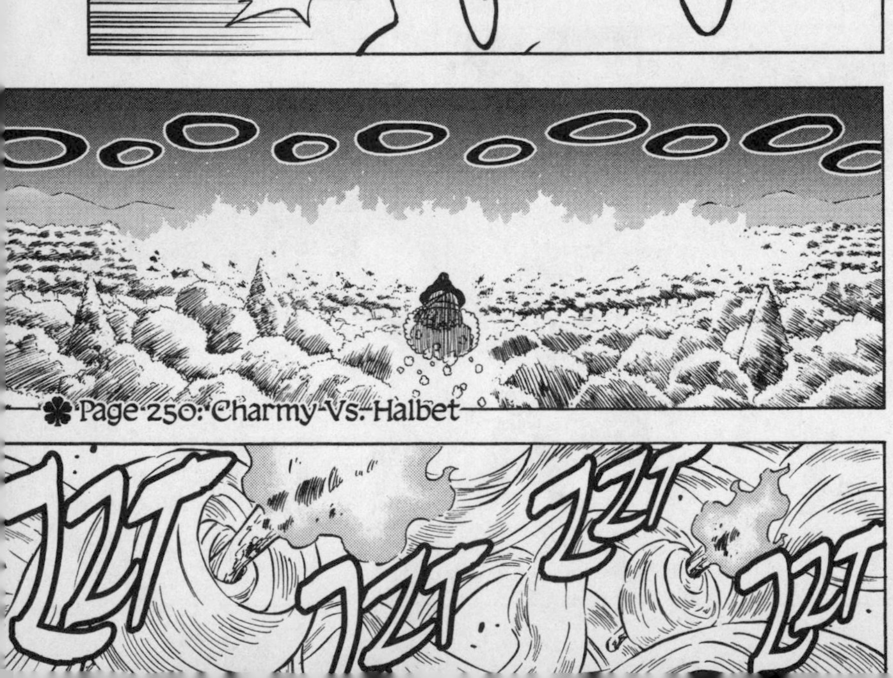
ZZZT
ZZT
ZZZT
ZZZT

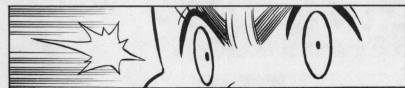

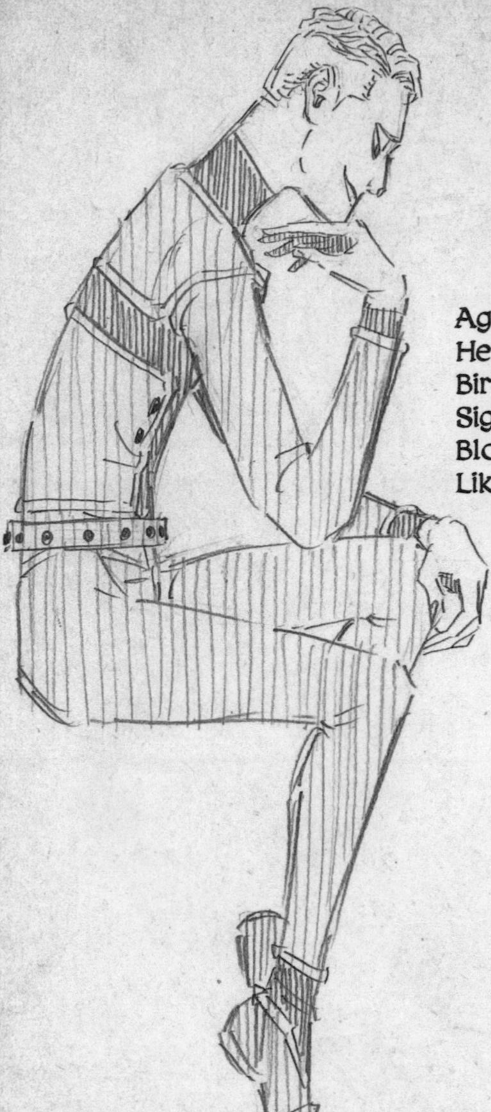

Sivoir Snyle

Age: 25
Height: 179 cm
Birthday: September 14
Sign: Virgo
Blood Type: A
Likes: Sniping, finding fault with things

Character Profile

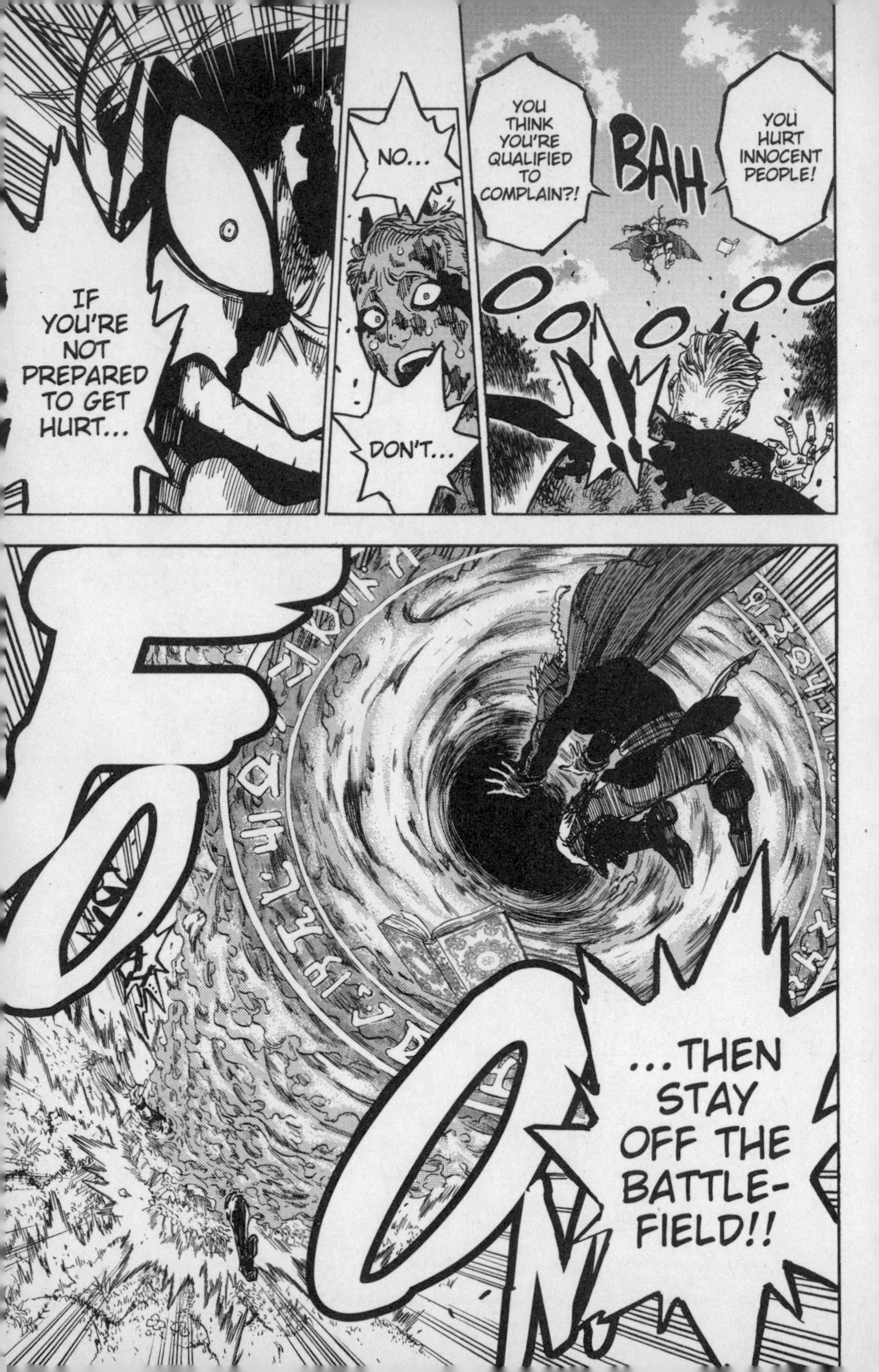
YOU HURT INNOCENT PEOPLE!
BAH
YOU THINK YOU'RE QUALIFIED TO COMPLAIN?!
NO...
DON'T...
IF YOU'RE NOT PREPARED TO GET HURT...
...THEN STAY OFF THE BATTLE-FIELD!!

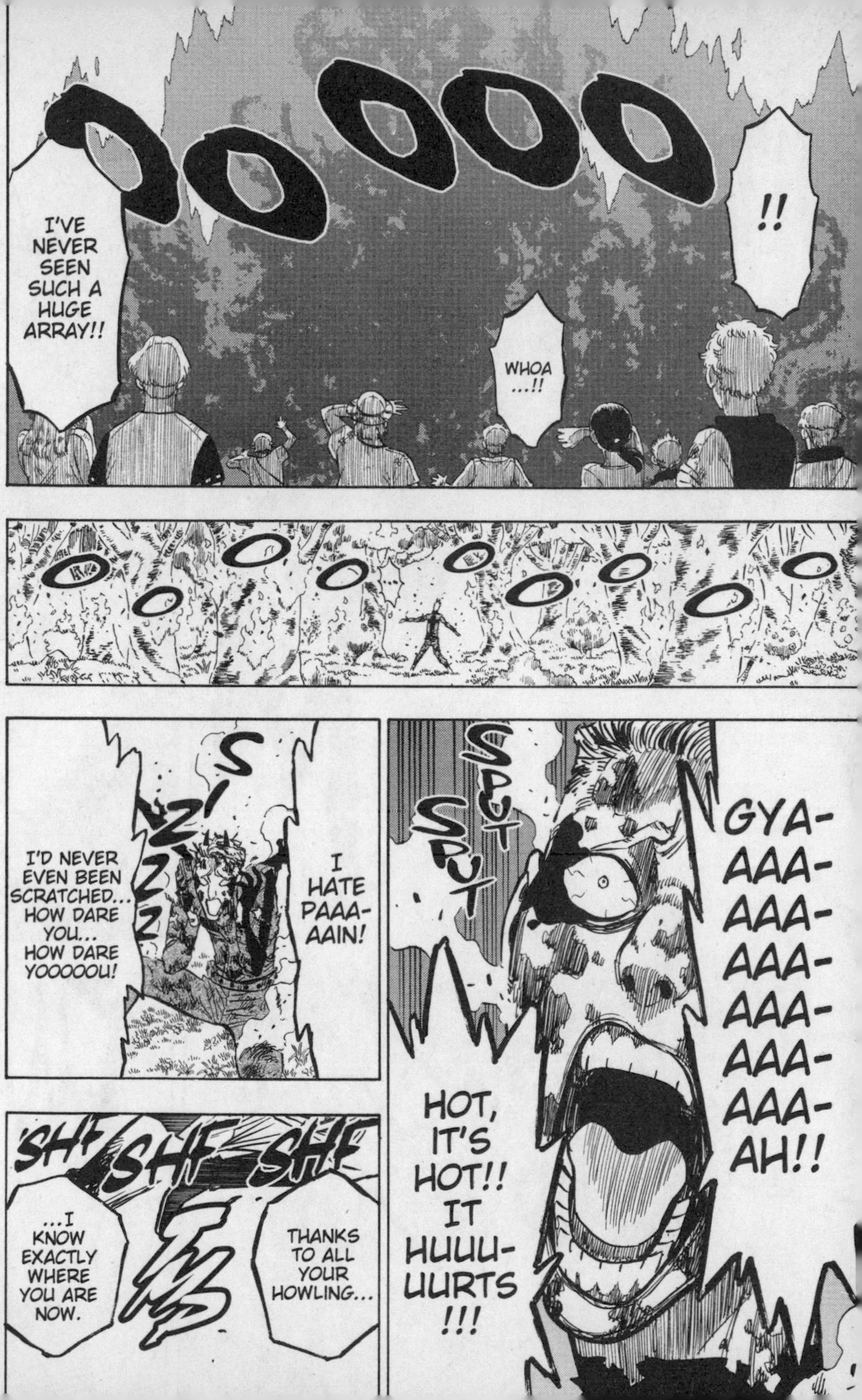
!!
WHOA ...!!
I'VE NEVER SEEN SUCH A HUGE ARRAY!!
SPUT SPUT
GYA-AAA-AAA-AAA-AAA-AAA-AAA-AH!!
HOT, IT'S HOT!! IT HUUU-UURTS!!!
SIZZZZ
I HATE PAAAA-AAIN!
I'D NEVER EVEN BEEN SCRATCHED... HOW DARE YOU... HOW DARE YOOOOOU!
SHF SHF SHF
THANKS TO ALL YOUR HOWLING...
...I KNOW EXACTLY WHERE YOU ARE NOW.

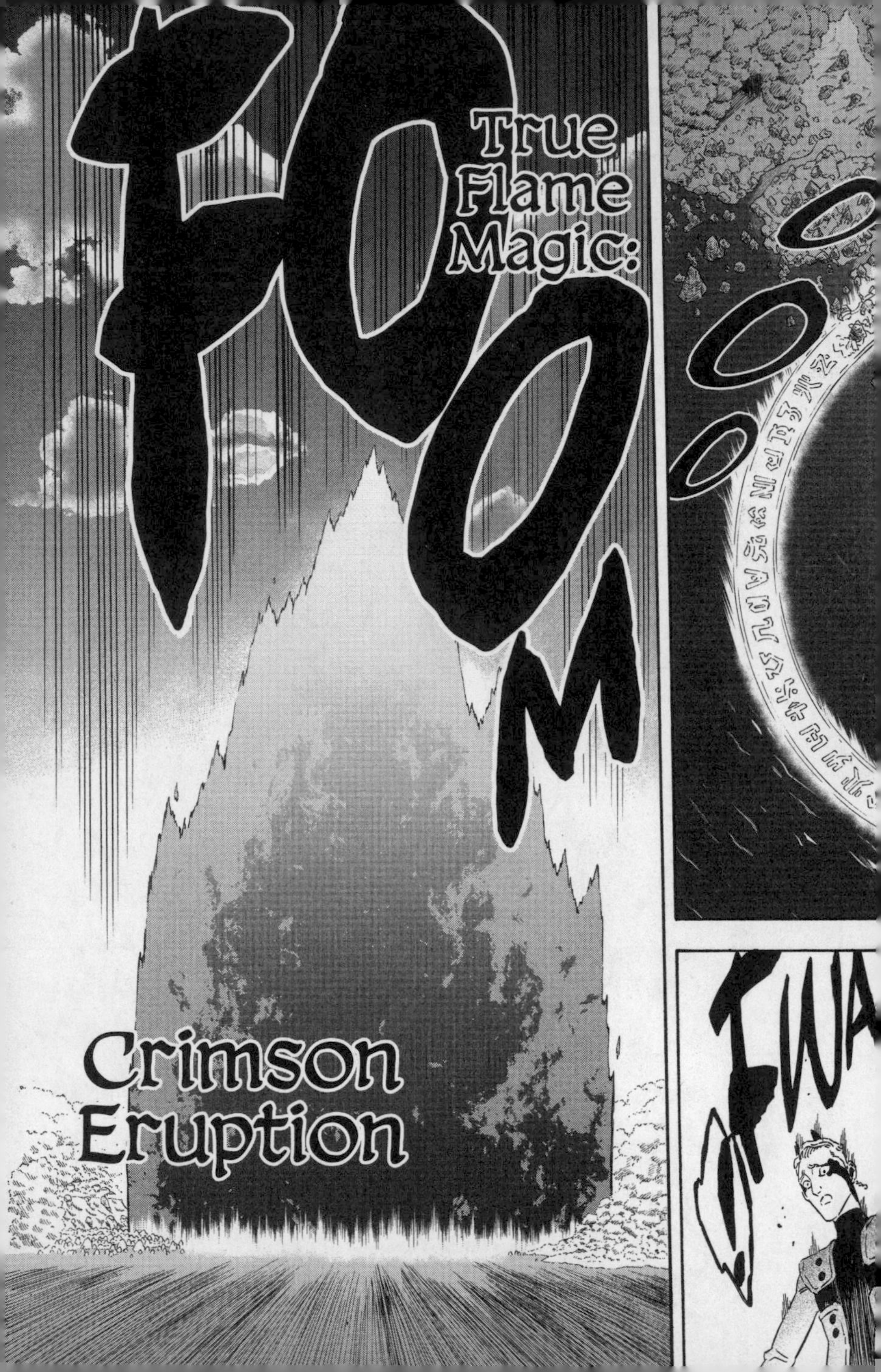
FOOOM
True Flame Magic:
Crimson Eruption
FWA

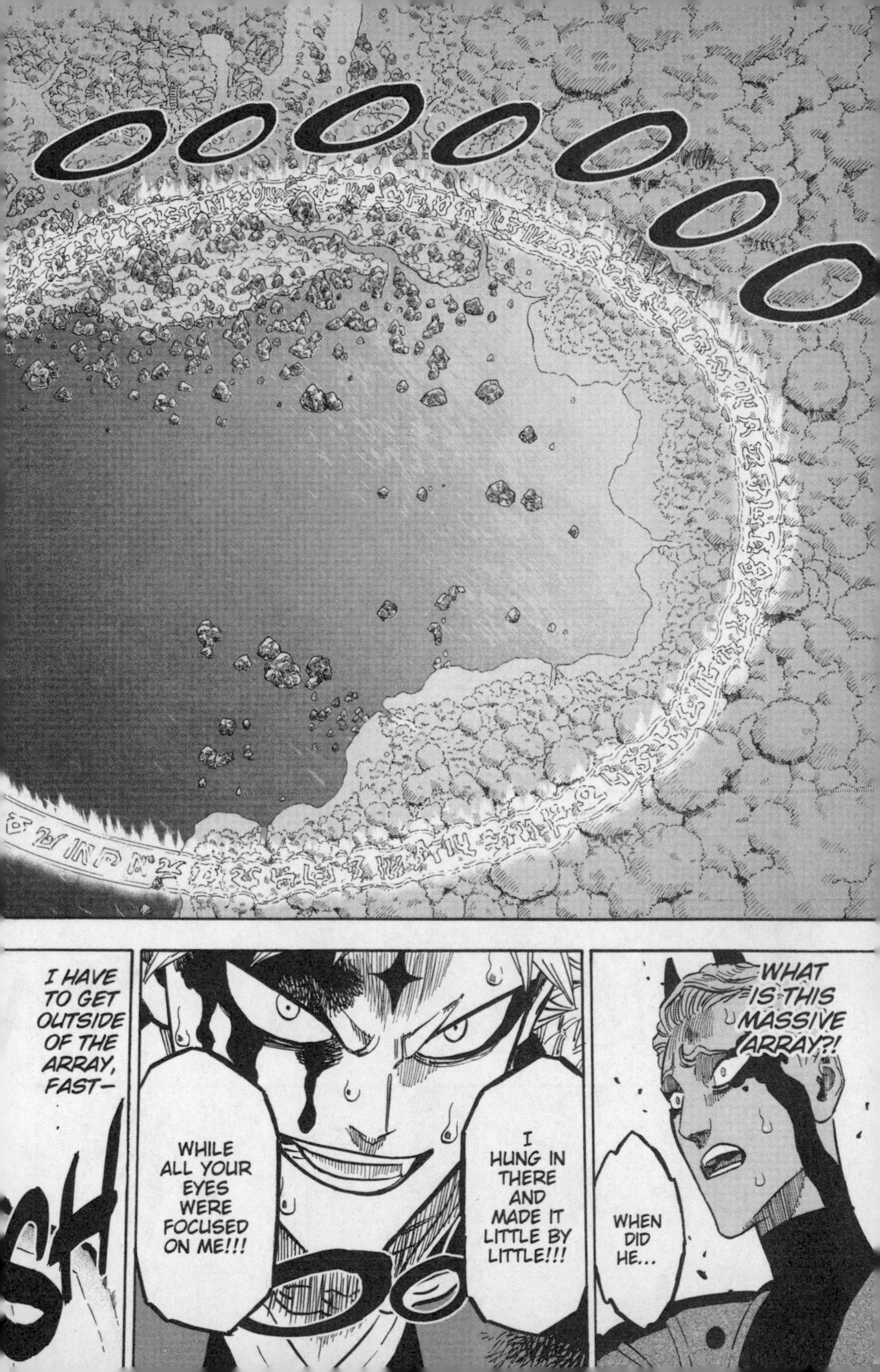
OOOOOOOO
WHAT IS THIS MASSIVE ARRAY?!
WHEN DID HE...
I HUNG IN THERE AND MADE IT LITTLE BY LITTLE!!!
WHILE ALL YOUR EYES WERE FOCUSED ON ME!!!
I HAVE TO GET OUTSIDE OF THE ARRAY, FAST—
SH

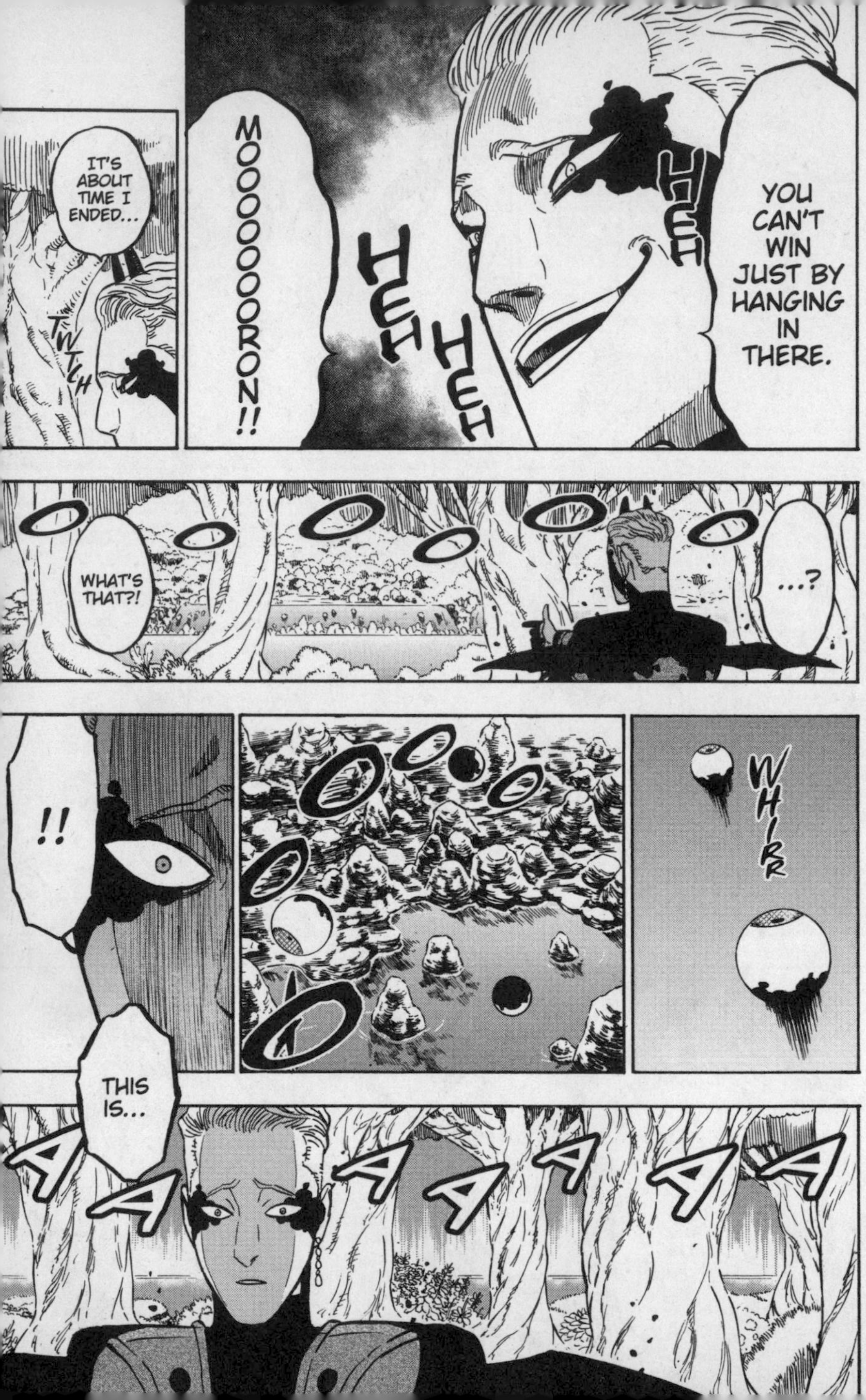
YOU CAN'T WIN JUST BY HANGING IN THERE.
HEH
HEH
HEH
MOOOOOOOORON!!
IT'S ABOUT TIME I ENDED...
TWITCH
...?
WHAT'S THAT?!
WHIRR
!!
THIS IS...
AAAAAAAAA

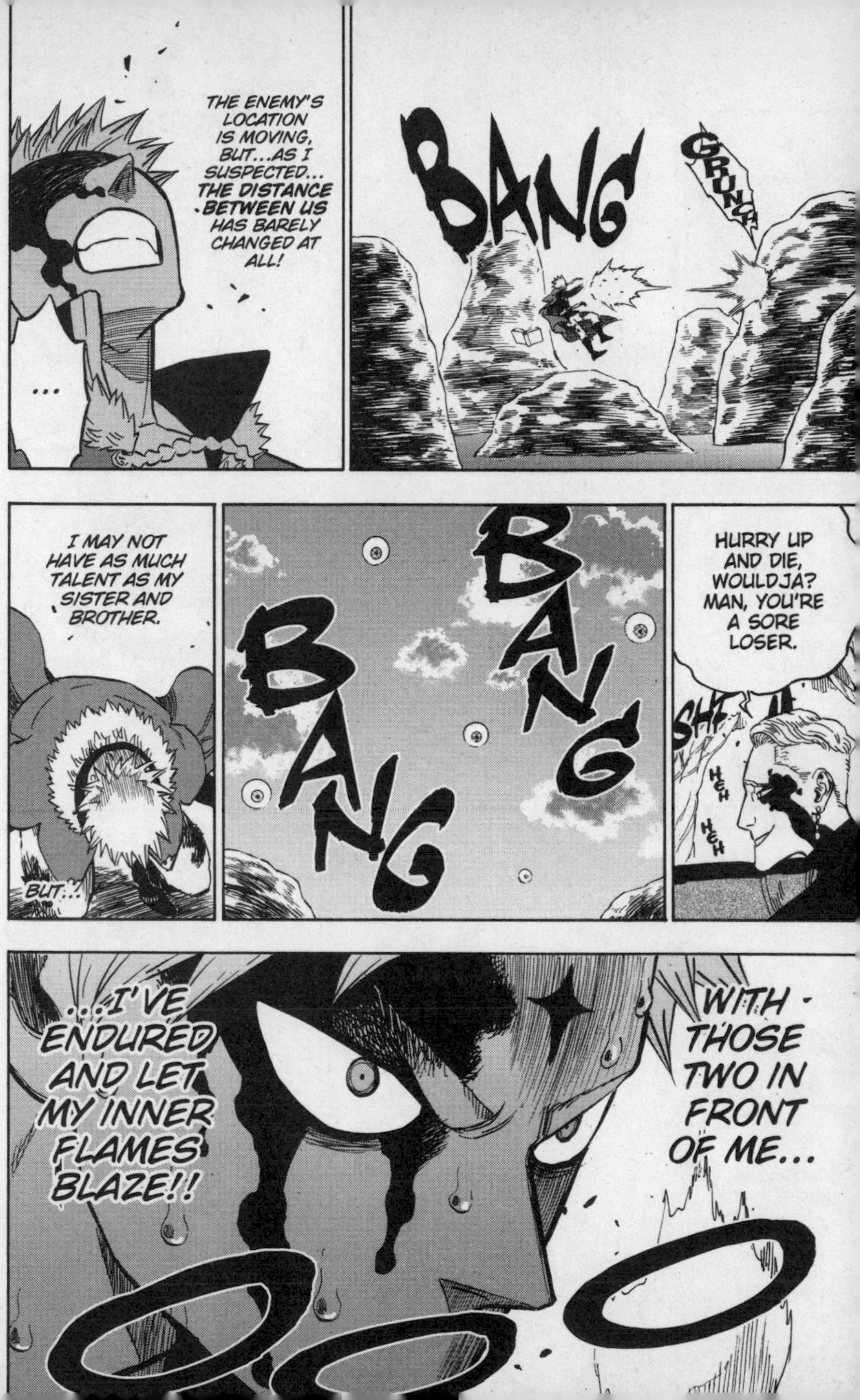
BANG
GRUNCH
THE ENEMY'S LOCATION IS MOVING, BUT...AS I SUSPECTED... THE DISTANCE BETWEEN US HAS BARELY CHANGED AT ALL!
...
HURRY UP AND DIE, WOULDJA? MAN, YOU'RE A SORE LOSER.
HEH HEH
BANG
BANG
I MAY NOT HAVE AS MUCH TALENT AS MY SISTER AND BROTHER.
BUT...
WITH THOSE TWO IN FRONT OF ME...
...I'VE ENDURED AND LET MY INNER FLAMES BLAZE!!

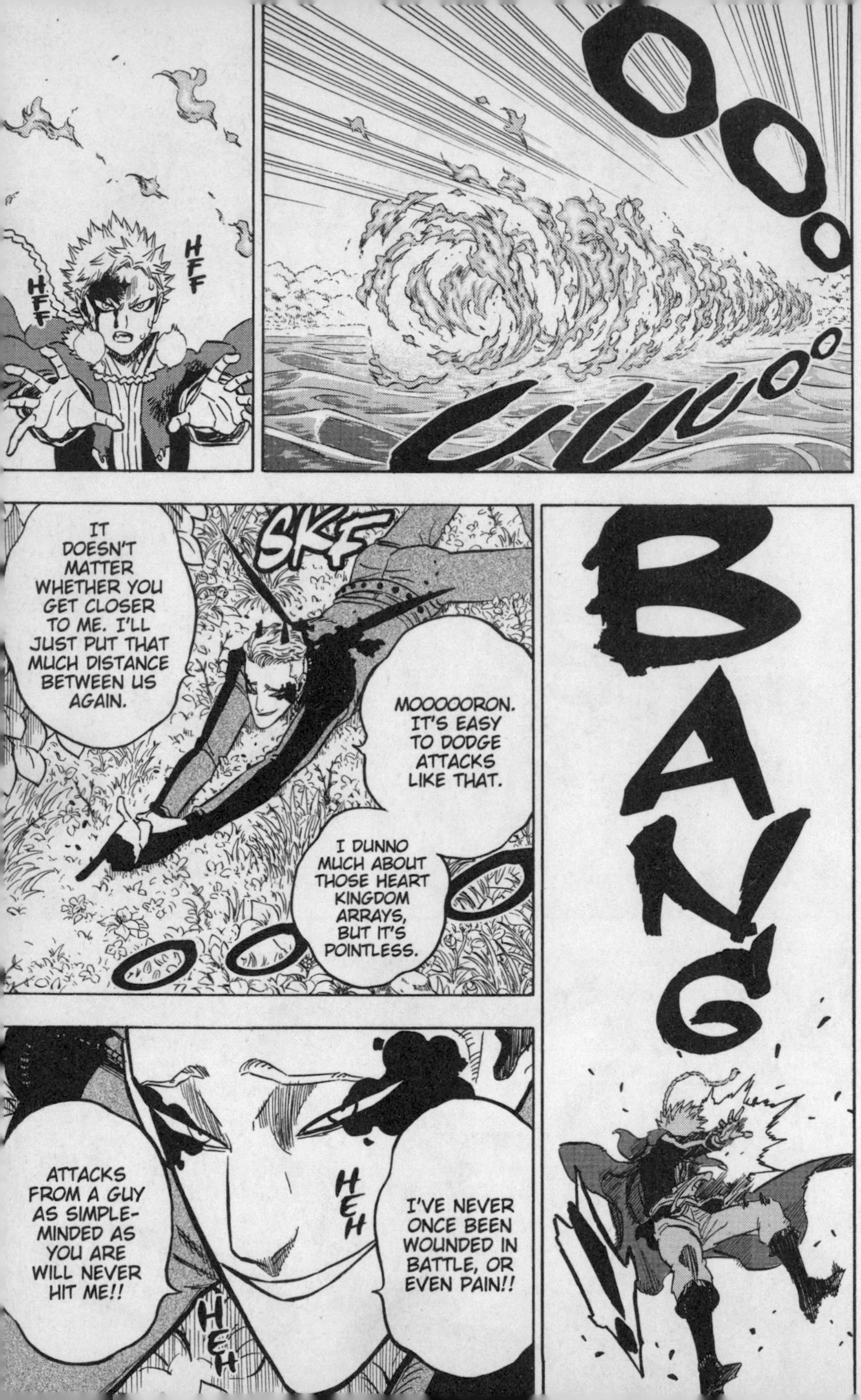
HFF
HFF
BANG
SKF
MOOOOORON. IT'S EASY TO DODGE ATTACKS LIKE THAT.
I DUNNO MUCH ABOUT THOSE HEART KINGDOM ARRAYS, BUT IT'S POINTLESS.
IT DOESN'T MATTER WHETHER YOU GET CLOSER TO ME. I'LL JUST PUT THAT MUCH DISTANCE BETWEEN US AGAIN.
I'VE NEVER ONCE BEEN WOUNDED IN BATTLE, OR EVEN PAIN!!
HEH
HEH
ATTACKS FROM A GUY AS SIMPLE-MINDED AS YOU ARE WILL NEVER HIT ME!!

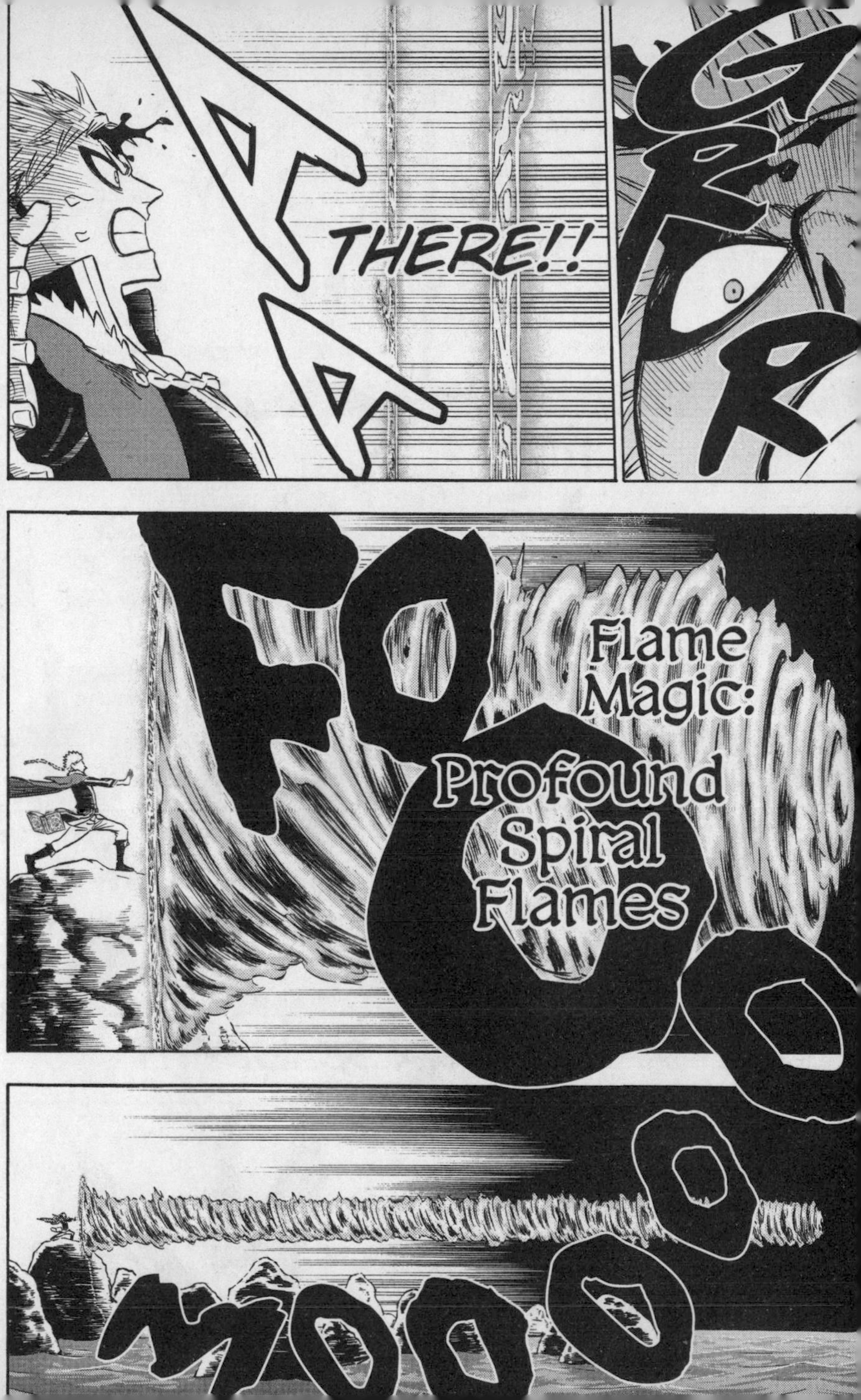
THERE!!
Flame Magic:
Profound Spiral Flames

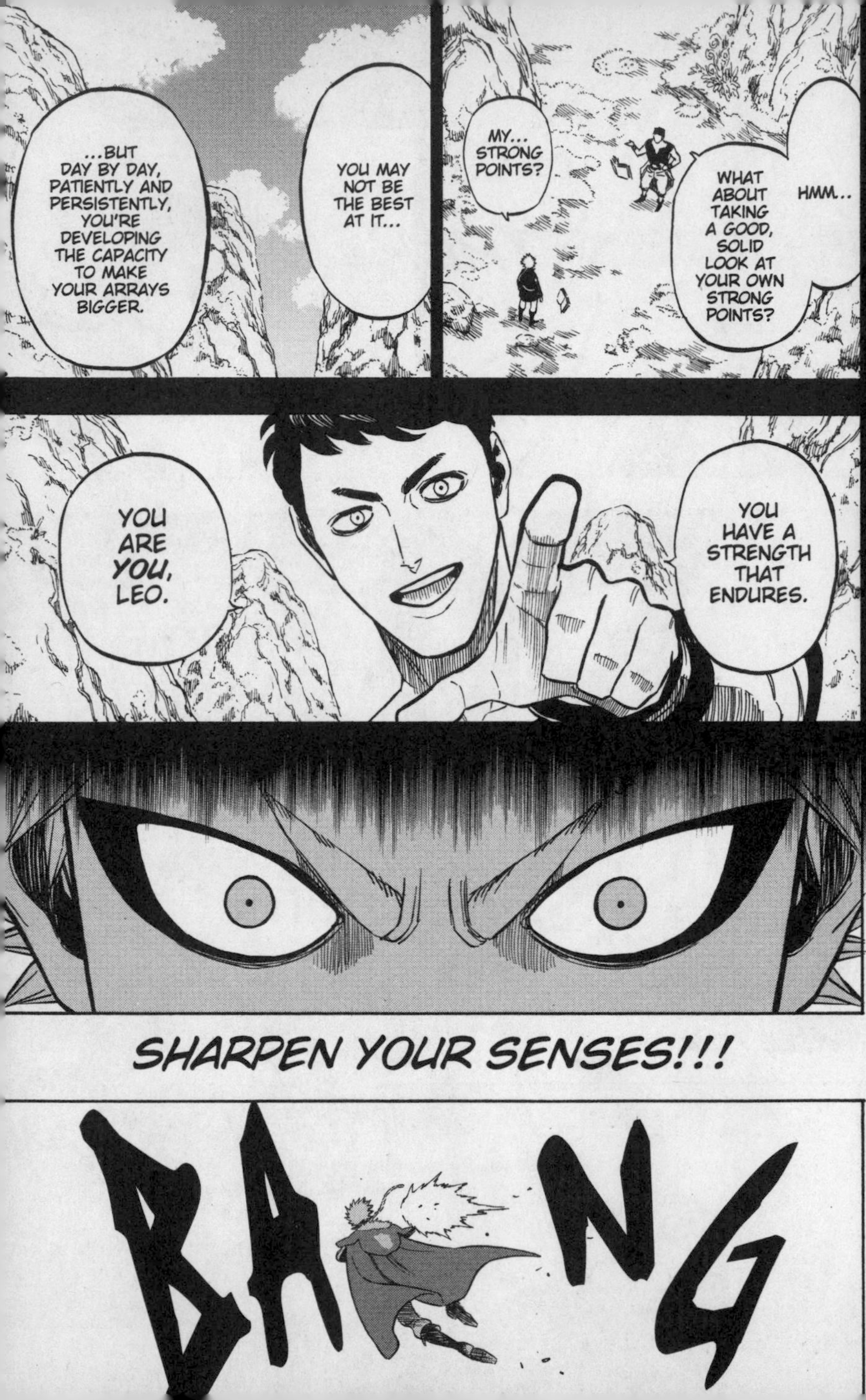
HMM...
WHAT ABOUT TAKING A GOOD, SOLID LOOK AT YOUR OWN STRONG POINTS?
MY... STRONG POINTS?
YOU MAY NOT BE THE BEST AT IT...
...BUT DAY BY DAY, PATIENTLY AND PERSISTENTLY, YOU'RE DEVELOPING THE CAPACITY TO MAKE YOUR ARRAYS BIGGER.
YOU HAVE A STRENGTH THAT ENDURES.
YOU ARE *YOU*, LEO.
SHARPEN YOUR SENSES!!!
BANG

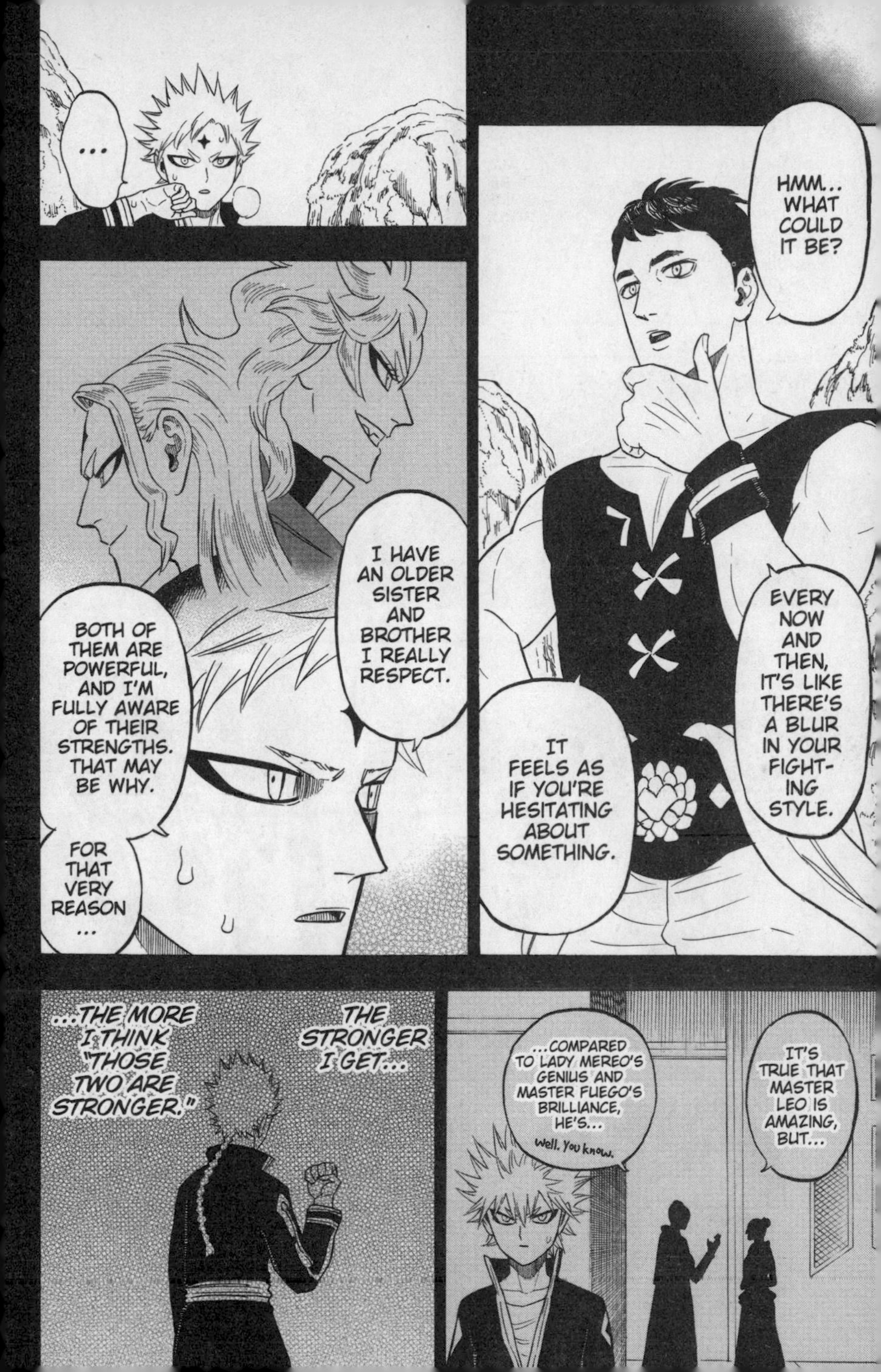
HMM... WHAT COULD IT BE?
EVERY NOW AND THEN, IT'S LIKE THERE'S A BLUR IN YOUR FIGHTING STYLE.
IT FEELS AS IF YOU'RE HESITATING ABOUT SOMETHING.
...
I HAVE AN OLDER SISTER AND BROTHER I REALLY RESPECT.
BOTH OF THEM ARE POWERFUL, AND I'M FULLY AWARE OF THEIR STRENGTHS. THAT MAY BE WHY.
FOR THAT VERY REASON...
IT'S TRUE THAT MASTER LEO IS AMAZING, BUT...
...COMPARED TO LADY MEREO'S GENIUS AND MASTER FUEGO'S BRILLIANCE, HE'S...
Well. You know.
THE STRONGER I GET...
...THE MORE I THINK "THOSE TWO ARE STRONGER."

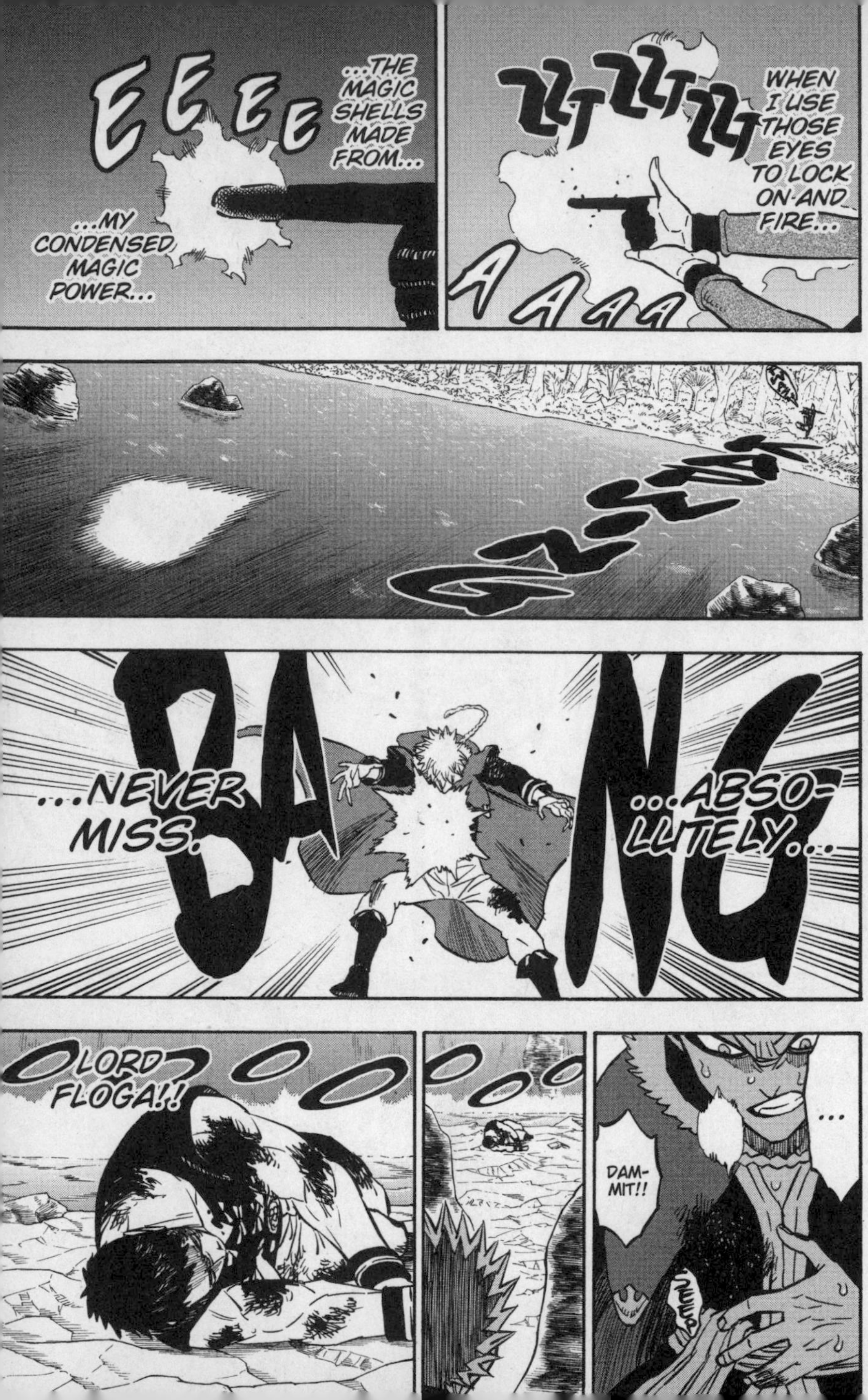
ZZZT ZZZT ZZZT
WHEN I USE THOSE EYES TO LOCK ON AND FIRE...
AAAA
...THE MAGIC SHELLS MADE FROM...
EEEE
...MY CONDENSED MAGIC POWER...
BANG
...ABSOLUTELY...
...NEVER MISS.
...
DAM-MIT!!
OOOO
LORD FLOGA!!
OOOO

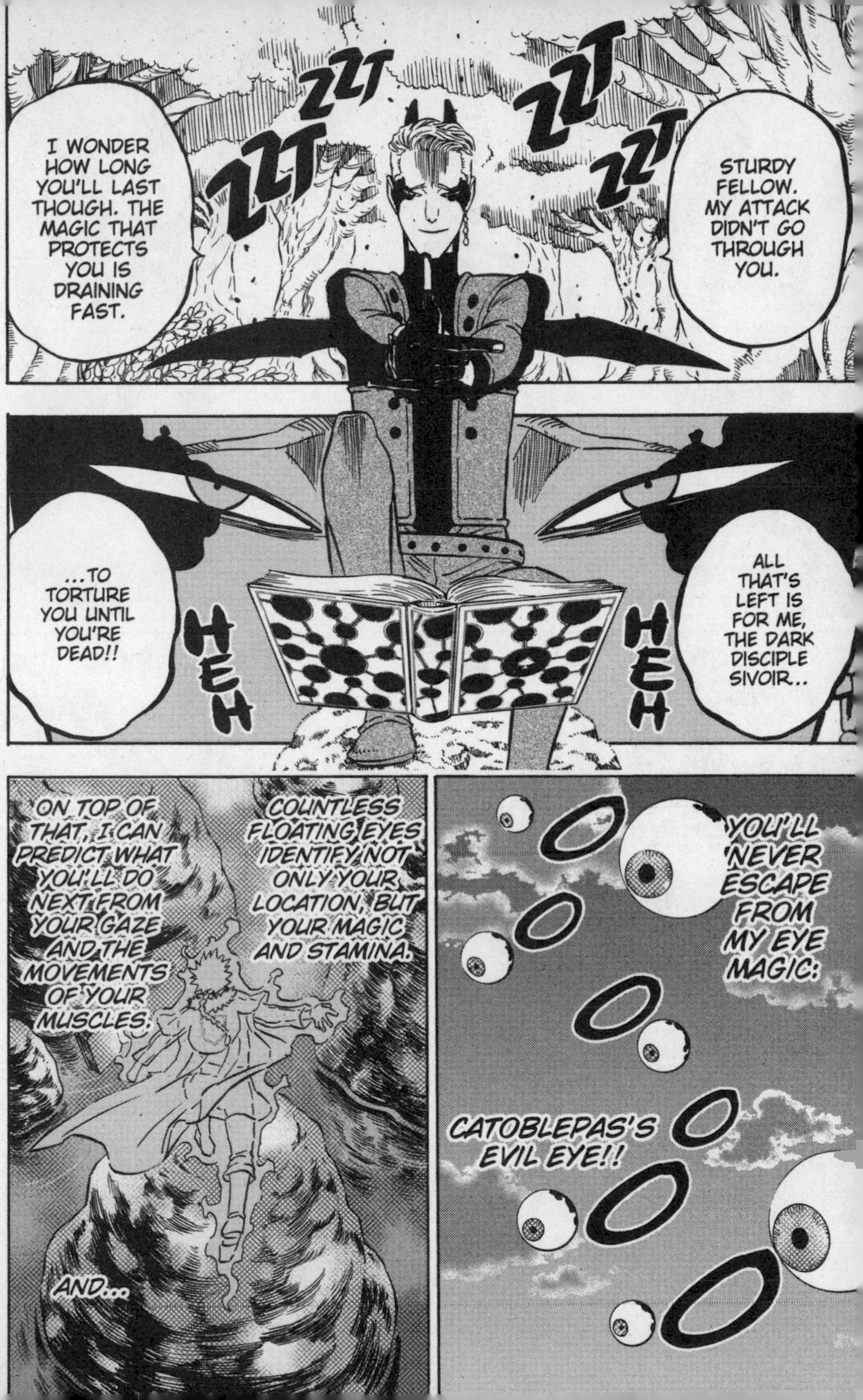
STURDY FELLOW. MY ATTACK DIDN'T GO THROUGH YOU.
ZZZT ZZZT
ZZZT ZZZT
I WONDER HOW LONG YOU'LL LAST THOUGH. THE MAGIC THAT PROTECTS YOU IS DRAINING FAST.
ALL THAT'S LEFT IS FOR ME, THE DARK DISCIPLE SIVOIR...
HEH HEH
HEH HEH
...TO TORTURE YOU UNTIL YOU'RE DEAD!!
YOU'LL NEVER ESCAPE FROM MY EYE MAGIC:
CATOBLEPAS'S EVIL EYE!!
COUNTLESS FLOATING EYES IDENTIFY NOT ONLY YOUR LOCATION, BUT YOUR MAGIC AND STAMINA.
ON TOP OF THAT, I CAN PREDICT WHAT YOU'LL DO NEXT FROM YOUR GAZE AND THE MOVEMENTS OF YOUR MUSCLES.
AND...

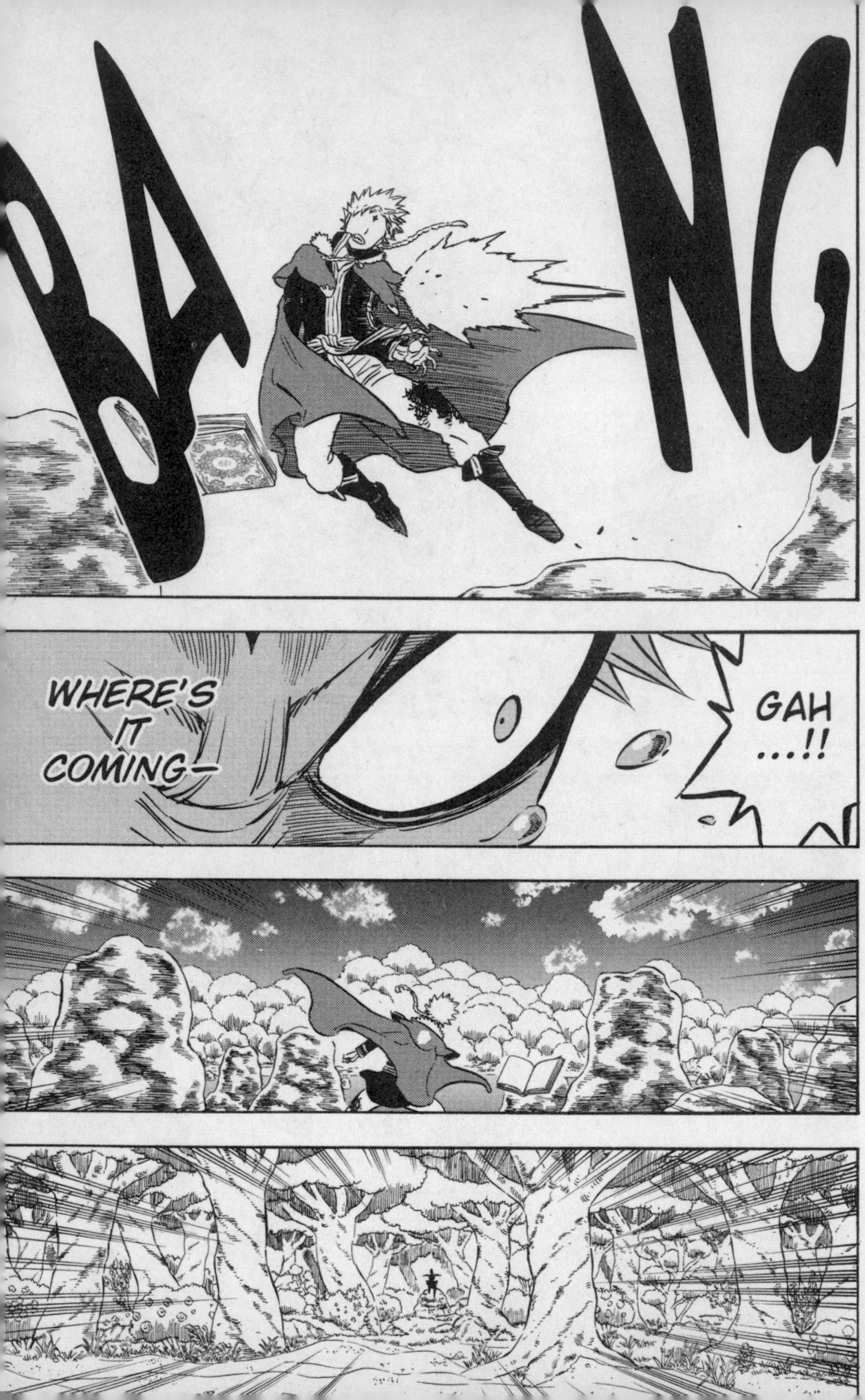
BANG
GAH...!!
WHERE'S IT COMING-

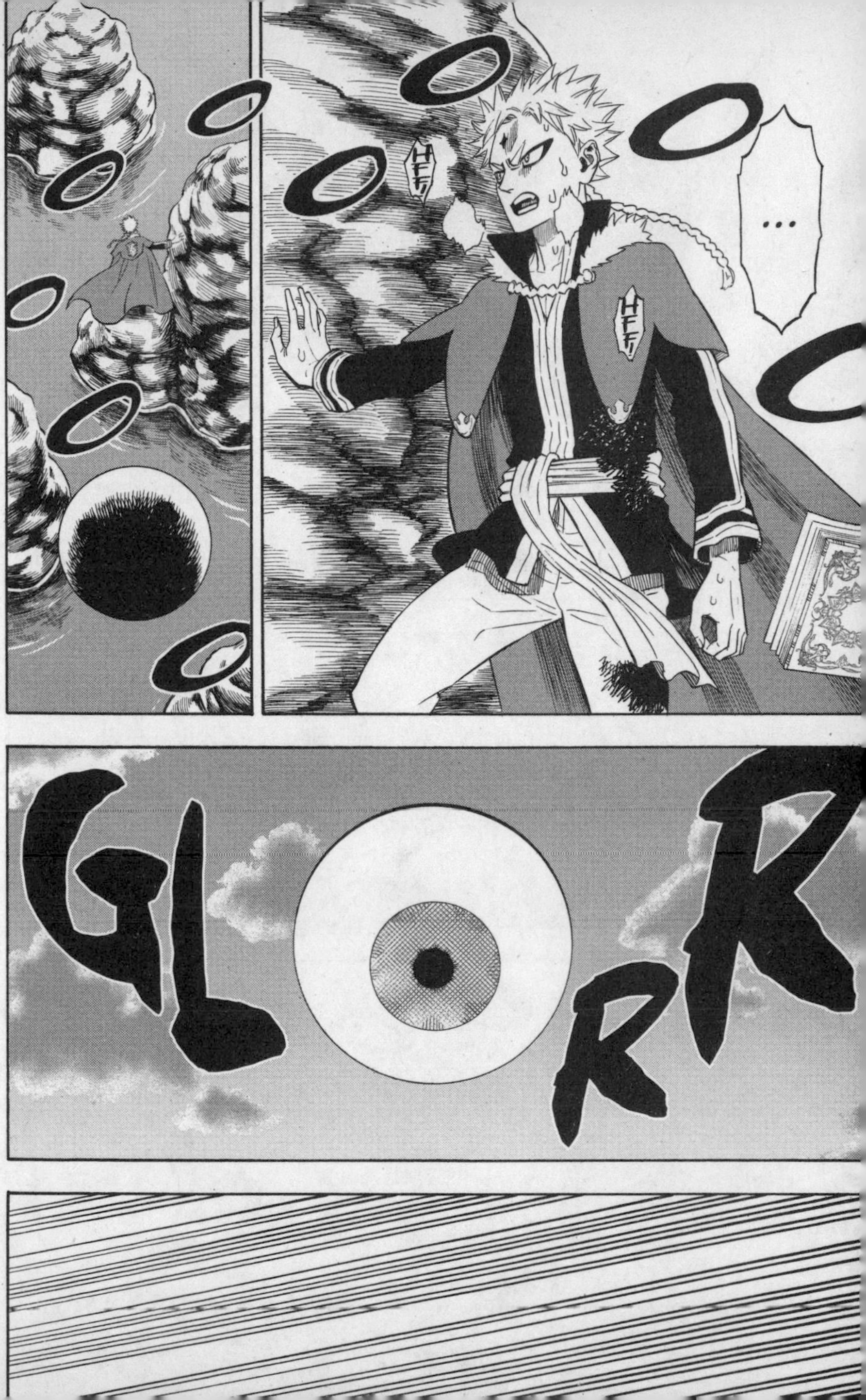
...
HFF!
HFF!
GLORR

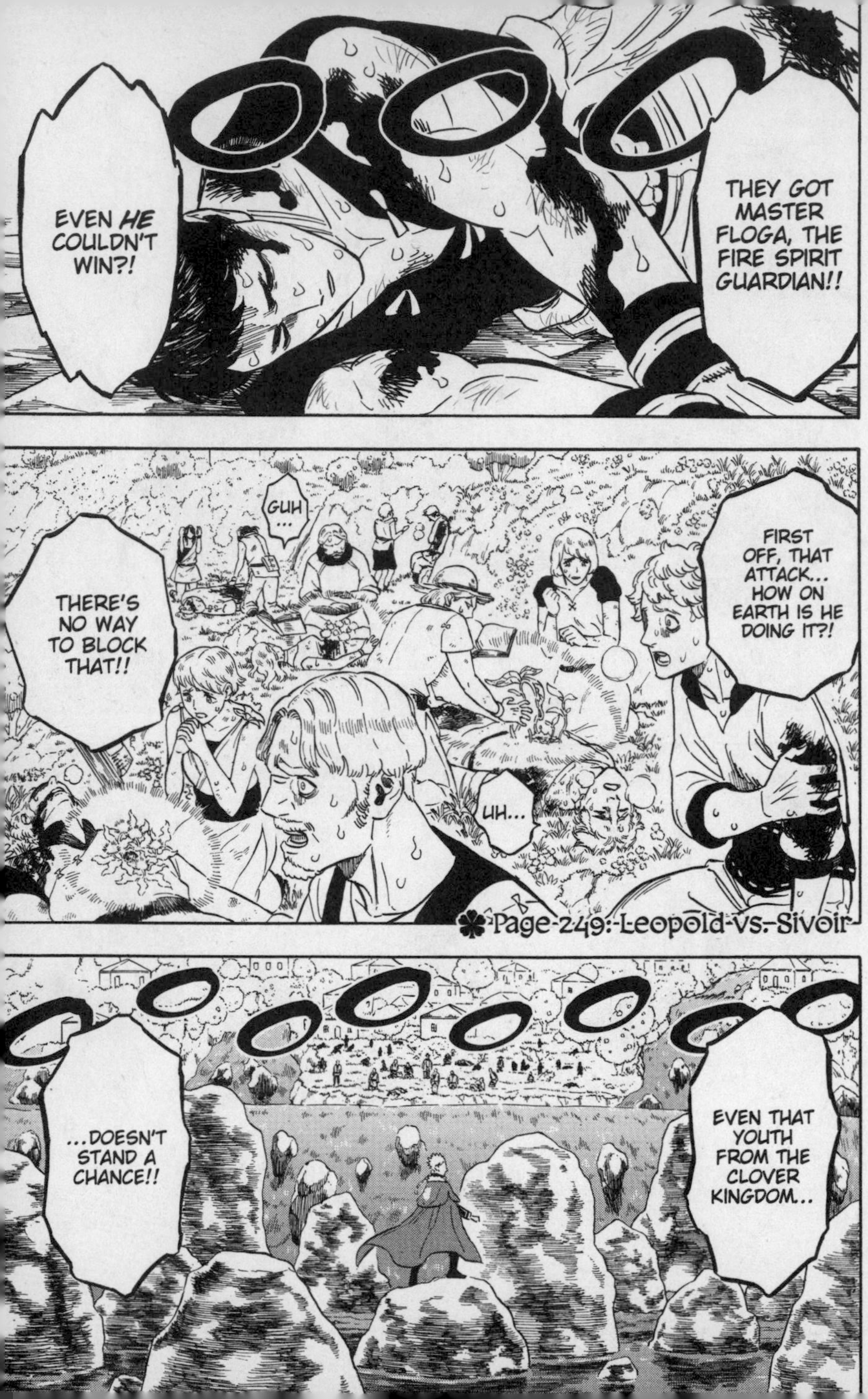
THEY GOT MASTER FLOGA, THE FIRE SPIRIT GUARDIAN!!
EVEN HE COULDN'T WIN?!
FIRST OFF, THAT ATTACK... HOW ON EARTH IS HE DOING IT?!
GUH...
UH...
THERE'S NO WAY TO BLOCK THAT!!
Page 249: Leopold vs. Sivoir
EVEN THAT YOUTH FROM THE CLOVER KINGDOM...
...DOESN'T STAND A CHANCE!!

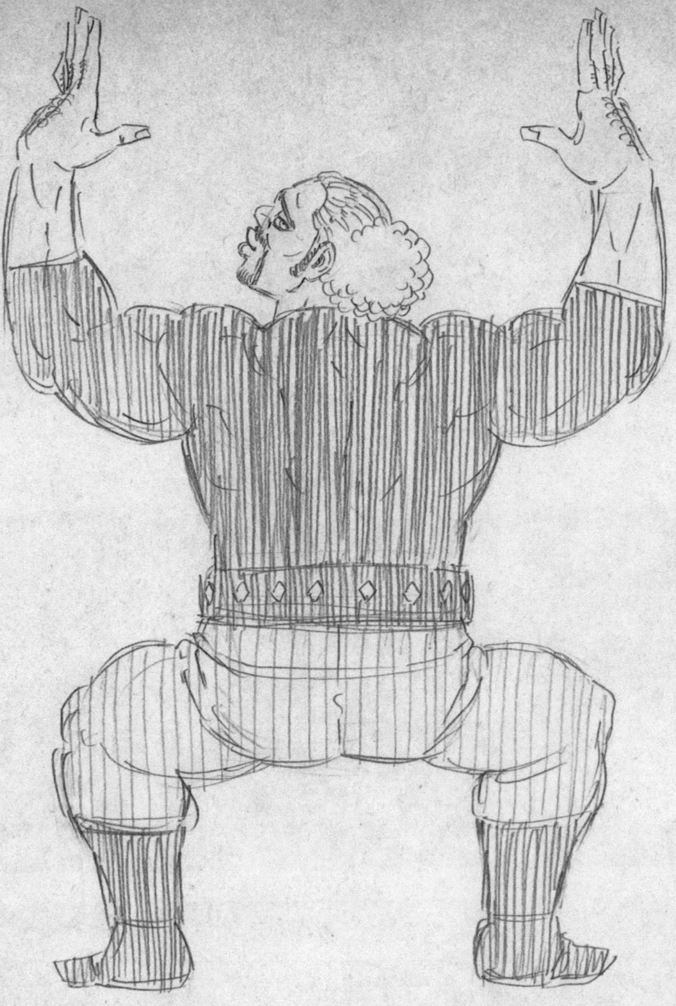

Svenkin Gatard

Age: 27 Height: 201 cm
Birthday: April 21 Sign: Taurus Blood Type: O
Likes: Vanica, bodybuilding

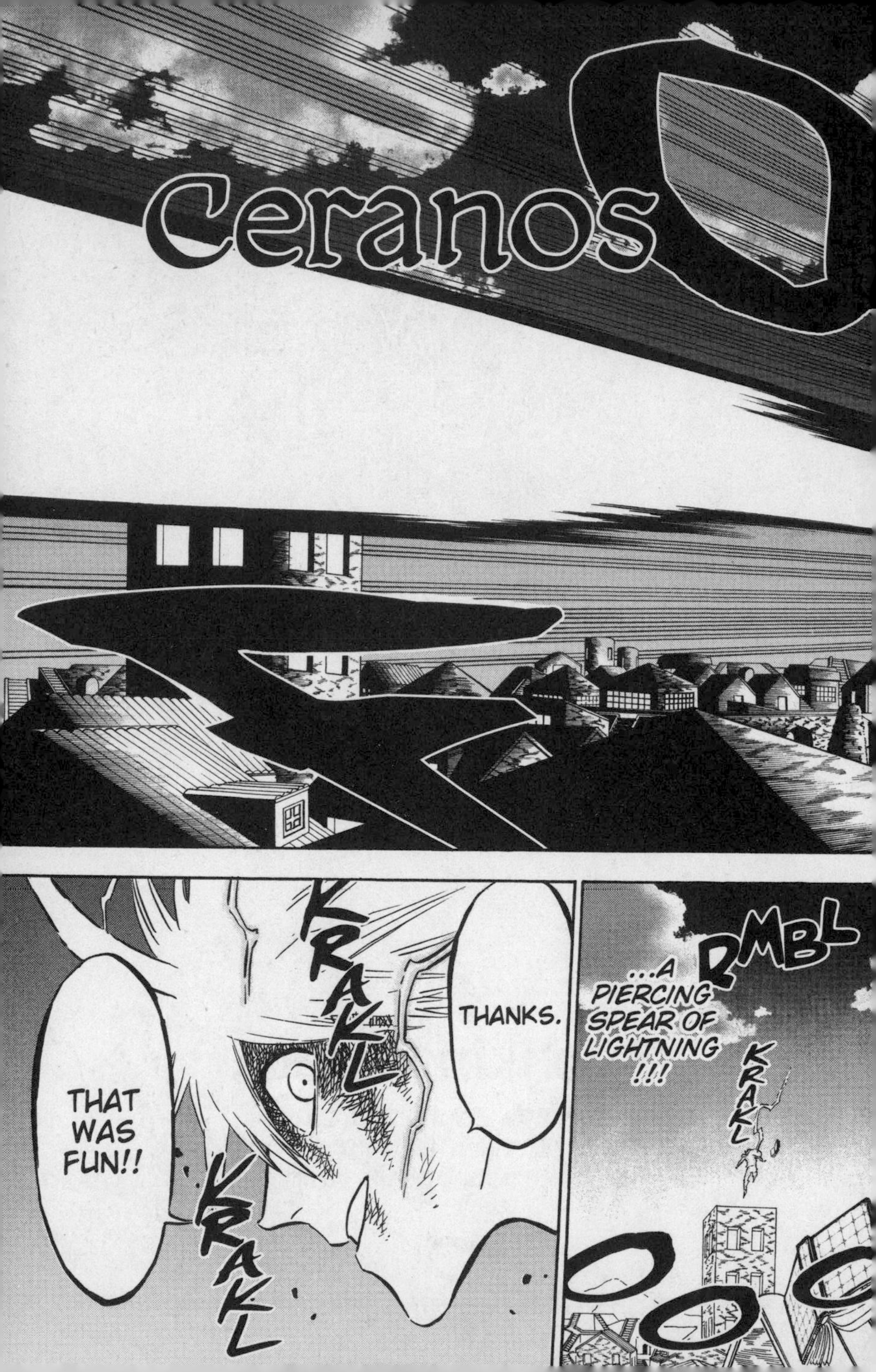
Ceranos
RMBL
...A PIERCING SPEAR OF LIGHTNING!!!
KRAKL
THANKS.
KRAKL
THAT WAS FUN!!
KRAKL

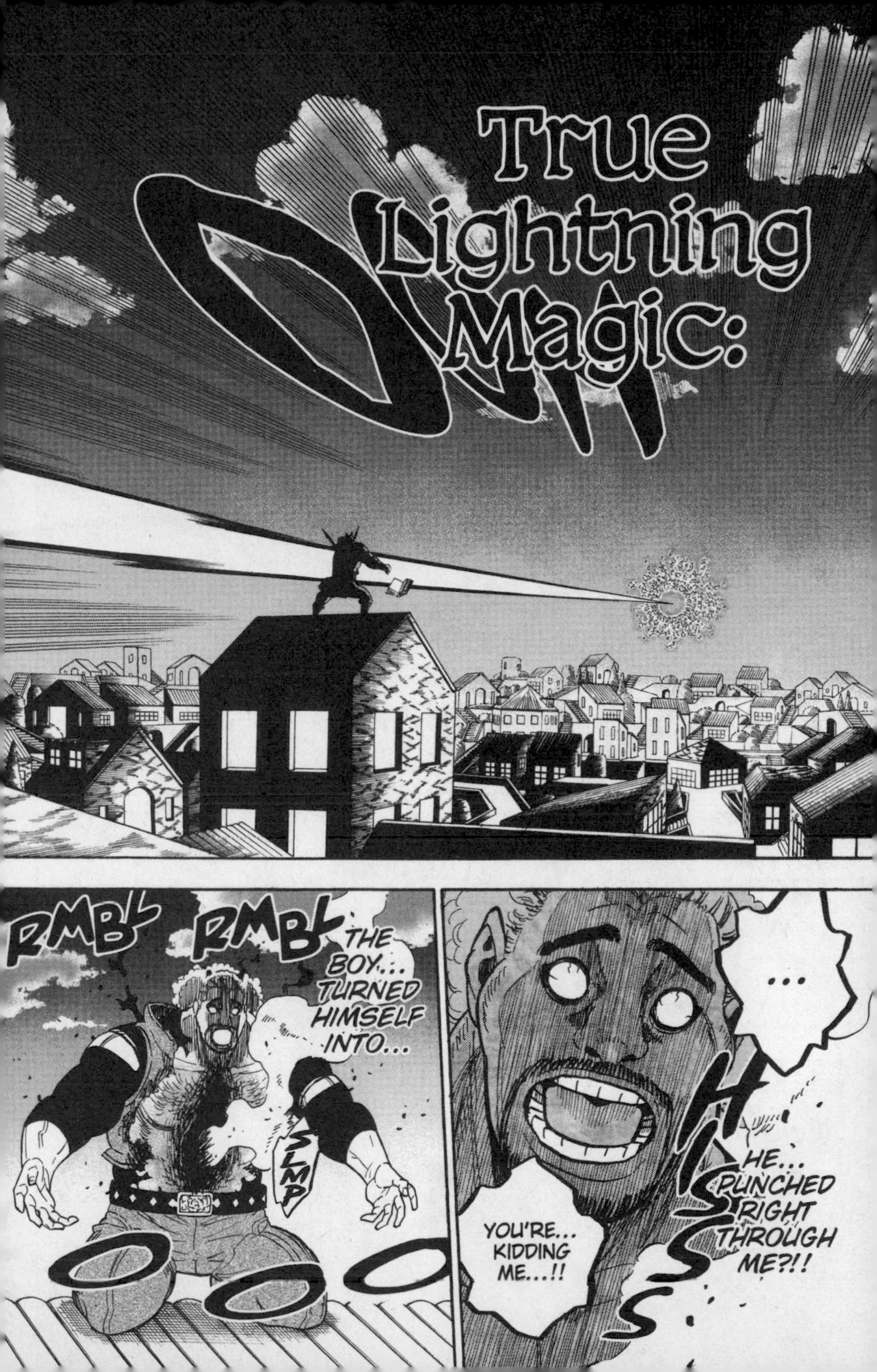
True Lightning Magic:
...
HE... PUNCHED RIGHT THROUGH ME?!!
HISSS
YOU'RE... KIDDING ME...!!
RMBL RMBL
THE BOY... TURNED HIMSELF INTO...
SLMP

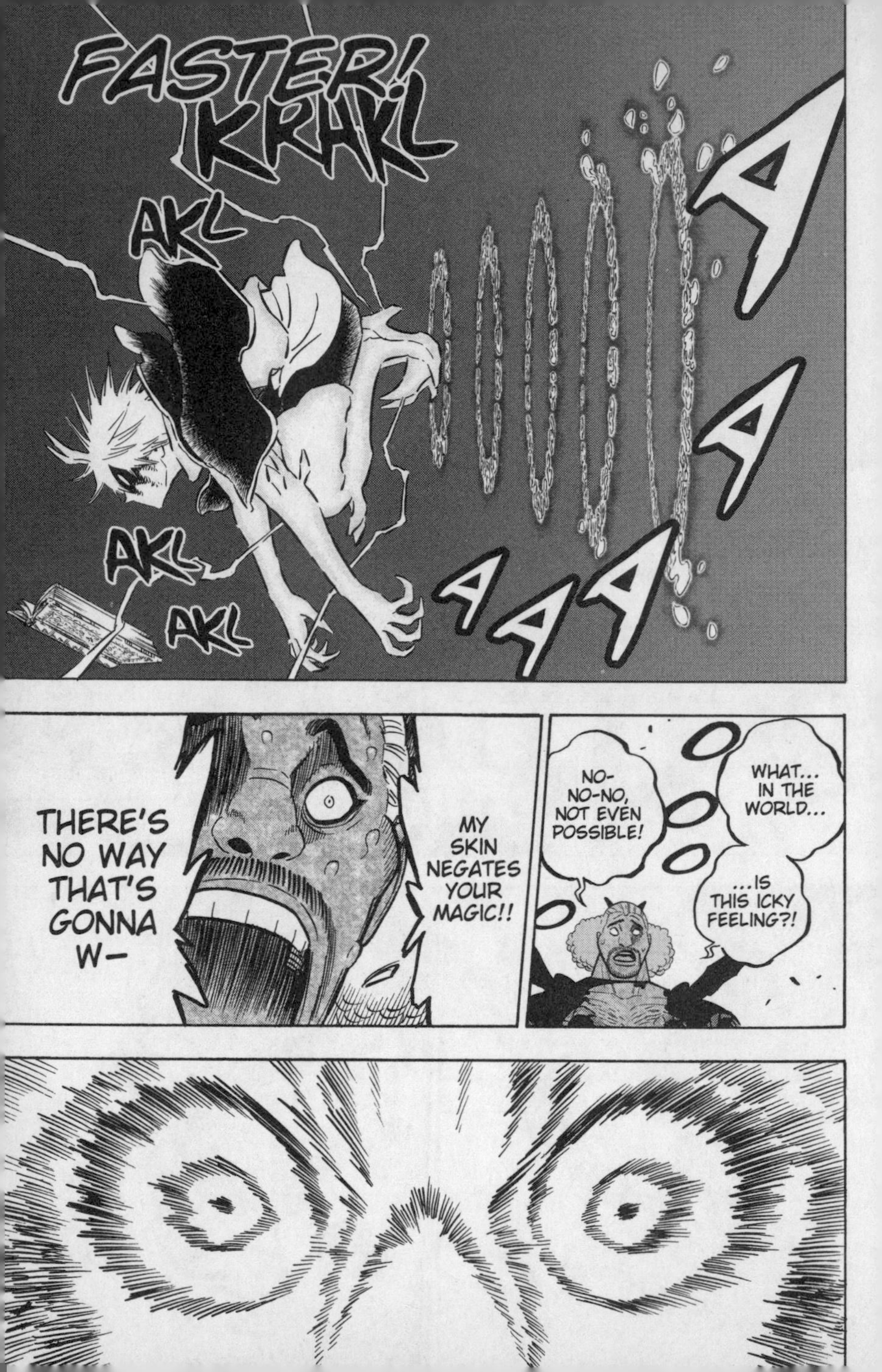
FASTER!
KRAKL
AKL
AKL
AKL
AAAAAA
WHAT... IN THE WORLD...
...IS THIS ICKY FEELING?!
NO-NO-NO, NOT EVEN POSSIBLE!
MY SKIN NEGATES YOUR MAGIC!!
THERE'S NO WAY THAT'S GONNA W—

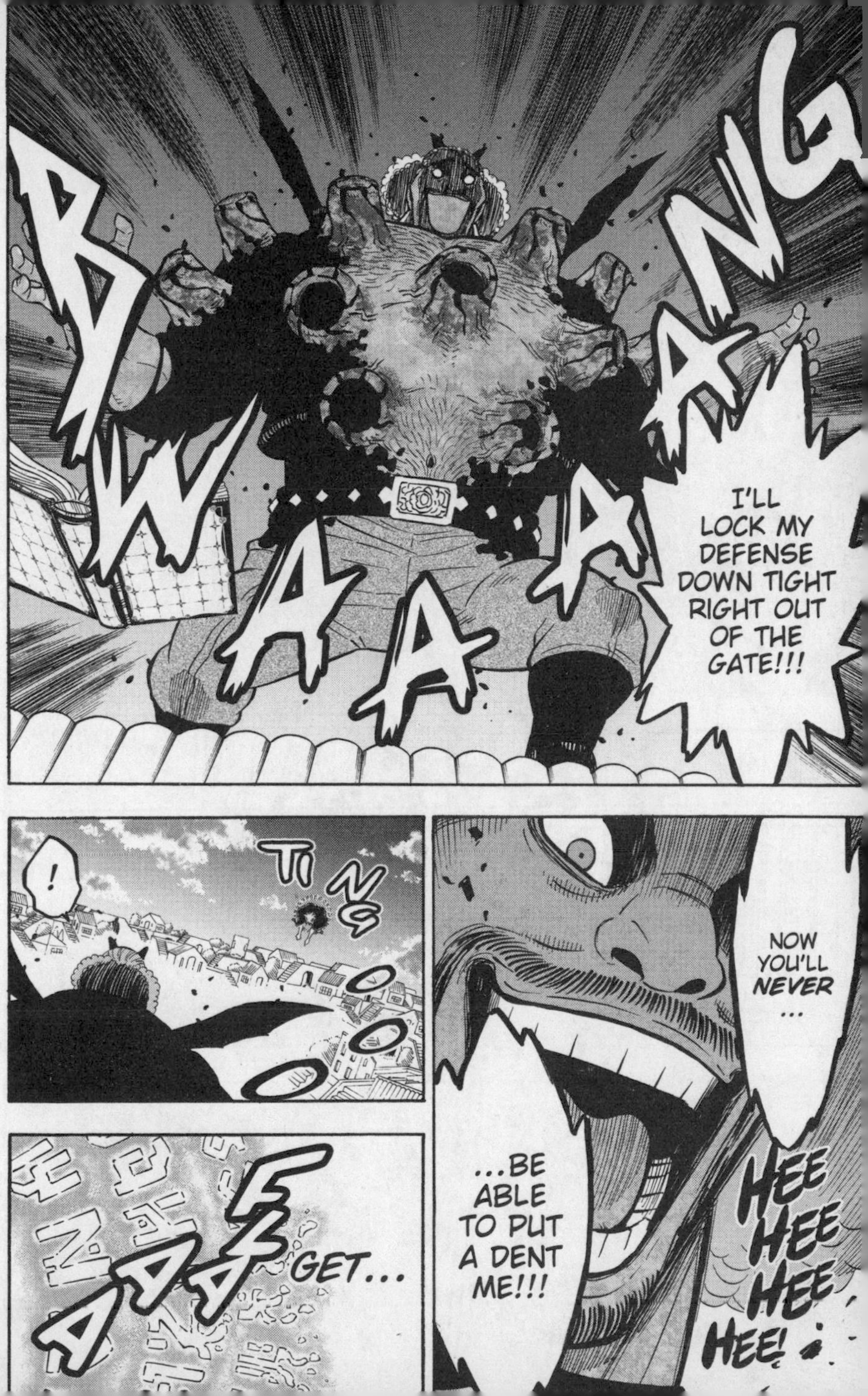
BAWAAAAANG
I'LL LOCK MY DEFENSE DOWN TIGHT RIGHT OUT OF THE GATE!!!
NOW YOU'LL NEVER...
...BE ABLE TO PUT A DENT ME!!!
HEE HEE HEE HEE!
!
TING
GET...
FAAAA

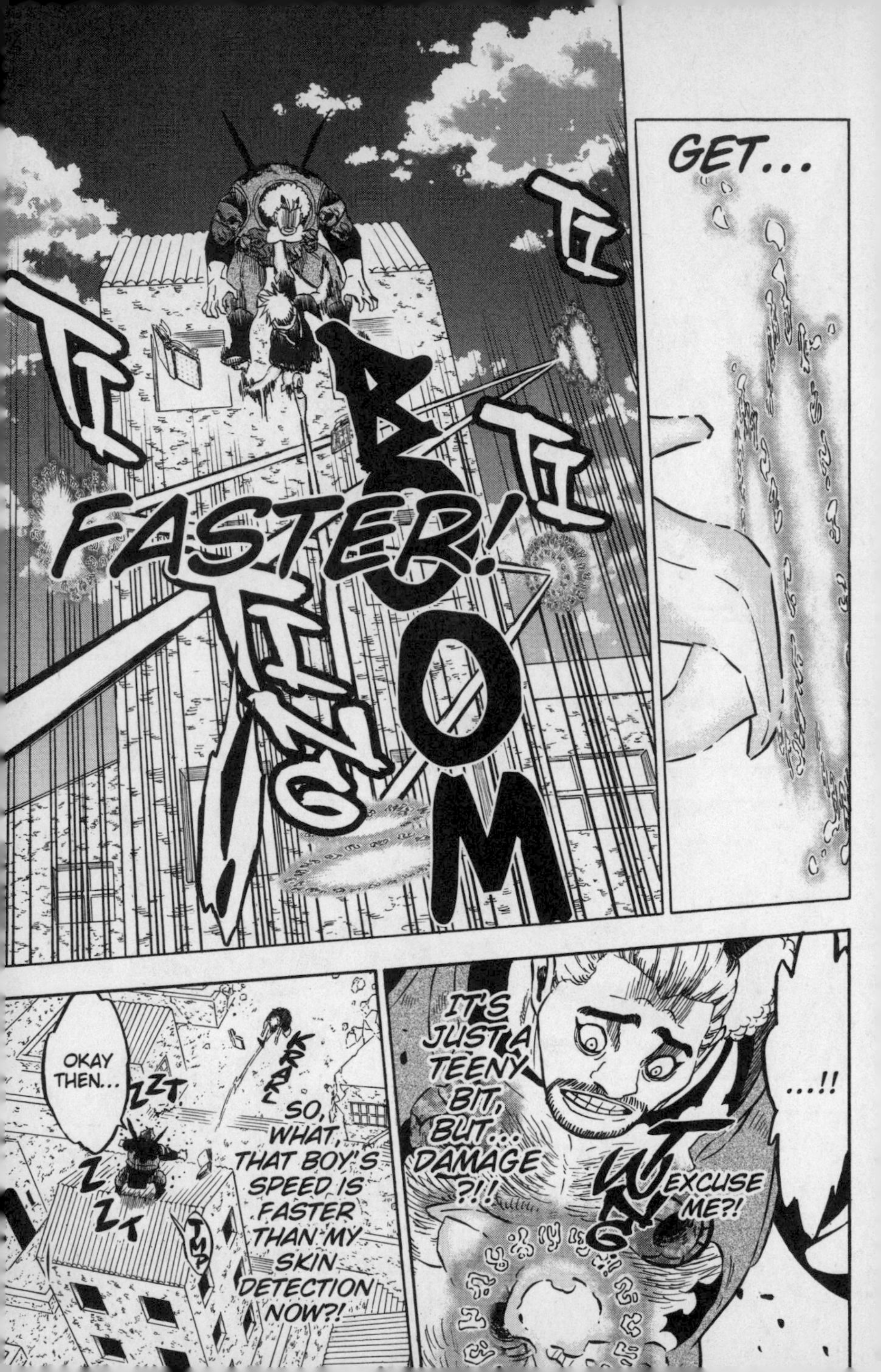
GET...
TI
TI
TI
BOOM
FASTER!
TING
...!!
IT'S JUST A TEENY BIT, BUT... DAMAGE?!!
EXCUSE ME?!
WING
KRAK!
SO, WHAT, THAT BOY'S SPEED IS FASTER THAN MY SKIN DETECTION NOW?!
OKAY THEN...
ZZZT
ZZZT
TMP

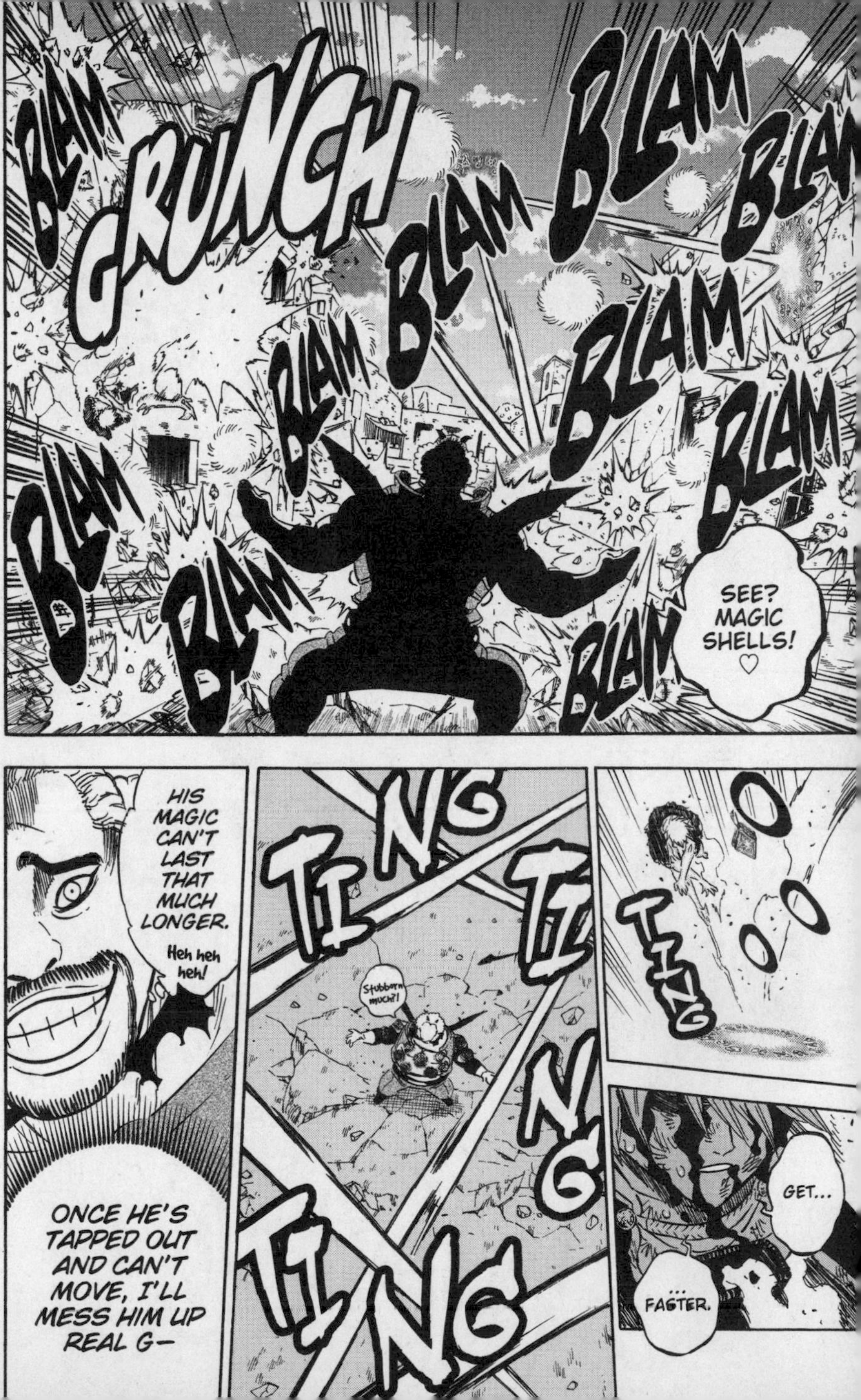
BLAM
SEE? MAGIC SHELLS! ♡
BLAM
BLAM
BLAM
BLAM
BLAM
BLAM
BLAM
BLAM
CRUNCH
BLAM
BLAM
TING
GET...
...FASTER.
TING
TING
Stubborn much?!
TING
TING
HIS MAGIC CAN'T LAST THAT MUCH LONGER.
Heh heh heh!
ONCE HE'S TAPPED OUT AND CAN'T MOVE, I'LL MESS HIM UP REAL G—

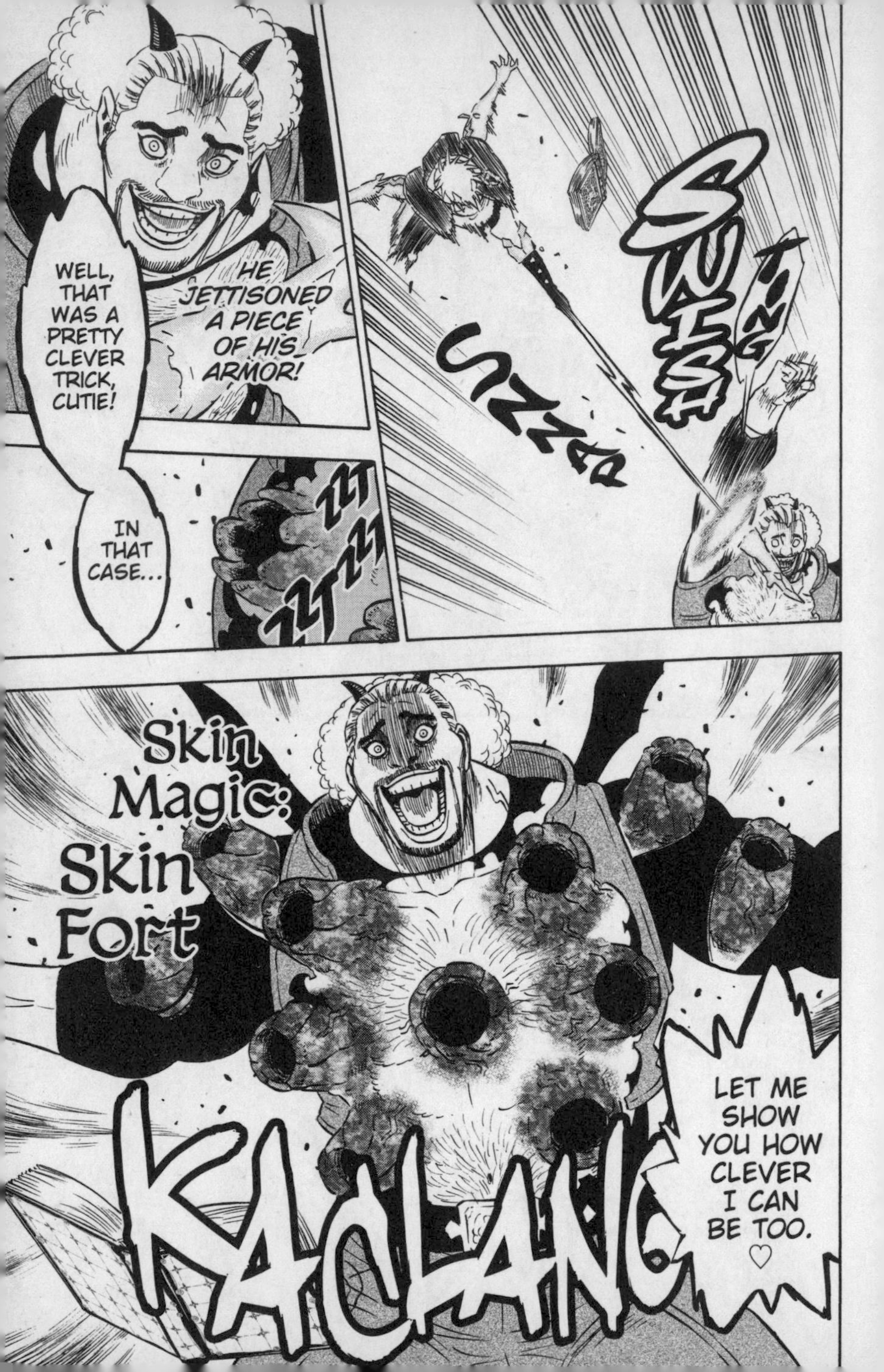
SWISH
TING
ZZZAP
HE JETTISONED A PIECE OF HIS ARMOR!
WELL, THAT WAS A PRETTY CLEVER TRICK, CUTIE!
ZZZT
IN THAT CASE...
LET ME SHOW YOU HOW CLEVER I CAN BE TOO. ♡
Skin Magic: Skin Fort
KACLANG

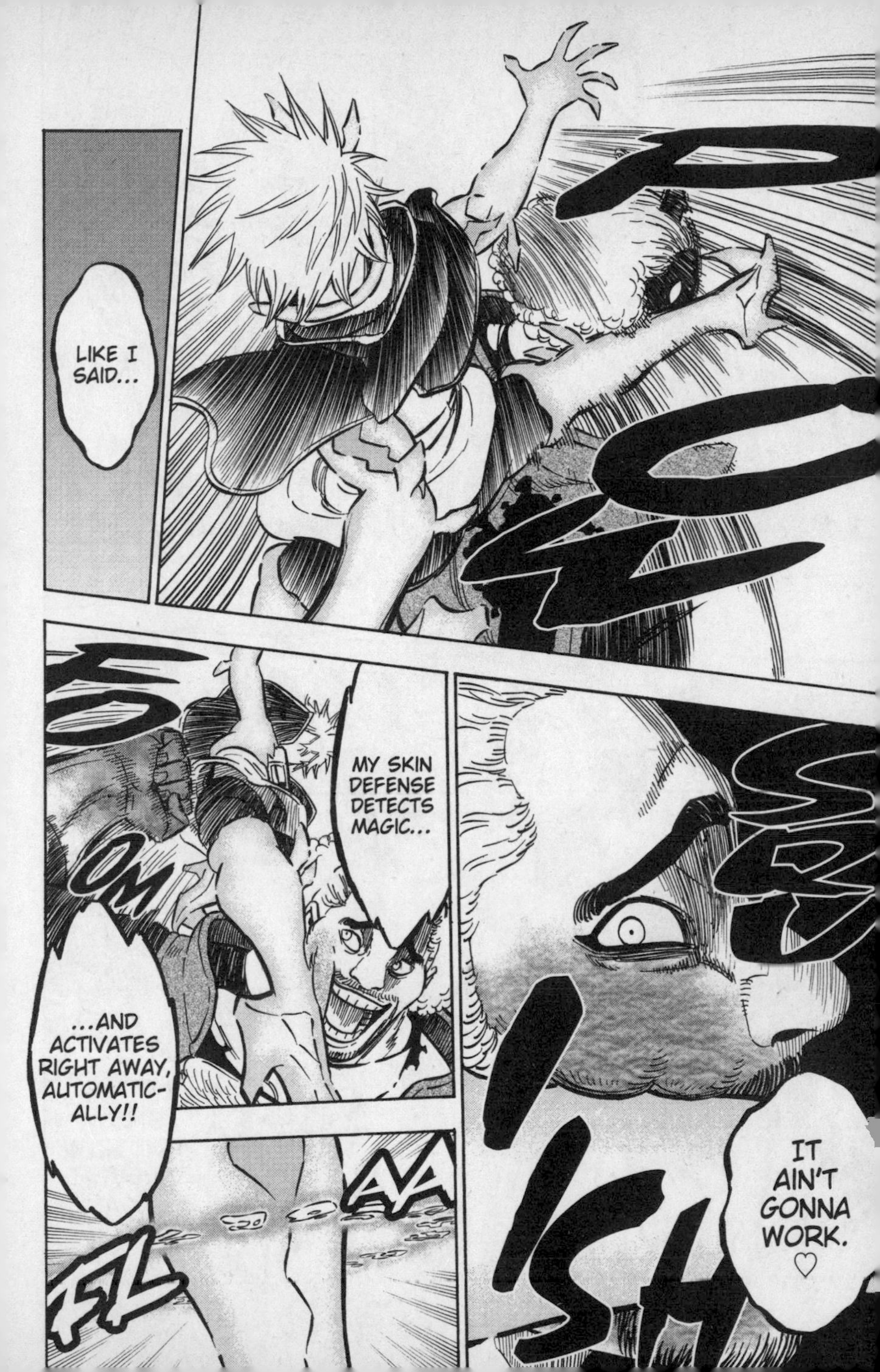
LIKE I SAID...
IT AIN'T GONNA WORK. ♡
MY SKIN DEFENSE DETECTS MAGIC...
...AND ACTIVATES RIGHT AWAY, AUTOMATIC-ALLY!!

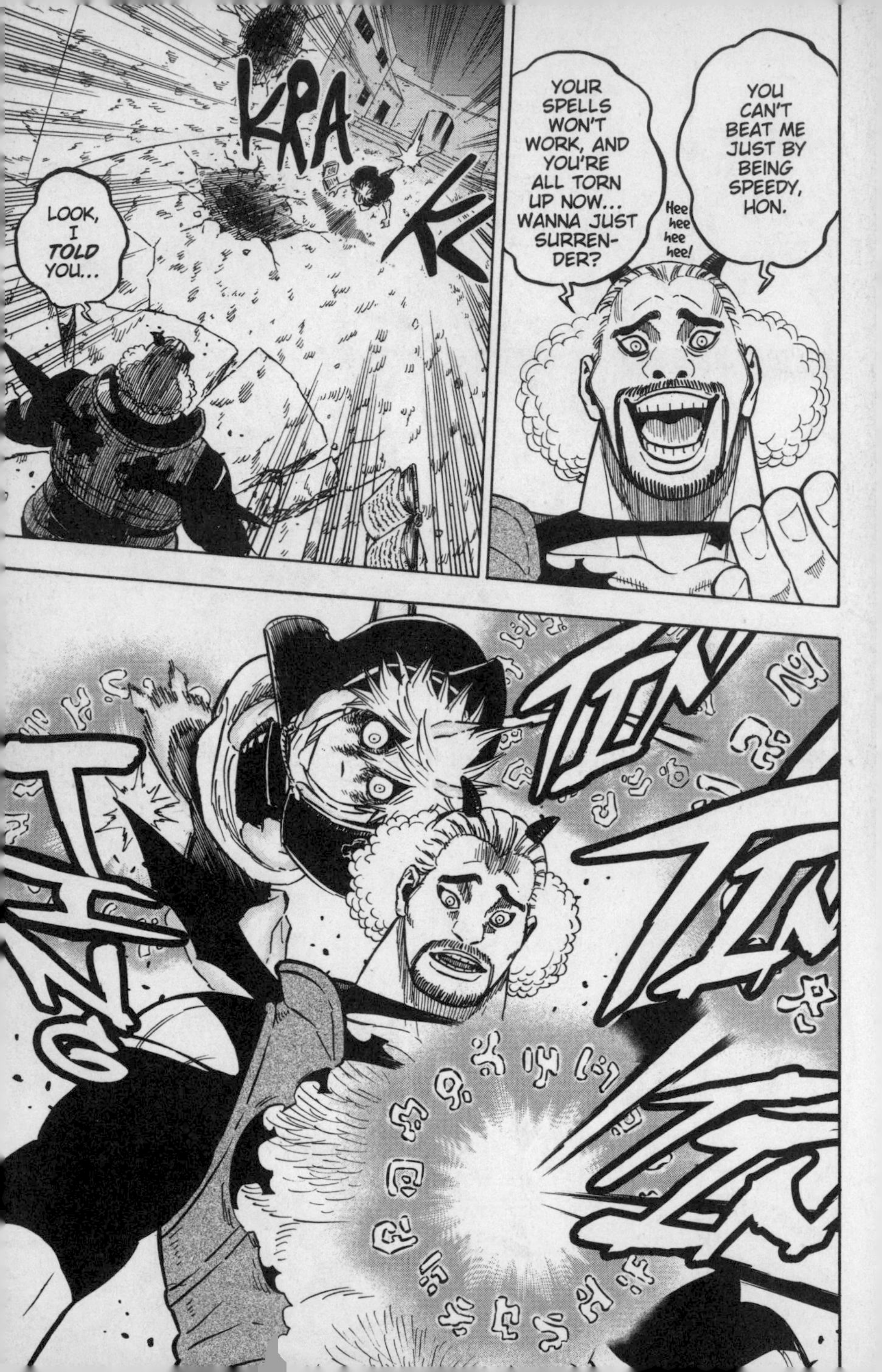
YOU CAN'T BEAT ME JUST BY BEING SPEEDY, HON.
Hee hee hee hee!
YOUR SPELLS WON'T WORK, AND YOU'RE ALL TORN UP NOW... WANNA JUST SURRENDER?
KRAKK
LOOK, I TOLD YOU...

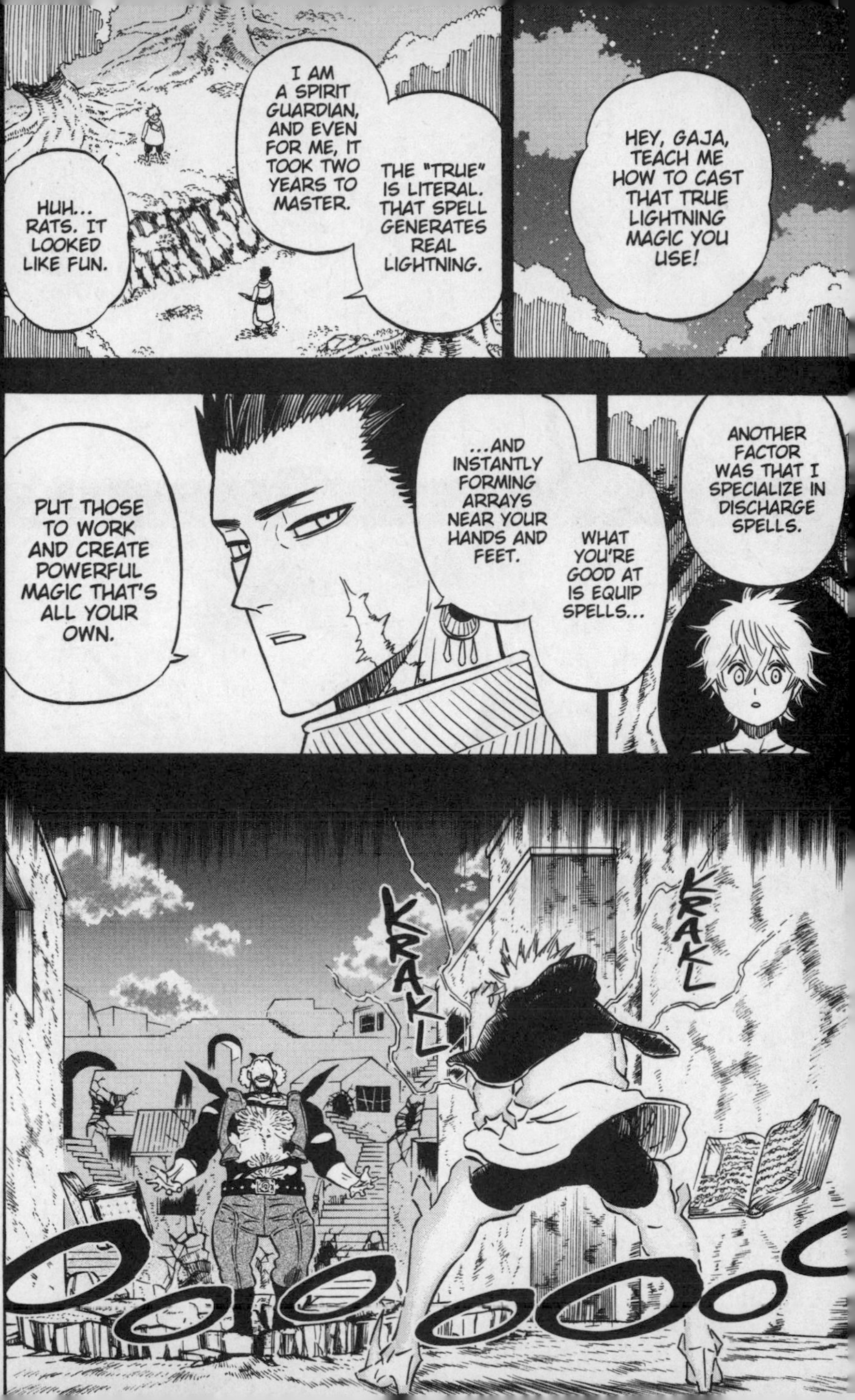
HEY, GAJA, TEACH ME HOW TO CAST THAT TRUE LIGHTNING MAGIC YOU USE!
THE "TRUE" IS LITERAL. THAT SPELL GENERATES REAL LIGHTNING.
I AM A SPIRIT GUARDIAN, AND EVEN FOR ME, IT TOOK TWO YEARS TO MASTER.
HUH... RATS. IT LOOKED LIKE FUN.
ANOTHER FACTOR WAS THAT I SPECIALIZE IN DISCHARGE SPELLS.
WHAT YOU'RE GOOD AT IS EQUIP SPELLS...
...AND INSTANTLY FORMING ARRAYS NEAR YOUR HANDS AND FEET.
PUT THOSE TO WORK AND CREATE POWERFUL MAGIC THAT'S ALL YOUR OWN.
KRAKL
KRAKL

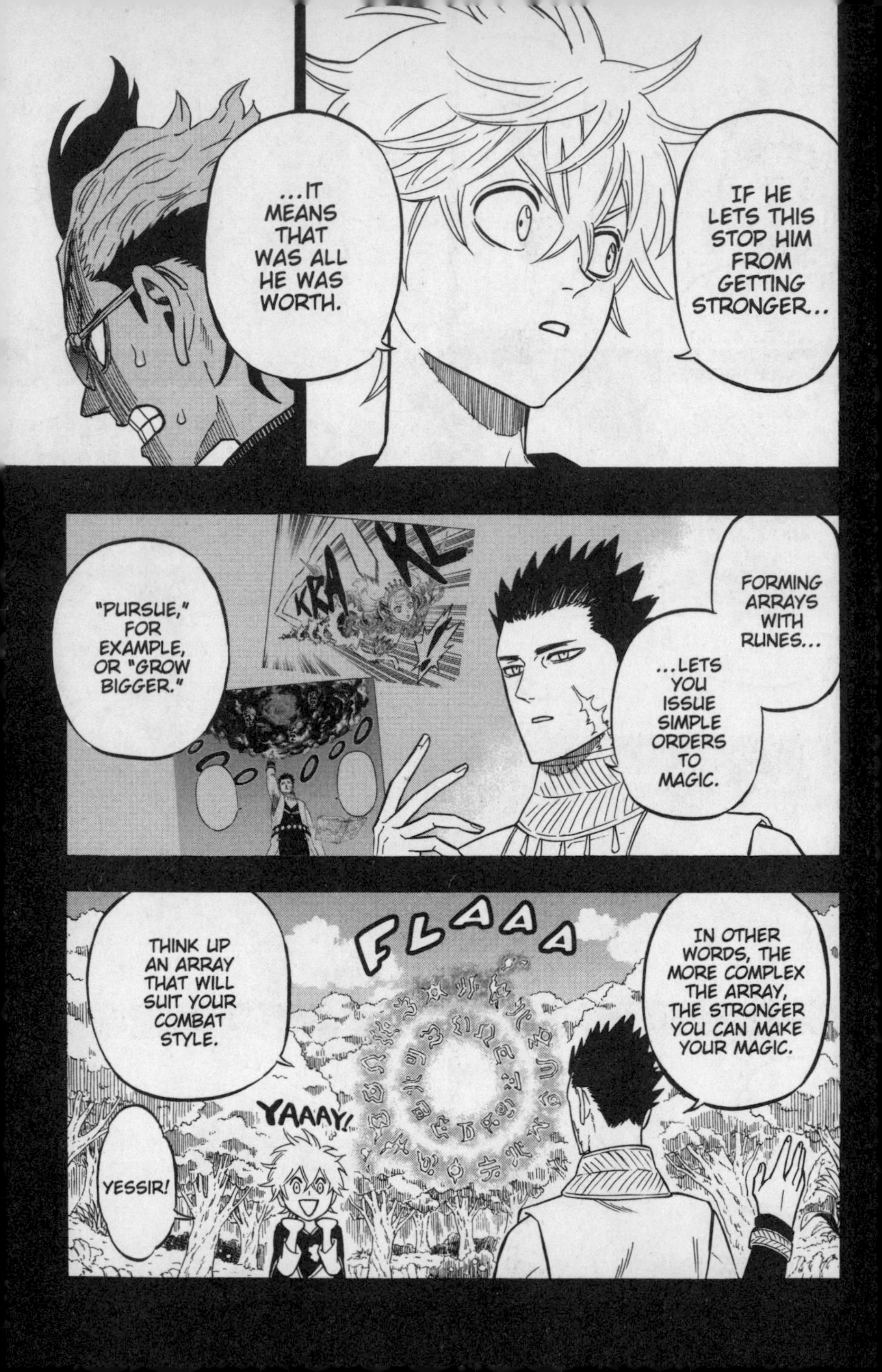
IF HE LETS THIS STOP HIM FROM GETTING STRONGER...
...IT MEANS THAT WAS ALL HE WAS WORTH.
FORMING ARRAYS WITH RUNES...
...LETS YOU ISSUE SIMPLE ORDERS TO MAGIC.
KRA KL
"PURSUE," FOR EXAMPLE, OR "GROW BIGGER."
IN OTHER WORDS, THE MORE COMPLEX THE ARRAY, THE STRONGER YOU CAN MAKE YOUR MAGIC.
FLAAAA
THINK UP AN ARRAY THAT WILL SUIT YOUR COMBAT STYLE.
YAAAY!
YESSIR!

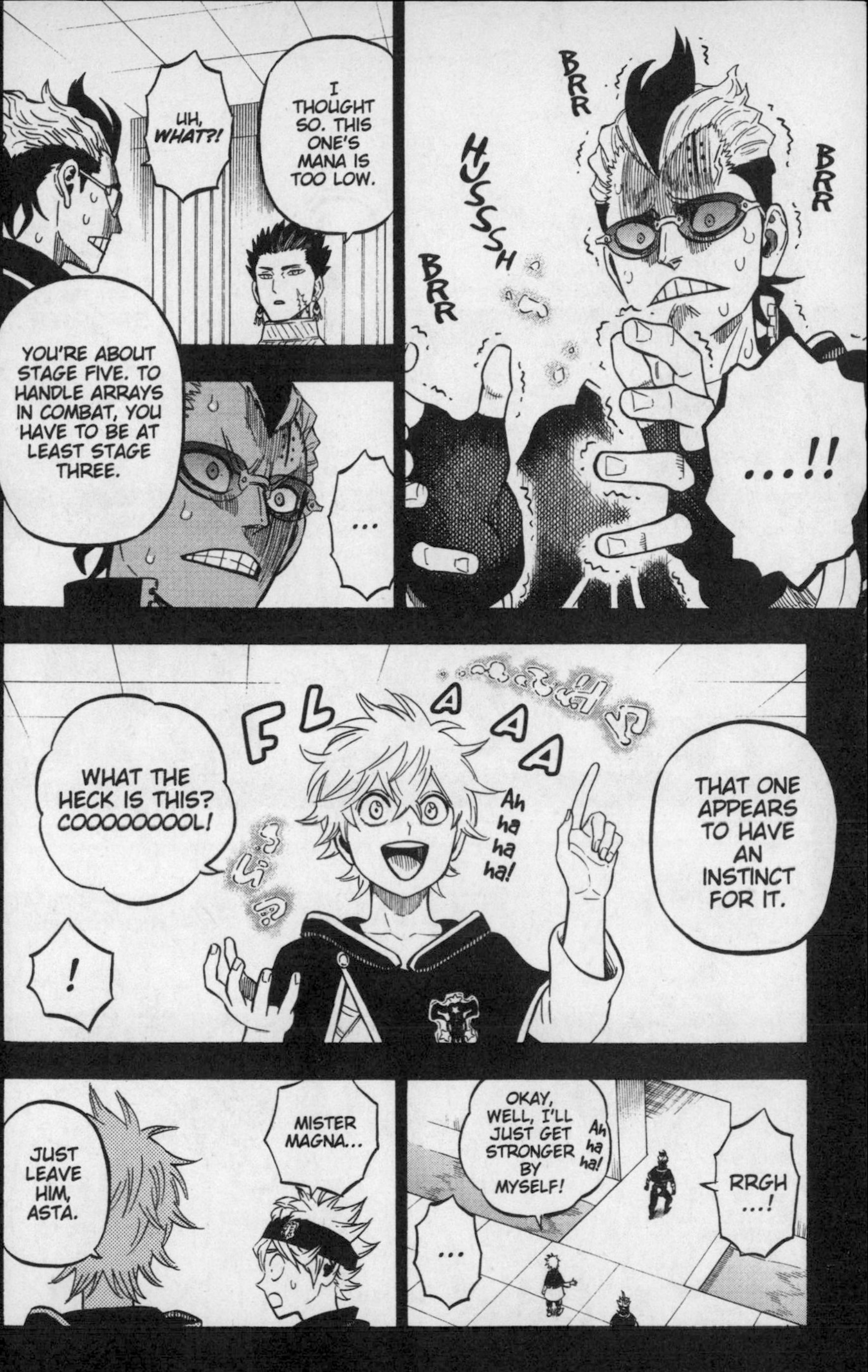
BRR
BRR
HUSSSH
BRR
...!!
I THOUGHT SO. THIS ONE'S MANA IS TOO LOW.
UH, WHAT?!
YOU'RE ABOUT STAGE FIVE. TO HANDLE ARRAYS IN COMBAT, YOU HAVE TO BE AT LEAST STAGE THREE.
...
THAT ONE APPEARS TO HAVE AN INSTINCT FOR IT.
FLAAAA
Ah ha ha ha!
WHAT THE HECK IS THIS? COOOOOOOOL!
!
RRGH ...!
OKAY, WELL, I'LL JUST GET STRONGER BY MYSELF!
Ah ha ha!
...
MISTER MAGNA...
JUST LEAVE HIM, ASTA.

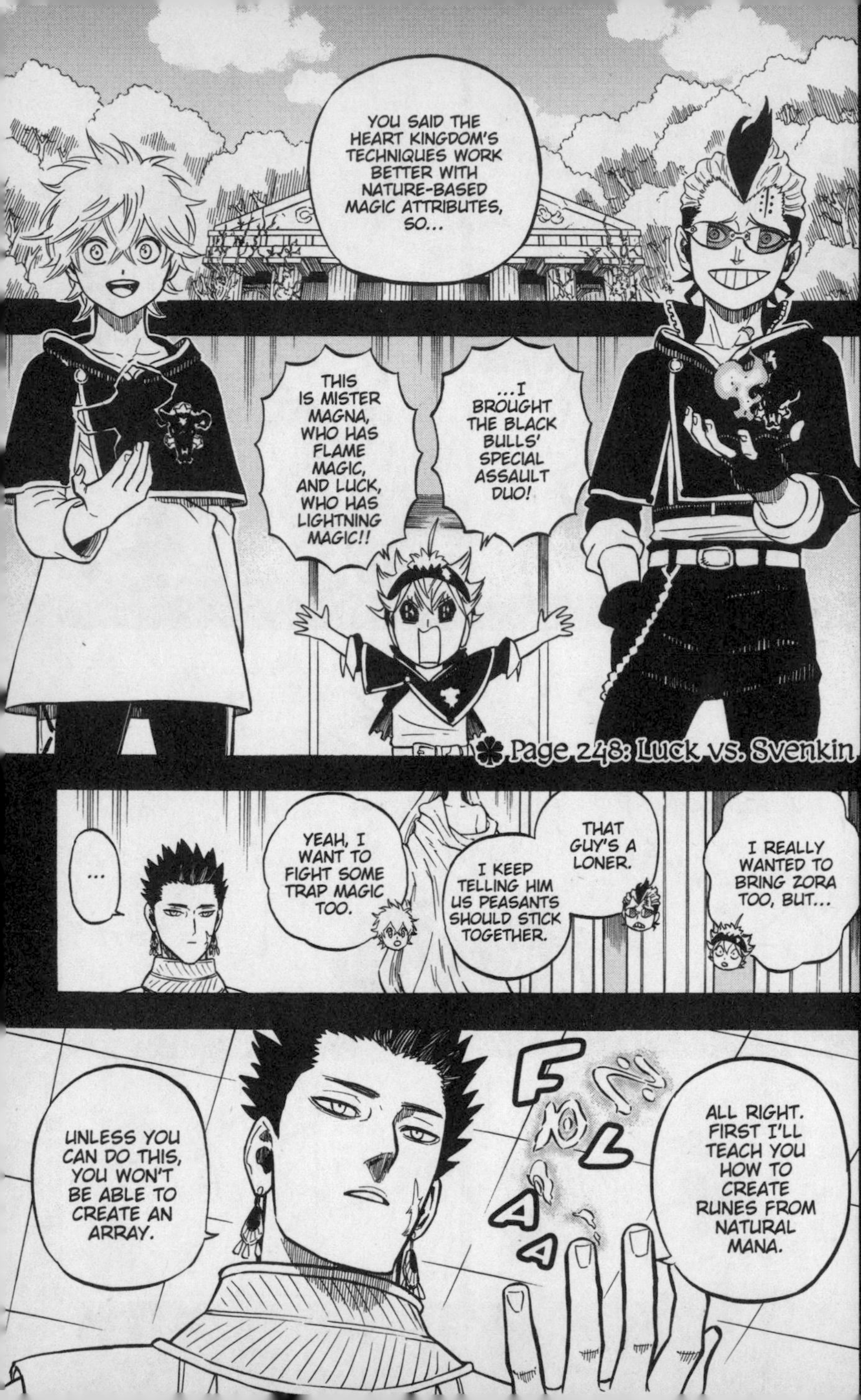
YOU SAID THE HEART KINGDOM'S TECHNIQUES WORK BETTER WITH NATURE-BASED MAGIC ATTRIBUTES, SO...
...I BROUGHT THE BLACK BULLS' SPECIAL ASSAULT DUO!
THIS IS MISTER MAGNA, WHO HAS FLAME MAGIC, AND LUCK, WHO HAS LIGHTNING MAGIC!!
Page 248: Luck vs. Svenkin
I REALLY WANTED TO BRING ZORA TOO, BUT...
THAT GUY'S A LONER.
I KEEP TELLING HIM US PEASANTS SHOULD STICK TOGETHER.
YEAH, I WANT TO FIGHT SOME TRAP MAGIC TOO.
...
ALL RIGHT. FIRST I'LL TEACH YOU HOW TO CREATE RUNES FROM NATURAL MANA.
FLAA
UNLESS YOU CAN DO THIS, YOU WON'T BE ABLE TO CREATE AN ARRAY.

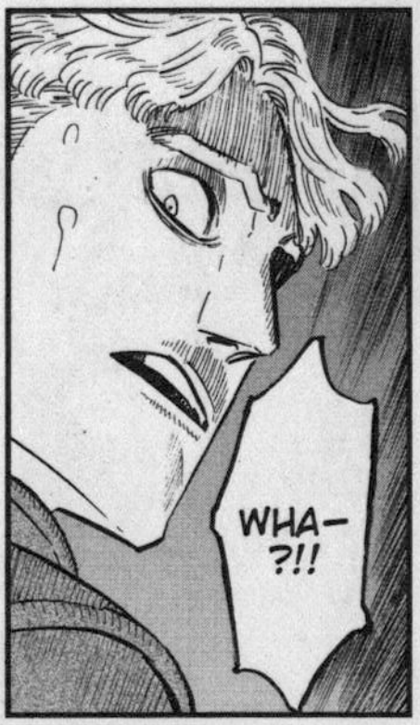
WHA-
?!!

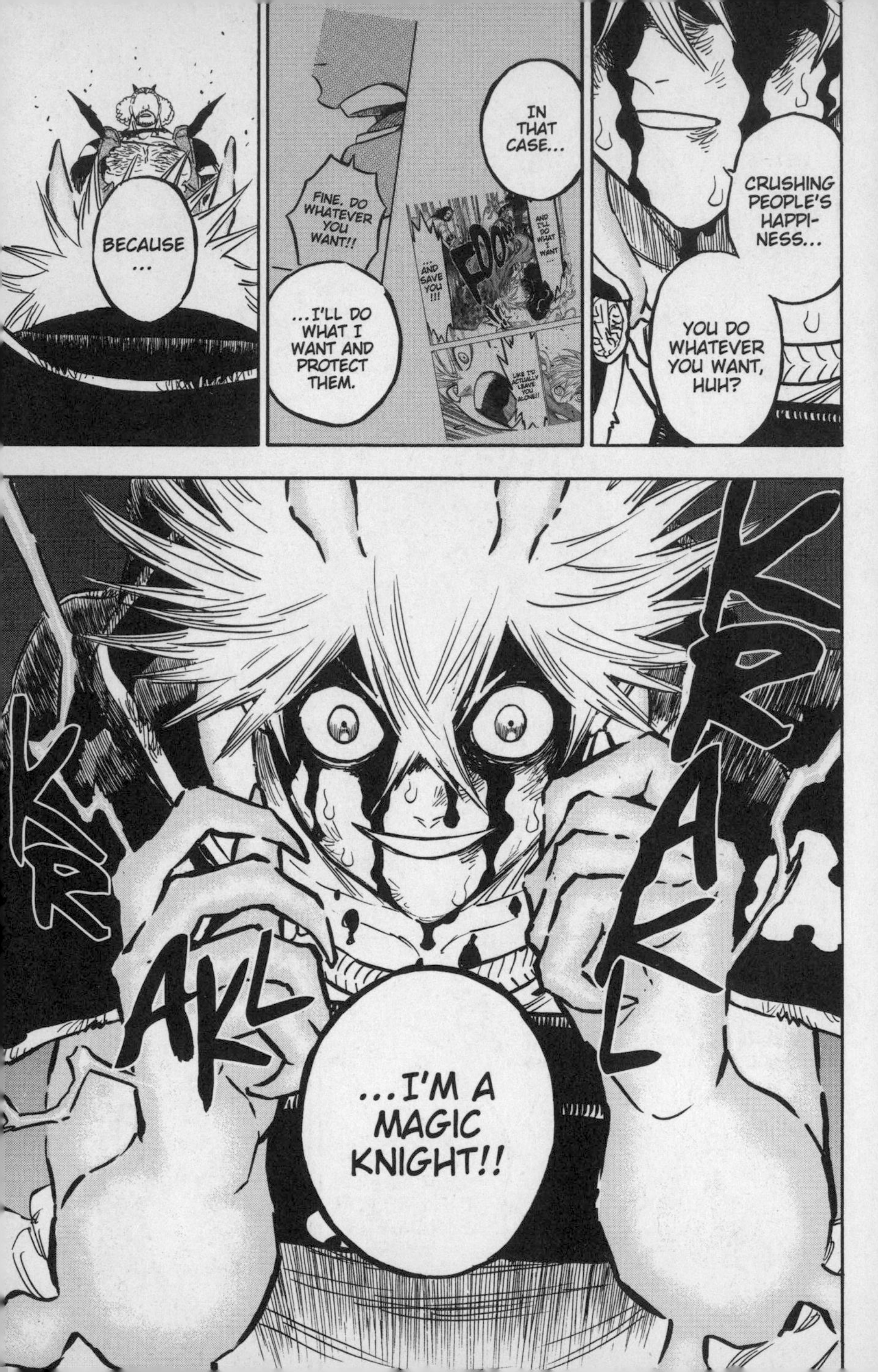
CRUSHING PEOPLE'S HAPPINESS...
YOU DO WHATEVER YOU WANT, HUH?
IN THAT CASE...
AND I'LL DO WHAT I WANT...
FOOM
...AND SAVE YOU!!!
LIKE I'D ACTUALLY LEAVE YOU ALONE!!
FINE. DO WHATEVER YOU WANT!!
...I'LL DO WHAT I WANT AND PROTECT THEM.
BECAUSE ...
KRAKL
KRAKL
...I'M A MAGIC KNIGHT!!

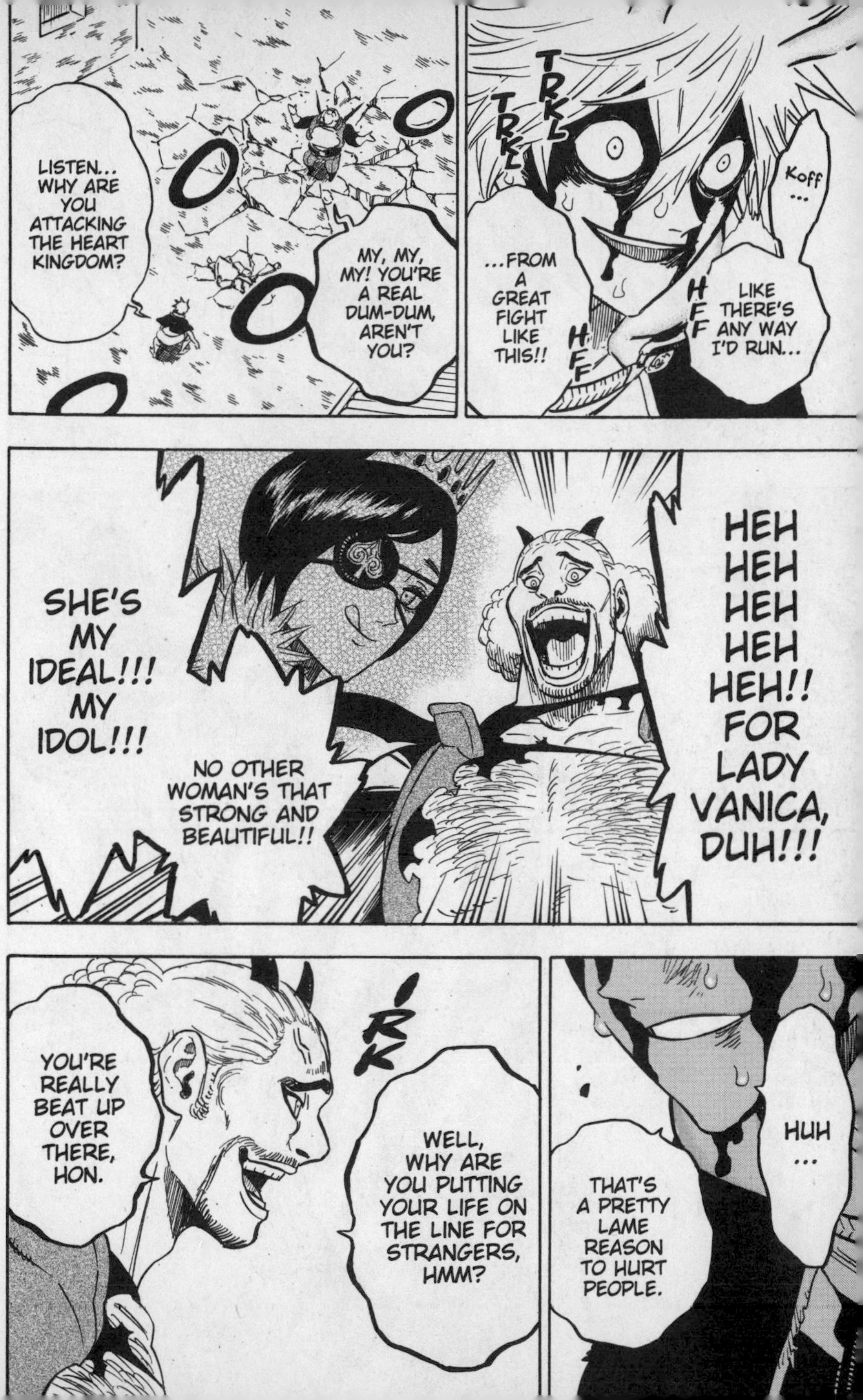
TRKL TRKL
Koff ...
LIKE THERE'S ANY WAY I'D RUN...
HFF HFF
...FROM A GREAT FIGHT LIKE THIS!!
LISTEN... WHY ARE YOU ATTACKING THE HEART KINGDOM?
MY, MY, MY! YOU'RE A REAL DUM-DUM, AREN'T YOU?
HEH HEH HEH HEH HEH!! FOR LADY VANICA, DUH!!!
SHE'S MY IDEAL!!! MY IDOL!!!
NO OTHER WOMAN'S THAT STRONG AND BEAUTIFUL!!
HUH ...
THAT'S A PRETTY LAME REASON TO HURT PEOPLE.
IRK
YOU'RE REALLY BEAT UP OVER THERE, HON.
WELL, WHY ARE YOU PUTTING YOUR LIFE ON THE LINE FOR STRANGERS, HMM?

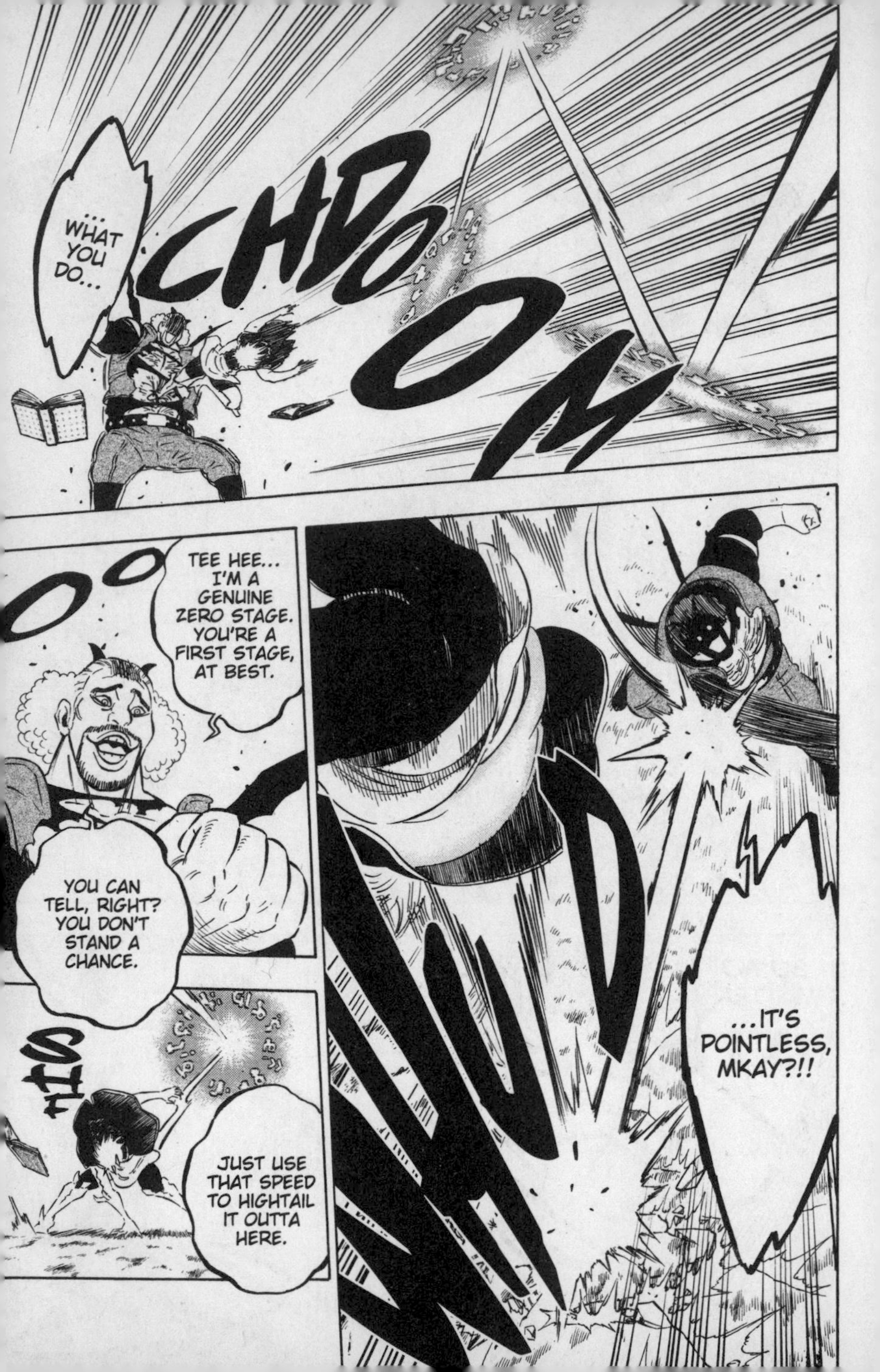
CHDOOM
...WHAT YOU DO...
...IT'S POINTLESS, MKAY?!!
TEE HEE... I'M A GENUINE ZERO STAGE. YOU'RE A FIRST STAGE, AT BEST.
YOU CAN TELL, RIGHT? YOU DON'T STAND A CHANCE.
JUST USE THAT SPEED TO HIGHTAIL IT OUTTA HERE.

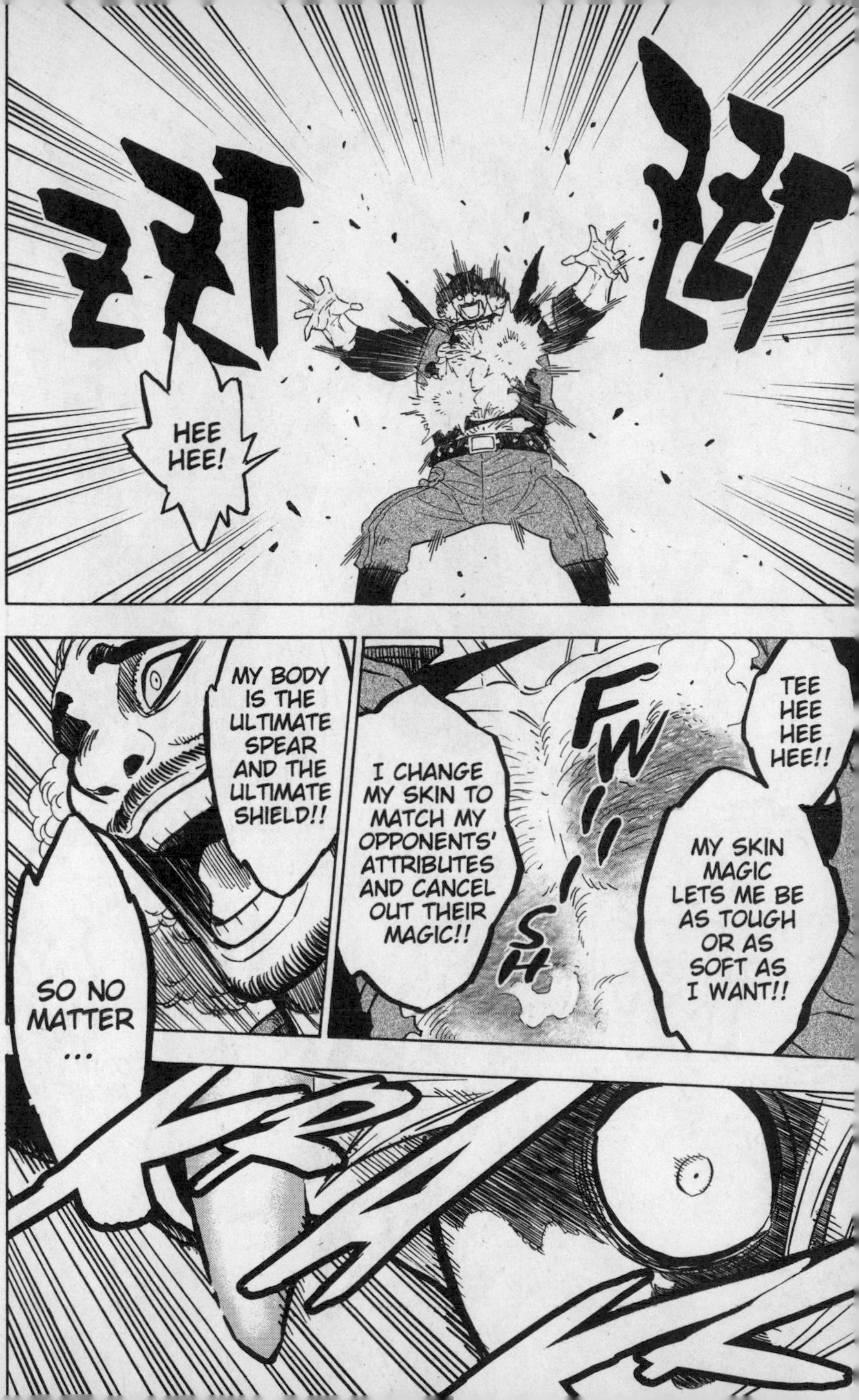
HEE HEE!
TEE HEE HEE HEE!!
MY SKIN MAGIC LETS ME BE AS TOUGH OR AS SOFT AS I WANT!!
FWISH
I CHANGE MY SKIN TO MATCH MY OPPONENTS' ATTRIBUTES AND CANCEL OUT THEIR MAGIC!!
MY BODY IS THE ULTIMATE SPEAR AND THE ULTIMATE SHIELD!!
SO NO MATTER ...

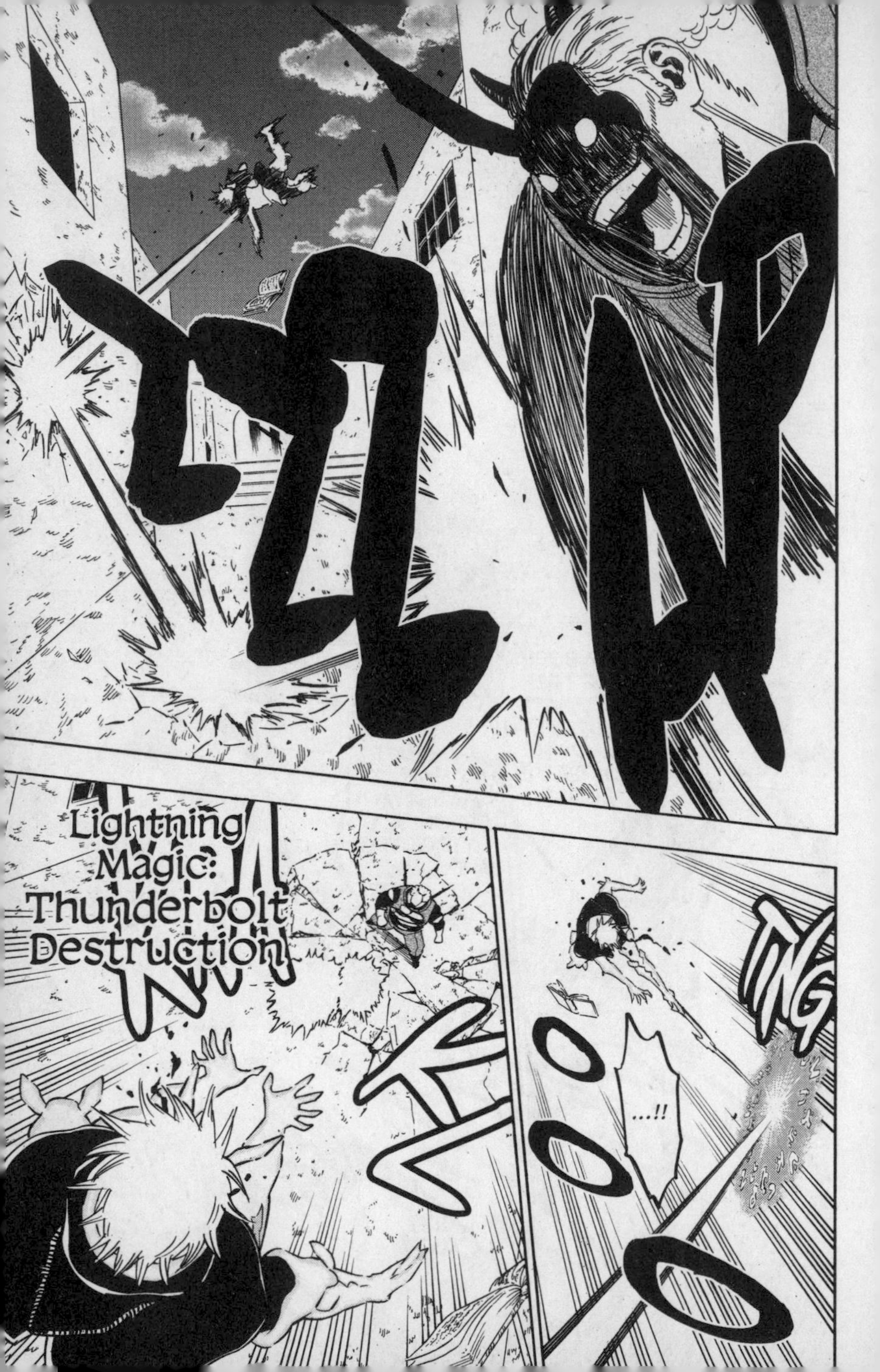
TING
...!!
Lightning Magic: Thunderbolt Destruction

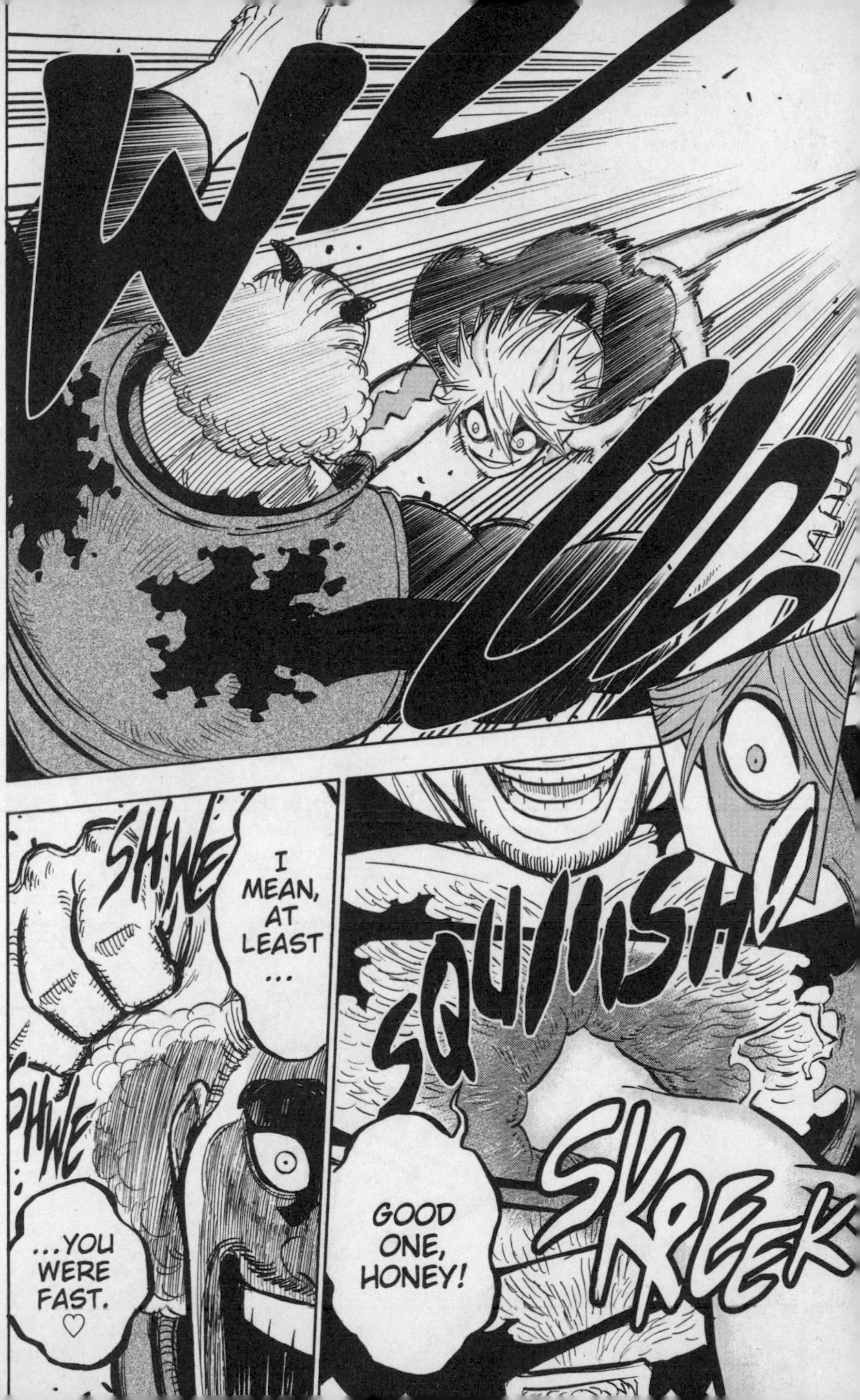
WHUD
SQUIISH!
SKREEK
GOOD ONE, HONEY!
I MEAN, AT LEAST...
SHWE
SHWE
...YOU WERE FAST. ♡

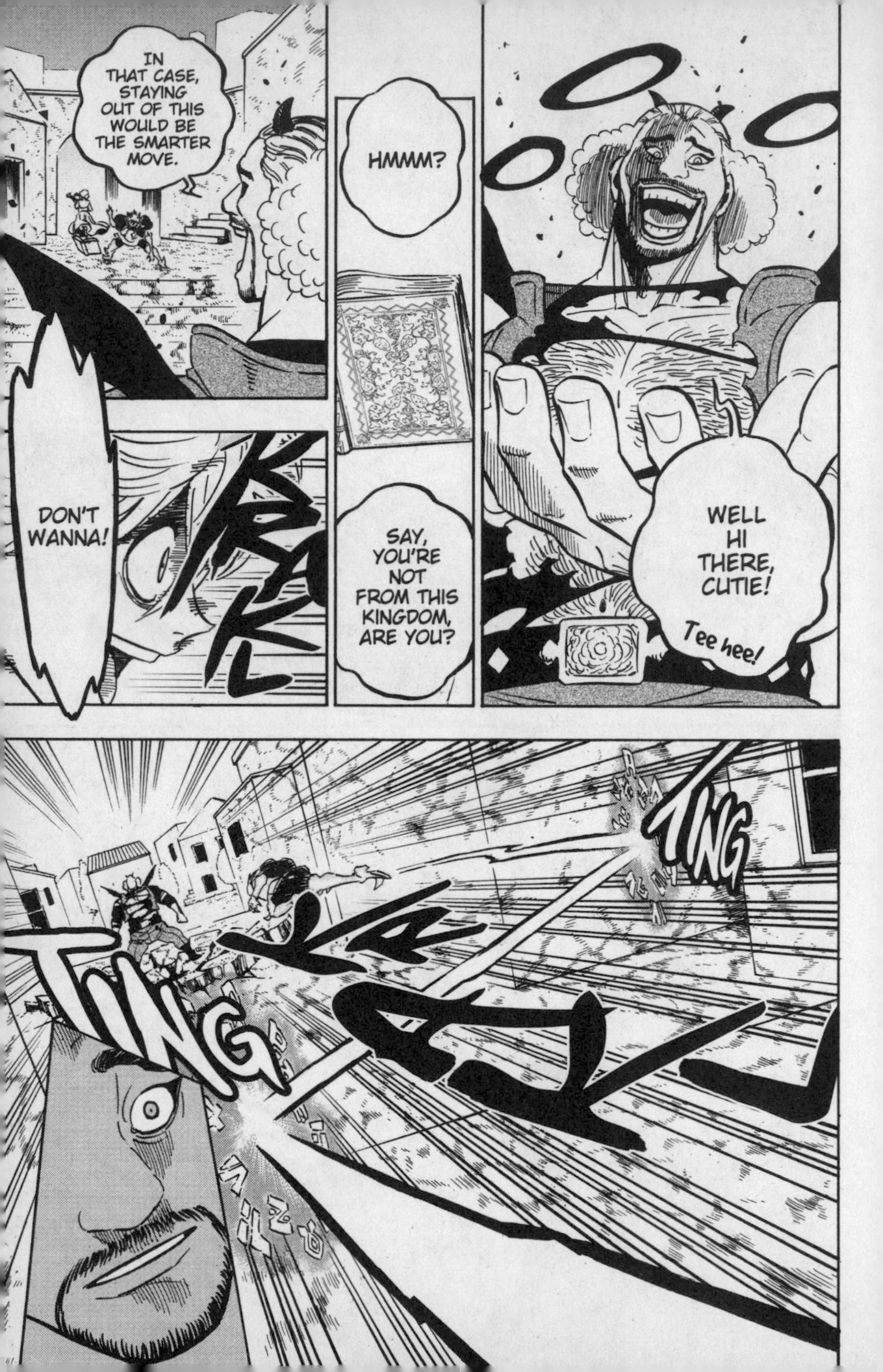
WELL HI THERE, CUTIE!
Tee hee!
HMMM?
SAY, YOU'RE NOT FROM THIS KINGDOM, ARE YOU?
IN THAT CASE, STAYING OUT OF THIS WOULD BE THE SMARTER MOVE.
DON'T WANNA!
TING
TIING

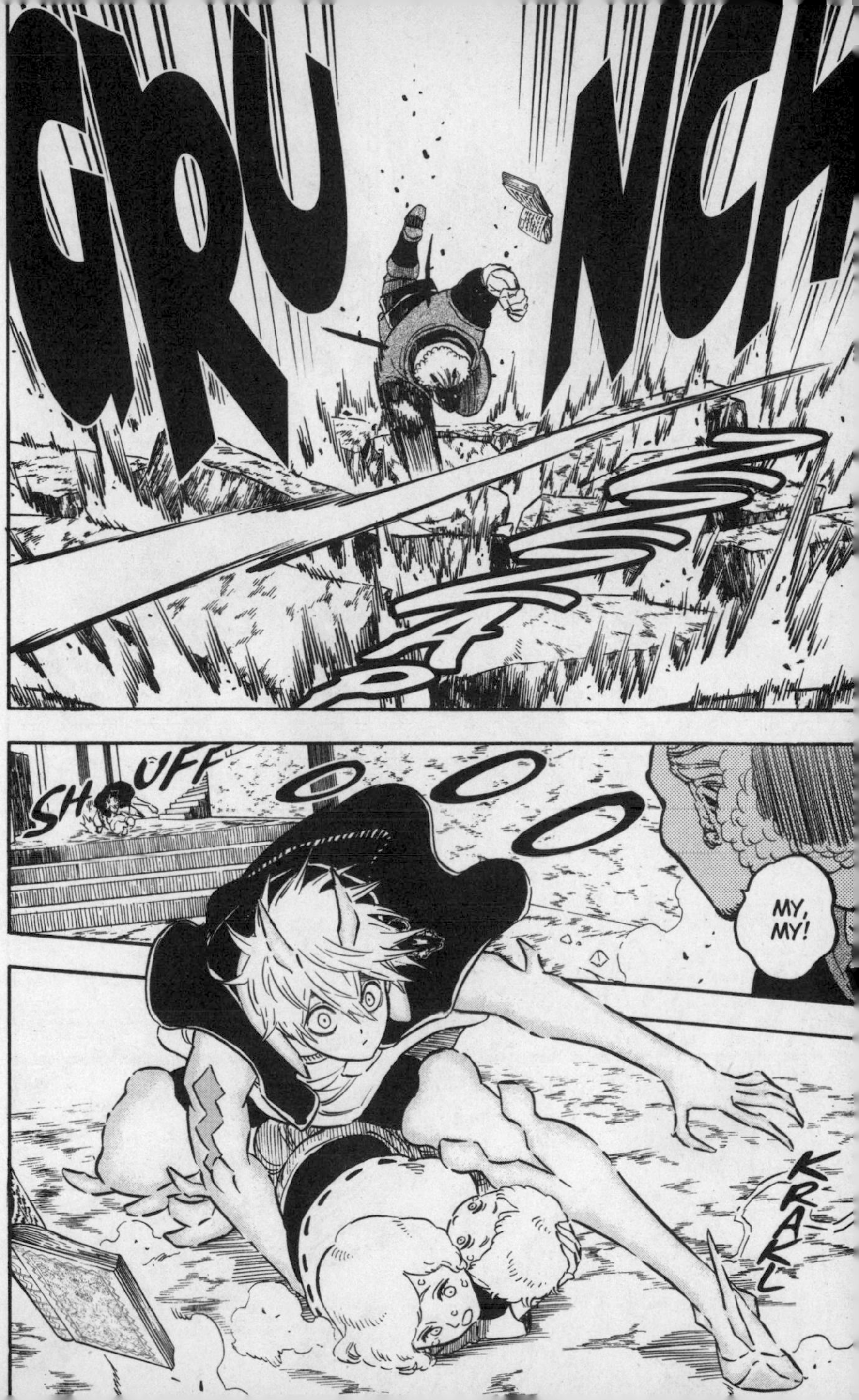
GRUNCH!
SHUFF
MY, MY!
KRAKL

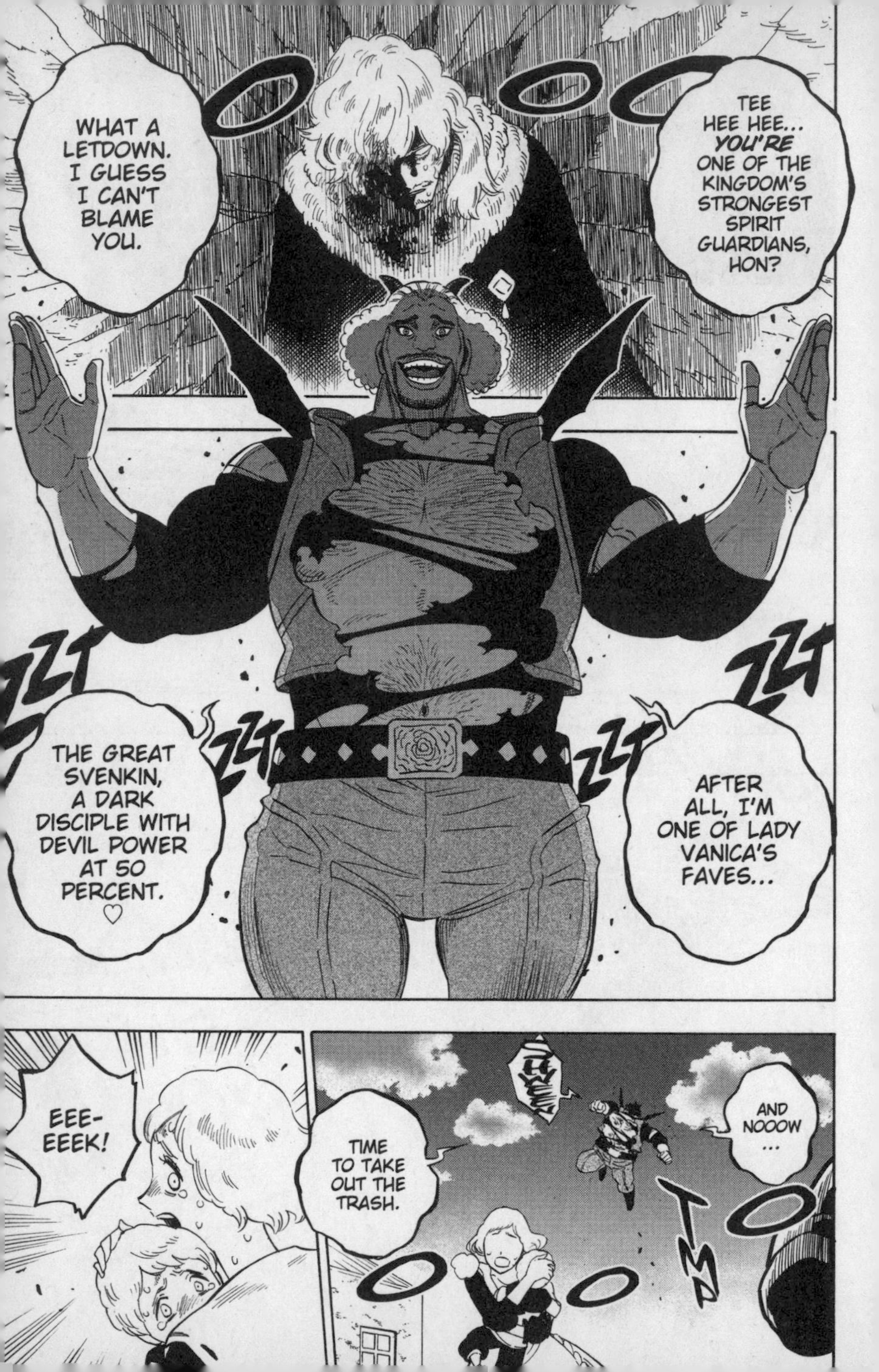
TEE HEE HEE... YOU'RE ONE OF THE KINGDOM'S STRONGEST SPIRIT GUARDIANS, HON?
WHAT A LETDOWN. I GUESS I CAN'T BLAME YOU.
ZZT
AFTER ALL, I'M ONE OF LADY VANICA'S FAVES...
ZZT
THE GREAT SVENKIN, A DARK DISCIPLE WITH DEVIL POWER AT 50 PERCENT. ♡
AND NOOOW ...
TMP
TIME TO TAKE OUT THE TRASH.
EEE-EEEK!

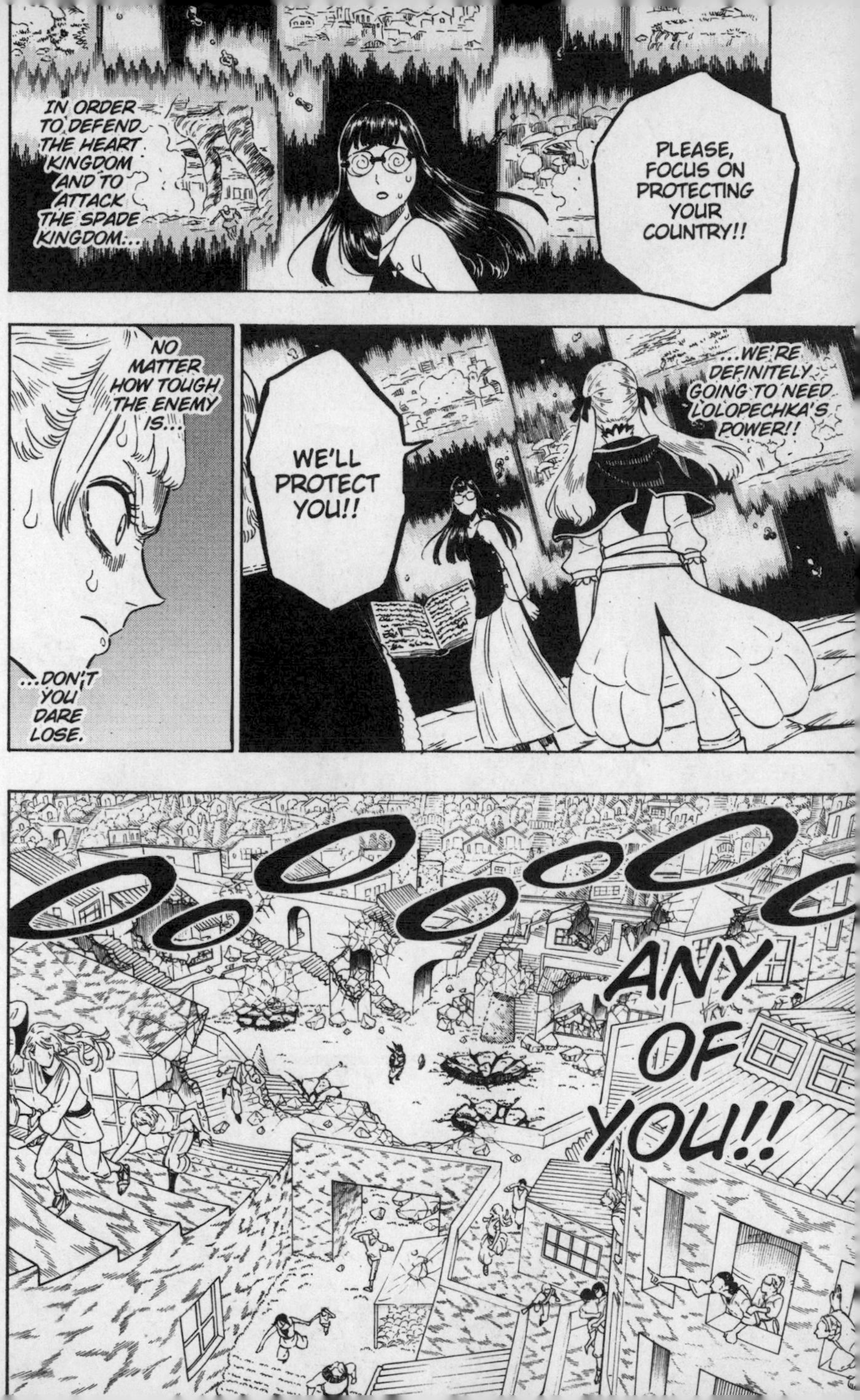
PLEASE, FOCUS ON PROTECTING YOUR COUNTRY!!
IN ORDER TO DEFEND THE HEART KINGDOM AND TO ATTACK THE SPADE KINGDOM...
...WE'RE DEFINITELY GOING TO NEED LOLOPECHKA'S POWER!!
WE'LL PROTECT YOU!!
NO MATTER HOW TOUGH THE ENEMY IS...
...DON'T YOU DARE LOSE.
ANY OF YOU!!

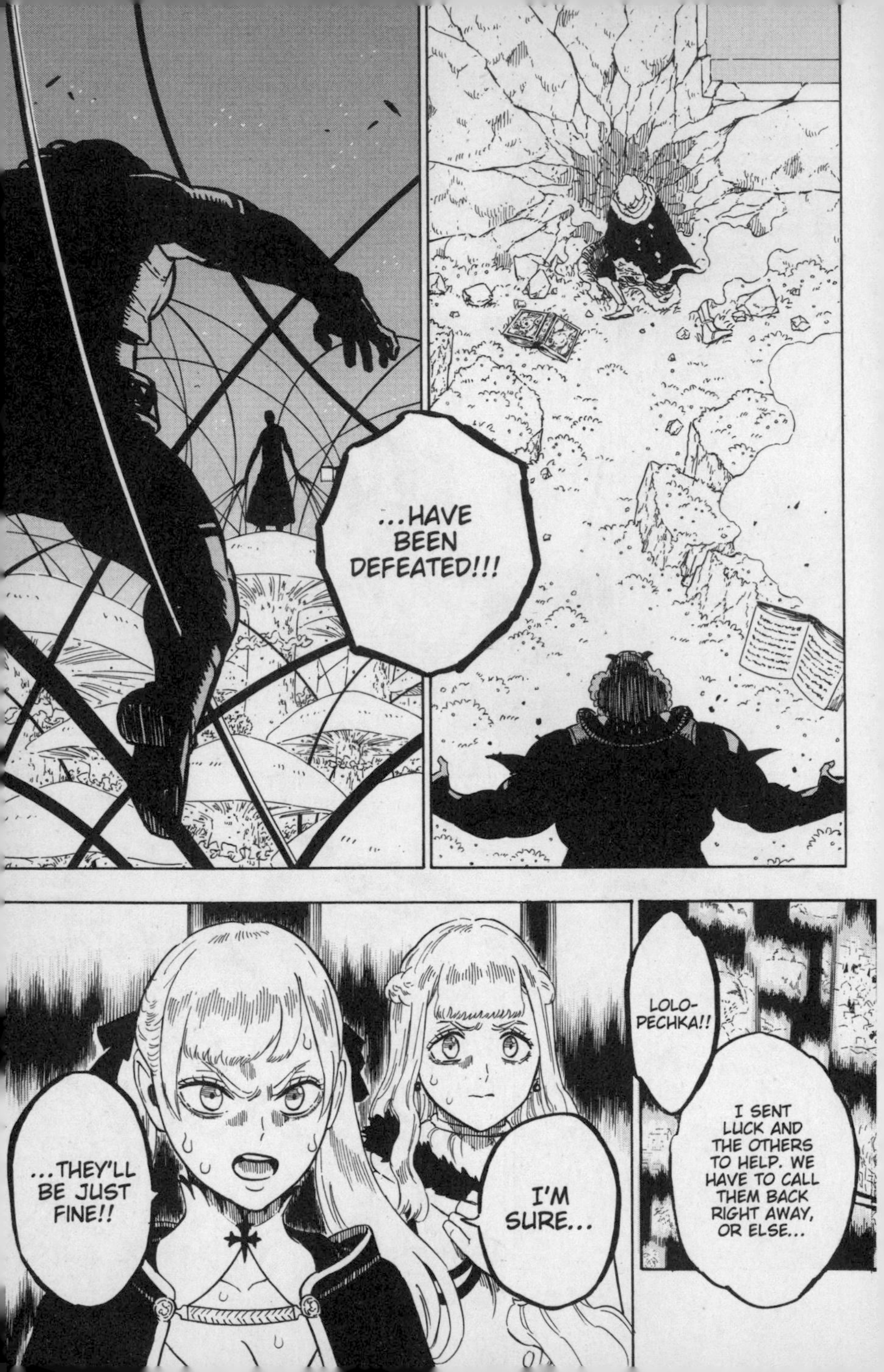
...HAVE BEEN DEFEATED!!!
LOLO-PECHKA!!
I SENT LUCK AND THE OTHERS TO HELP. WE HAVE TO CALL THEM BACK RIGHT AWAY, OR ELSE...
I'M SURE...
...THEY'LL BE JUST FINE!!

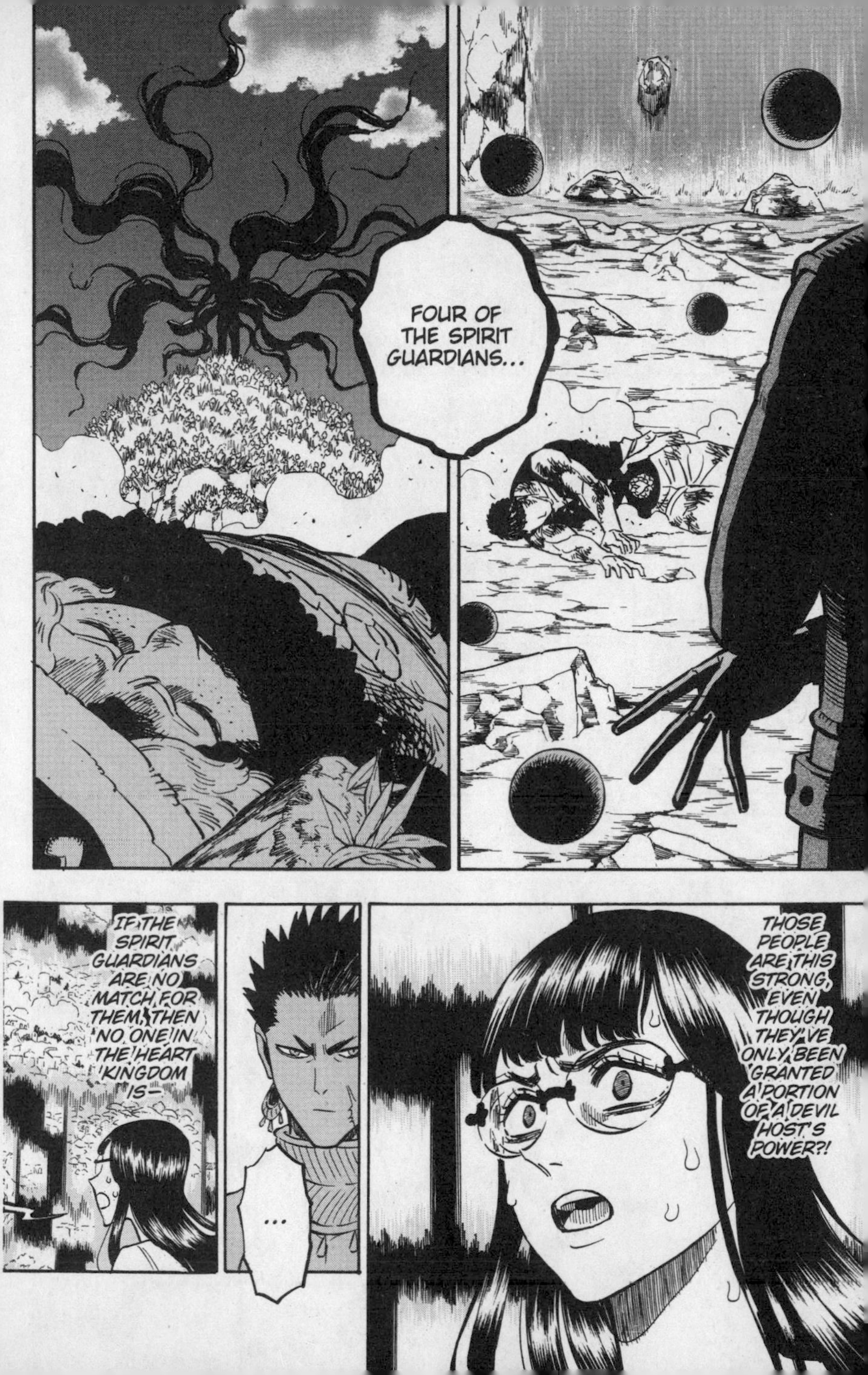
FOUR OF THE SPIRIT GUARDIANS...
THOSE PEOPLE ARE THIS STRONG, EVEN THOUGH THEY'VE ONLY BEEN GRANTED A PORTION OF A DEVIL HOST'S POWER?!
...
IF THE SPIRIT GUARDIANS ARE NO MATCH FOR THEM, THEN NO ONE IN THE HEART KINGDOM IS—

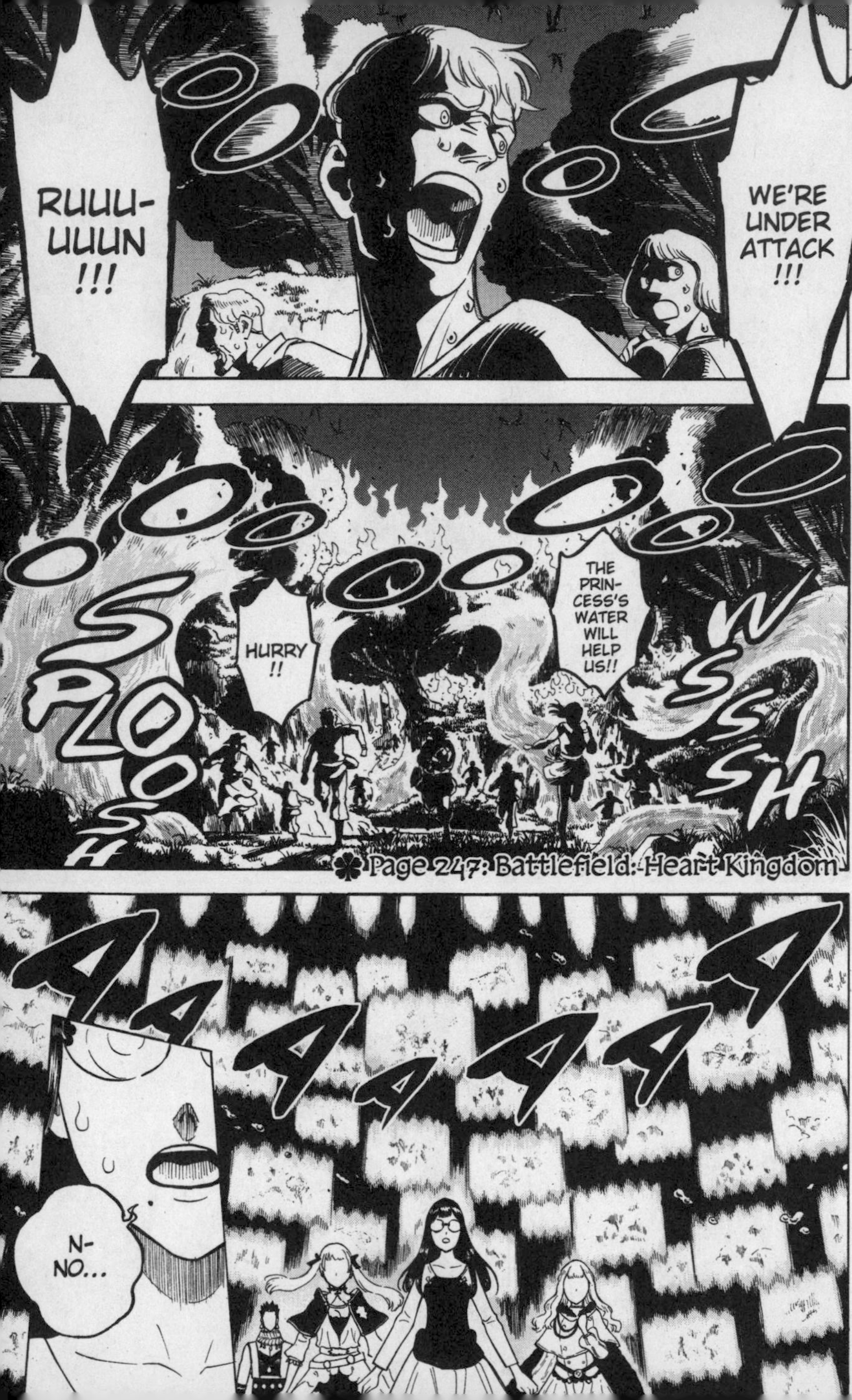
WE'RE UNDER ATTACK!!!
RUUUUUUN!!!
THE PRINCESS'S WATER WILL HELP US!!
HURRY!!
WSSSH
SPLOOSH
Page 247: Battlefield: Heart Kingdom
N-NO...

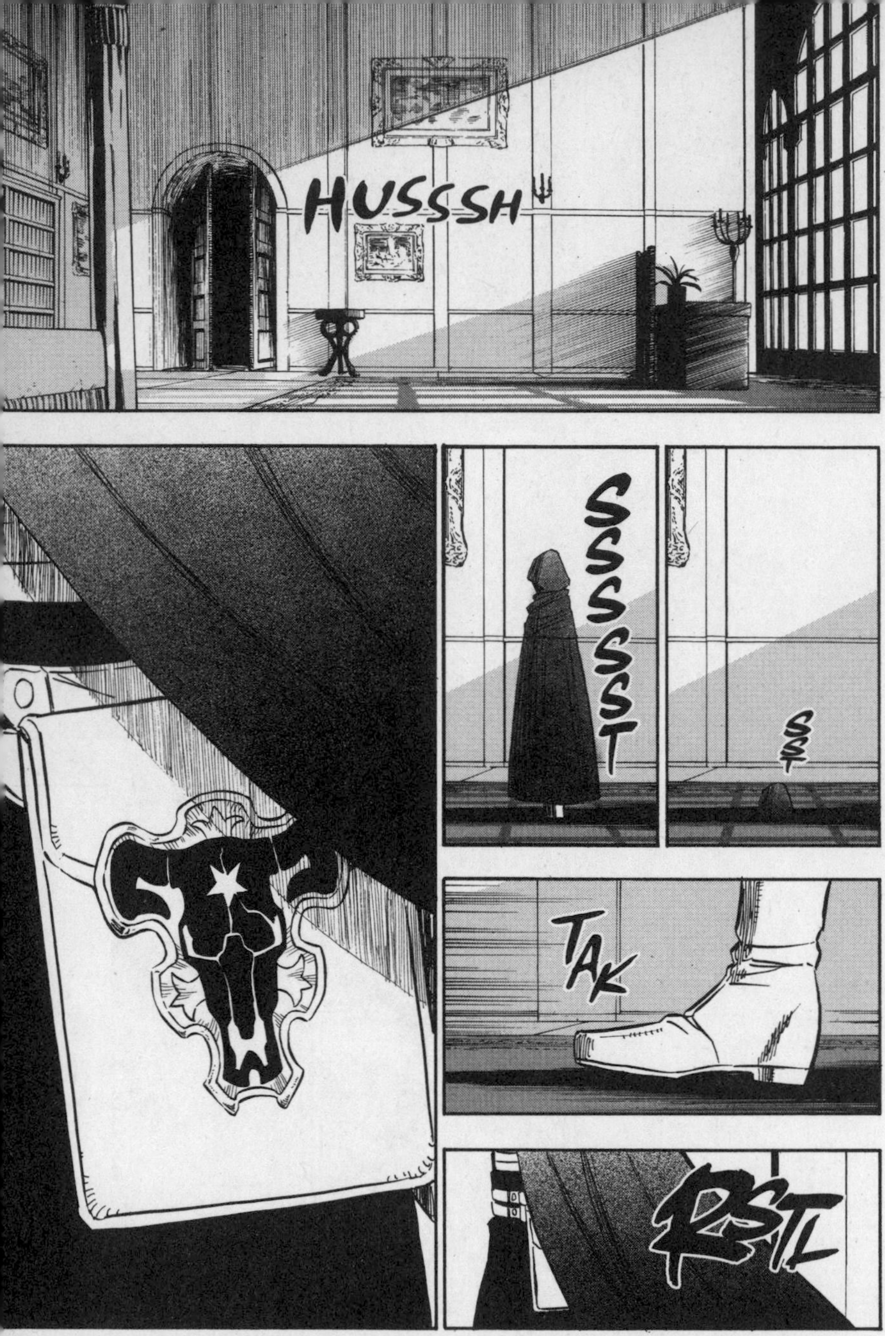
HUSSSH
SST
SSSSST
TAK
RSTL

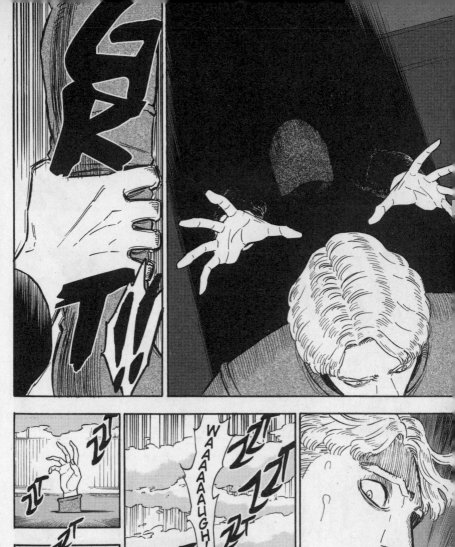

ZZT ZZT

ZZT

ZZT

WAAAAAUGH!

ZZT ZZT ZZT

ZZT

ZZT ZZT

ZZT

ZZT

BLOOP!

WHA— ?!!

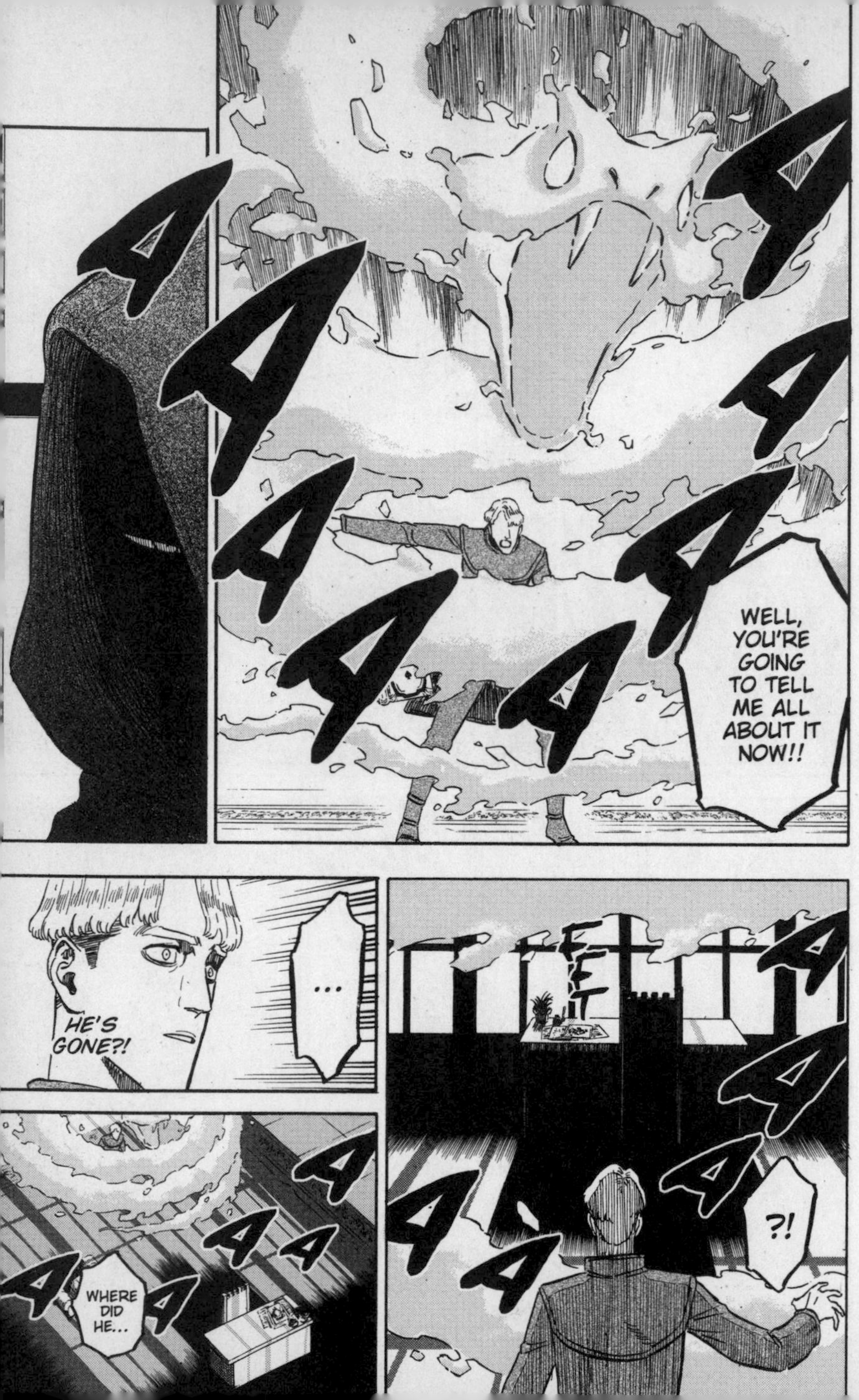
WELL, YOU'RE GOING TO TELL ME ALL ABOUT IT NOW!!
FFT
?!
...
HE'S GONE?!
WHERE DID HE...

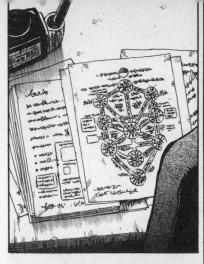

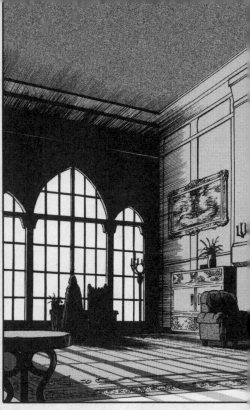

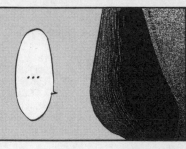

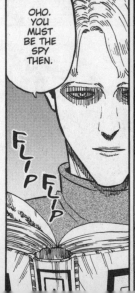

...
HEY. YOU.
WHAT ARE YOU DOING IN LORD DANTE'S ROOM?!
OHO. YOU MUST BE THE SPY THEN.
FLIP FLIP

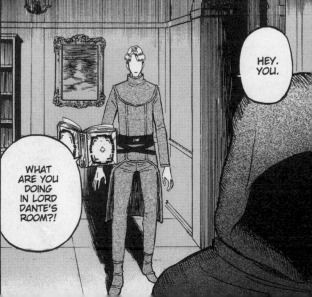

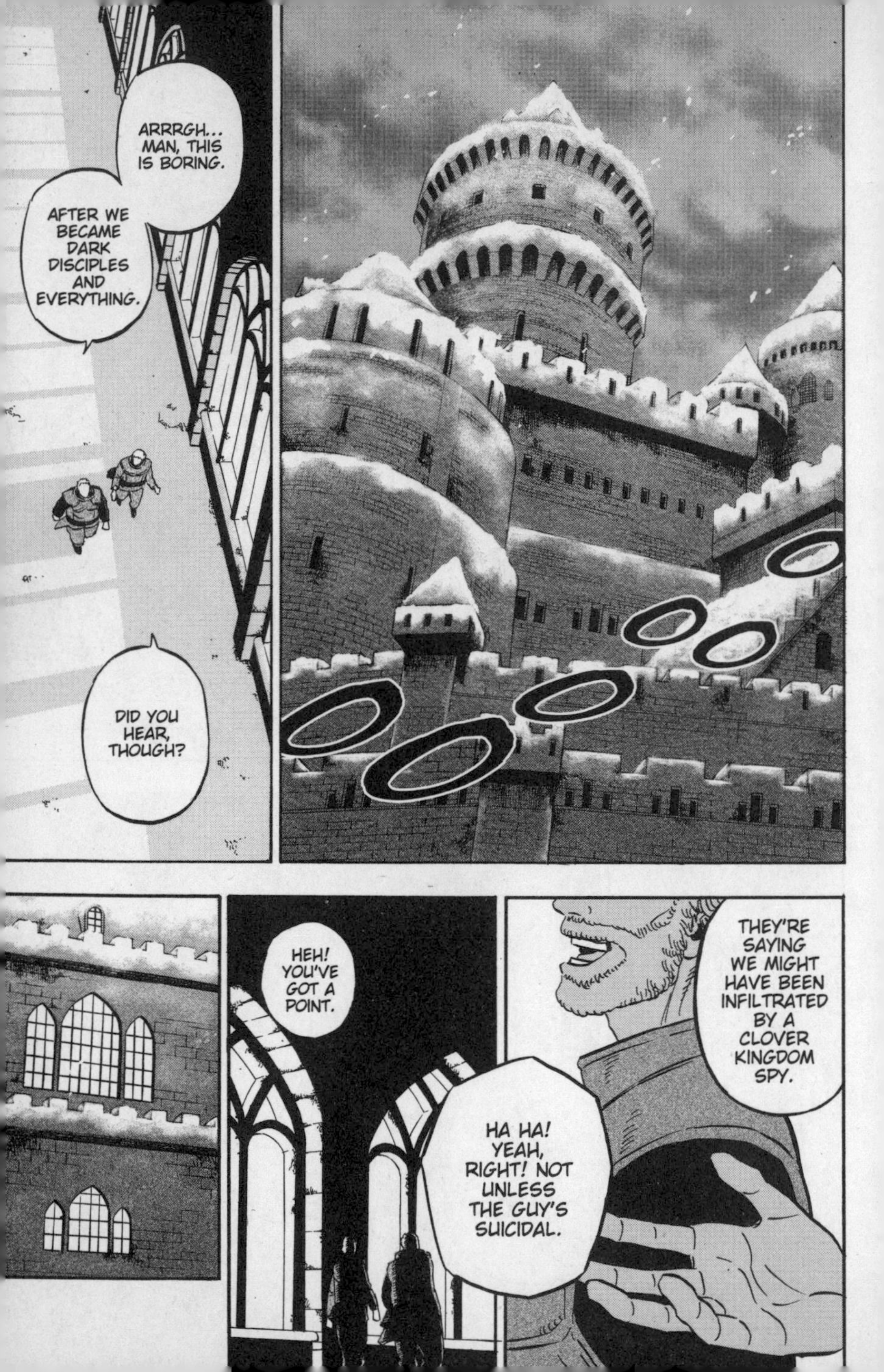
ARRRGH... MAN, THIS IS BORING.
AFTER WE BECAME DARK DISCIPLES AND EVERYTHING.
DID YOU HEAR, THOUGH?
THEY'RE SAYING WE MIGHT HAVE BEEN INFILTRATED BY A CLOVER KINGDOM SPY.
HA HA! YEAH, RIGHT! NOT UNLESS THE GUY'S SUICIDAL.
HEH! YOU'VE GOT A POINT.

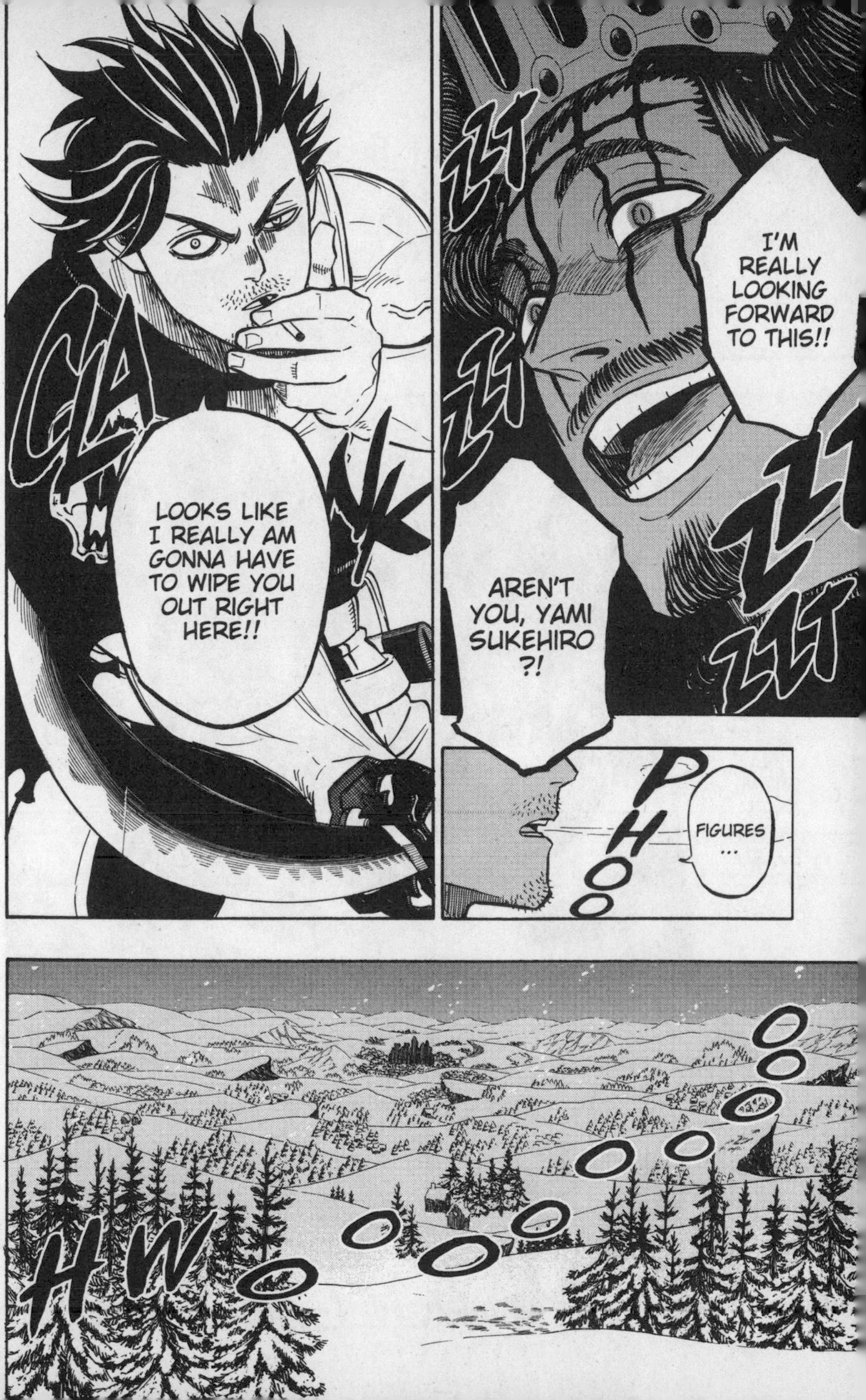
I'M REALLY LOOKING FORWARD TO THIS!!
ARE'N'T YOU, YAMI SUKEHIRO ?!
PHOO
FIGURES ...
LOOKS LIKE I REALLY AM GONNA HAVE TO WIPE YOU OUT RIGHT HERE!!
HWOOOOOOOOOO

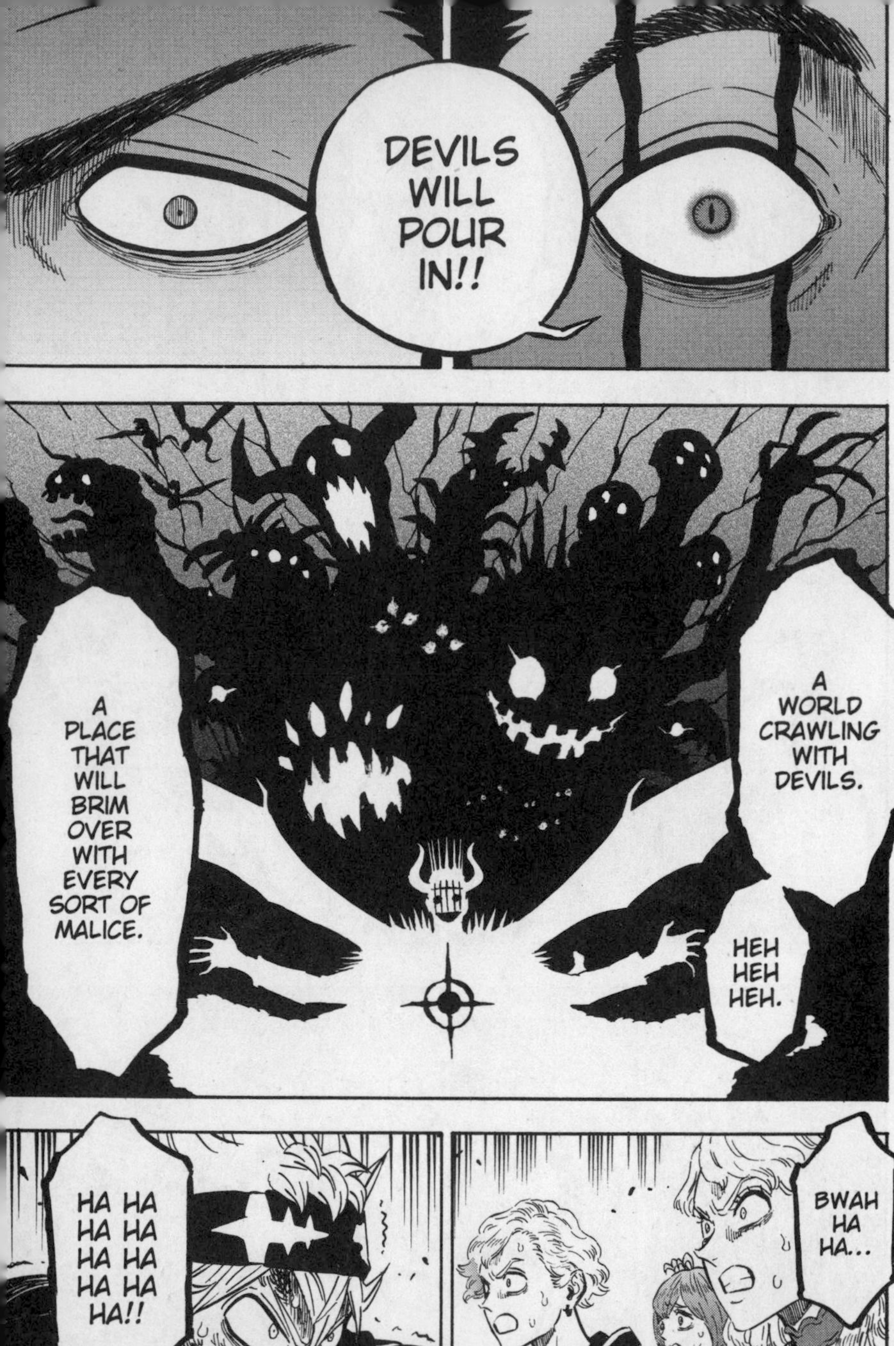
DEVILS WILL POUR IN!!
A WORLD CRAWLING WITH DEVILS.
A PLACE THAT WILL BRIM OVER WITH EVERY SORT OF MALICE.
HEH HEH HEH.
BWAH HA HA...
HA HA HA HA HA HA HA HA HA!!

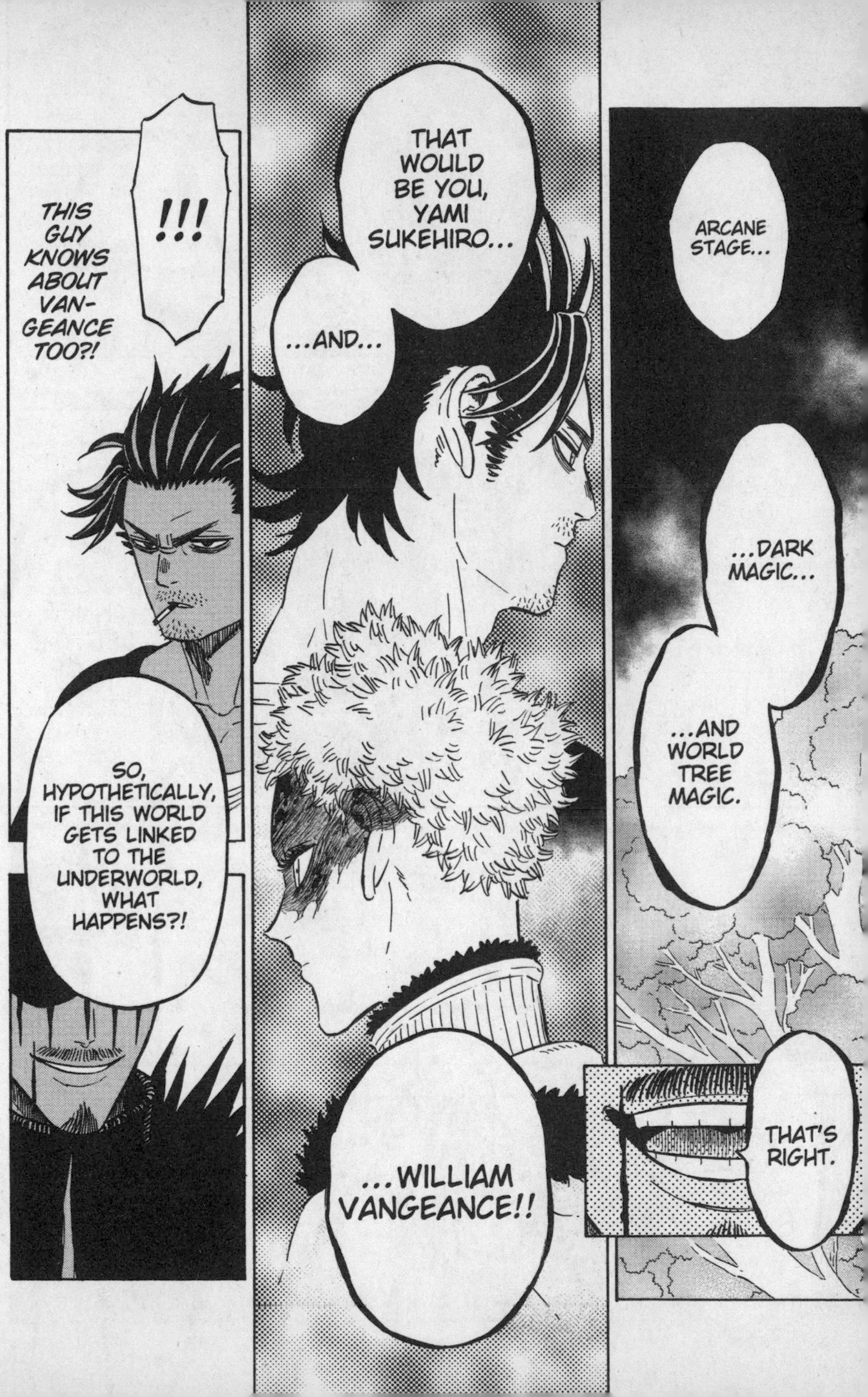
ARCANE STAGE...
...DARK MAGIC...
...AND WORLD TREE MAGIC.
THAT'S RIGHT.
THAT WOULD BE YOU, YAMI SUKEHIRO...
...AND...
...WILLIAM VANGEANCE!!
!!!
THIS GUY KNOWS ABOUT VAN-GEANCE TOO?!
SO, HYPOTHETICALLY, IF THIS WORLD GETS LINKED TO THE UNDERWORLD, WHAT HAPPENS?!

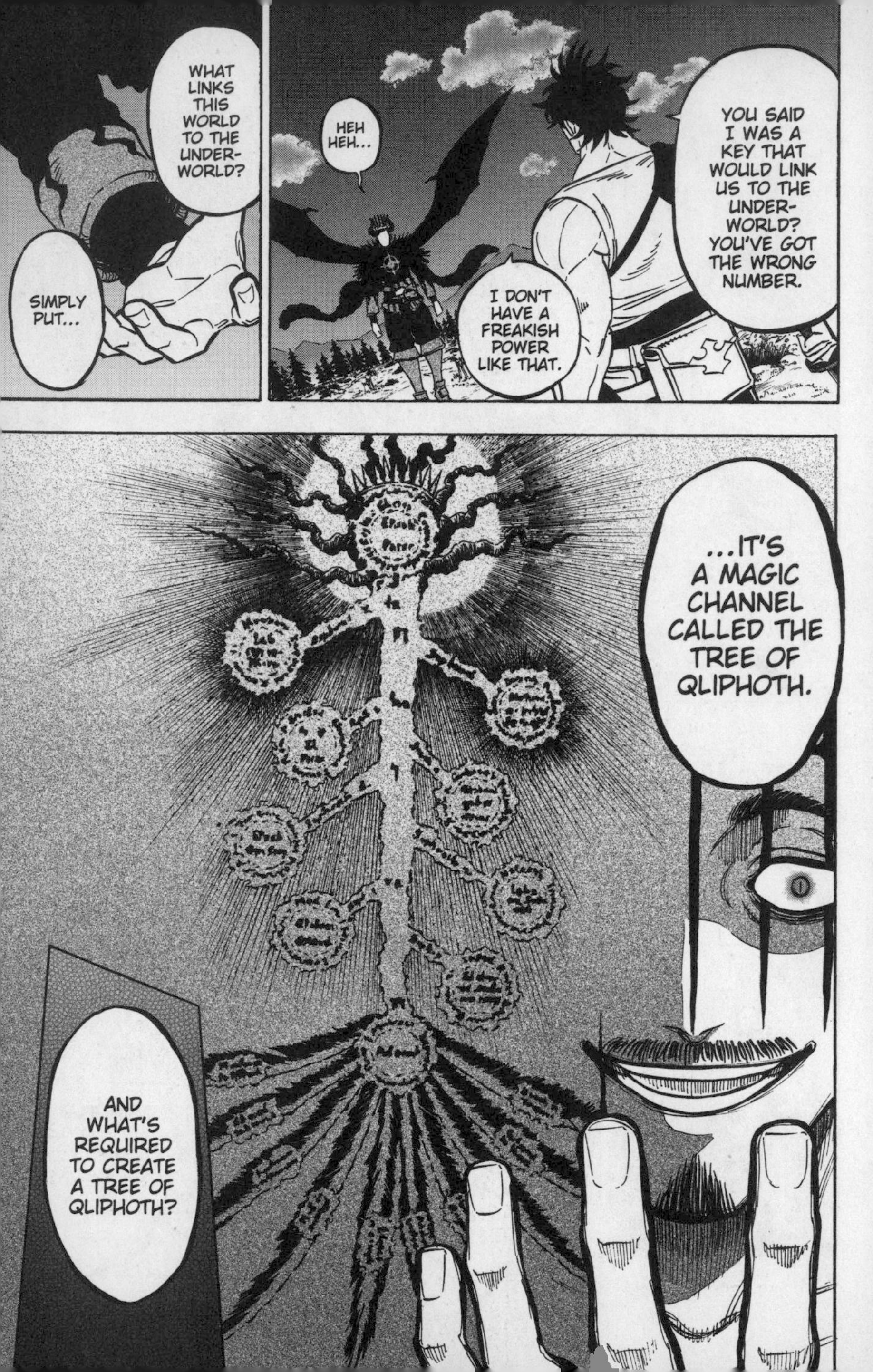
YOU SAID I WAS A KEY THAT WOULD LINK US TO THE UNDER-WORLD? YOU'VE GOT THE WRONG NUMBER.
I DON'T HAVE A FREAKISH POWER LIKE THAT.
HEH HEH...
WHAT LINKS THIS WORLD TO THE UNDER-WORLD?
SIMPLY PUT...
...IT'S A MAGIC CHANNEL CALLED THE TREE OF QLIPHOTH.
AND WHAT'S REQUIRED TO CREATE A TREE OF QLIPHOTH?

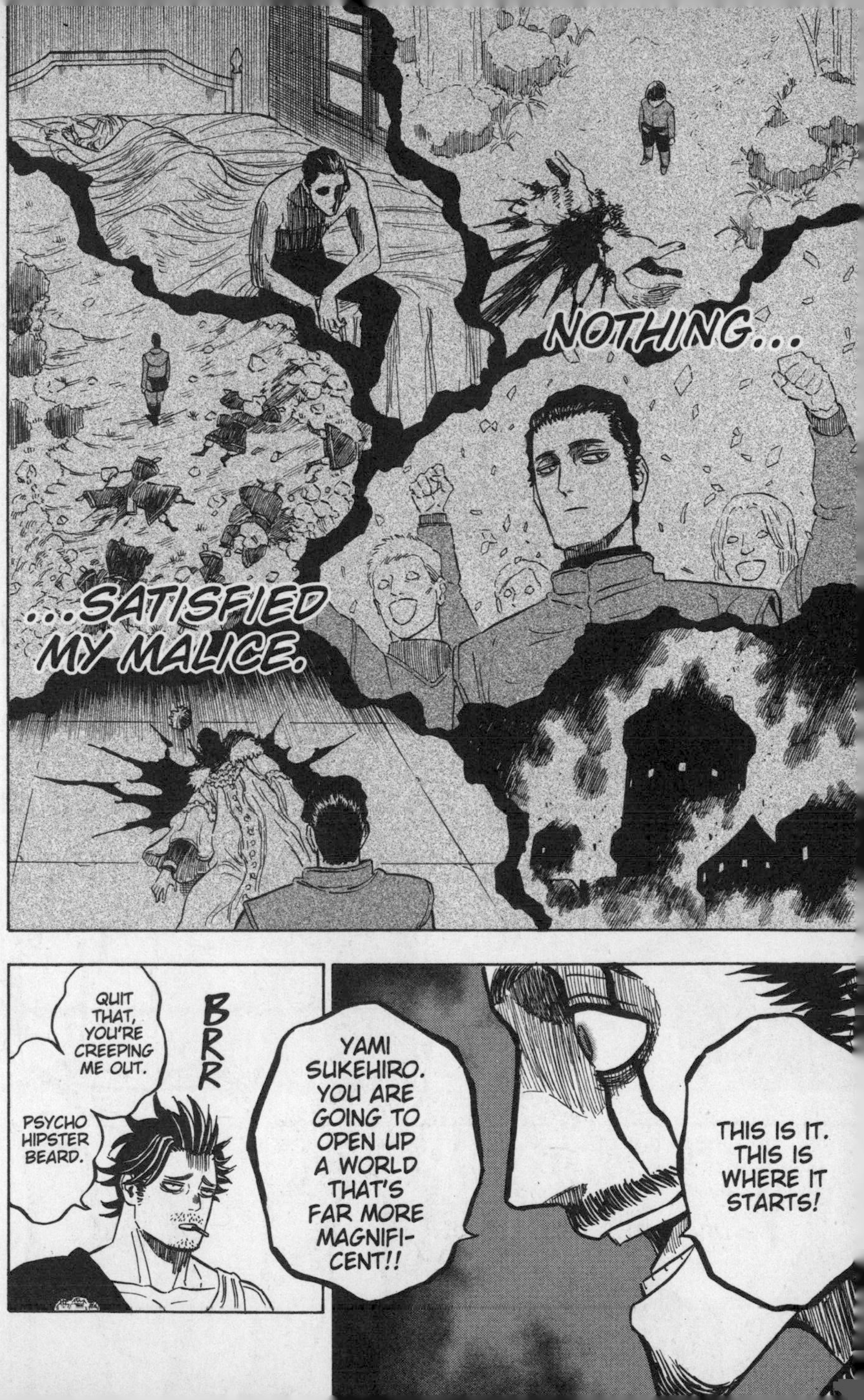
NOTHING...
...SATISFIED MY MALICE.
THIS IS IT. THIS IS WHERE IT STARTS!
YAMI SUKEHIRO. YOU ARE GOING TO OPEN UP A WORLD THAT'S FAR MORE MAGNIFI-CENT!!
BRR
QUIT THAT, YOU'RE CREEPING ME OUT.
PSYCHO HIPSTER BEARD.

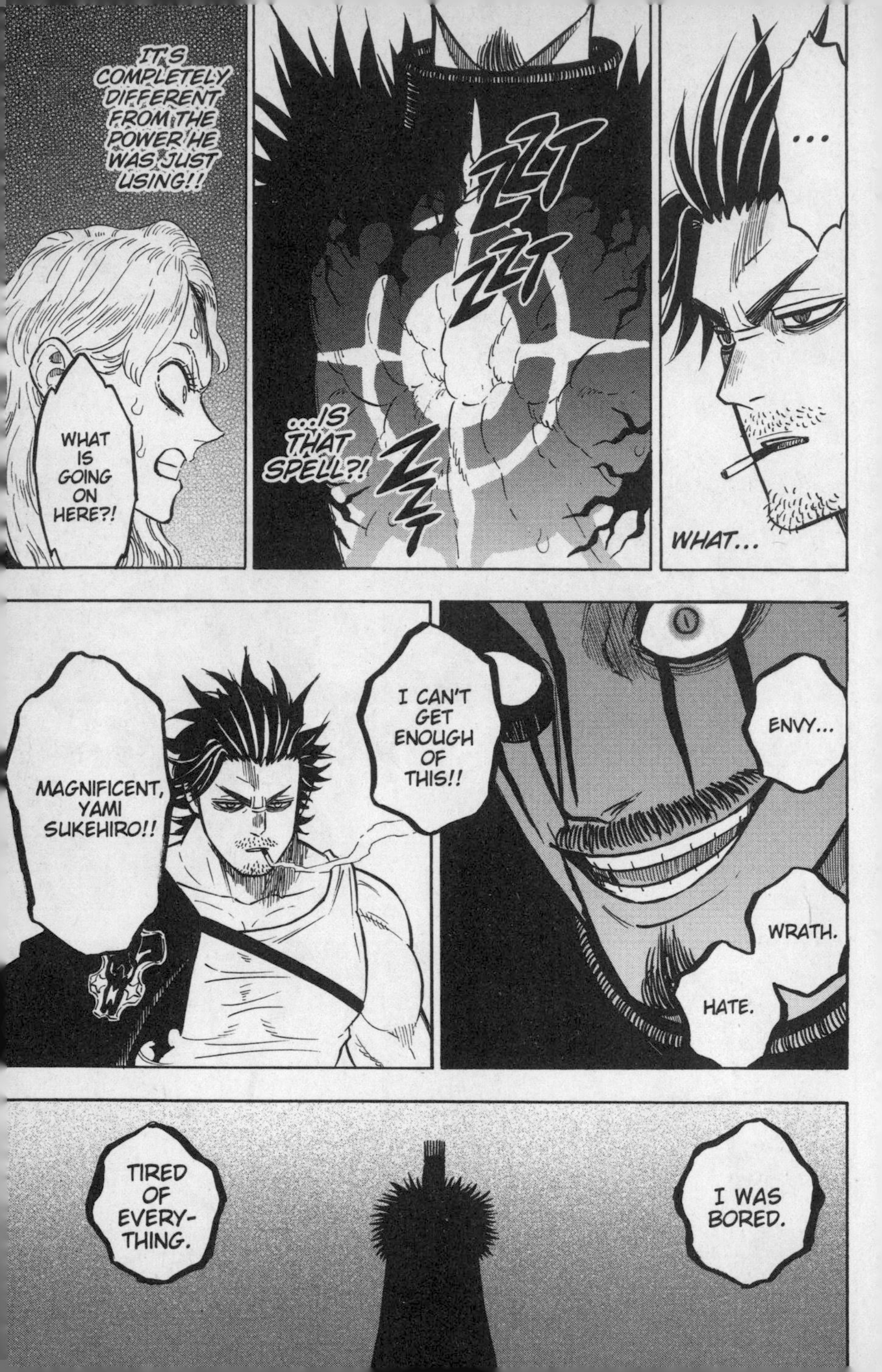
...
WHAT...
ZZZT ZZZT
...IS THAT SPELL?!
ZZZT
IT'S COMPLETELY DIFFERENT FROM THE POWER HE WAS JUST USING!!
WHAT IS GOING ON HERE?!
ENVY...
WRATH.
HATE.
I CAN'T GET ENOUGH OF THIS!!
MAGNIFICENT, YAMI SUKEHIRO!!
I WAS BORED.
TIRED OF EVERY-THING.

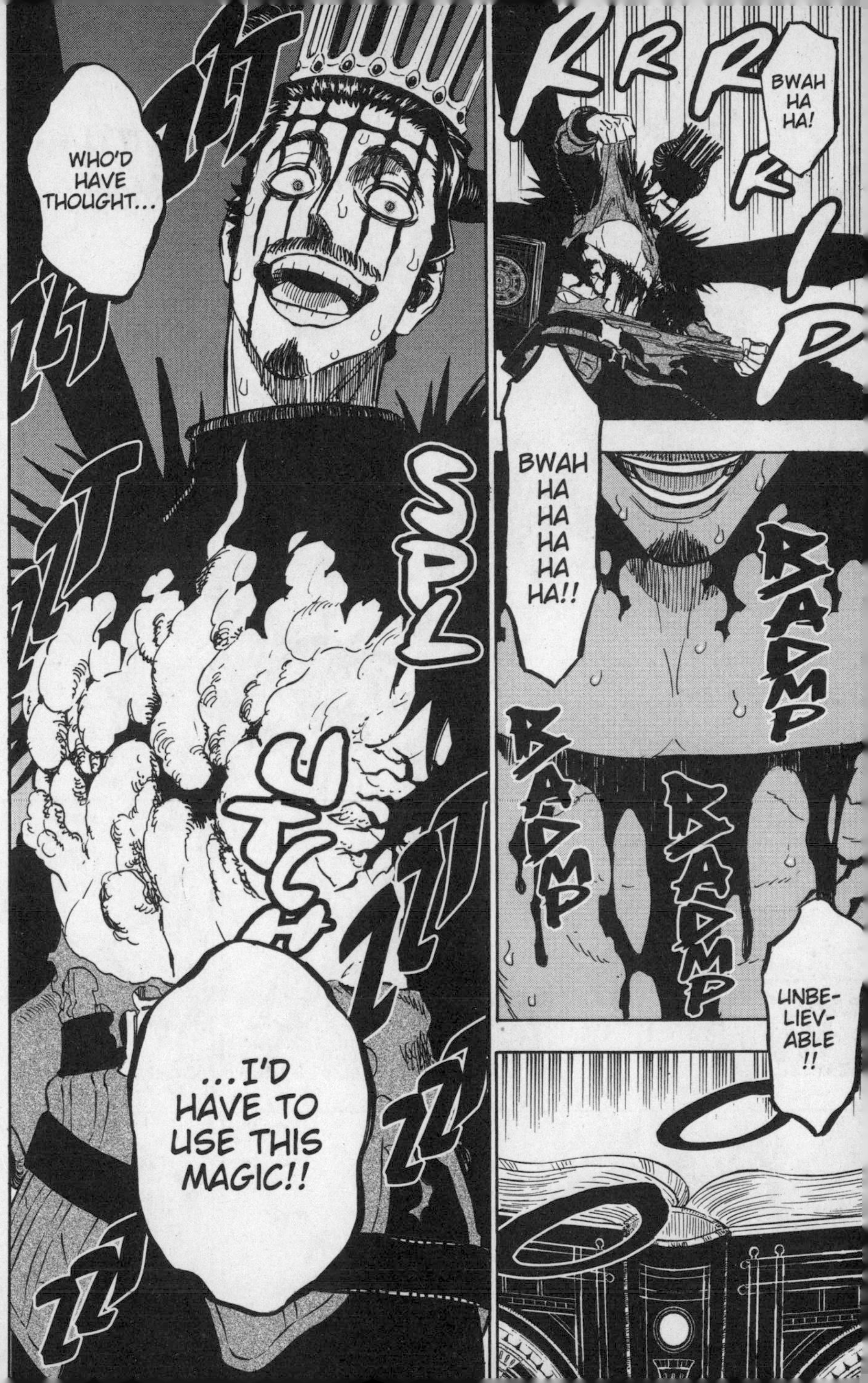
BWAH HA HA!
BWAH HA HA HA HA HA!!
BADMP
BADMP
BADMP
UNBE-LIEV-ABLE!!
WHO'D HAVE THOUGHT...
SPLUTCH
...I'D HAVE TO USE THIS MAGIC!!

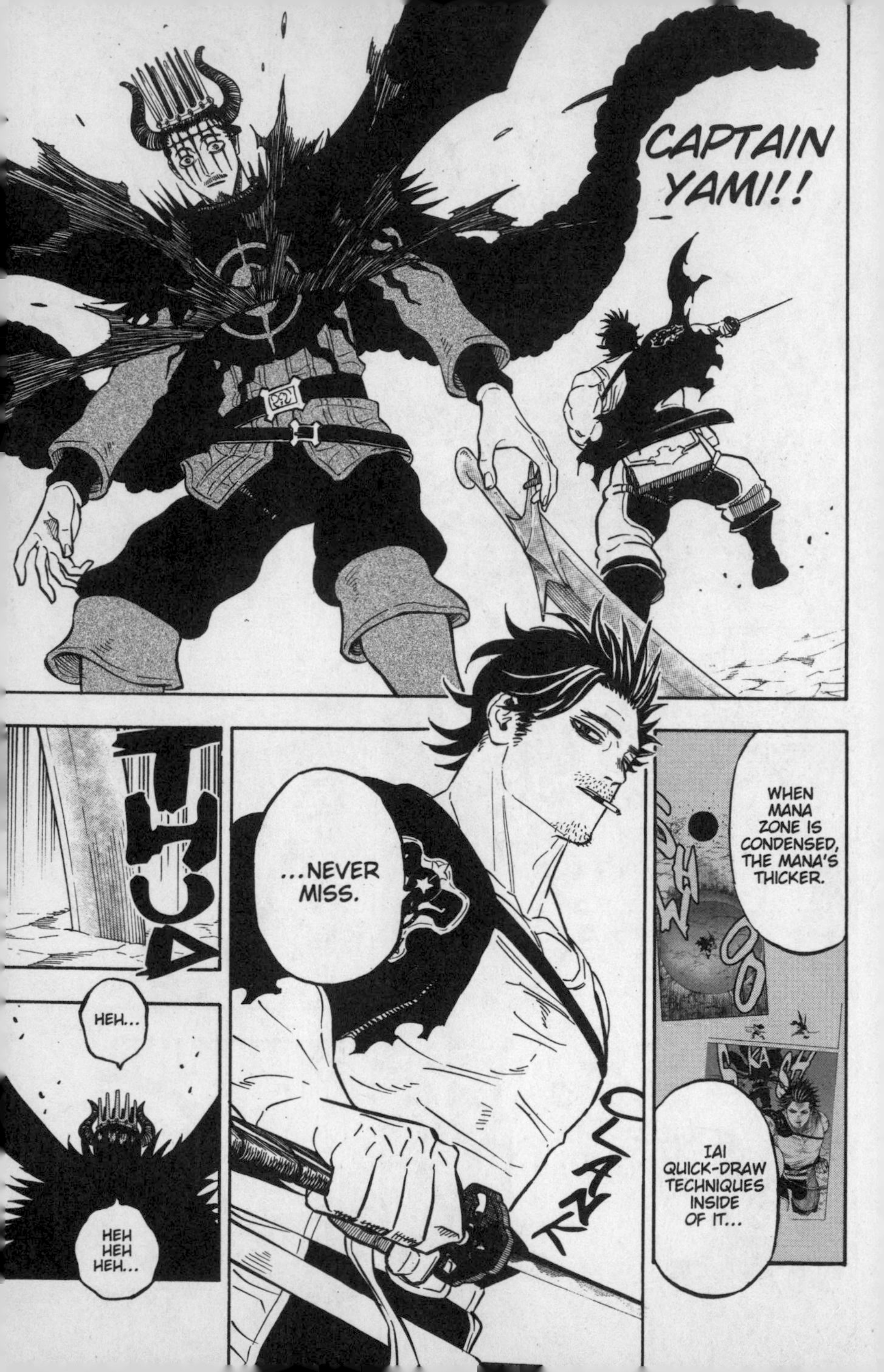
CAPTAIN YAMI!!
WHEN MANA ZONE IS CONDENSED, THE MANA'S THICKER.
IAI QUICK-DRAW TECHNIQUES INSIDE OF IT...
...NEVER MISS.
CLANK
HEH...
HEH HEH HEH...

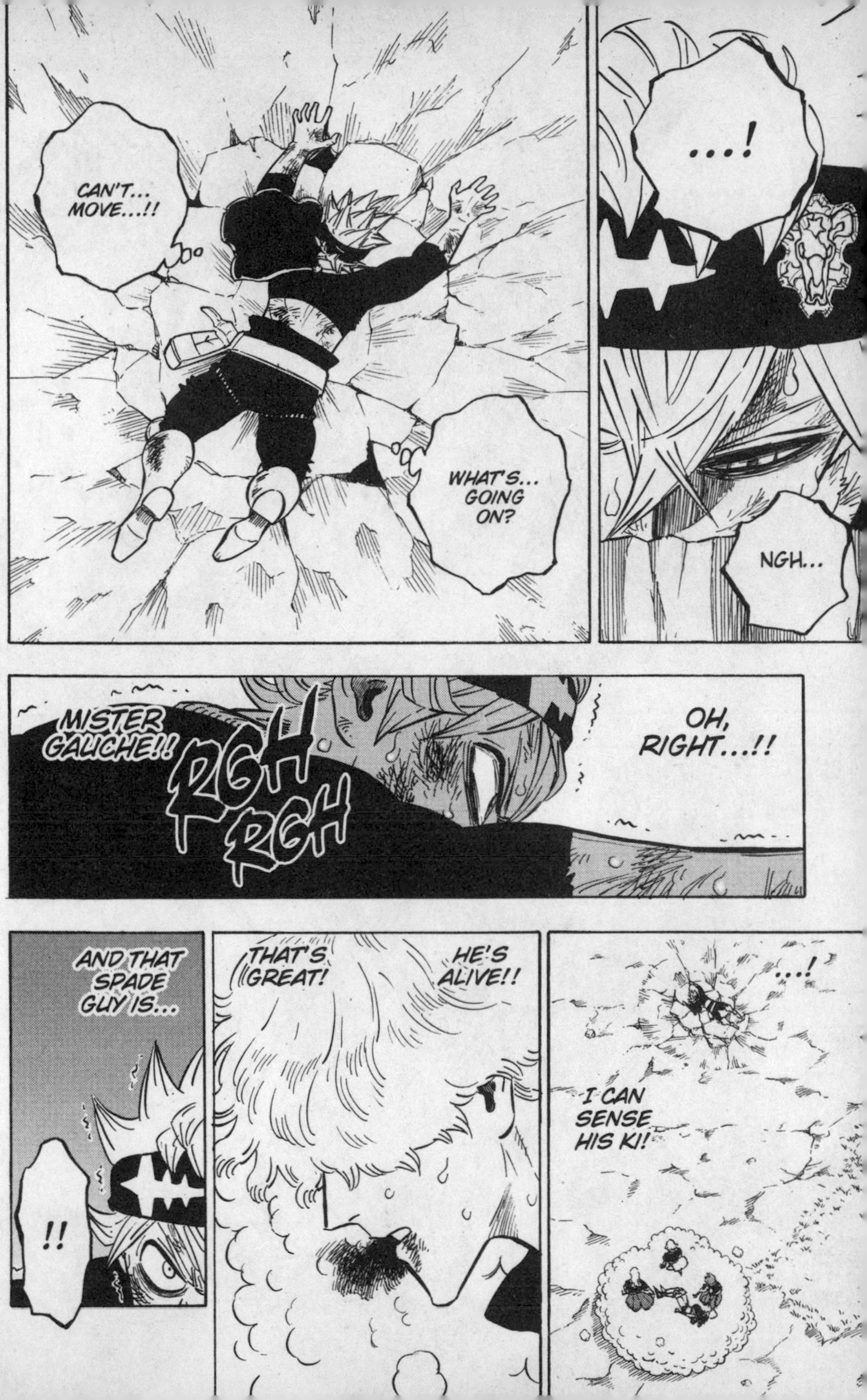
...!
NGH...
CAN'T... MOVE...!!
WHAT'S... GOING ON?
OH, RIGHT...!!
MISTER GAUCHE!!
RGH RGH
...!
I CAN SENSE HIS KI!
HE'S ALIVE!!
THAT'S GREAT!
AND THAT SPADE GUY IS...
!!

Page 246: The Tree of Qliphoth

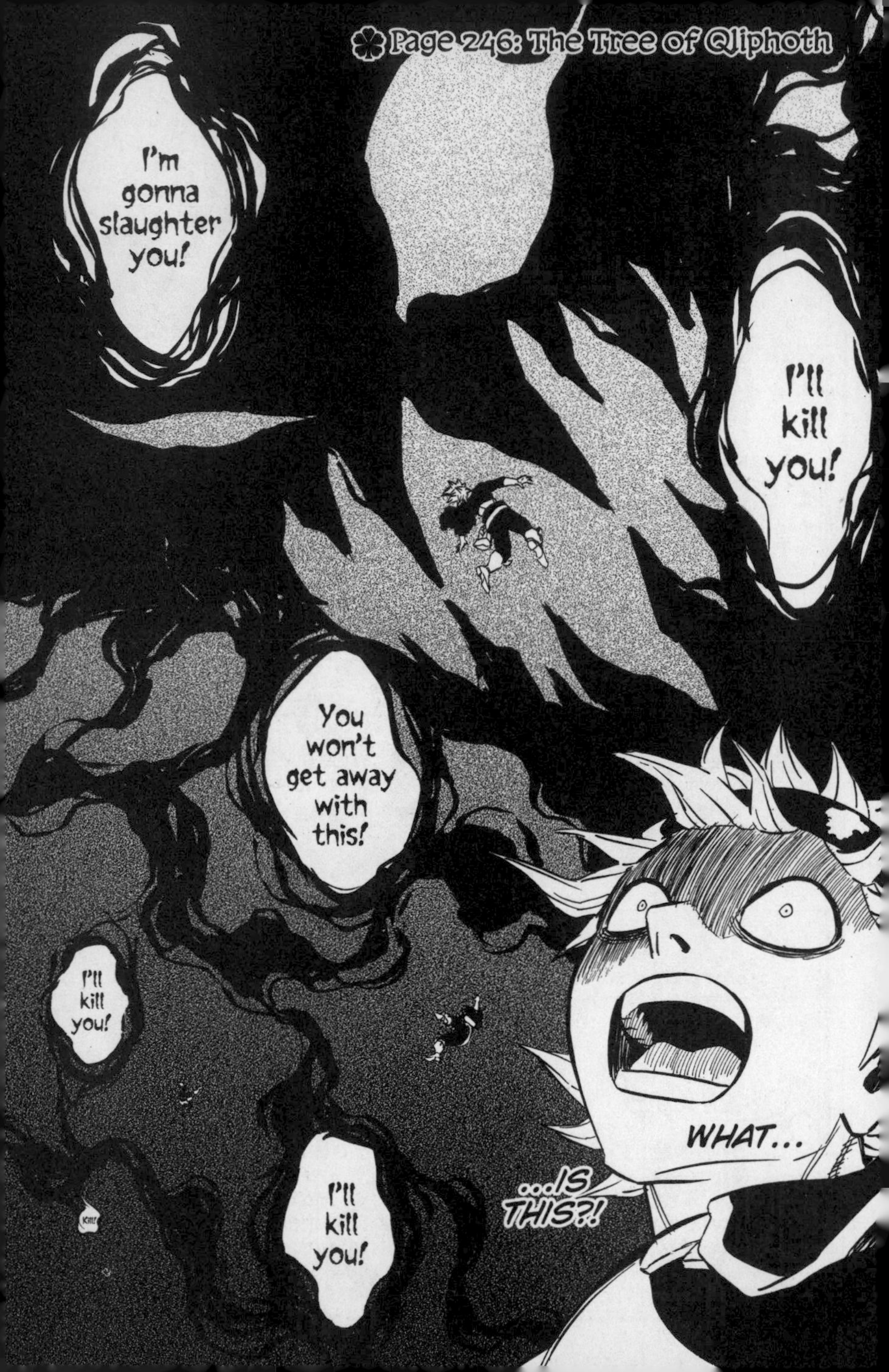

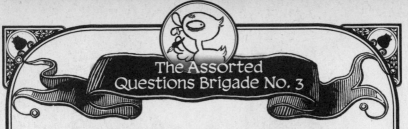

The Assorted Questions Brigade No. 3

Q: Can the recovery spells Mimosa and other mages use recover magic, as well as physical strength? (*Aoi Fujita*, Saitama) The next two questions are also from Aoi Fujita.

A: Nope, they can't! Physical strength and magic are two different things, and there aren't many mages who can recover magic. Charmy's the only one in the series at this point.

Sheep Cook: Head Chef
FLOOF
THWOKOKOK
SIZZZZ
POFF
POFF
WHY ?!!

Plant Recovery Magic: Princess-Healing Flower Paradise
AAAAAA
I CAN'T DO ANYTHING ABOUT YOUR MAGIC, BUT I CAN RECOVER YOUR STRENGTH FOR YOU.

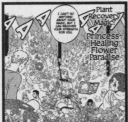

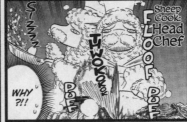

Q: If a mage uses up all their magic, what happens to them?

A: They temporarily stop being able to use spells! Their physical performance drops a little too. However, as with physical strength, if they take breaks or sleep, they gradually recover.

If they store magic in a magic item, like Gauche's left eye, they can use the stored stuff to cast spells when they don't have enough magic of their own. Magic items like that are rare though, and not many people have them.

LOOK...
...AT ME!!!

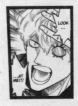

Q: Are you into any manga or anime lately?

A: There are all sorts of manga I'd like to read, but I'm currently only able to read *Weekly Shonen Jump*... As of now, June 2020, the final arc of *Haikyu!!* and the great war in *My Hero Academia* are insanely exciting every week!! As far as anime goes, up until a little while ago, my wife and I were both into *High Score Girl*.

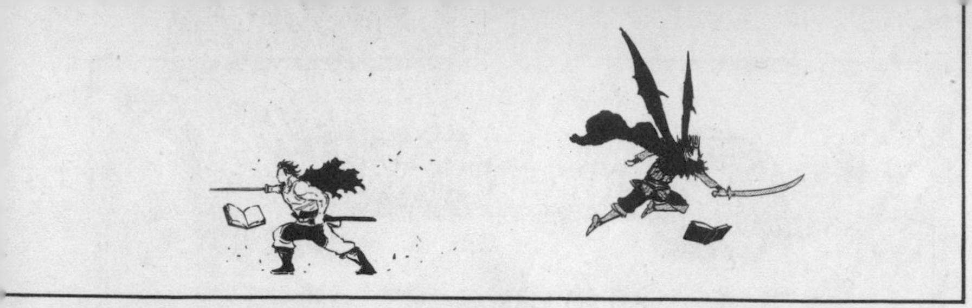
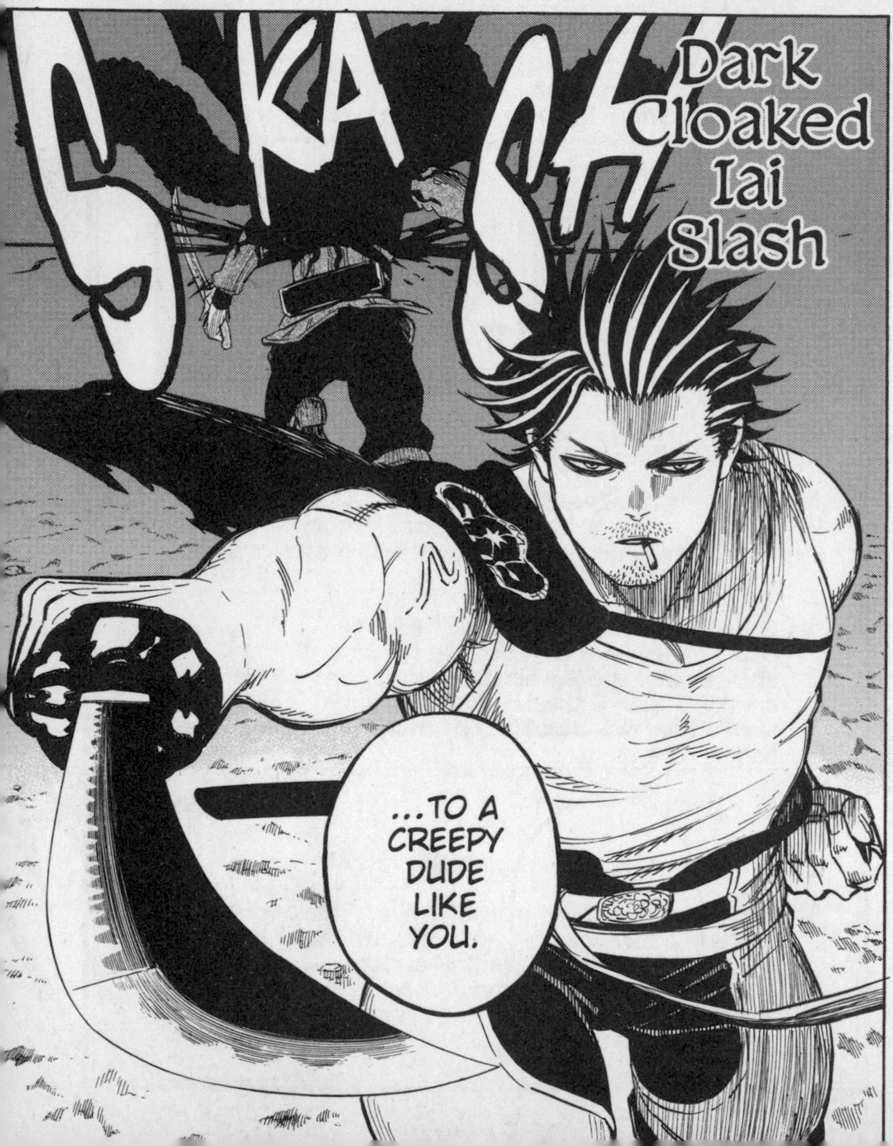
Dark Cloaked Iai Slash
...TO A CREEPY DUDE LIKE YOU.

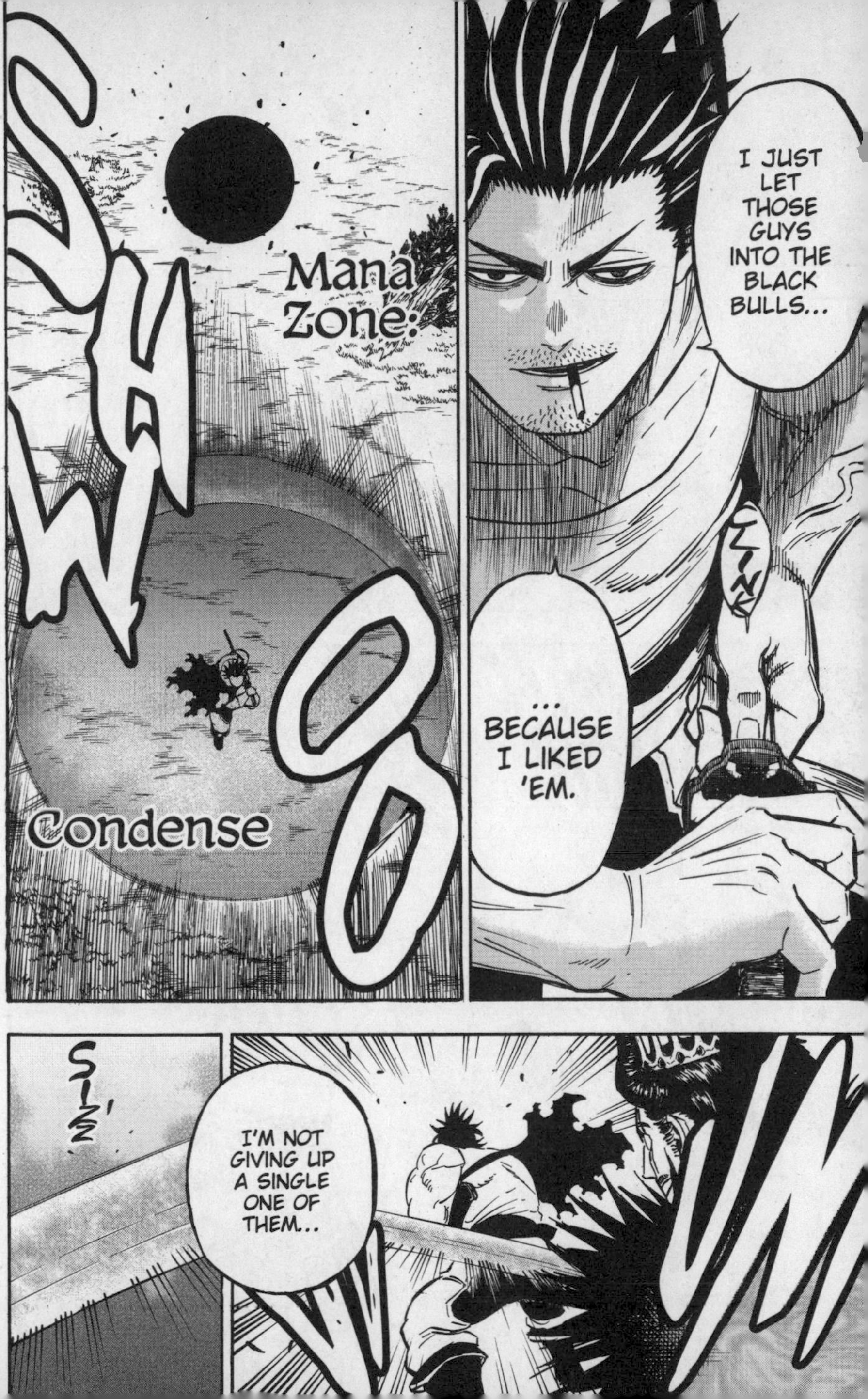
I JUST LET THOSE GUYS INTO THE BLACK BULLS...
ZLINK
...BECAUSE I LIKED 'EM.
Mana Zone:
Condense
I'M NOT GIVING UP A SINGLE ONE OF THEM...
SIZZ

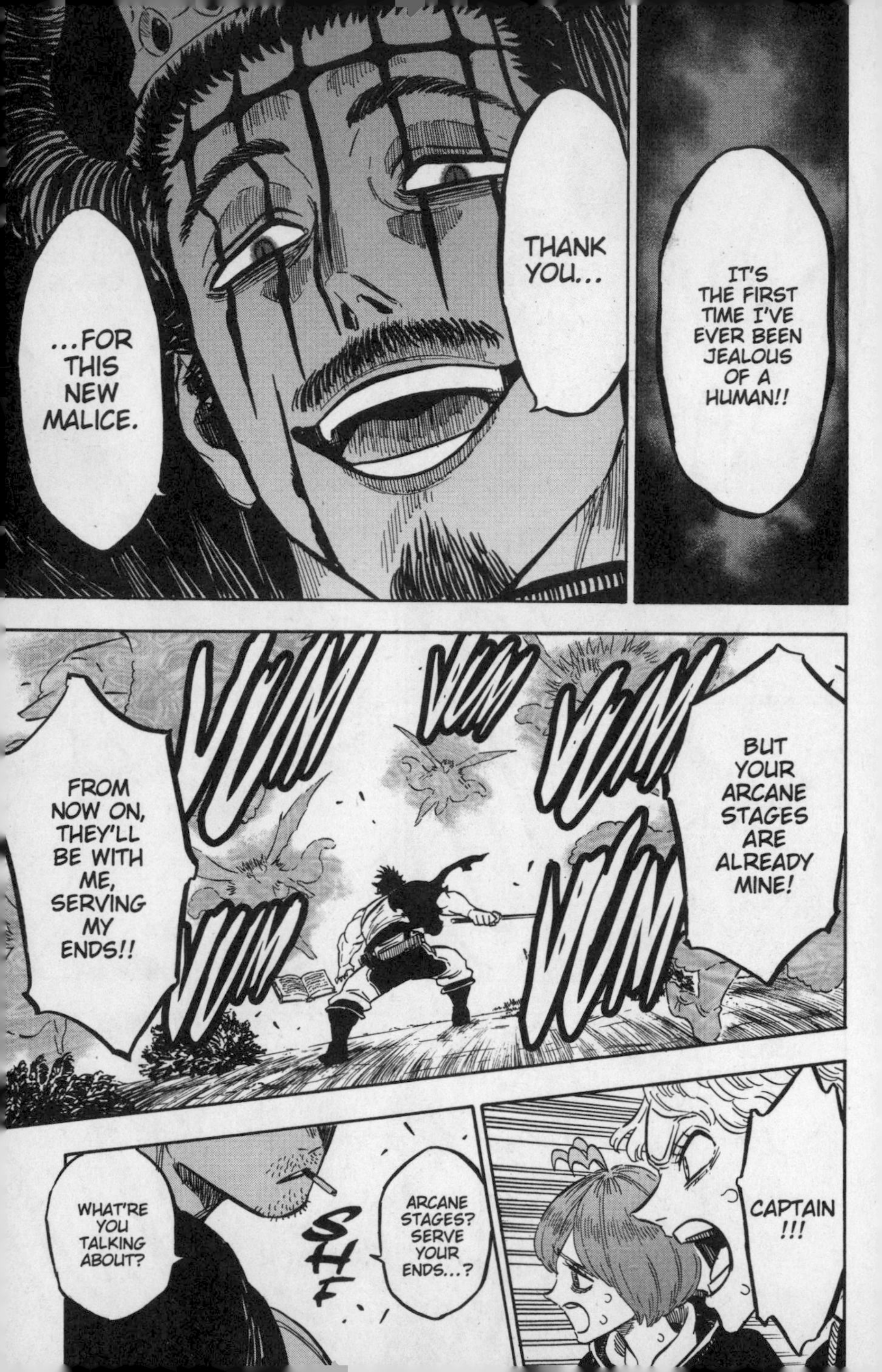
IT'S THE FIRST TIME I'VE EVER BEEN JEALOUS OF A HUMAN!!
THANK YOU...
...FOR THIS NEW MALICE.
BUT YOUR ARCANE STAGES ARE ALREADY MINE!
FROM NOW ON, THEY'LL BE WITH ME, SERVING MY ENDS!!
CAPTAIN!!!
ARCANE STAGES? SERVE YOUR ENDS...?
SHF
WHAT'RE YOU TALKING ABOUT?

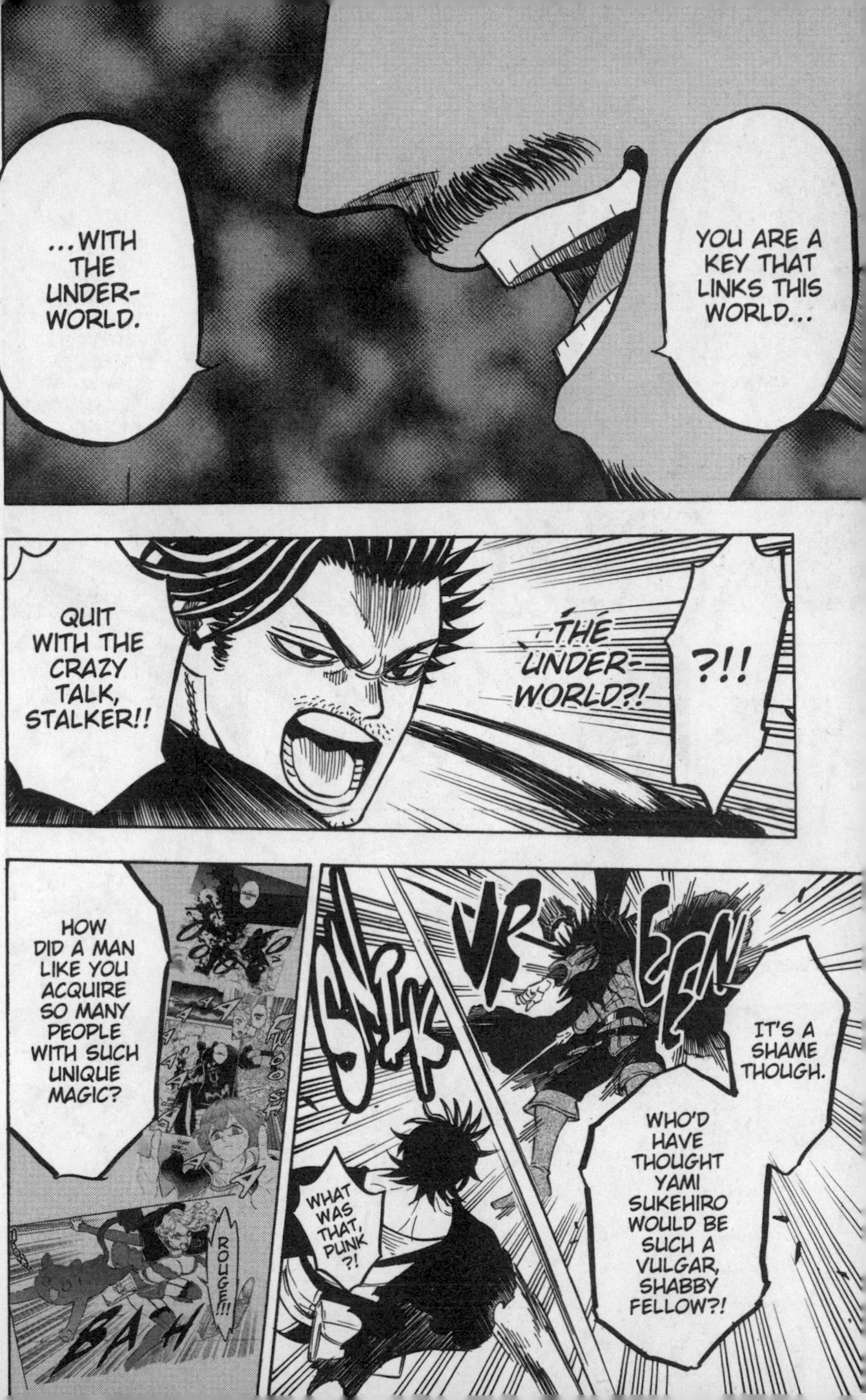
YOU ARE A KEY THAT LINKS THIS WORLD...
...WITH THE UNDER-WORLD.
?!!
THE UNDER-WORLD?!
QUIT WITH THE CRAZY TALK, STALKER!!
IT'S A SHAME THOUGH.
WHO'D HAVE THOUGHT YAMI SUKEHIRO WOULD BE SUCH A VULGAR, SHABBY FELLOW?!
WHAT WAS THAT, PUNK?!
HOW DID A MAN LIKE YOU ACQUIRE SO MANY PEOPLE WITH SUCH UNIQUE MAGIC?
ROUGE!!
BASH

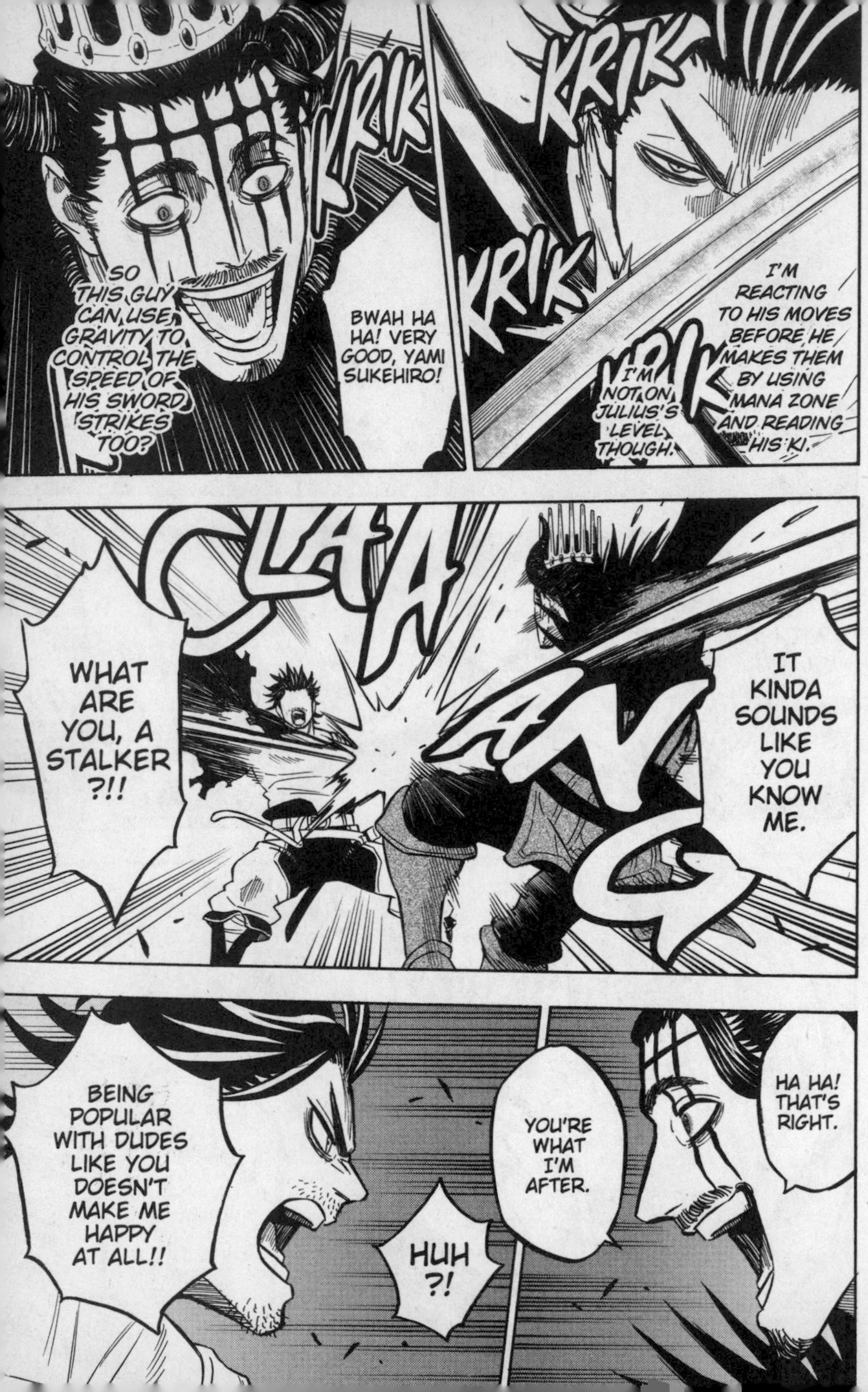
KRIK
KRIK
KRIK
I'M REACTING TO HIS MOVES BEFORE HE MAKES THEM BY USING MANA ZONE AND READING HIS KI.
I'M NOT ON JULIUS'S LEVEL THOUGH.
KRIK
BWAH HA HA! VERY GOOD, YAMI SUKEHIRO!
SO THIS GUY CAN USE GRAVITY TO CONTROL THE SPEED OF HIS SWORD STRIKES TOO?
IT KINDA SOUNDS LIKE YOU KNOW ME.
CLAANG
WHAT ARE YOU, A STALKER?!!
HA HA! THAT'S RIGHT.
YOU'RE WHAT I'M AFTER.
HUH?!
BEING POPULAR WITH DUDES LIKE YOU DOESN'T MAKE ME HAPPY AT ALL!!

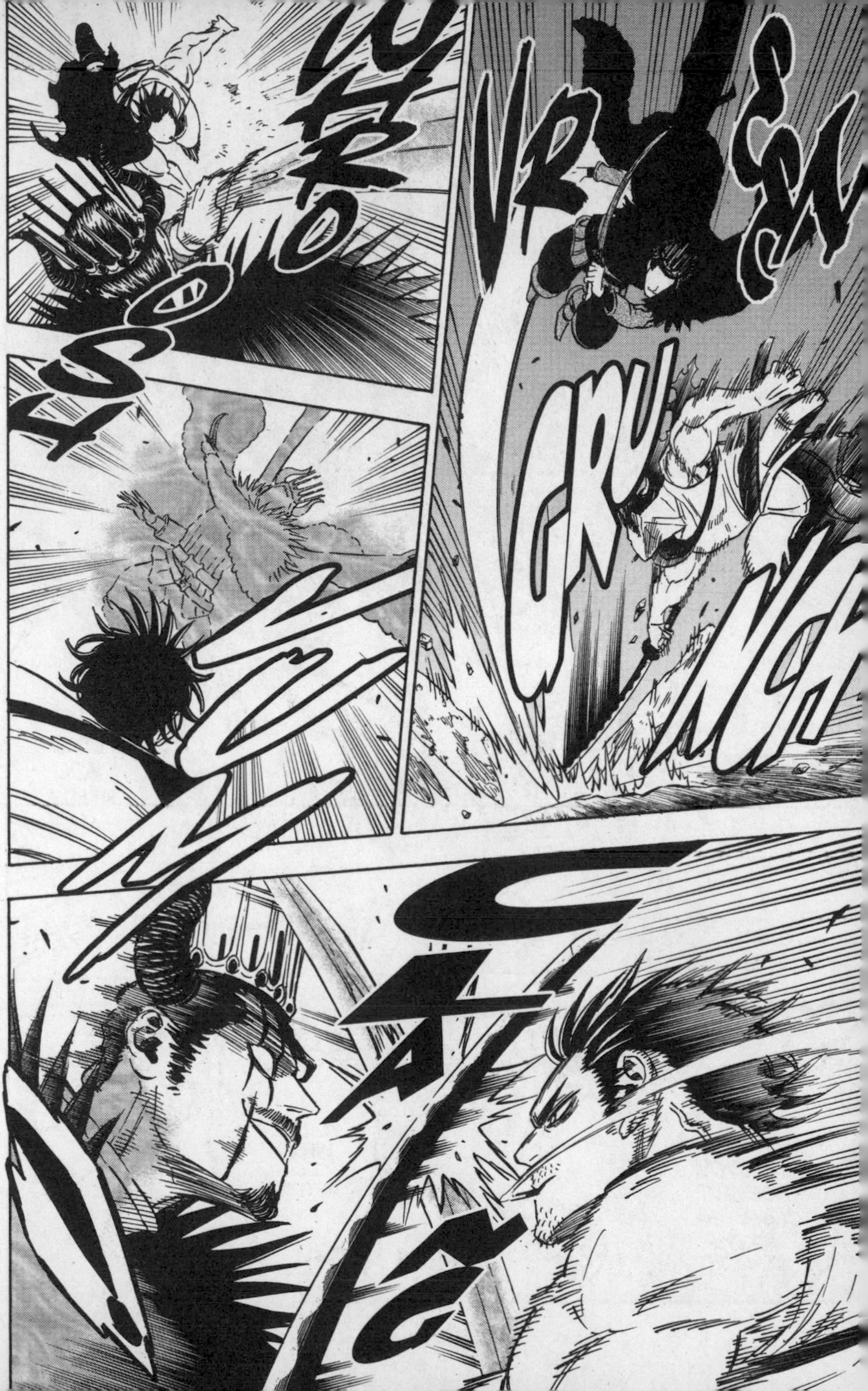
CRUNCH
CLANG

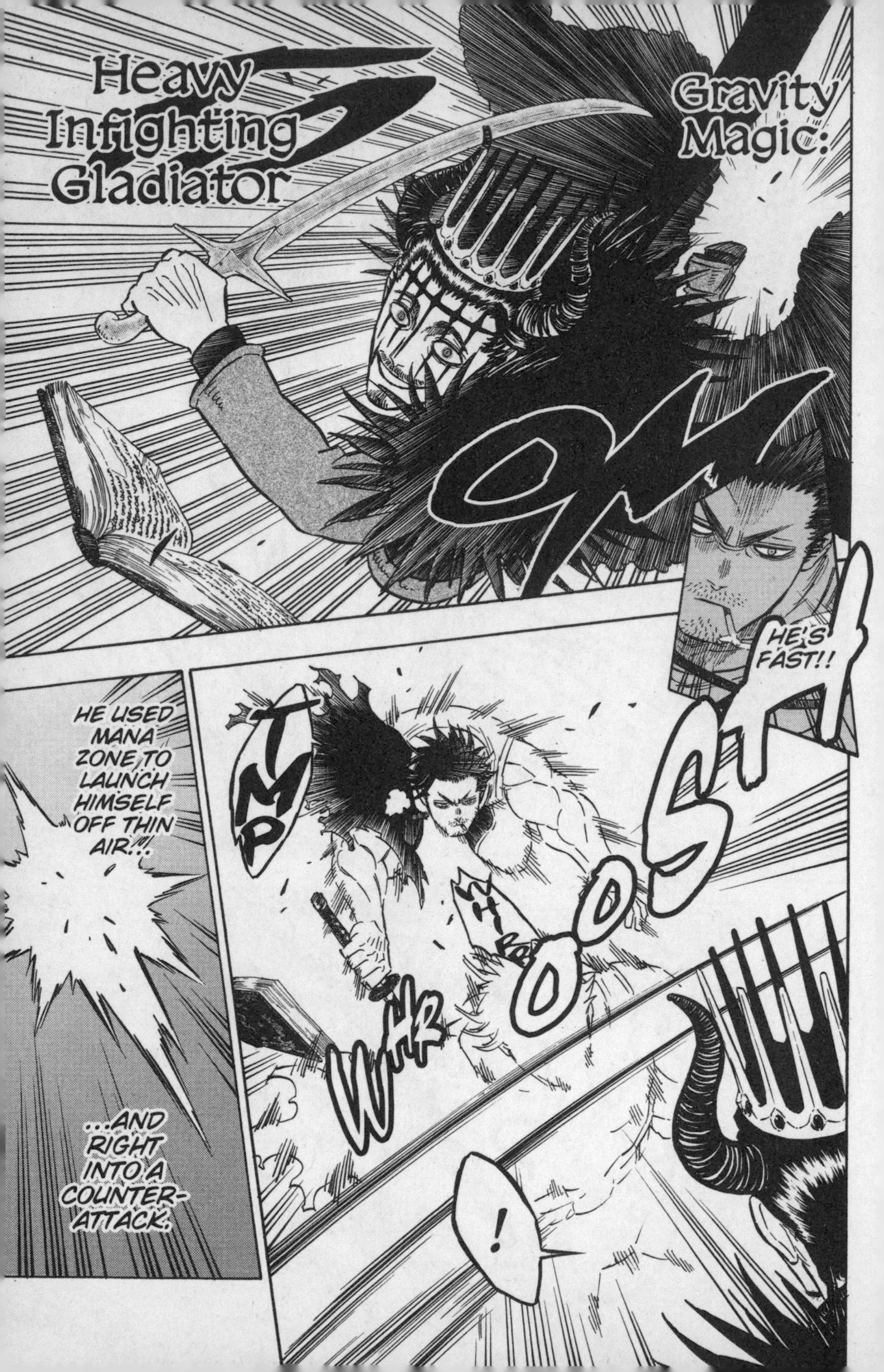
Gravity Magic:
Heavy Infighting Gladiator
HE'S FAST!!
WHOOOSH
TMP
!
HE USED MANA ZONE TO LAUNCH HIMSELF OFF THIN AIR...
...AND RIGHT INTO A COUNTER-ATTACK.

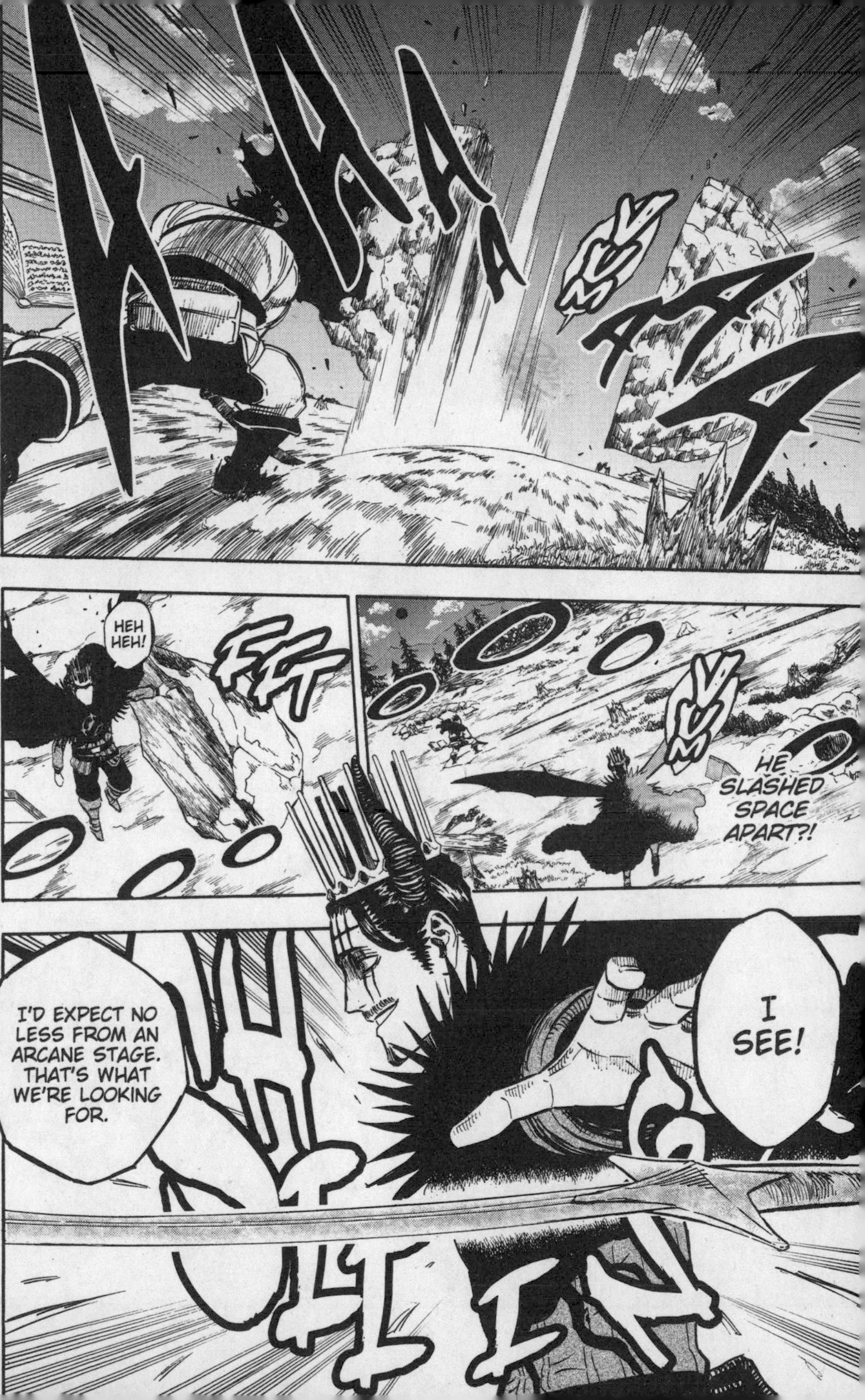
VUM
VUM
HE SLASHED SPACE APART?!
HEH HEH!
FFT
I SEE!
I'D EXPECT NO LESS FROM AN ARCANE STAGE. THAT'S WHAT WE'RE LOOKING FOR.

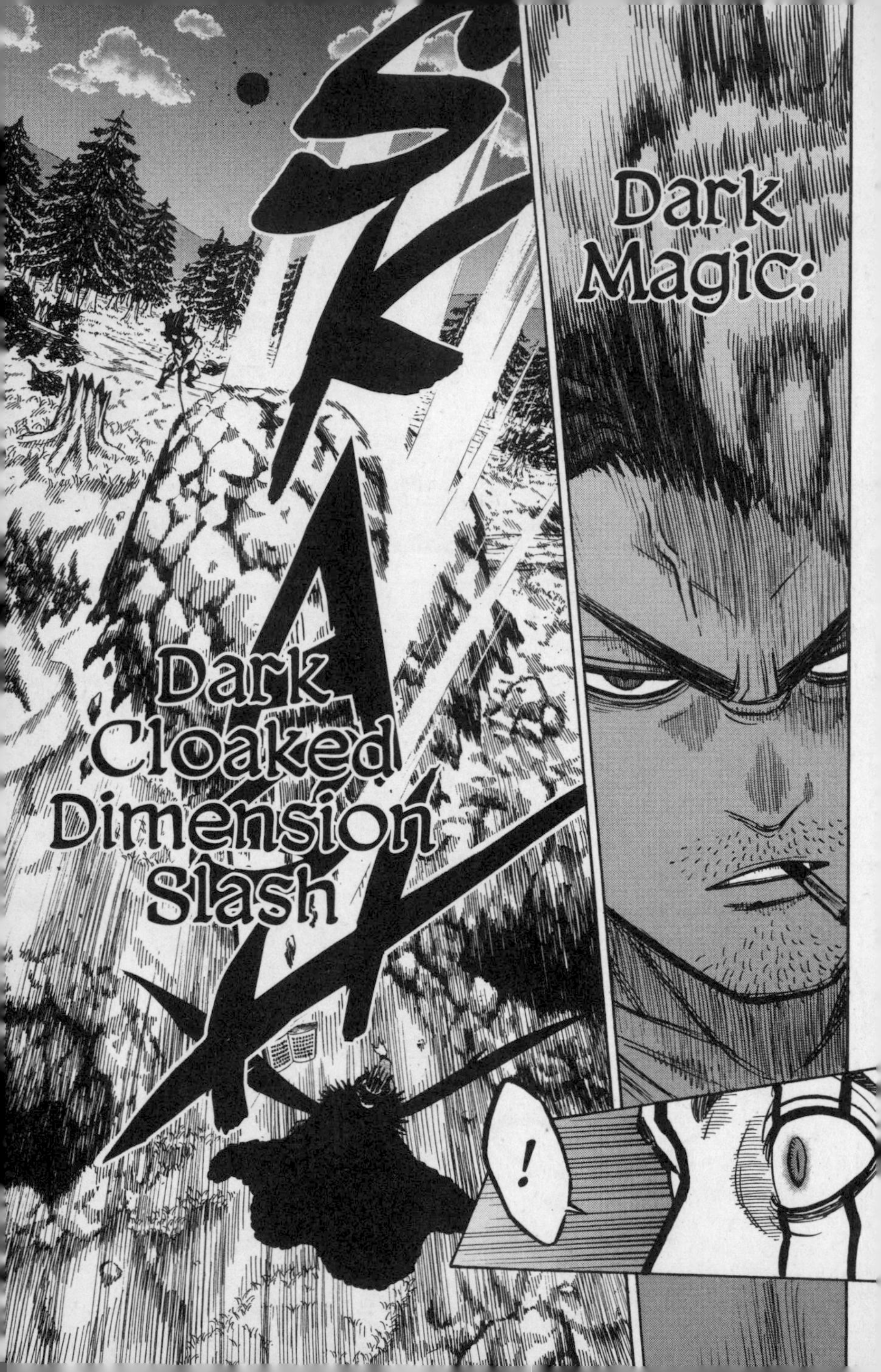
Dark Magic:
!
Dark Cloaked Dimension Slash

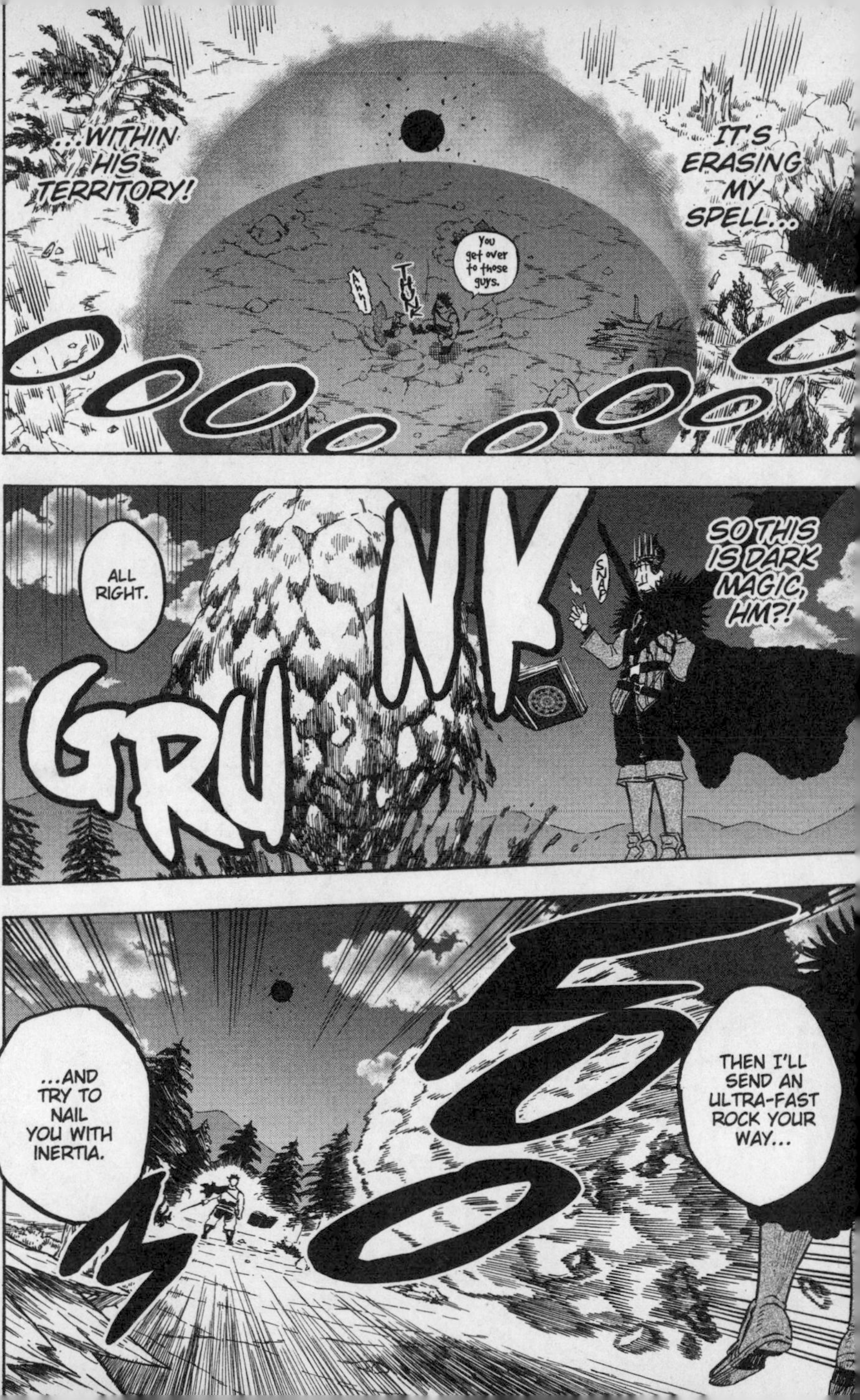
IT'S ERASING MY SPELL...
...WITHIN HIS TERRITORY!
You get over to those guys.
THUNK
SO THIS IS DARK MAGIC, HM?!
SNAP
GRUNK
ALL RIGHT.
THEN I'LL SEND AN ULTRA-FAST ROCK YOUR WAY...
...AND TRY TO NAIL YOU WITH INERTIA.

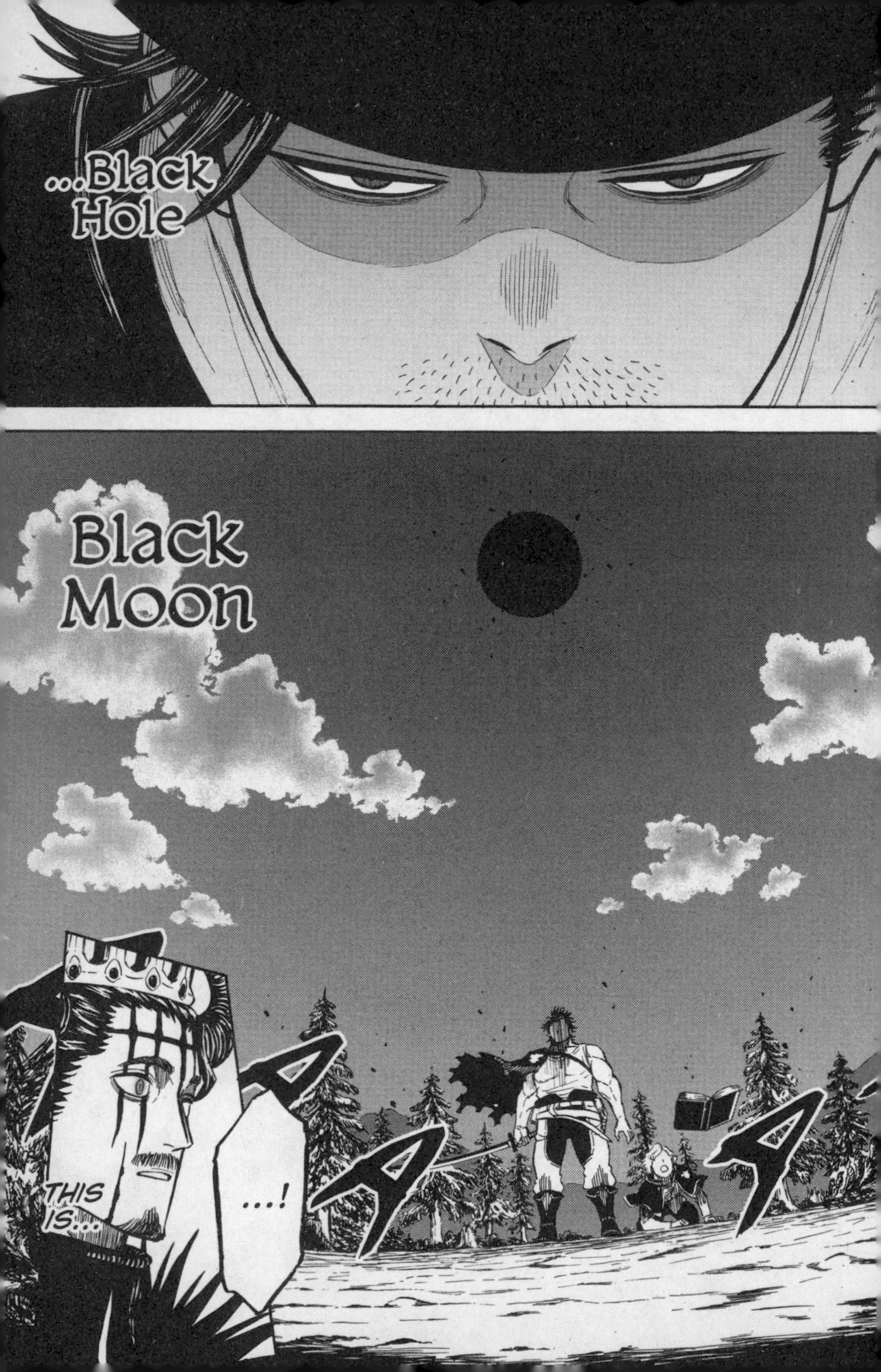
...Black Hole
Black Moon
...!
THIS IS...

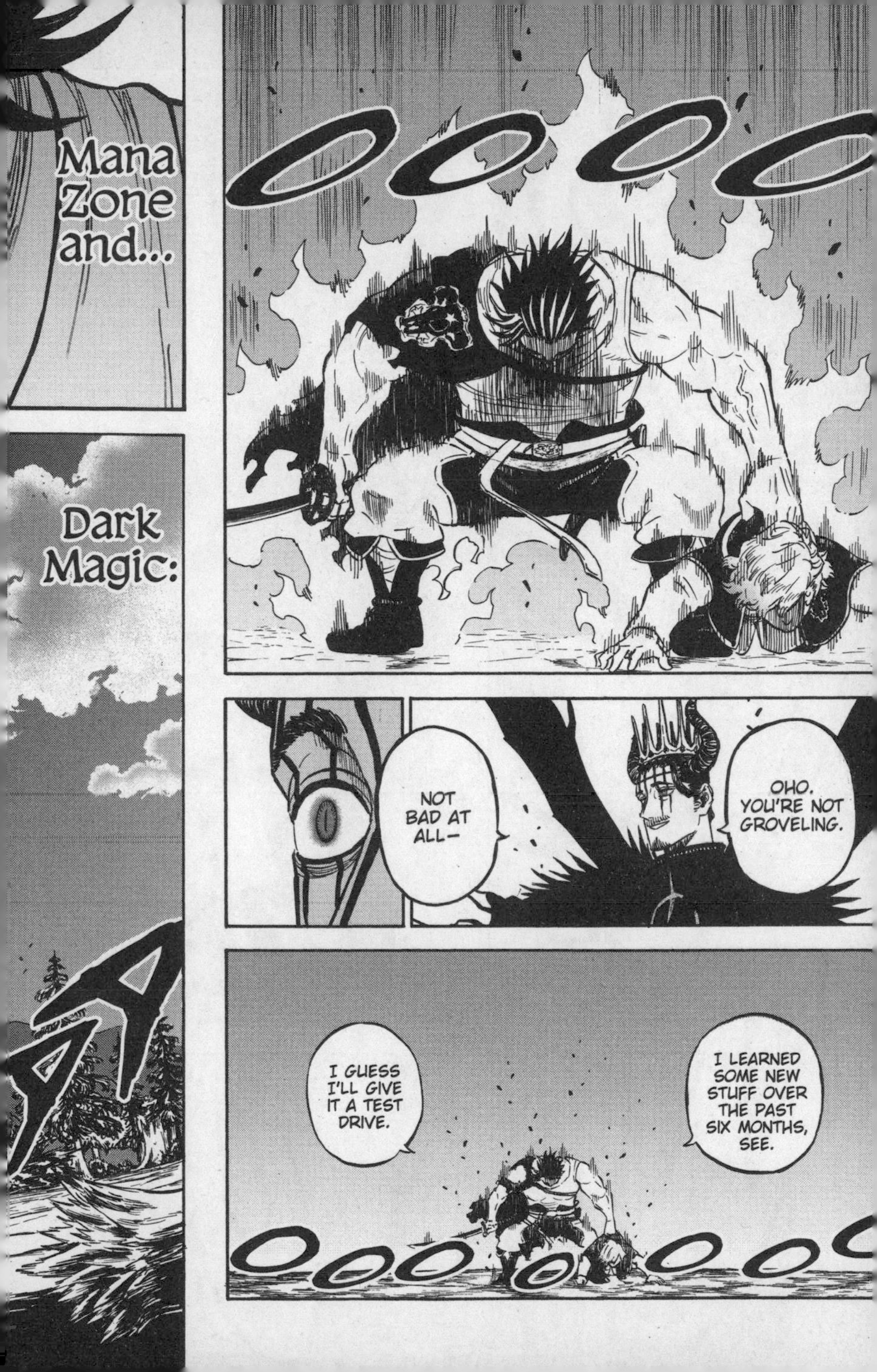
OHO. YOU'RE NOT GROVELING.
NOT BAD AT ALL—
I LEARNED SOME NEW STUFF OVER THE PAST SIX MONTHS, SEE.
I GUESS I'LL GIVE IT A TEST DRIVE.
Mana Zone and...
Dark Magic:

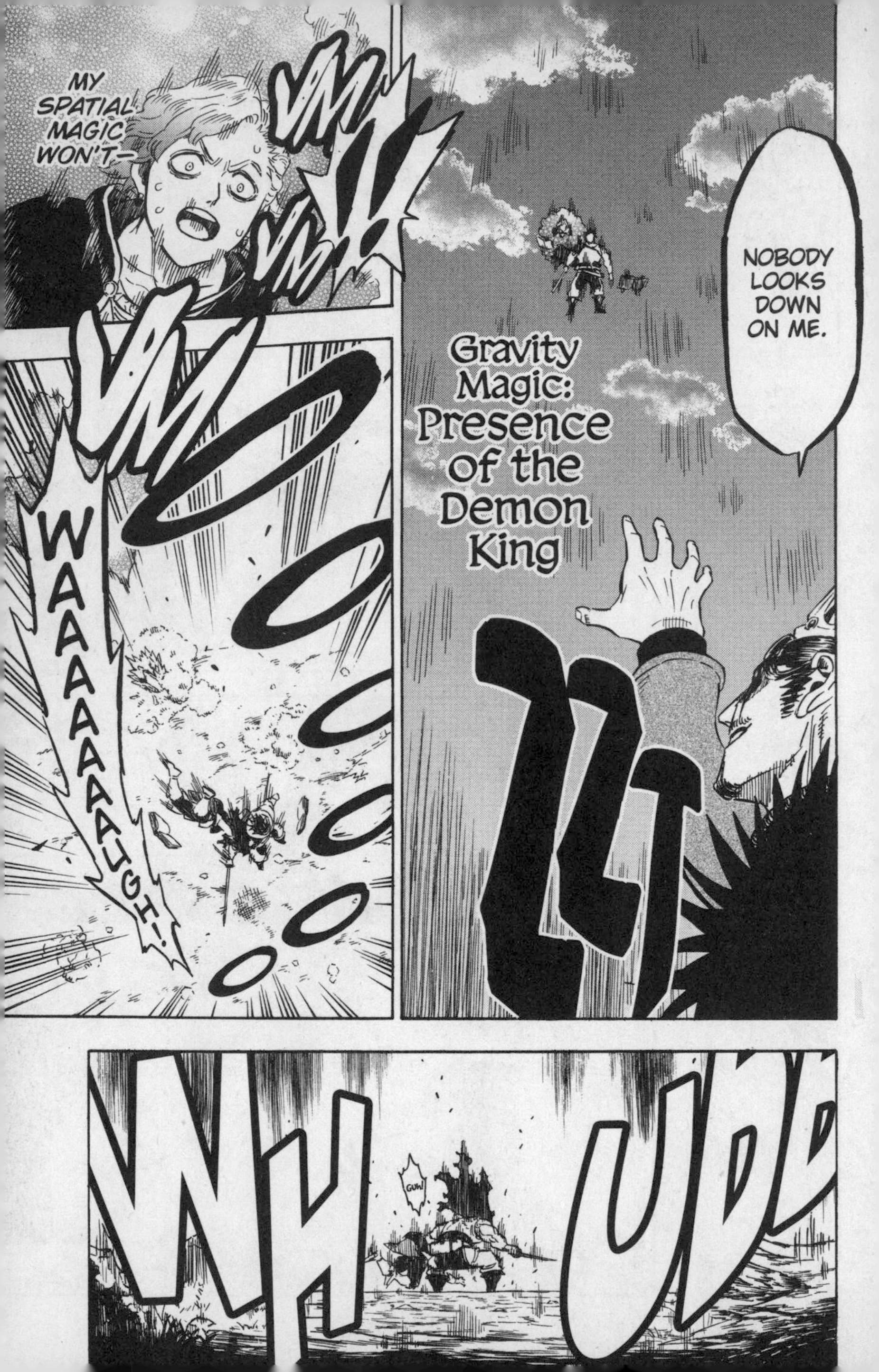
NOBODY LOOKS DOWN ON ME.
Gravity Magic: Presence of the Demon King
MY SPATIAL MAGIC WON'T—
WAAAAAAAAUGH!

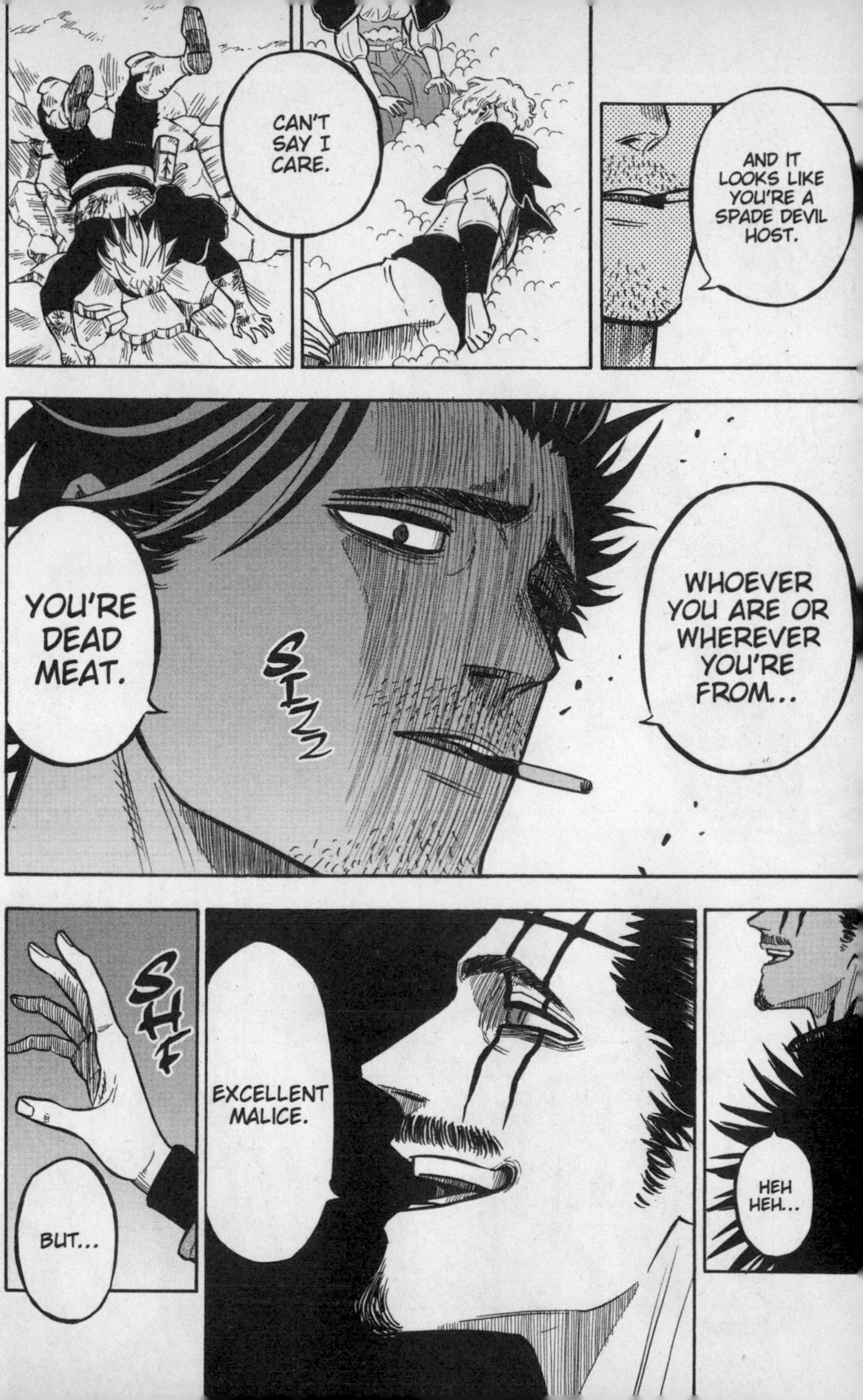
AND IT LOOKS LIKE YOU'RE A SPADE DEVIL HOST.
CAN'T SAY I CARE.
WHOEVER YOU ARE OR WHEREVER YOU'RE FROM...
SIZZ
YOU'RE DEAD MEAT.
HEH HEH...
EXCELLENT MALICE.
SHF
BUT...

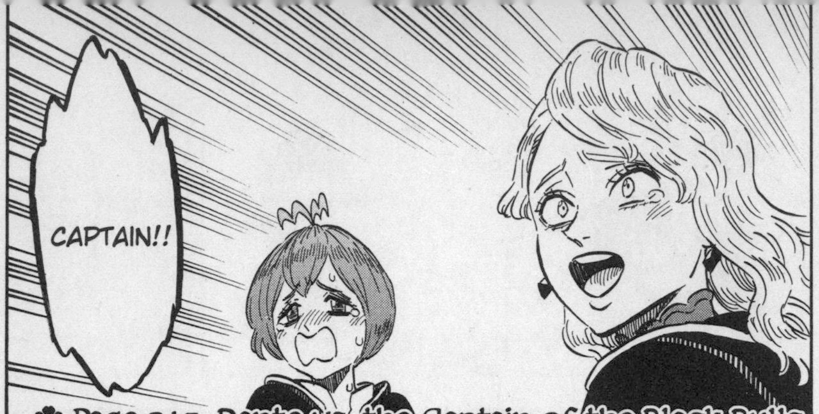
CAPTAIN!!

Page 245: Dante vs. the Captain of the Black Bulls

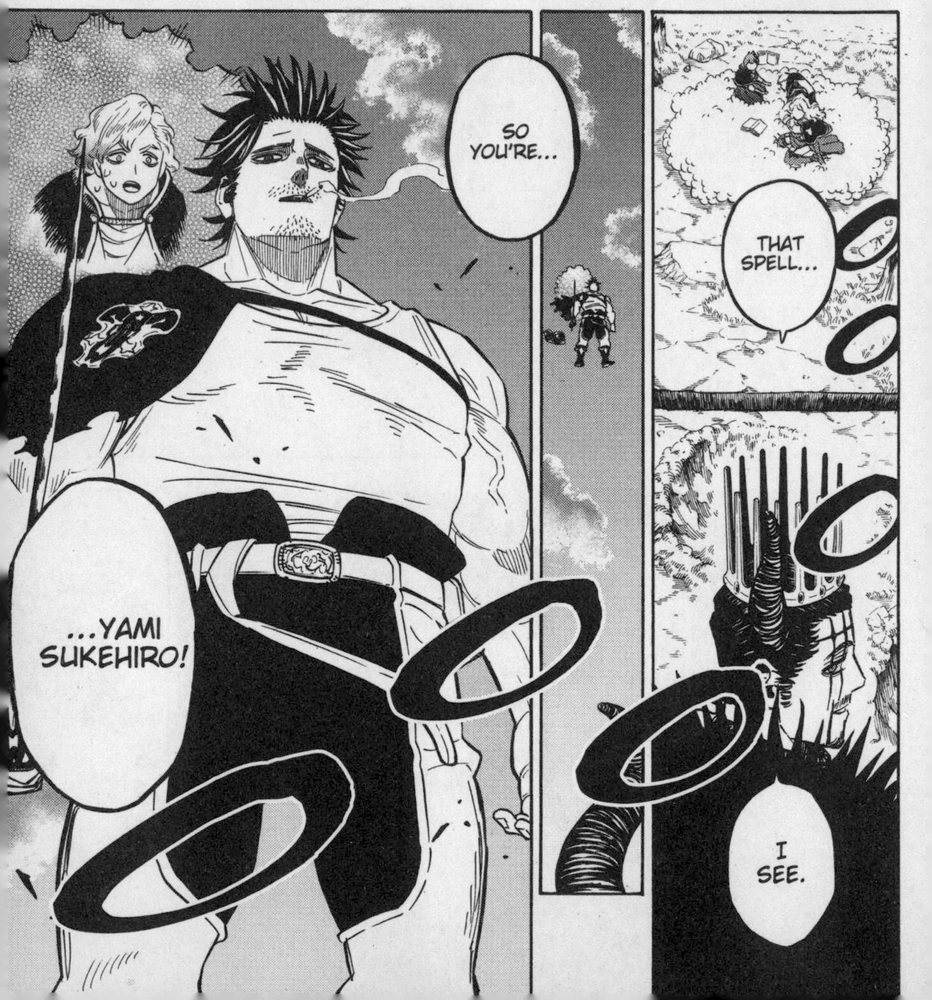
THAT SPELL...
I SEE.
SO YOU'RE...
...YAMI SUKEHIRO!

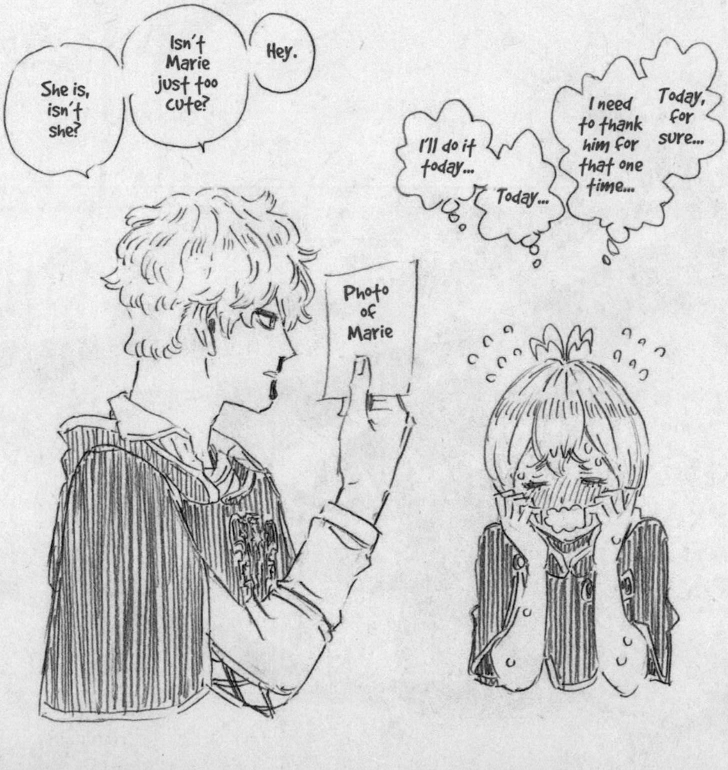
Today, for sure...
I need to thank him for that one time...
Today...
I'll do it today...
Hey.
Isn't Marie just too cute?
She is, isn't she?
Photo of Marie

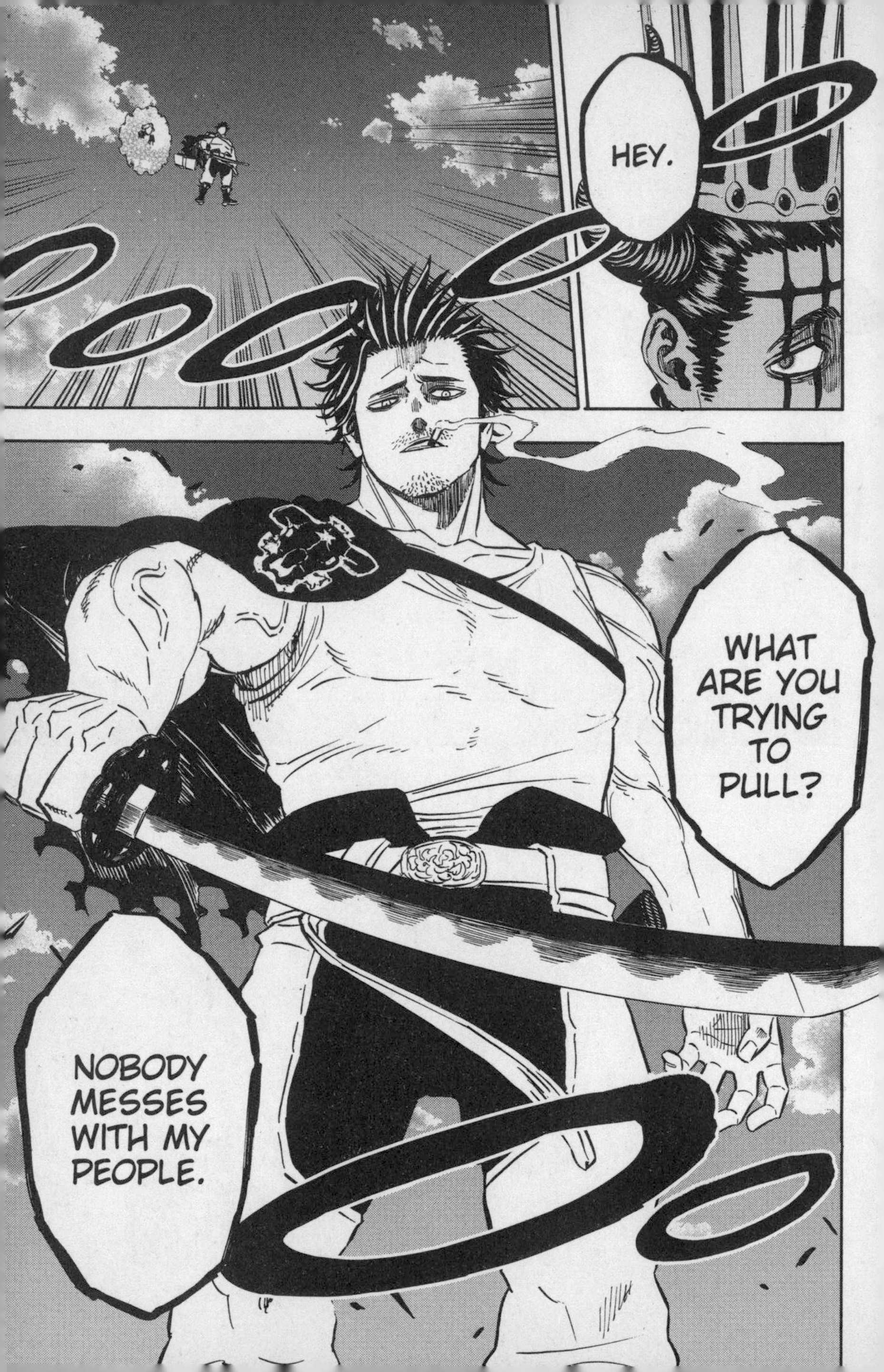
HEY.
WHAT ARE YOU TRYING TO PULL?
NOBODY MESSES WITH MY PEOPLE.

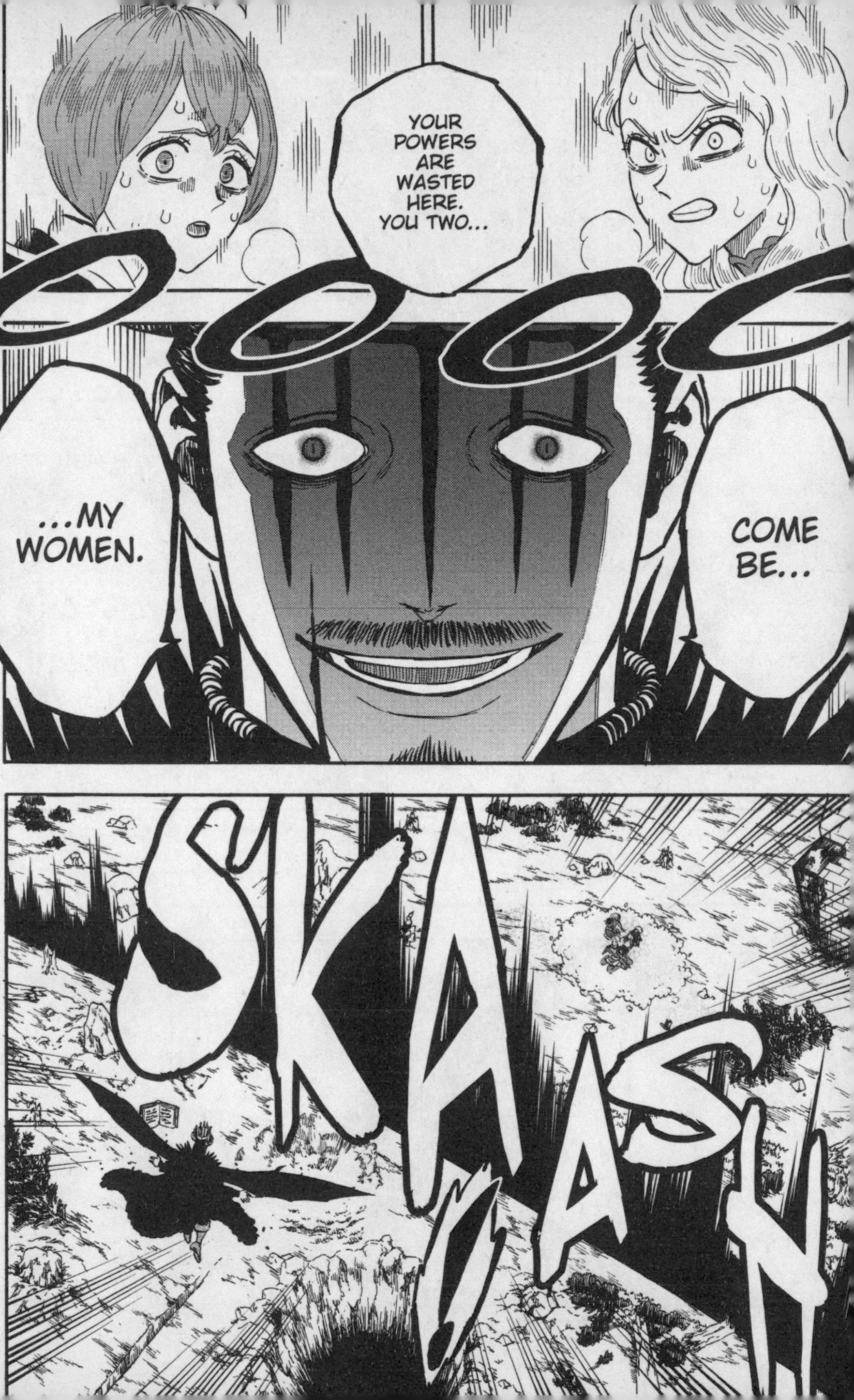
YOUR POWERS ARE WASTED HERE. YOU TWO...
COME BE...
...MY WOMEN.
SKASH

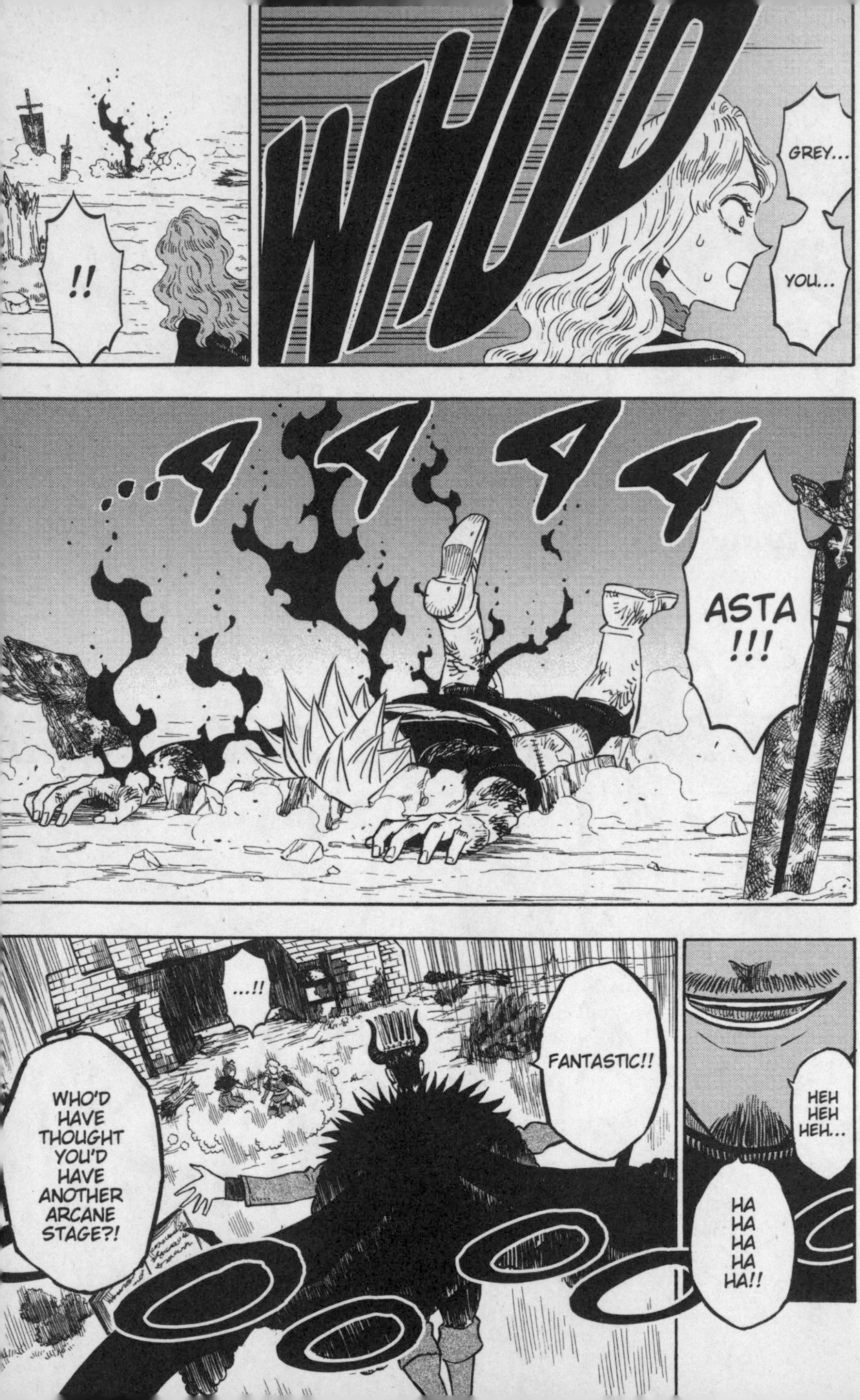
WHUD
GREY...
YOU...
!!
AAAA
ASTA!!!
HEH HEH HEH...
HA HA HA HA HA!!
FANTASTIC!!
...!!
WHO'D HAVE THOUGHT YOU'D HAVE ANOTHER ARCANE STAGE?!

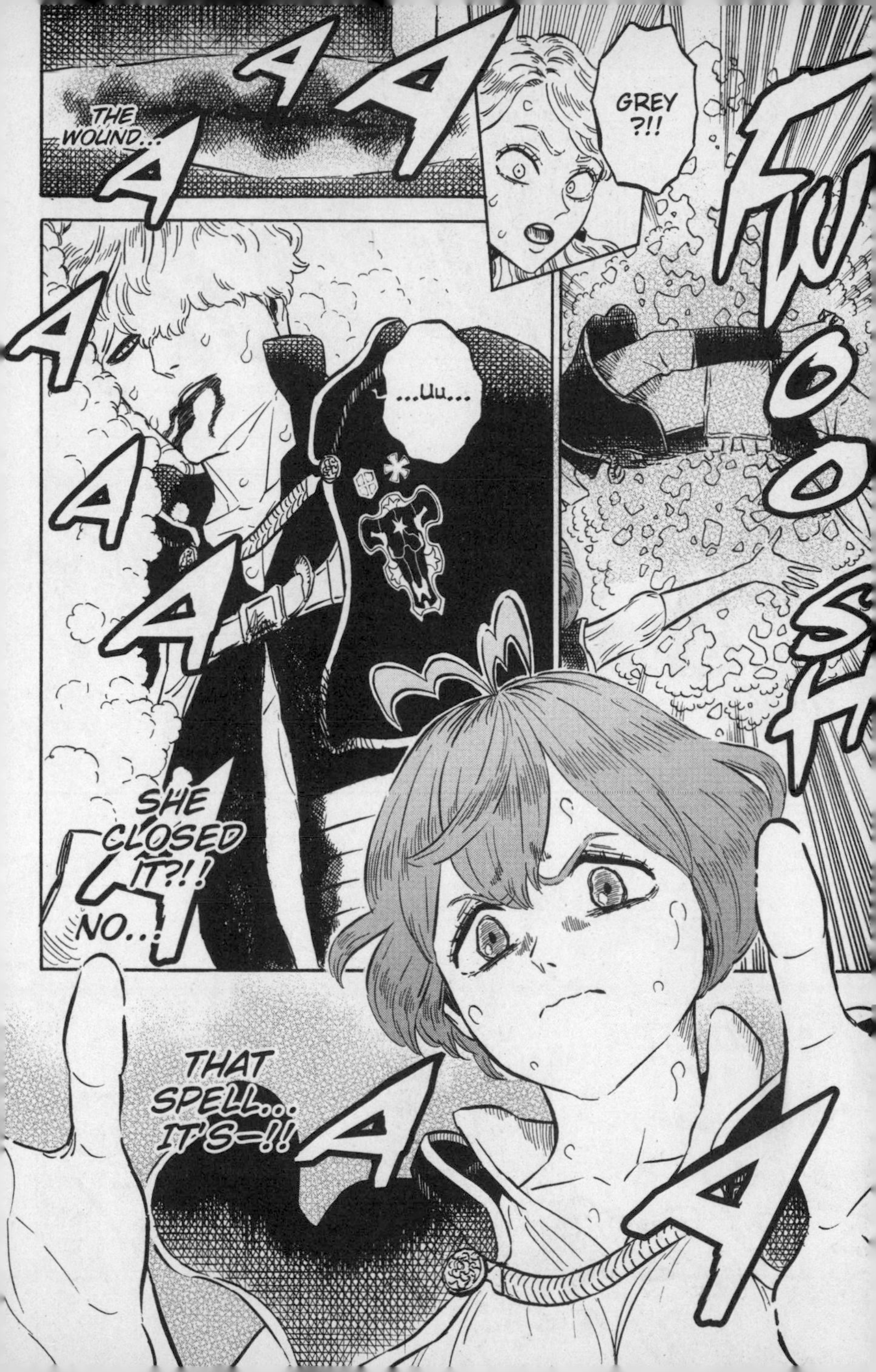
GREY ?!!
FWOOSH
THE WOUND...
...Uu...
SHE CLOSED IT?!!
NO...
THAT SPELL... IT'S—!!
AAAAAAAAA

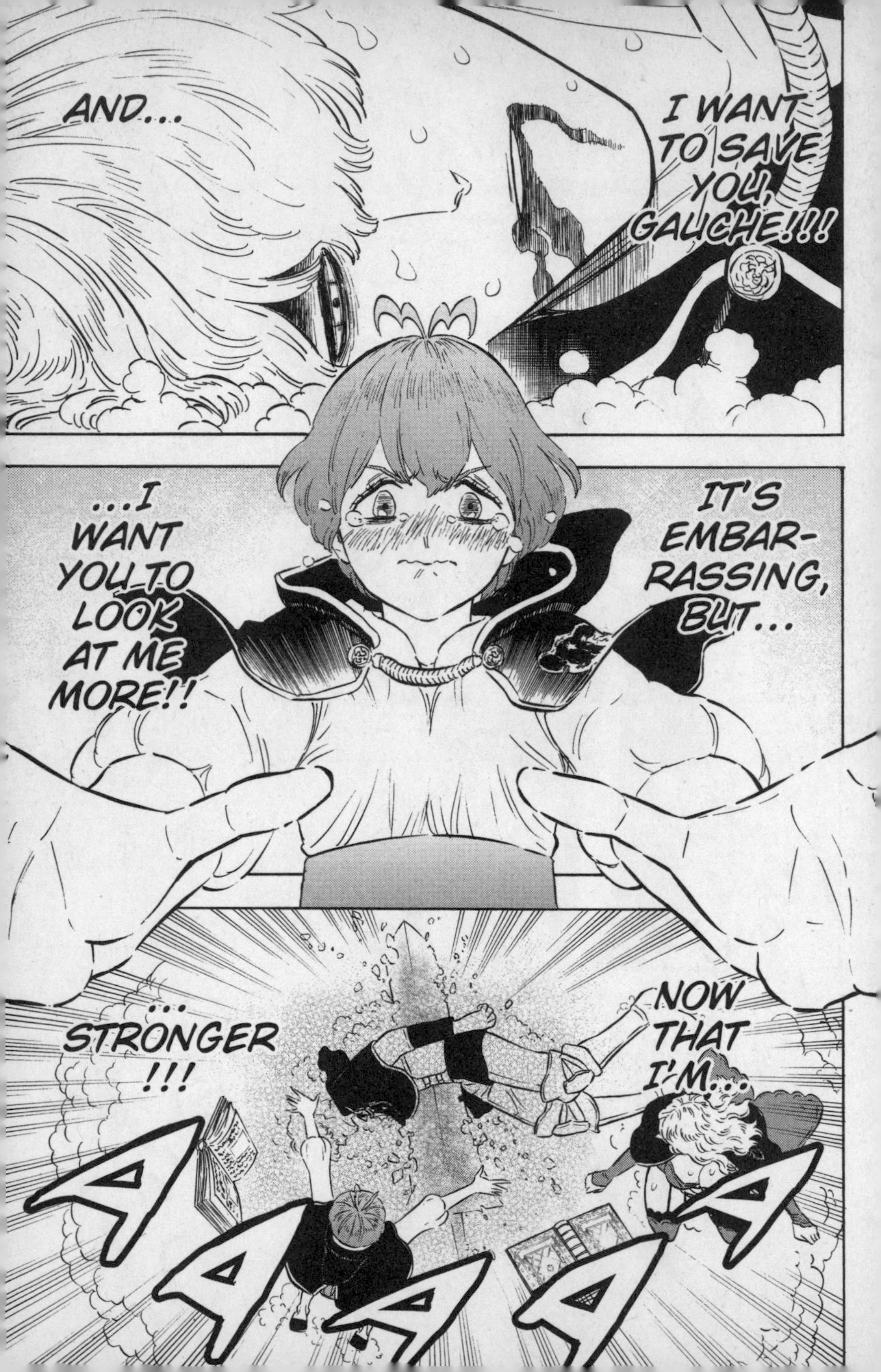
I WANT TO SAVE YOU, GAUCHE!!!
AND....
IT'S EMBARRASSING, BUT...
...I WANT YOU TO LOOK AT ME MORE!!
NOW THAT I'M...
...STRONGER!!!
AAAA

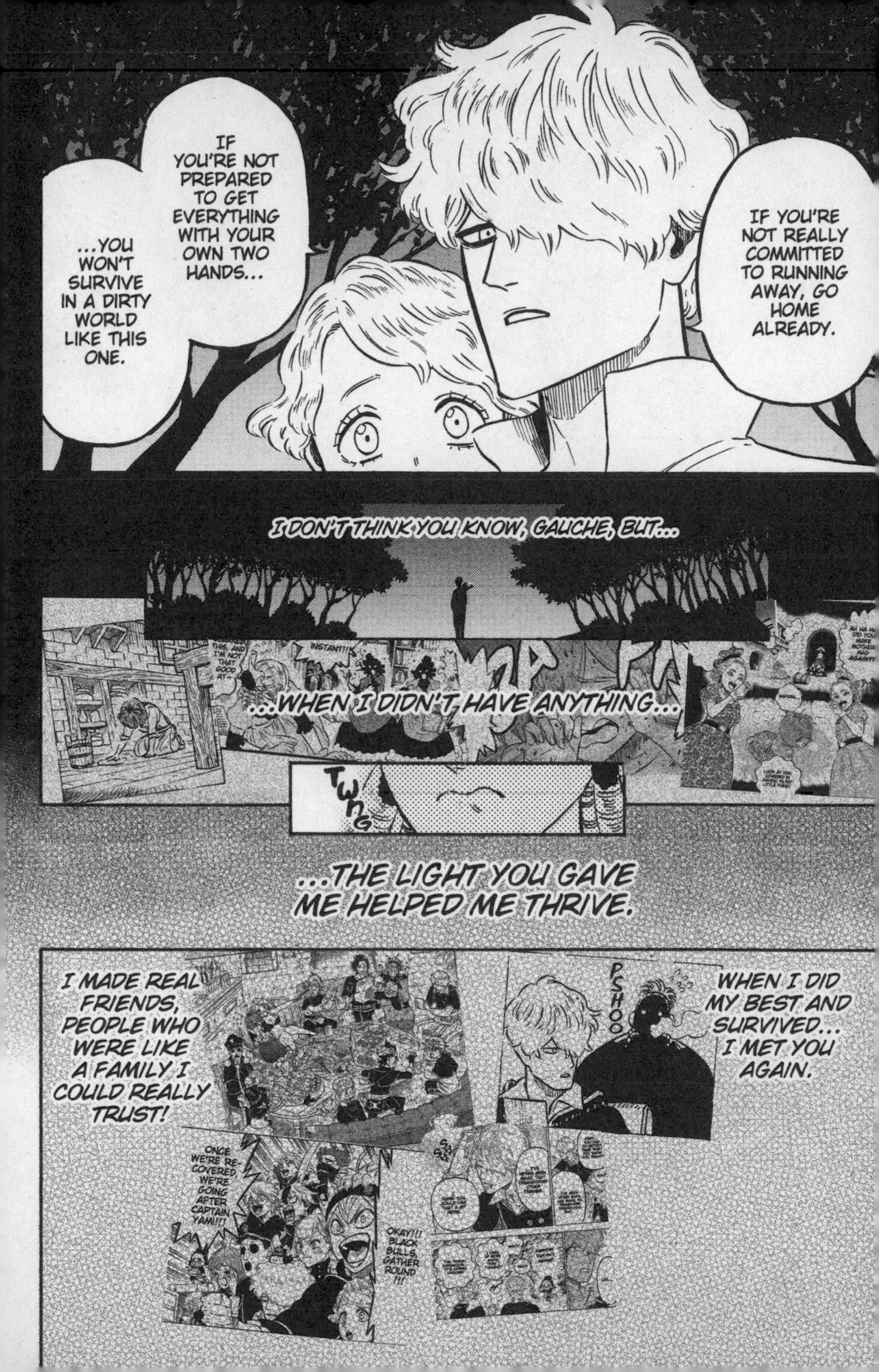
IF YOU'RE NOT REALLY COMMITTED TO RUNNING AWAY, GO HOME ALREADY.
IF YOU'RE NOT PREPARED TO GET EVERYTHING WITH YOUR OWN TWO HANDS...
...YOU WON'T SURVIVE IN A DIRTY WORLD LIKE THIS ONE.
I DON'T THINK YOU KNOW, GAUCHE, BUT...
INSTANT!!!
...WHEN I DIDN'T HAVE ANYTHING...
TWNG
...THE LIGHT YOU GAVE ME HELPED ME THRIVE.
PSHOO
WHEN I DID MY BEST AND SURVIVED... I MET YOU AGAIN.
I MADE REAL FRIENDS, PEOPLE WHO WERE LIKE A FAMILY I COULD REALLY TRUST!
ONCE WE'RE RE-COVERED, WE'RE GOING AFTER CAPTAIN YAMI!!!
OKAY!!! BLACK BULLS, GATHER ROUND!!!

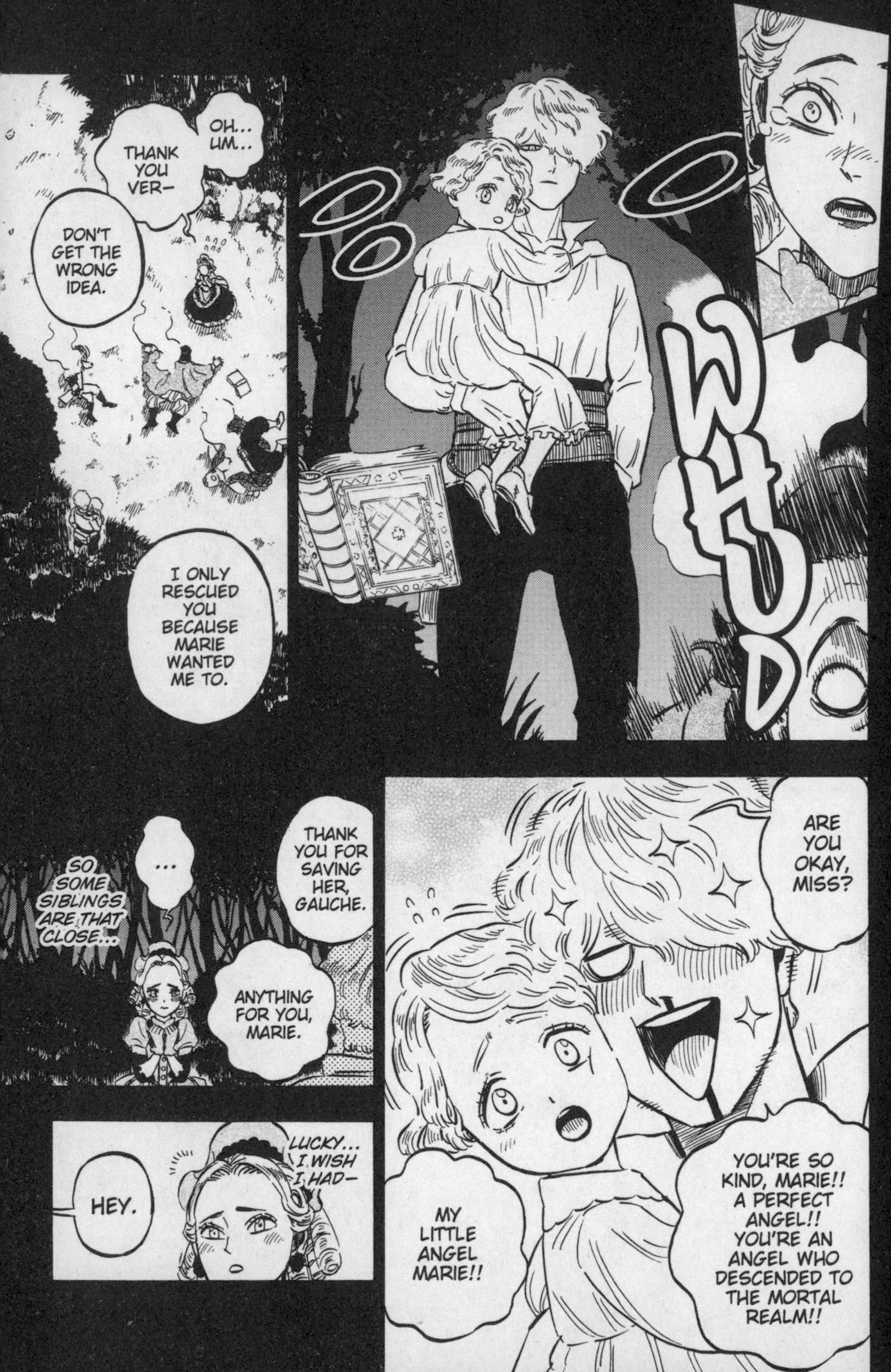
WHUD
OH... UM...
THANK YOU VER—
DON'T GET THE WRONG IDEA.
I ONLY RESCUED YOU BECAUSE MARIE WANTED ME TO.
ARE YOU OKAY, MISS?
YOU'RE SO KIND, MARIE!! A PERFECT ANGEL!! YOU'RE AN ANGEL WHO DESCENDED TO THE MORTAL REALM!!
MY LITTLE ANGEL MARIE!!
THANK YOU FOR SAVING HER, GAUCHE.
ANYTHING FOR YOU, MARIE.
...
SO SOME SIBLINGS ARE THAT CLOSE...
LUCKY... I WISH I HAD—
HEY.

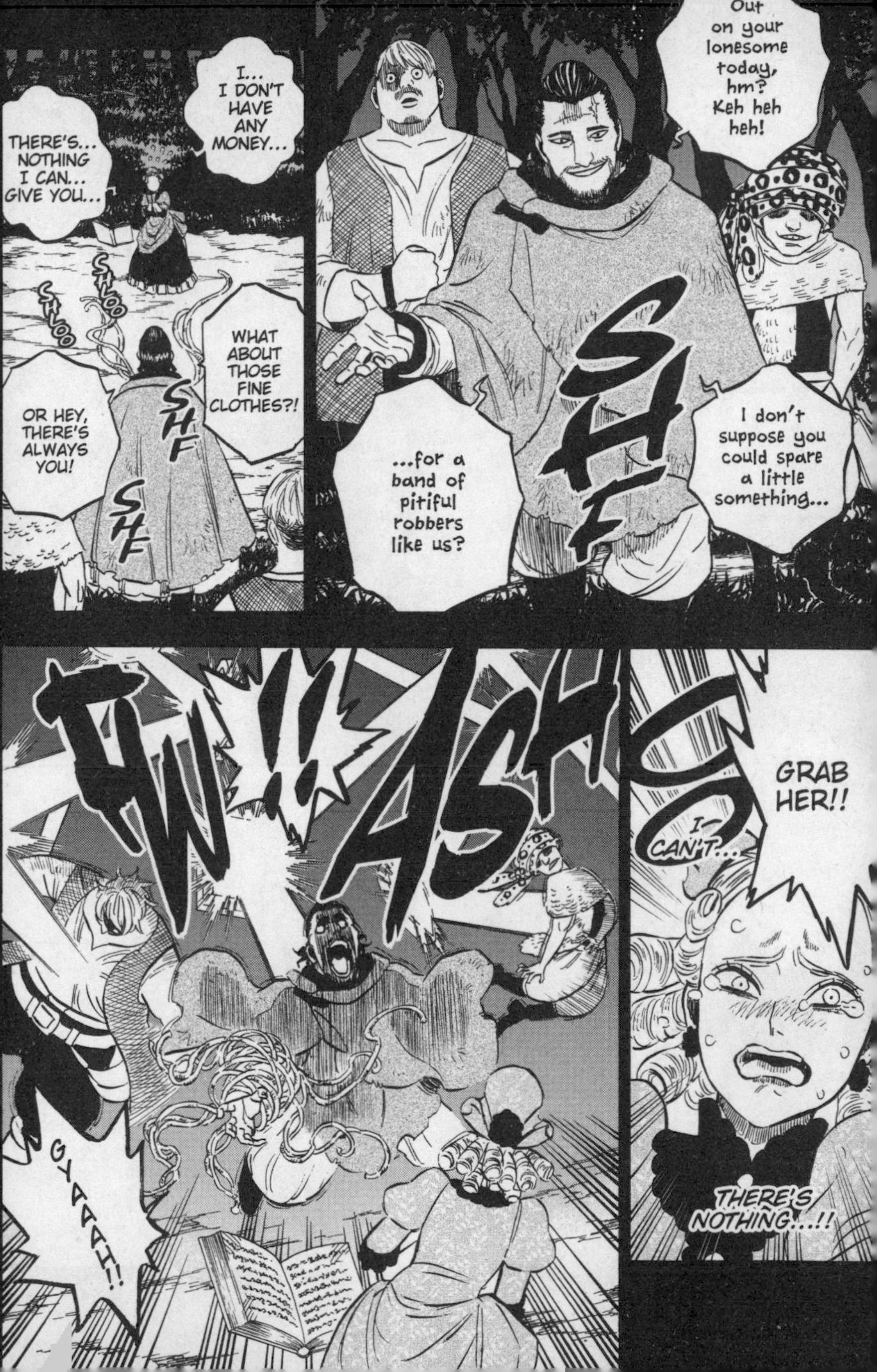
Out on your lonesome today, hm? Keh heh heh!
I don't suppose you could spare a little something...
SHF
...for a band of pitiful robbers like us?
I... I DON'T HAVE ANY MONEY...
THERE'S... NOTHING I CAN... GIVE YOU...
SHLOO
SHLOO
WHAT ABOUT THOSE FINE CLOTHES?!
SHF
SHF
OR HEY, THERE'S ALWAYS YOU!
GRAB HER!!
I CAN'T...
THERE'S NOTHING...!!
THWASH!!
GYAAAH!!

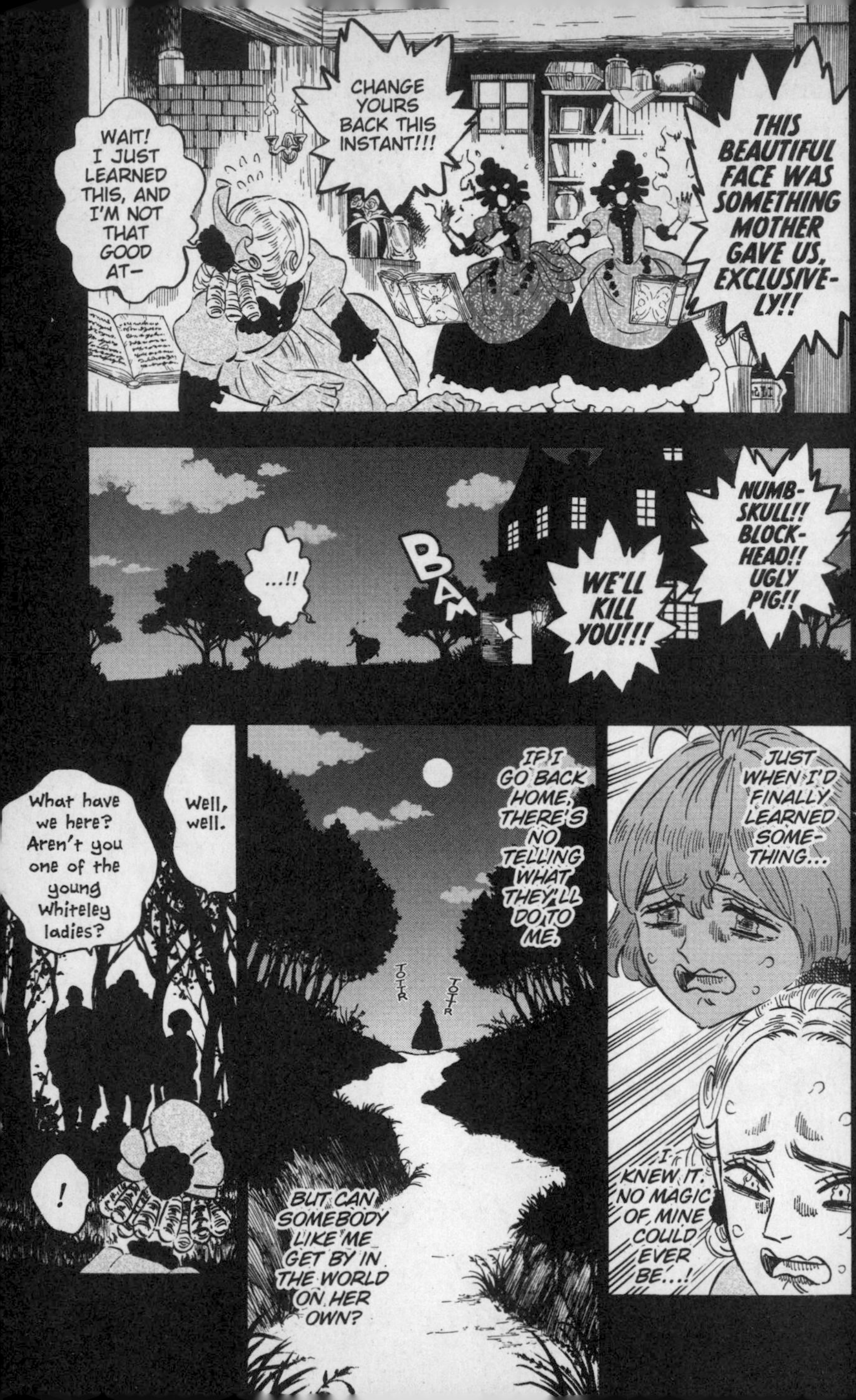
THIS BEAUTIFUL FACE WAS SOMETHING MOTHER GAVE US, EXCLUSIVE-LY!!
CHANGE YOURS BACK THIS INSTANT!!!
WAIT! I JUST LEARNED THIS, AND I'M NOT THAT GOOD AT—
NUMB-SKULL!! BLOCK-HEAD!! UGLY PIG!!
WE'LL KILL YOU!!!
BAM
...!!
JUST WHEN I'D FINALLY LEARNED SOME-THING...
I KNEW IT. NO MAGIC OF MINE COULD EVER BE...!
IF I GO BACK HOME, THERE'S NO TELLING WHAT THEY'LL DO TO ME.
TOTTR
TOTTR
BUT CAN SOMEBODY LIKE ME GET BY IN THE WORLD ON HER OWN?
Well, well.
What have we here? Aren't you one of the young Whiteley ladies?
!

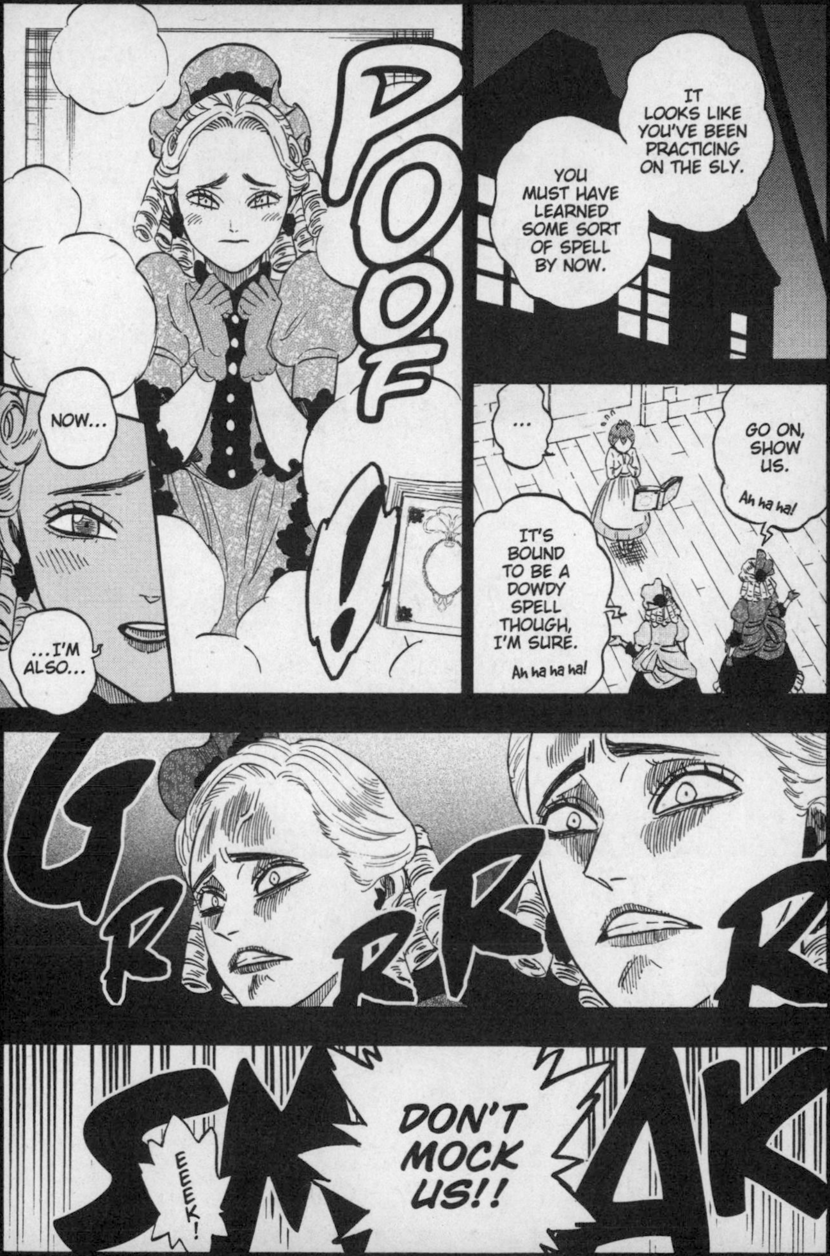
IT LOOKS LIKE YOU'VE BEEN PRACTICING ON THE SLY.
YOU MUST HAVE LEARNED SOME SORT OF SPELL BY NOW.
GO ON, SHOW US.
Ah ha ha!
...
IT'S BOUND TO BE A DOWDY SPELL THOUGH, I'M SURE.
Ah ha ha ha!
POOF
!
NOW...
...I'M ALSO...
URRRK
SMAK
DON'T MOCK US!!
EEEK!

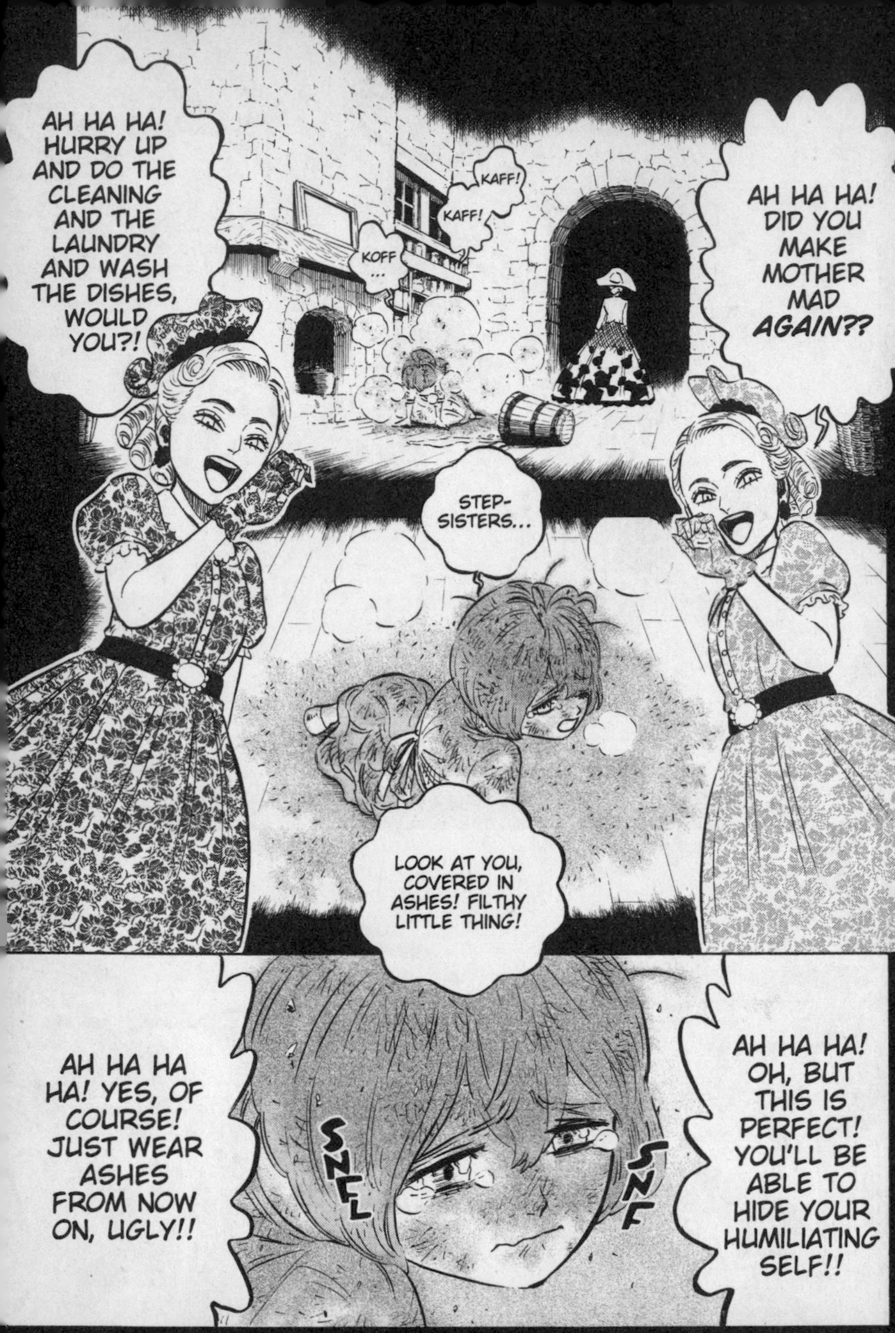
AH HA HA! DID YOU MAKE MOTHER MAD AGAIN??
KAFF!
KAFF!
KOFF...
AH HA HA! HURRY UP AND DO THE CLEANING AND THE LAUNDRY AND WASH THE DISHES, WOULD YOU?!
STEP-SISTERS...
LOOK AT YOU, COVERED IN ASHES! FILTHY LITTLE THING!
AH HA HA! OH, BUT THIS IS PERFECT! YOU'LL BE ABLE TO HIDE YOUR HUMILIATING SELF!!
SNF
SNFL
AH HA HA HA! YES, OF COURSE! JUST WEAR ASHES FROM NOW ON, UGLY!!

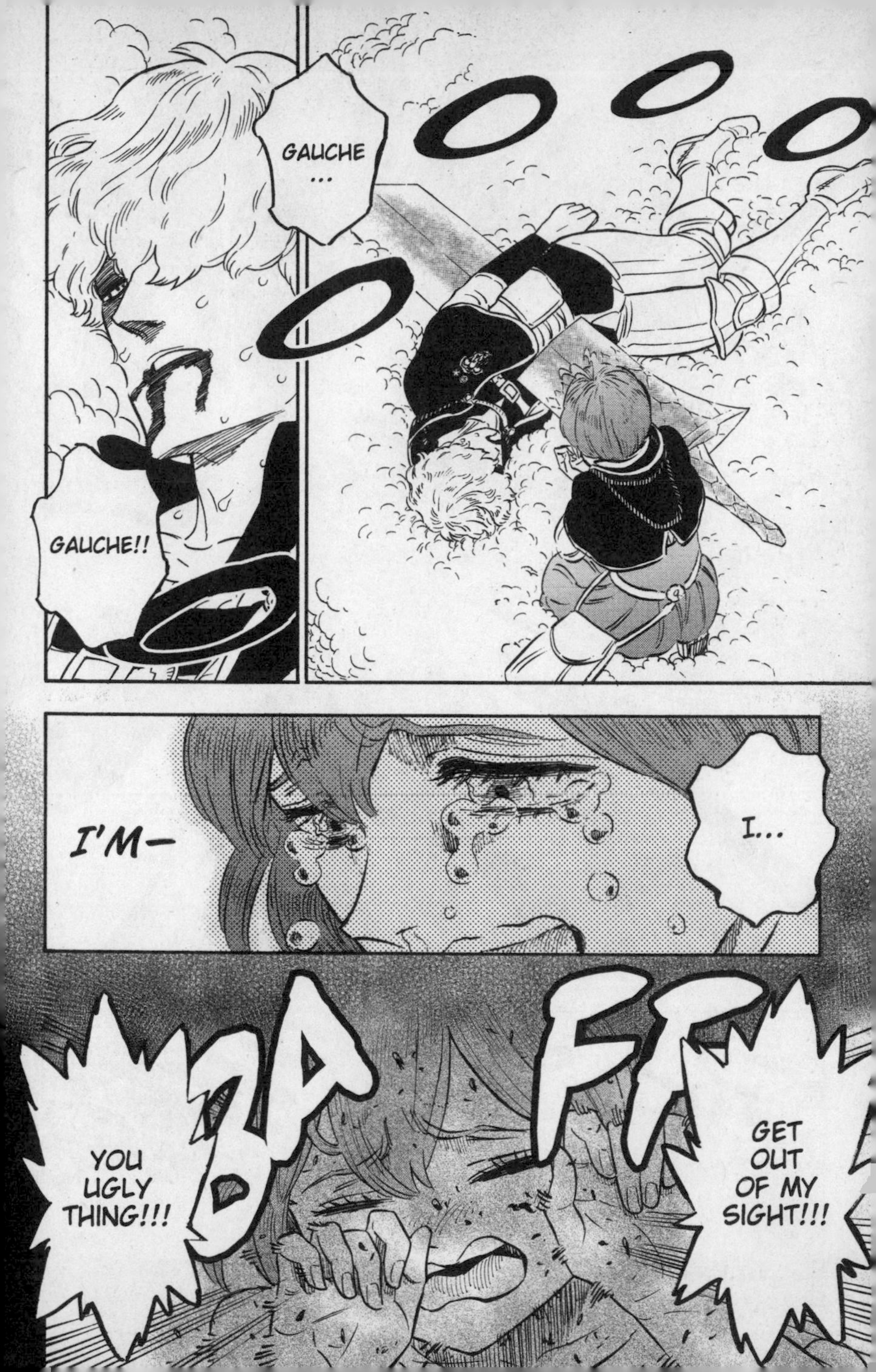
OOOOO
GAUCHE ...
GAUCHE!!
I...
I'M—
GET OUT OF MY SIGHT!!!
YOU UGLY THING!!!

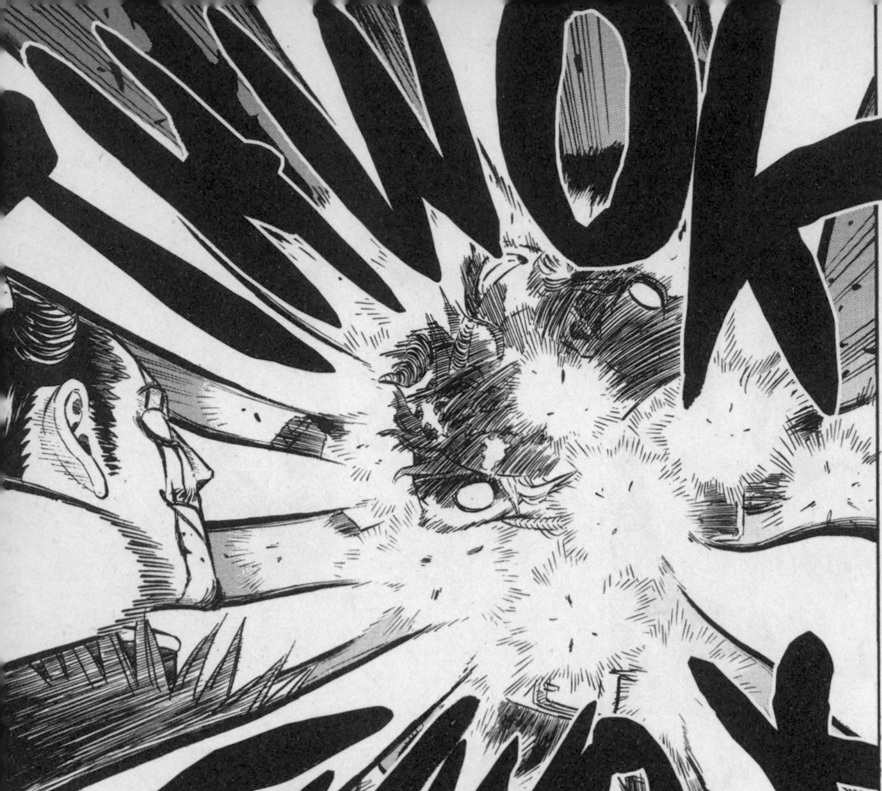
THWOK
THWOK
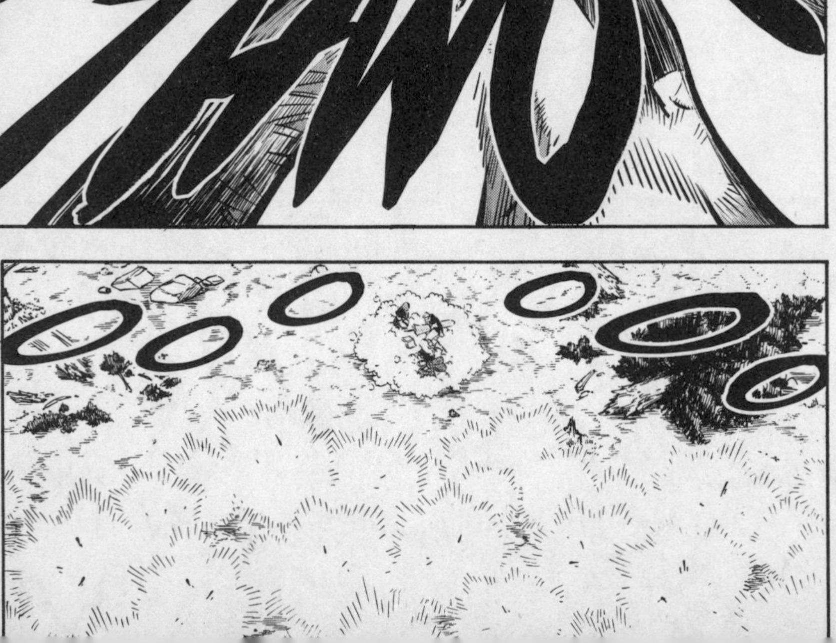

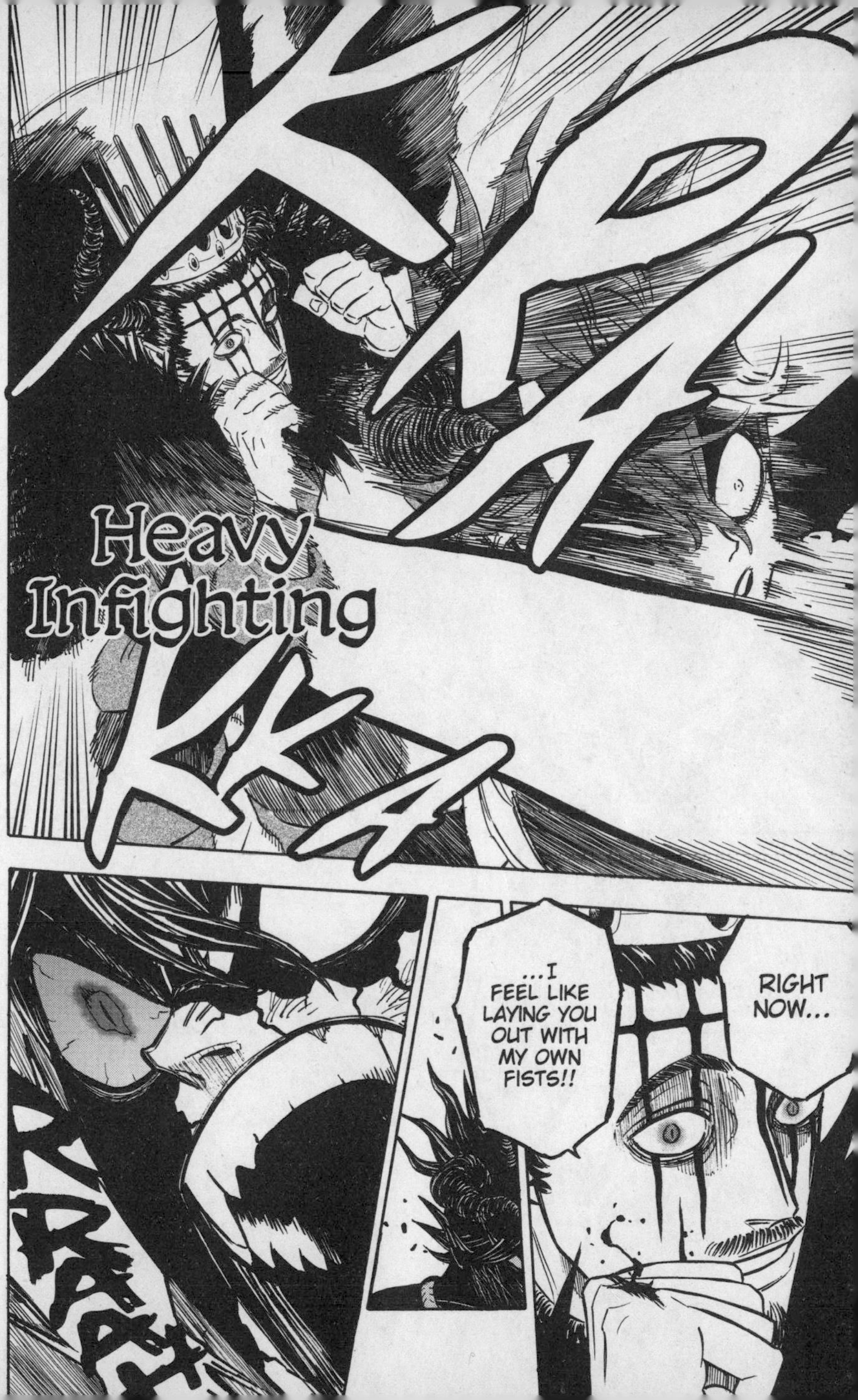
Heavy Infighting
RIGHT NOW...
...I FEEL LIKE LAYING YOU OUT WITH MY OWN FISTS!!

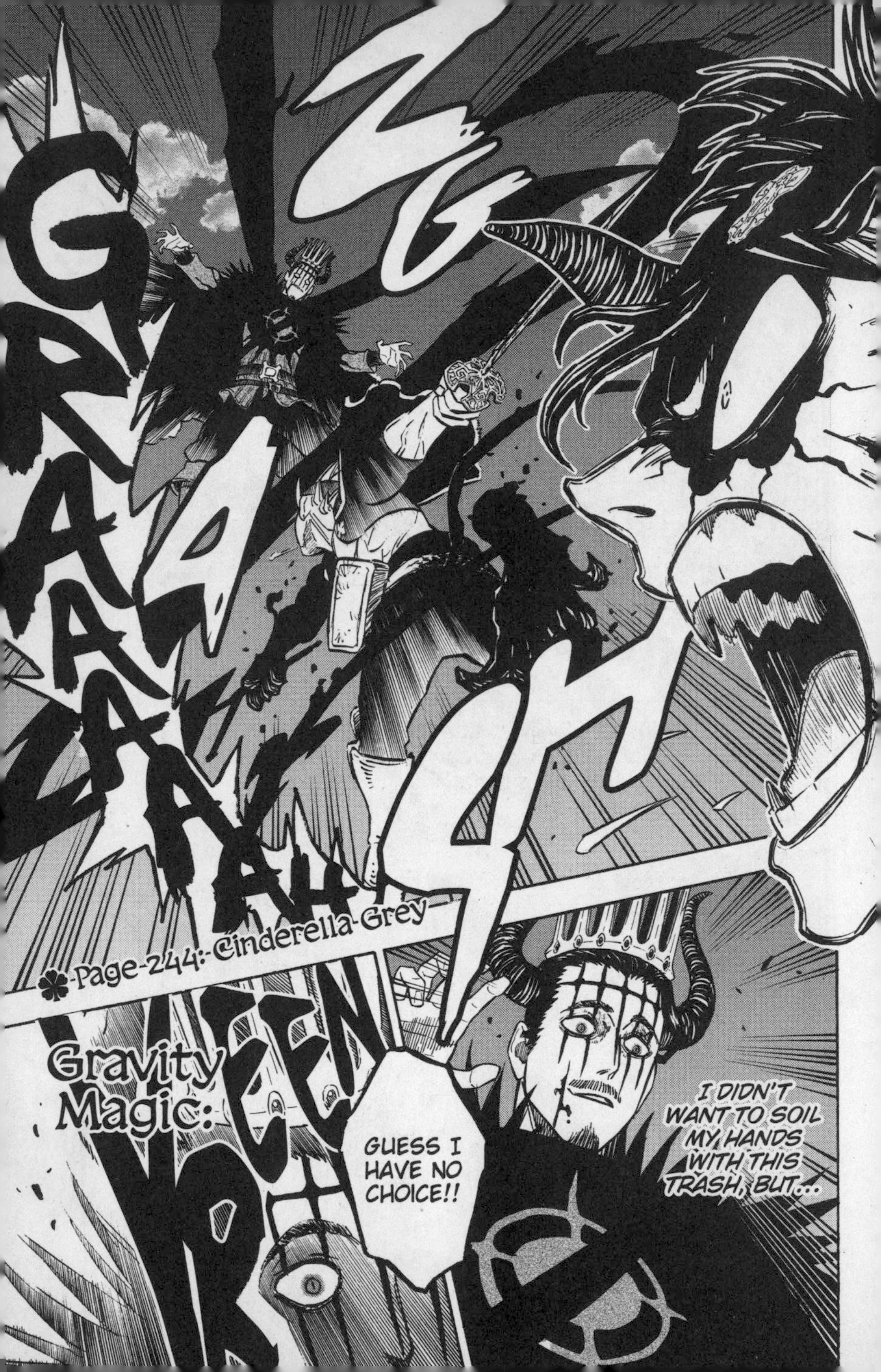
Page 244: Cinderella Grey
I DIDN'T WANT TO SOIL MY HANDS WITH THIS TRASH, BUT...
GUESS I HAVE NO CHOICE!!
Gravity Magic:

The Assorted Questions Brigade No. 2

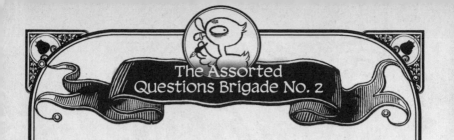

Q: Patry wasn't able to use someone else's grimoire, and yet in Page 202, the devil was able to use the grimoire he got (stole) from Patry. Why is that? (*N.S.*, Kanagawa)

A: It's something like "each soul has the right to own one grimoire." As a rule, mages only have the right to their own grimoire. That means they can't use grimoires that belong to other mages.

When Patry reincarnated and was in William Vangeance's body, there were two souls in one body, and each of them had the right to their own grimoire. Since that's the case, neither Patry nor William Vangeance can use the grimoire that belongs to the other one.

When Zagred (the Word Soul devil) stole Patry's grimoire, he stole William's right along with it, so he was able to use it. Basically, he turned someone else's grimoire into his own.

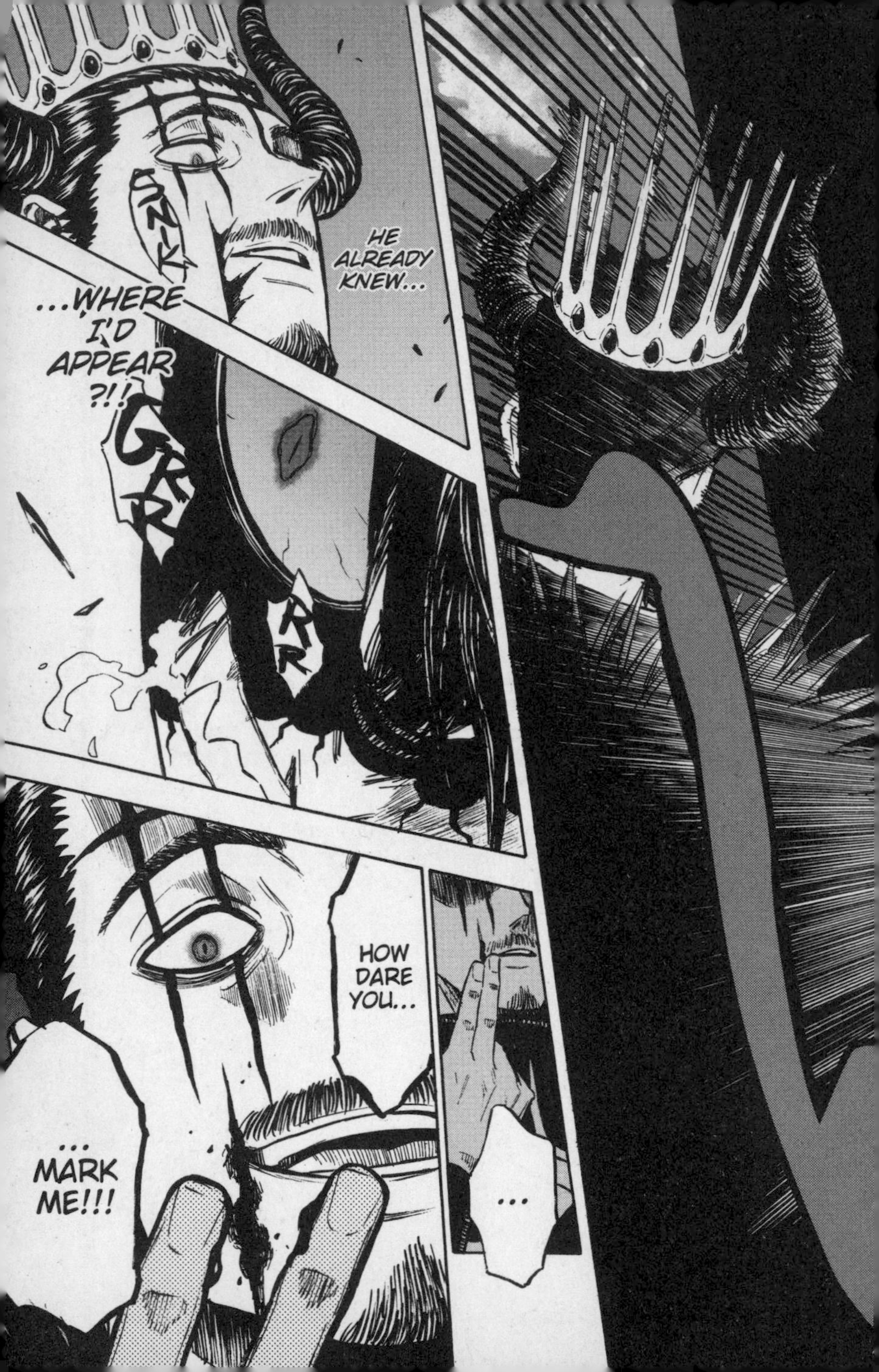
HE ALREADY KNEW...
SNIK
...WHERE I'D APPEAR?!!
GRR
RR
...
HOW DARE YOU...
...MARK ME!!!

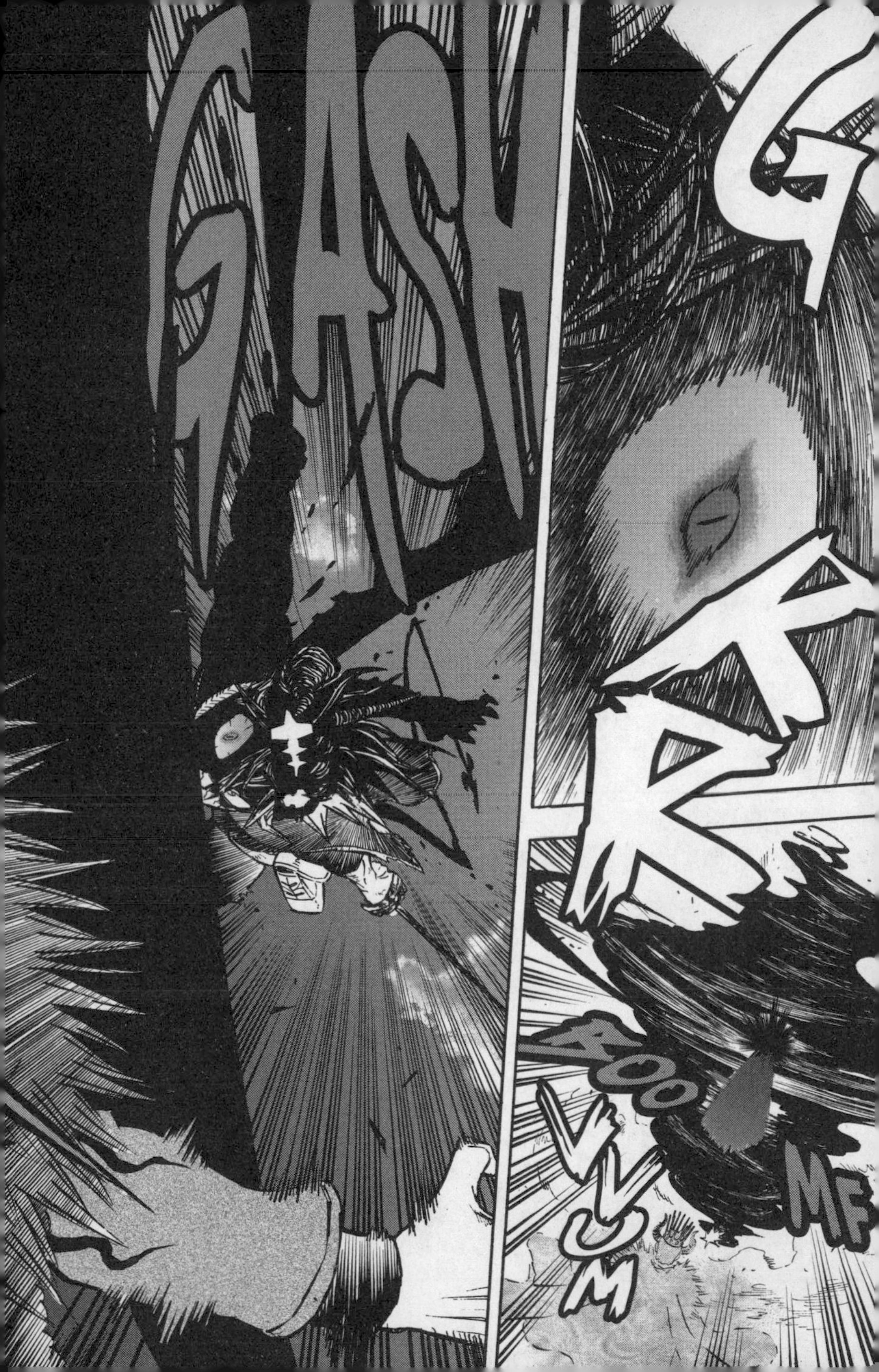
FOOO
VVVUM
MF
GASH

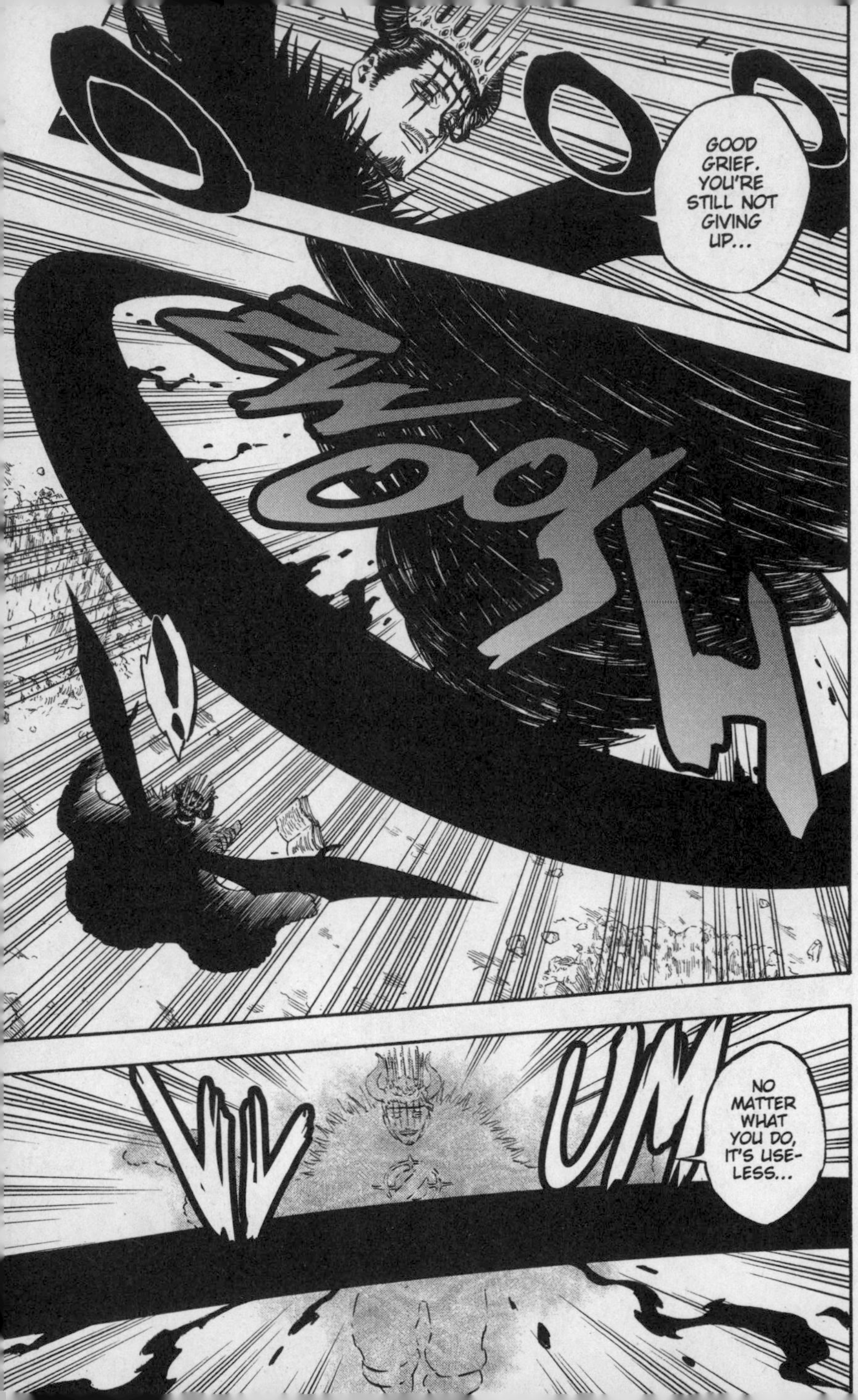
GOOD GRIEF. YOU'RE STILL NOT GIVING UP...
NO MATTER WHAT YOU DO, IT'S USELESS...

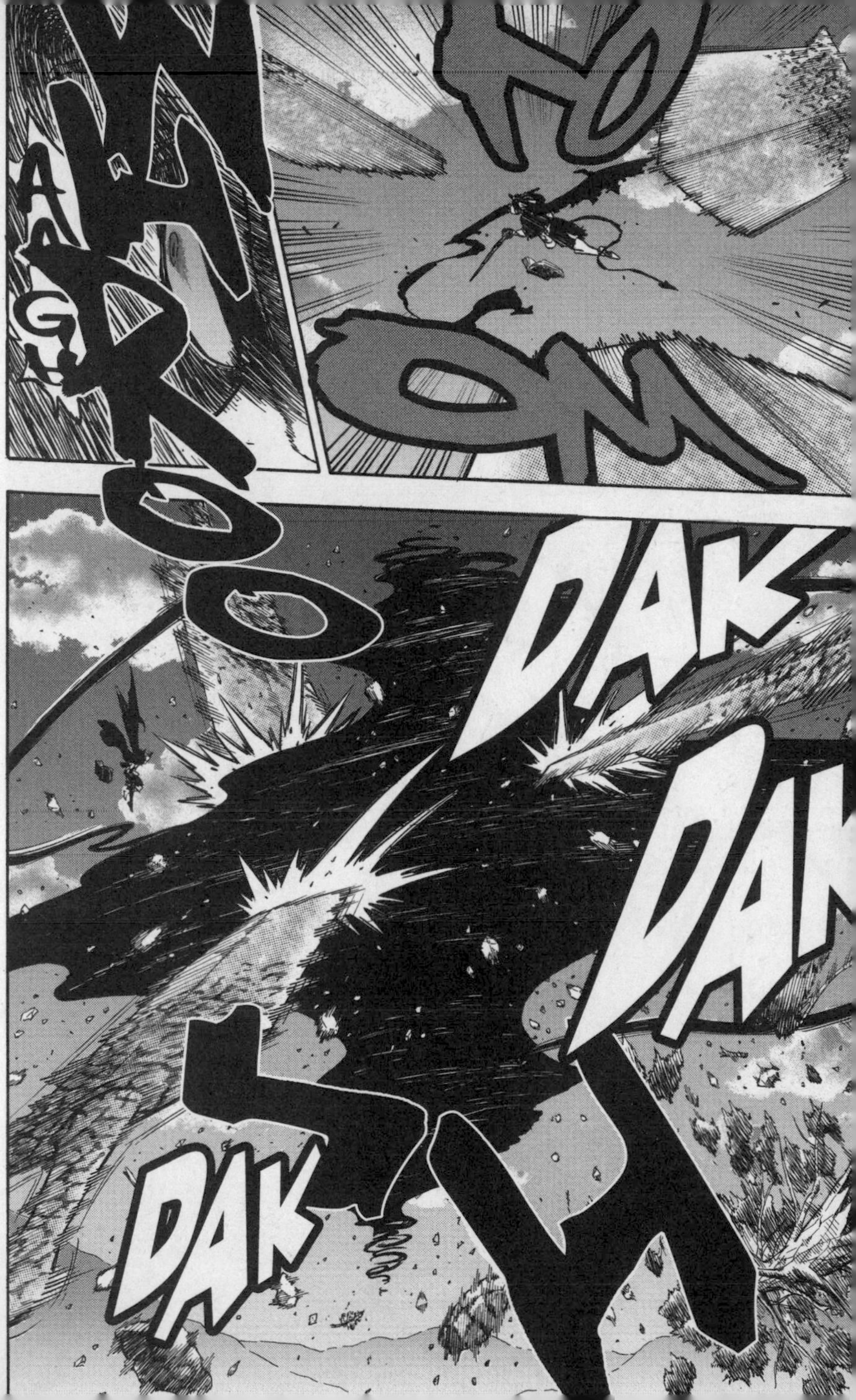
AAGH
DAK
DAK
DAK

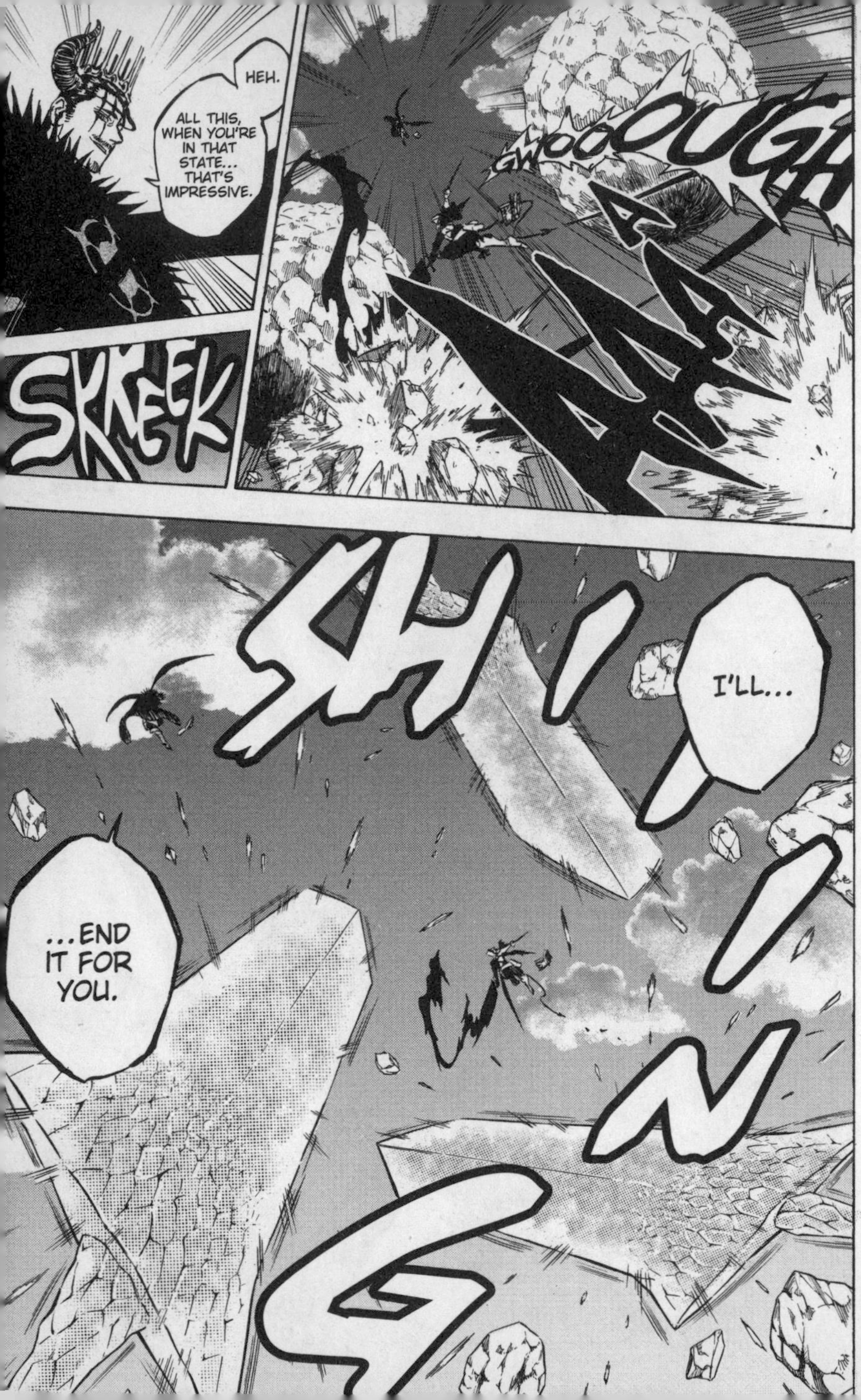
GWOOOOUGH
HEH.
ALL THIS, WHEN YOU'RE IN THAT STATE... THAT'S IMPRESSIVE.
SKREEEK
I'LL...
SHIIING
...END IT FOR YOU.

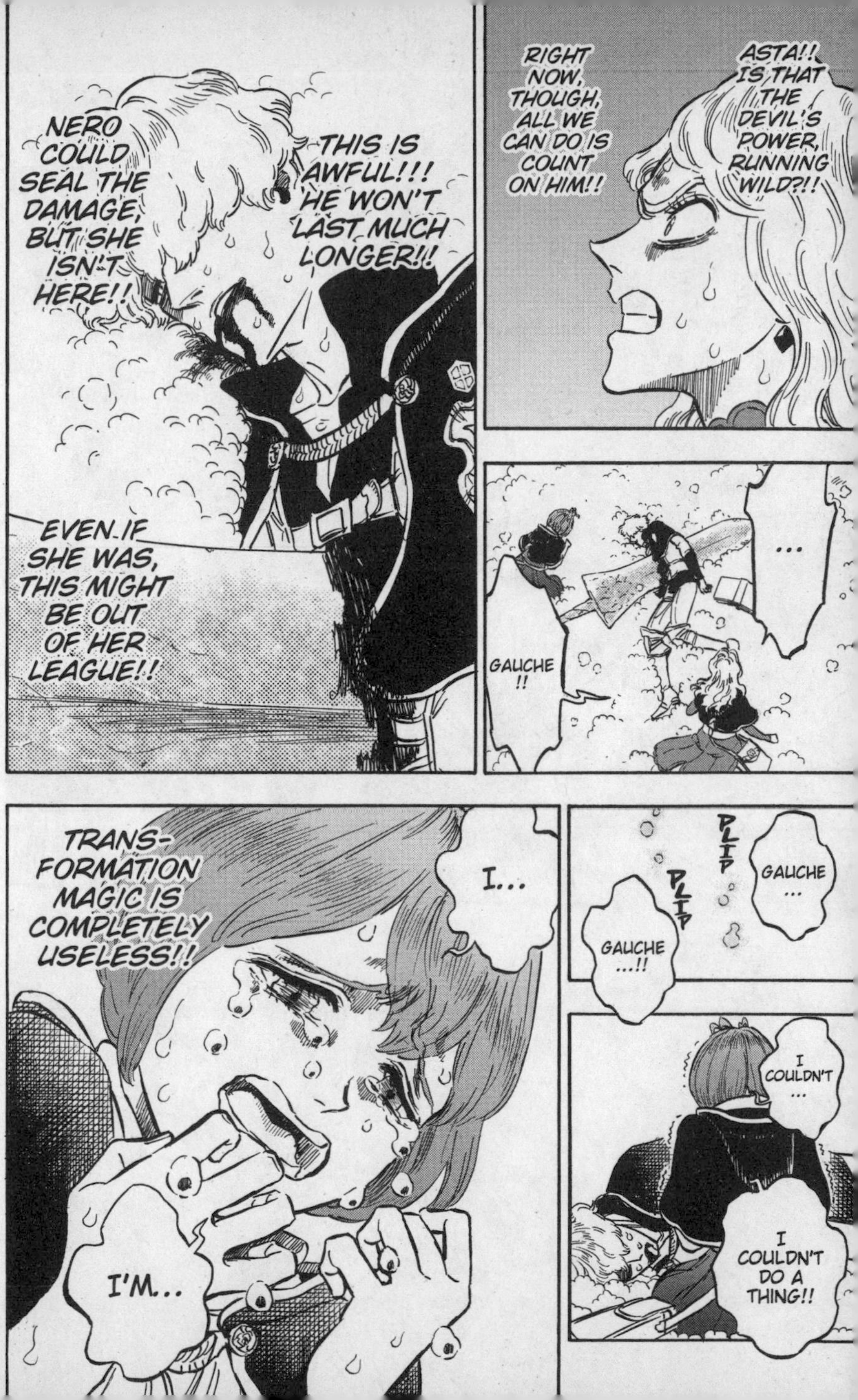
ASTA!! IS THAT THE DEVIL'S POWER, RUNNING WILD?!!
RIGHT NOW, THOUGH, ALL WE CAN DO IS COUNT ON HIM!!
...
GAUCHE !!
THIS IS AWFUL!!! HE WON'T LAST MUCH LONGER!!
NERO COULD SEAL THE DAMAGE, BUT SHE ISN'T HERE!!
EVEN IF SHE WAS, THIS MIGHT BE OUT OF HER LEAGUE!!
GAUCHE ...
PLIP
PLIP
GAUCHE ...!!
I COULDN'T ...
I COULDN'T DO A THING!!
I...
TRANS-FORMATION MAGIC IS COMPLETELY USELESS!!
I'M...

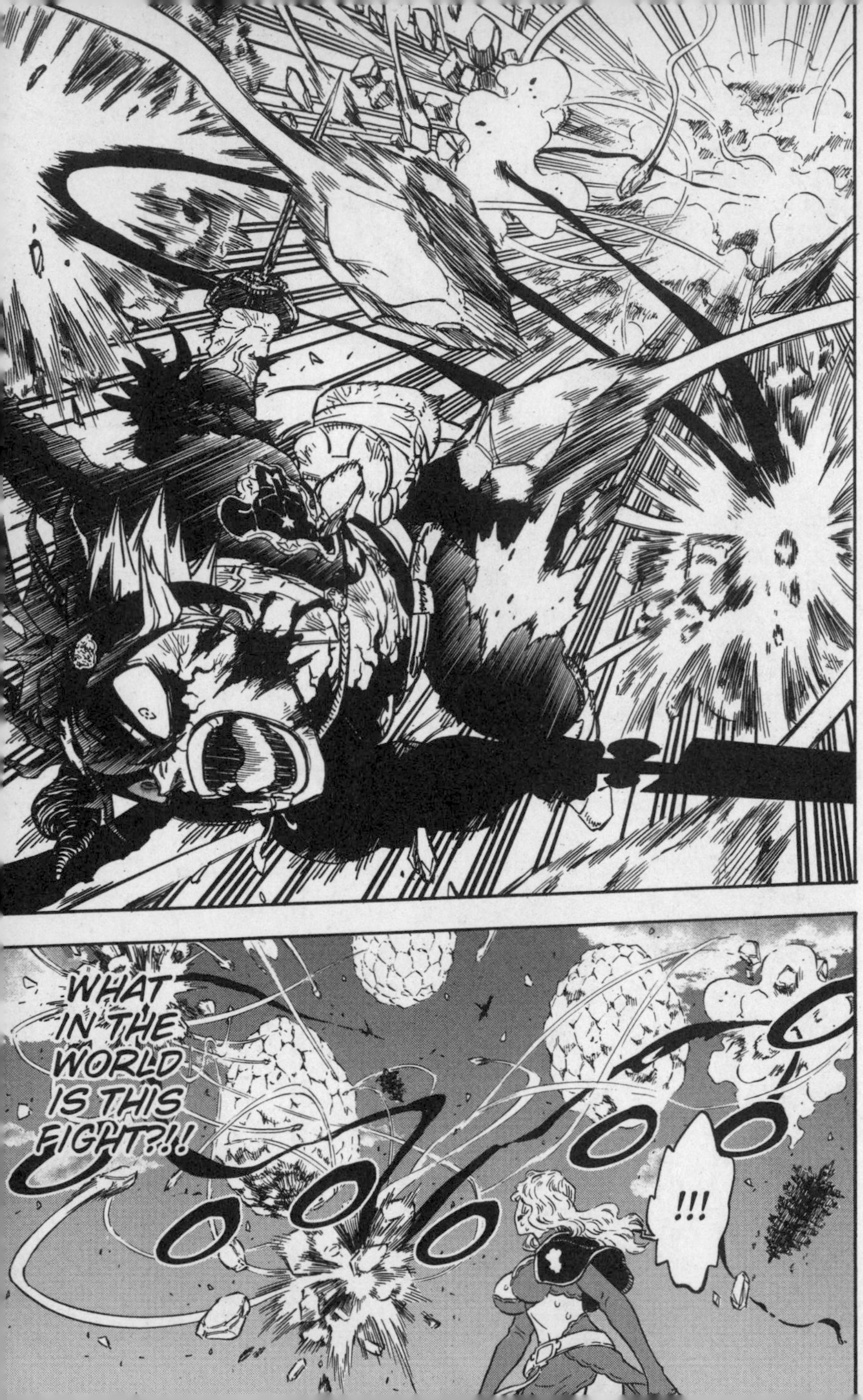
!!!
WHAT IN THE WORLD IS THIS FIGHT?!!

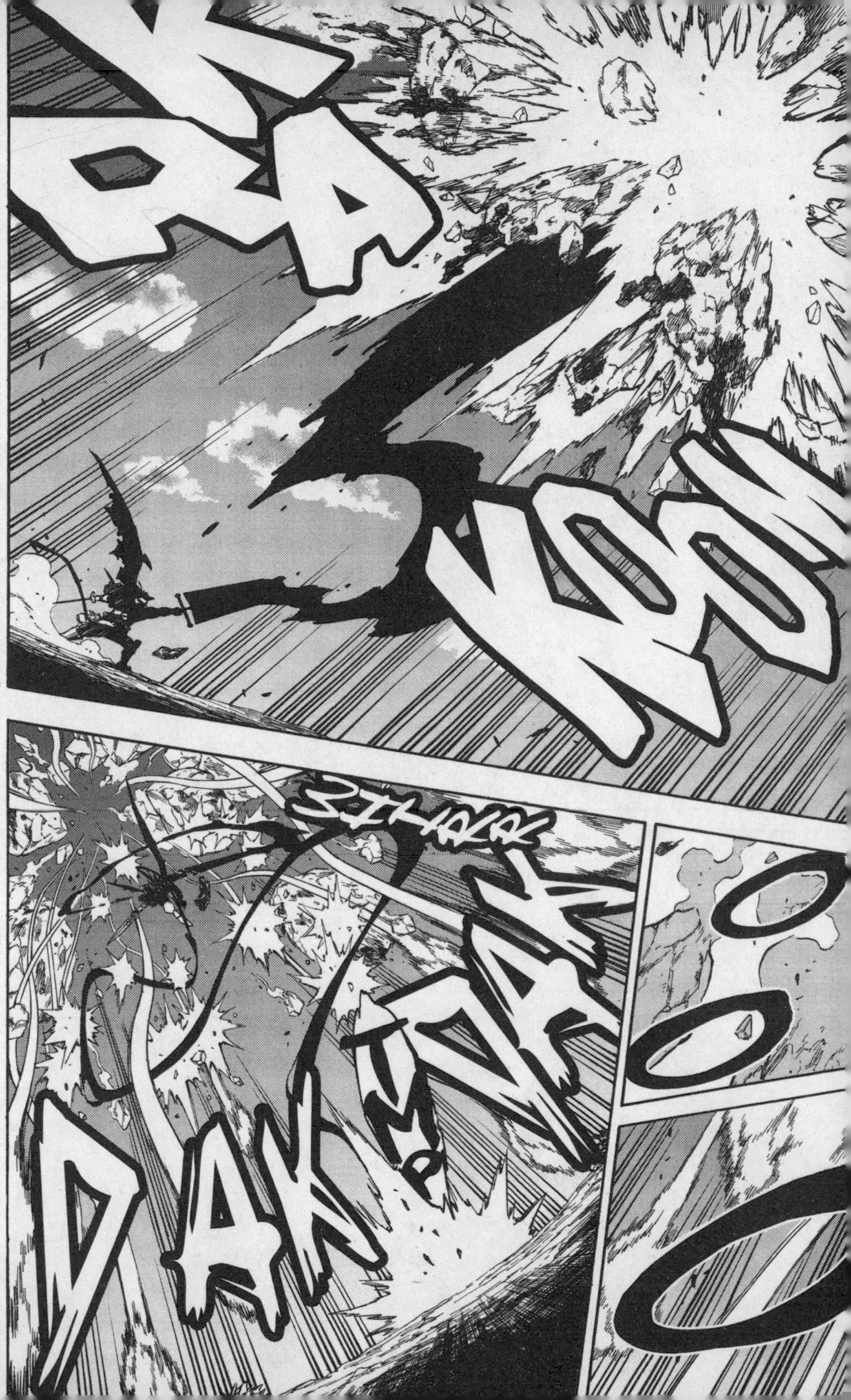

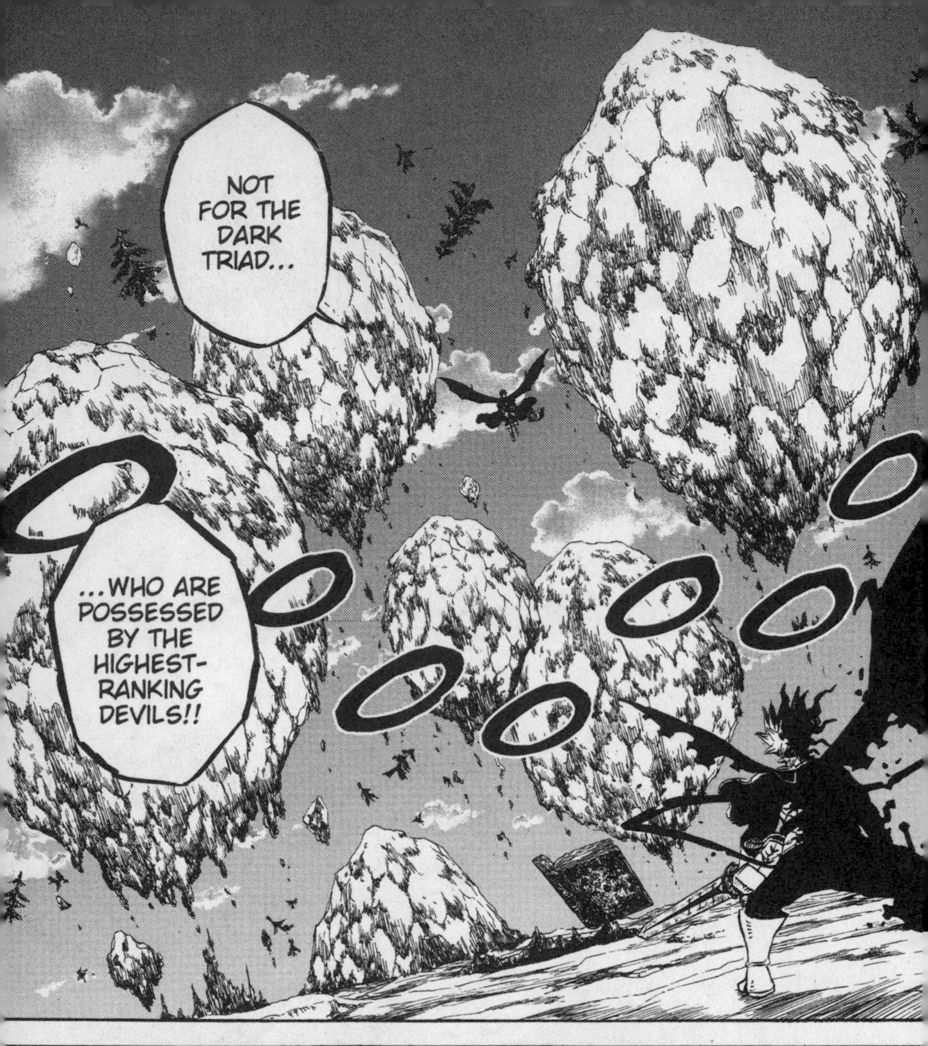
NOT FOR THE DARK TRIAD...
...WHO ARE POSSESSED BY THE HIGHEST-RANKING DEVILS!!
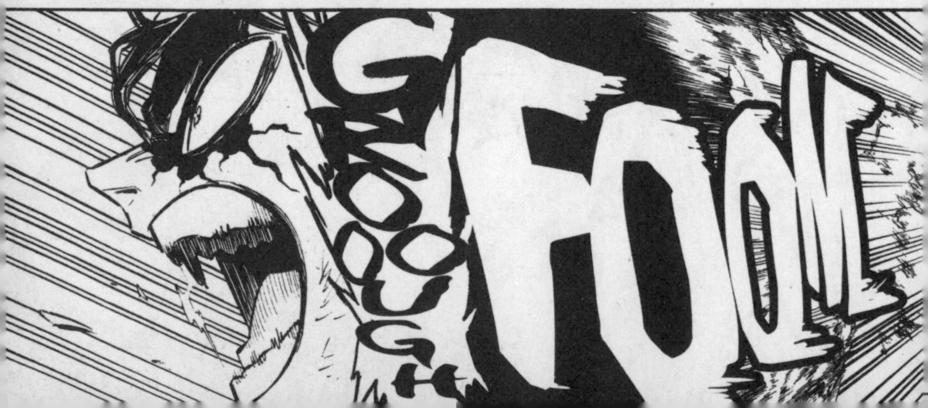
FOOM
GWOOOUG

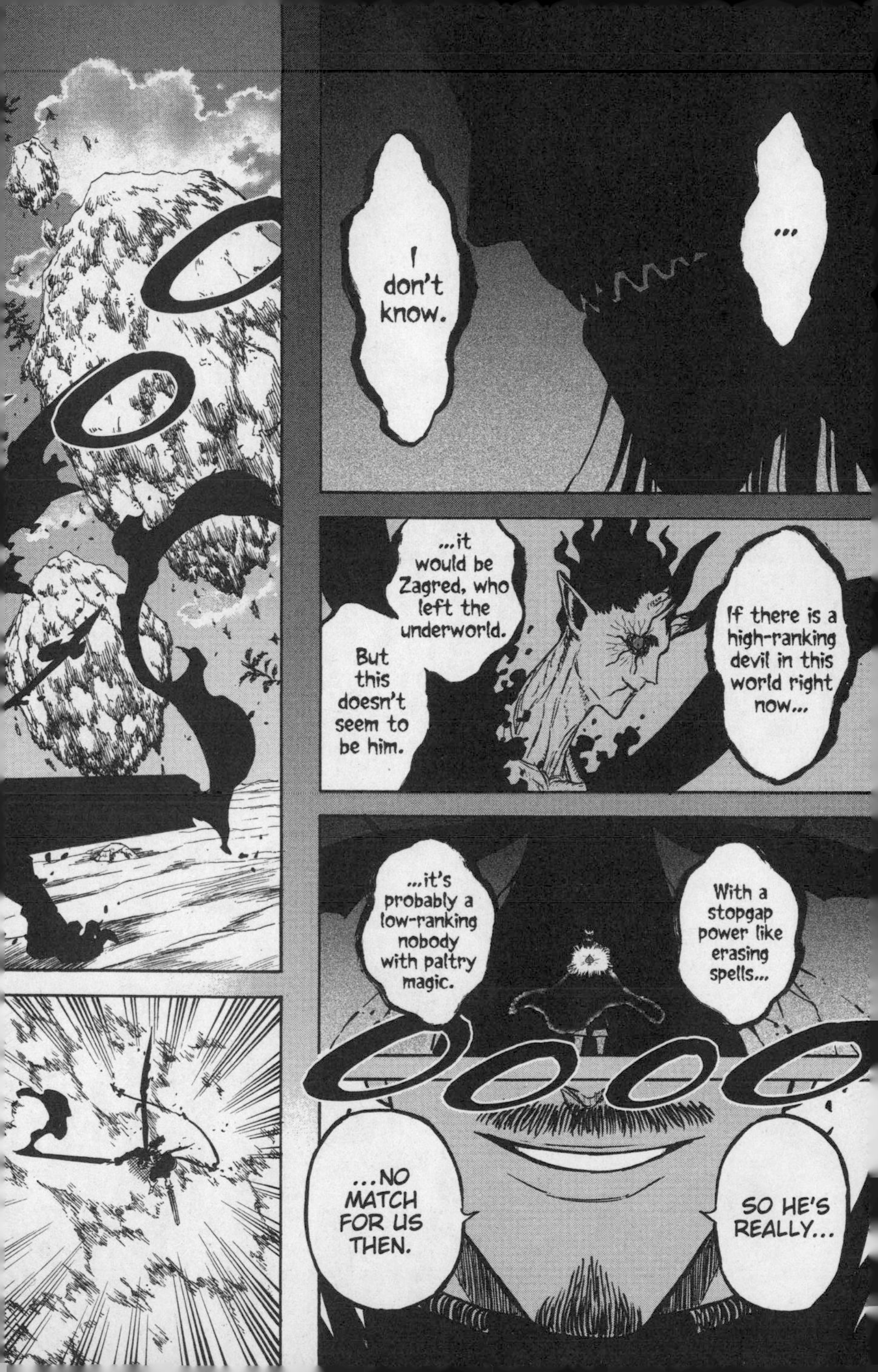
...
I don't know.
If there is a high-ranking devil in this world right now...
...it would be Zagred, who left the underworld.
But this doesn't seem to be him.
With a stopgap power like erasing spells...
...it's probably a low-ranking nobody with paltry magic.
SO HE'S REALLY...
...NO MATCH FOR US THEN.

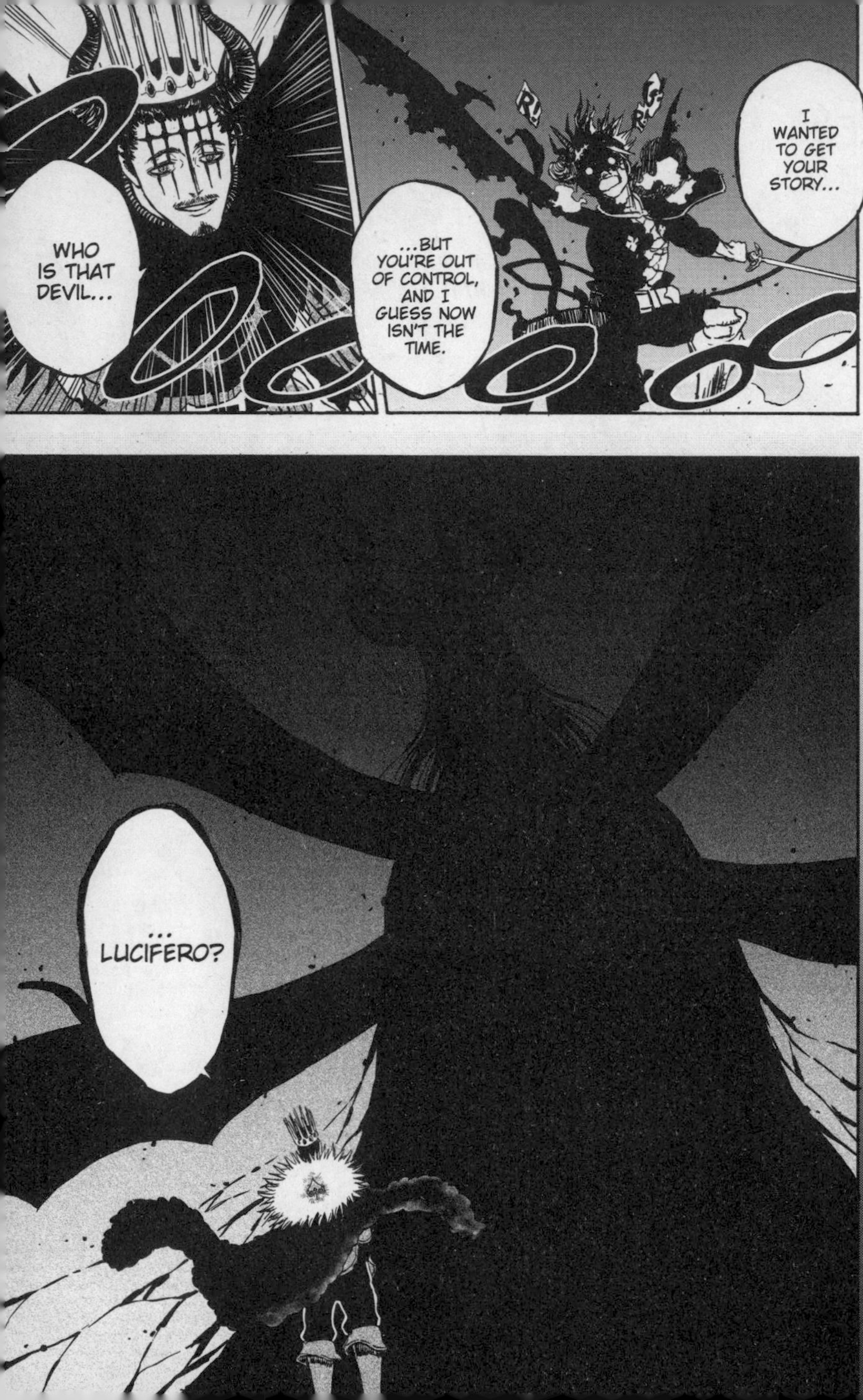
I WANTED TO GET YOUR STORY...
...BUT YOU'RE OUT OF CONTROL, AND I GUESS NOW ISN'T THE TIME.
WHO IS THAT DEVIL...
...LUCIFERO?

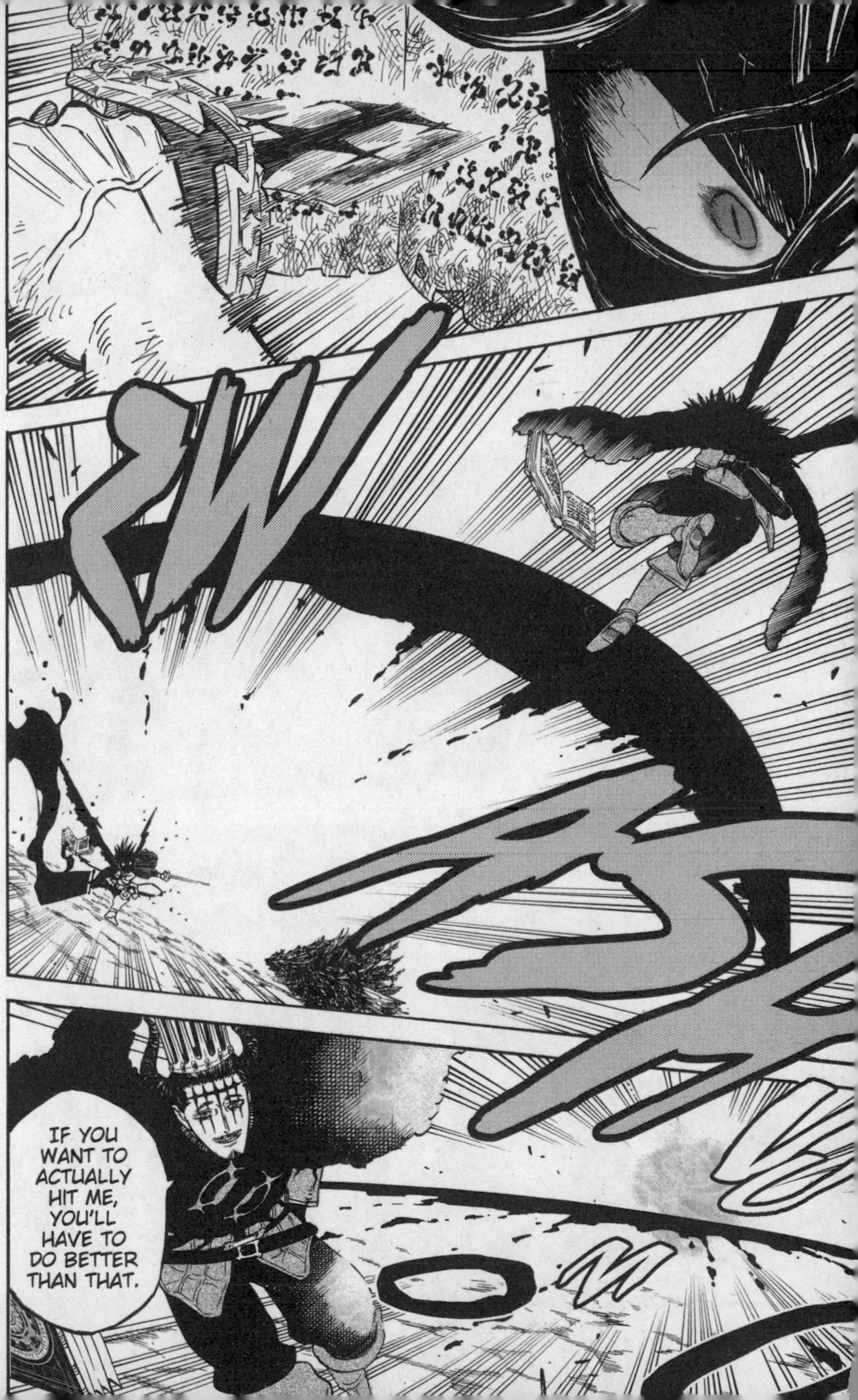
IF YOU WANT TO ACTUALLY HIT ME, YOU'LL HAVE TO DO BETTER THAN THAT.

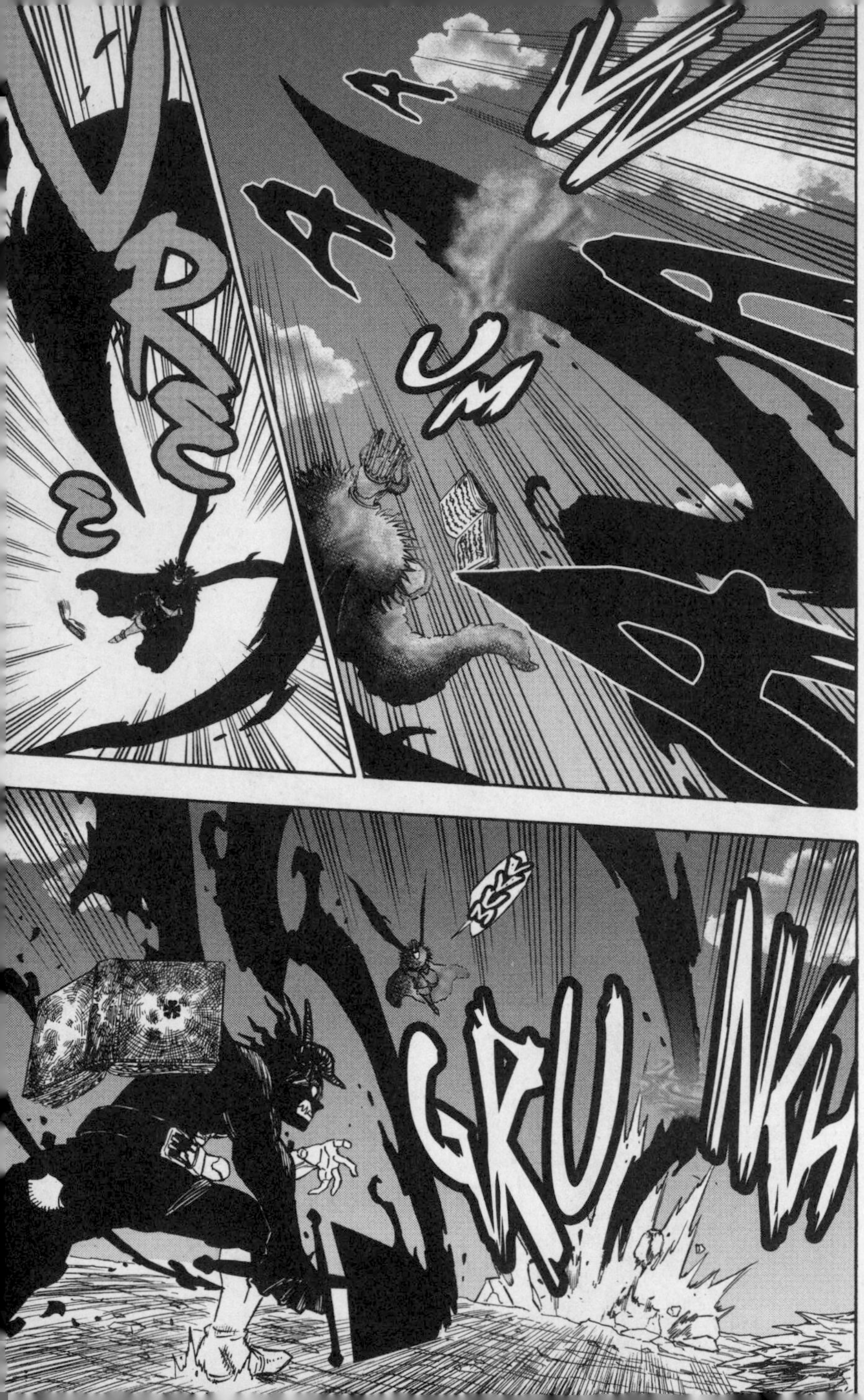
GRUNK

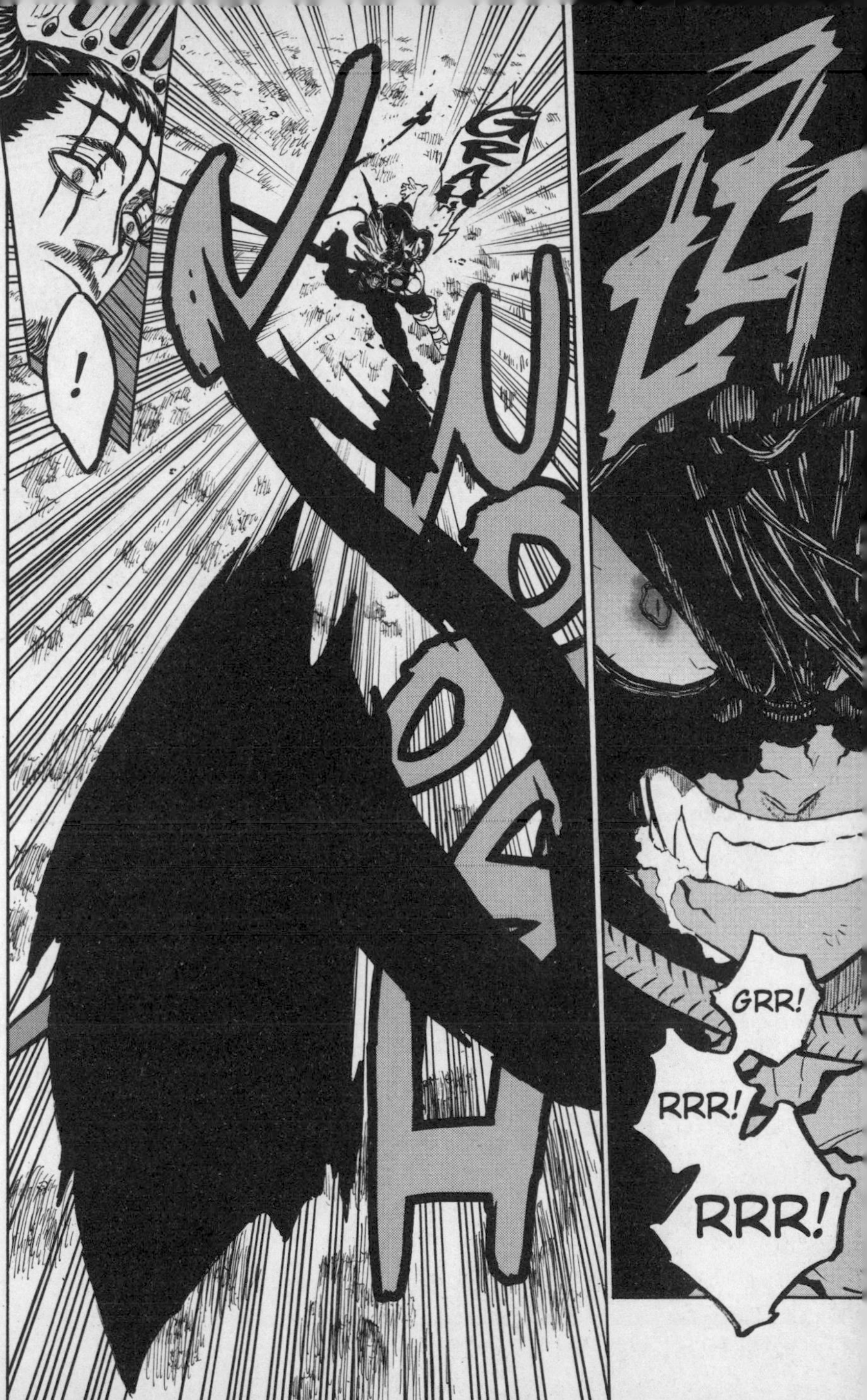
GRR!
RRR!
RRR!
!

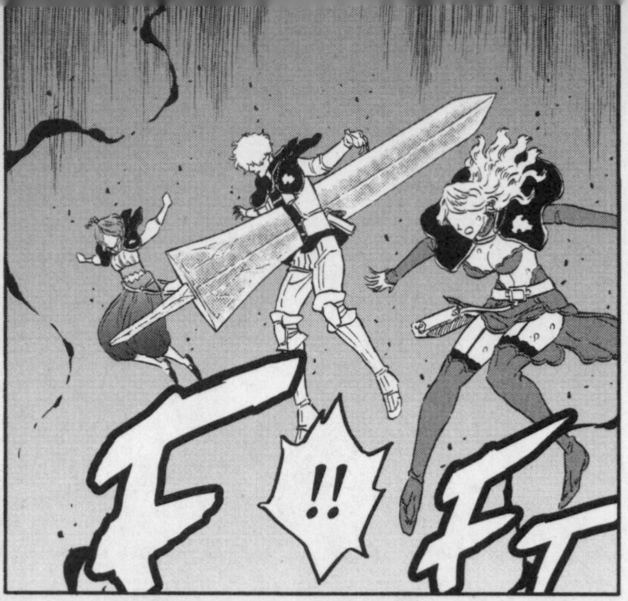
F
!!
FT
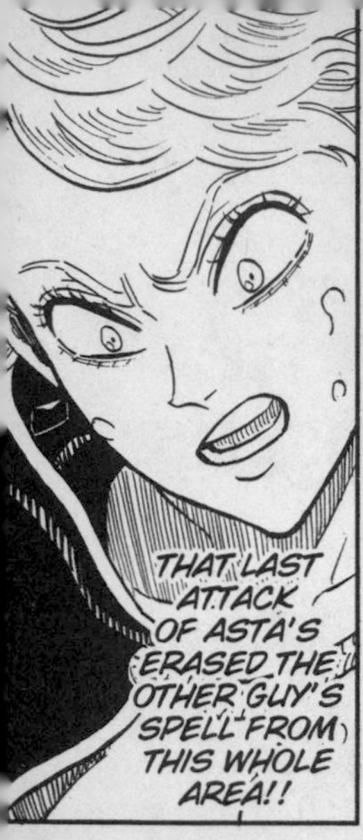
THAT LAST ATTACK OF ASTA'S ERASED THE OTHER GUY'S SPELL FROM THIS WHOLE AREA!!
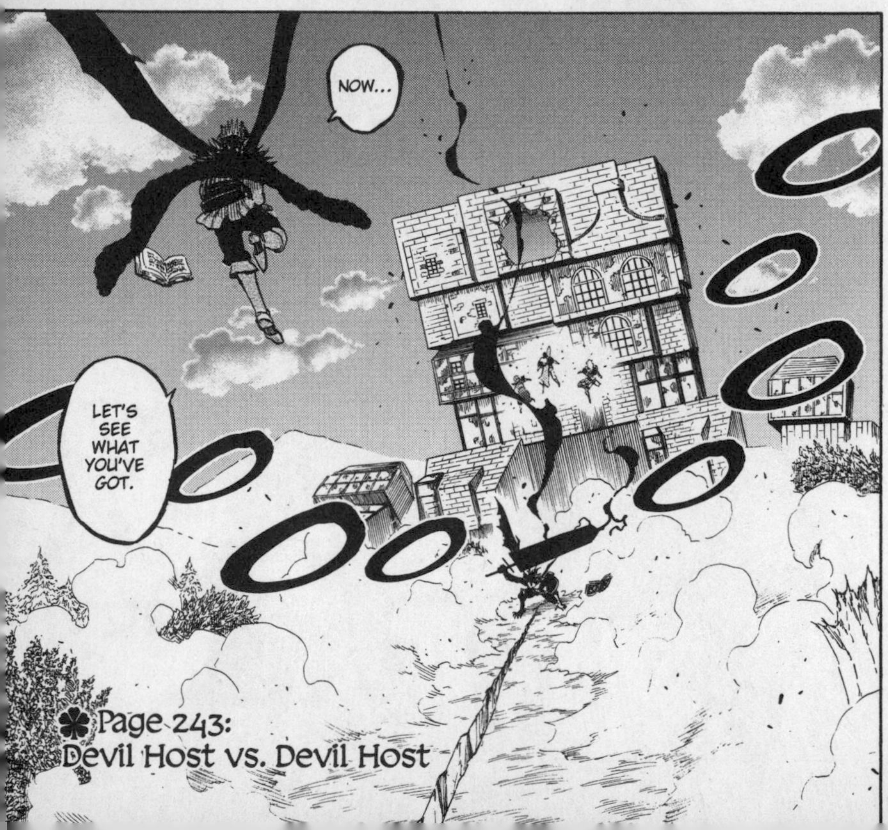
NOW...
LET'S SEE WHAT YOU'VE GOT.

Page 243: Devil Host vs. Devil Host

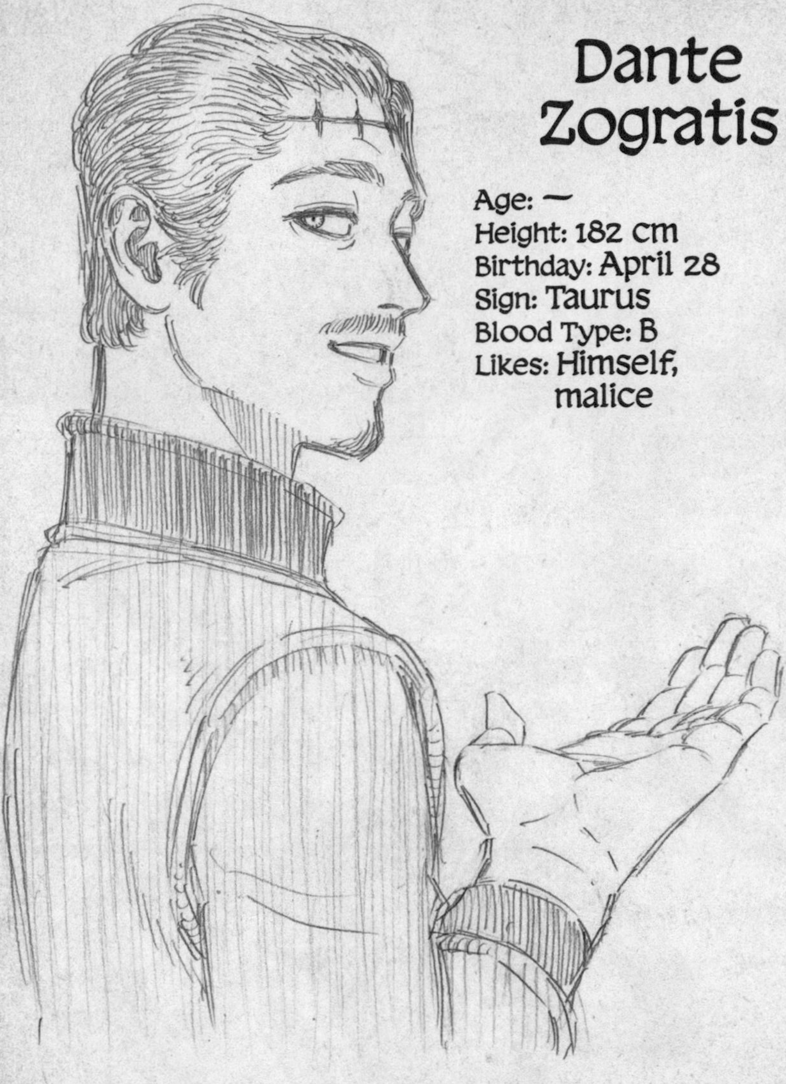

Dante Zogratis

Age: —
Height: 182 cm
Birthday: April 28
Sign: Taurus
Blood Type: B
Likes: Himself, malice

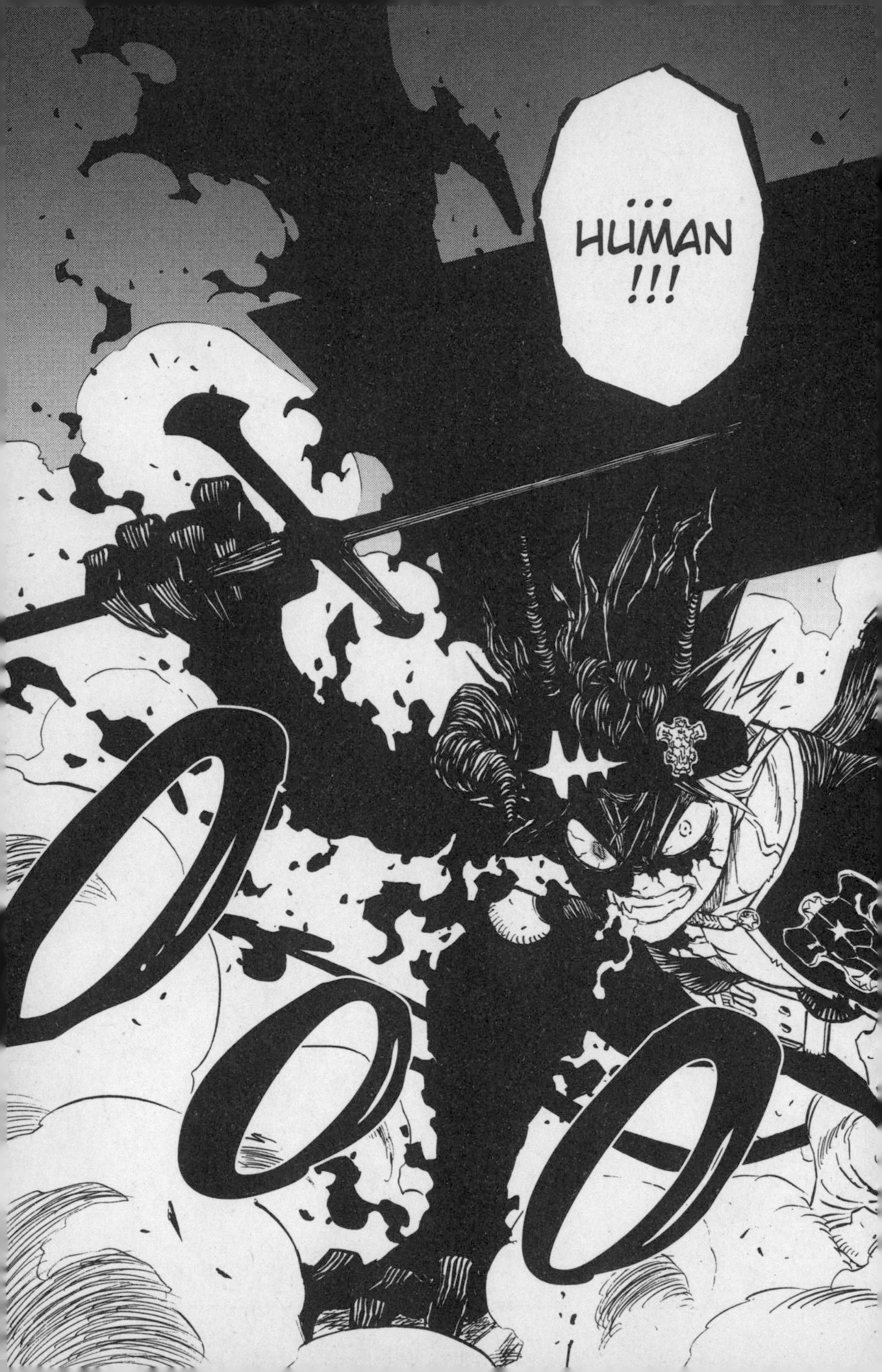
...HUMAN !!!

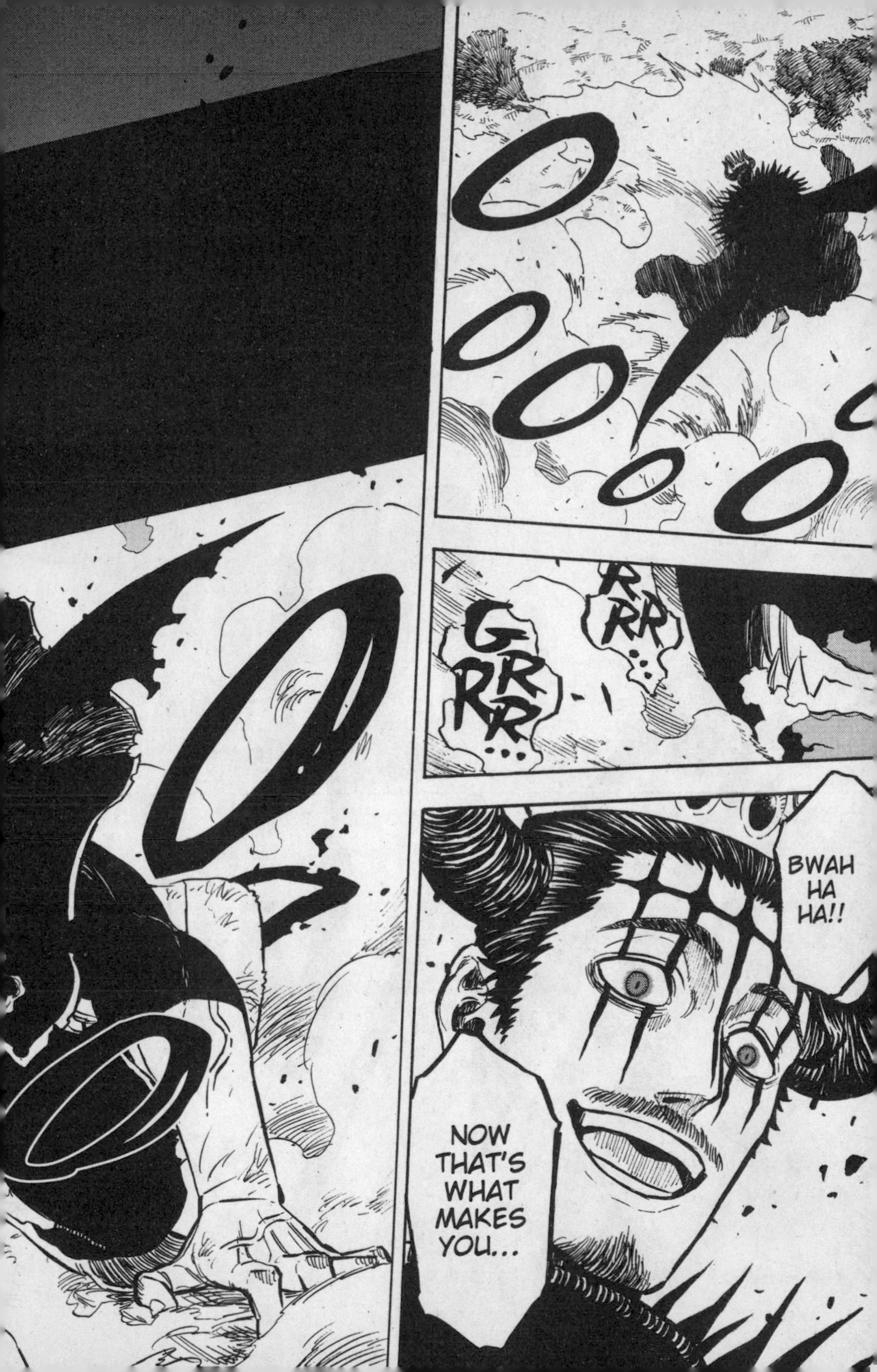
GRRR...
RRRR...
BWAH HA HA!!
NOW THAT'S WHAT MAKES YOU...

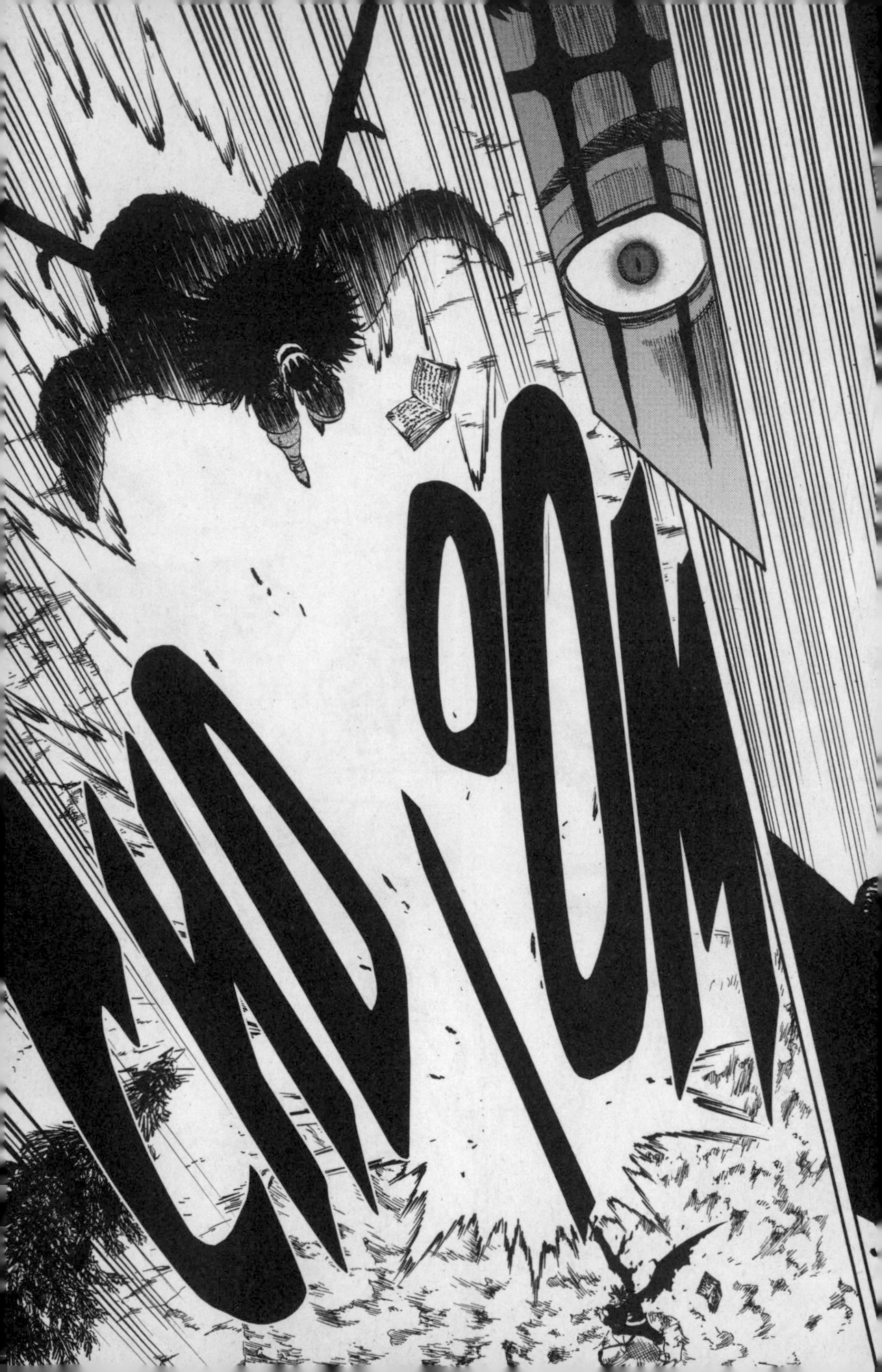

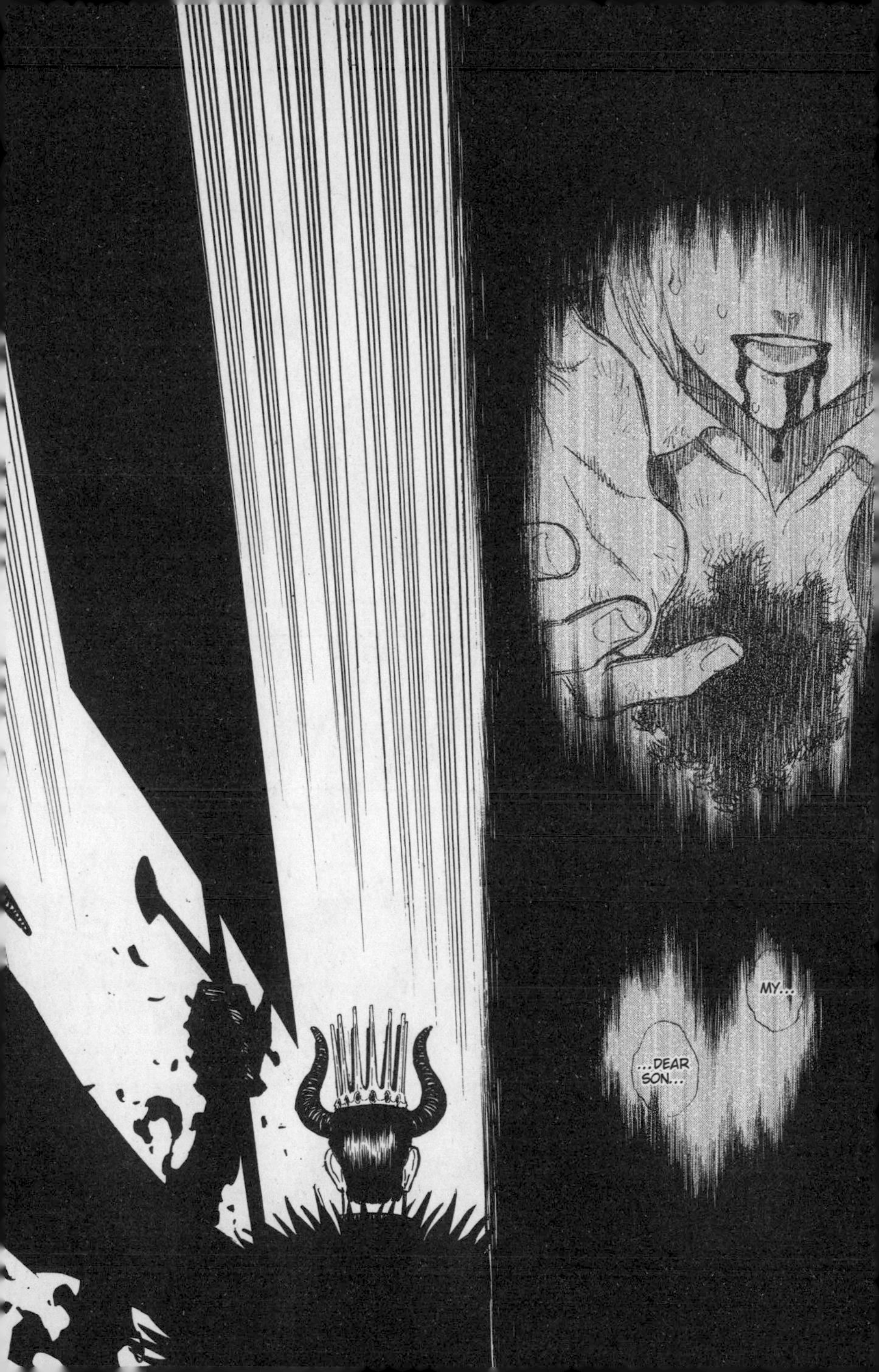
MY...
...DEAR SON...

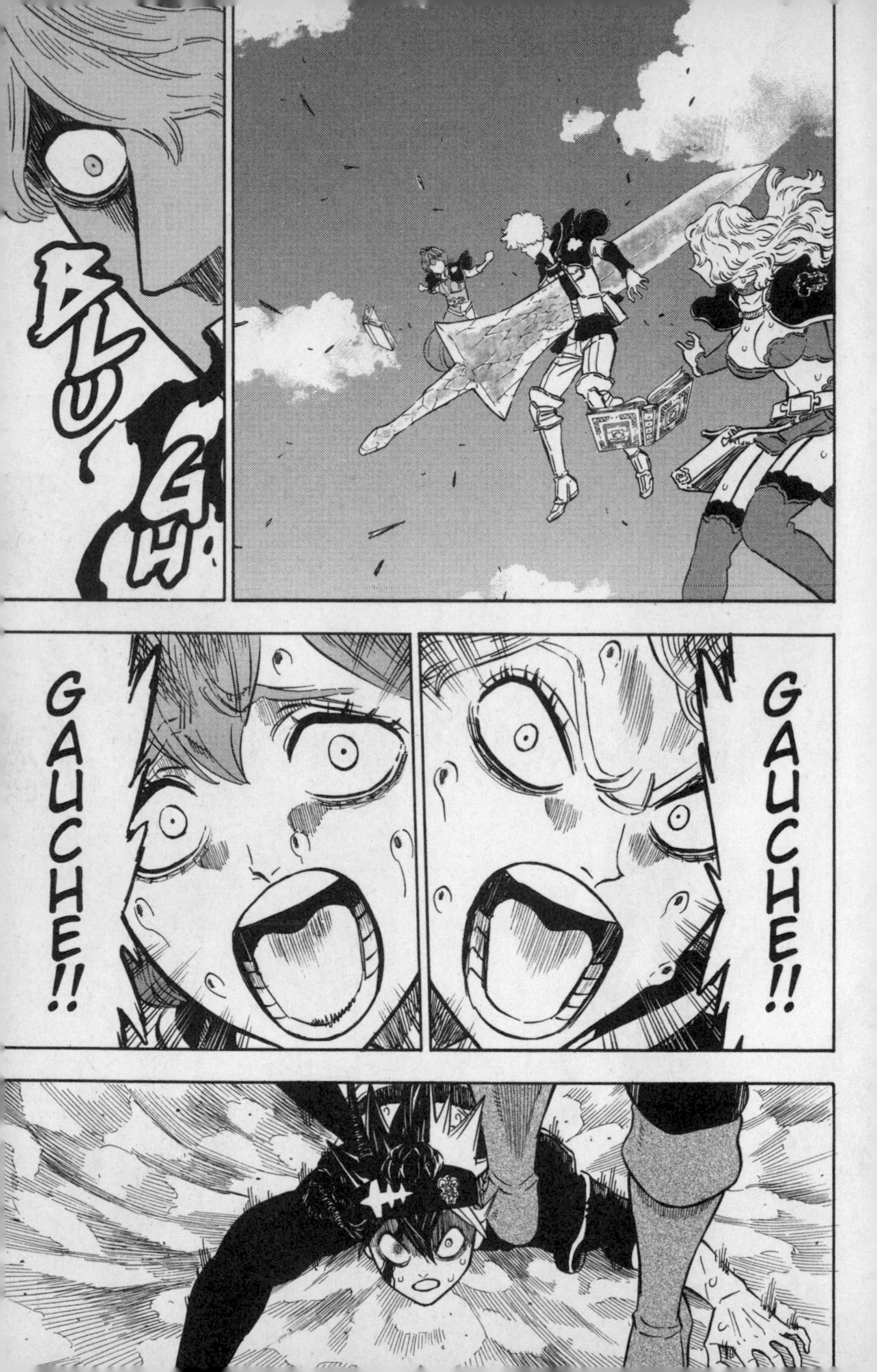
BLUGH
GAUCHE!!
GAUCHE!!

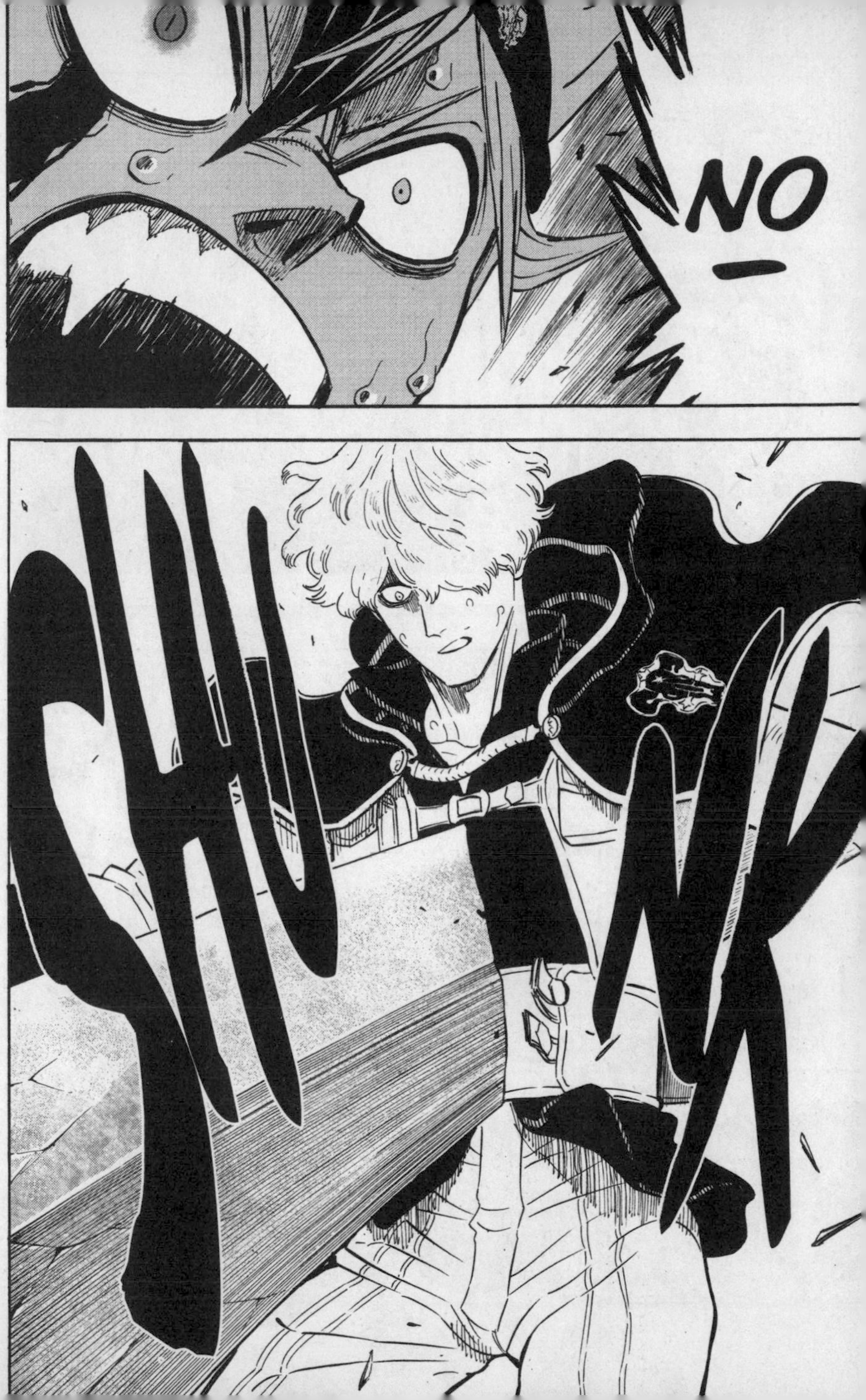
NO—
CHUNK

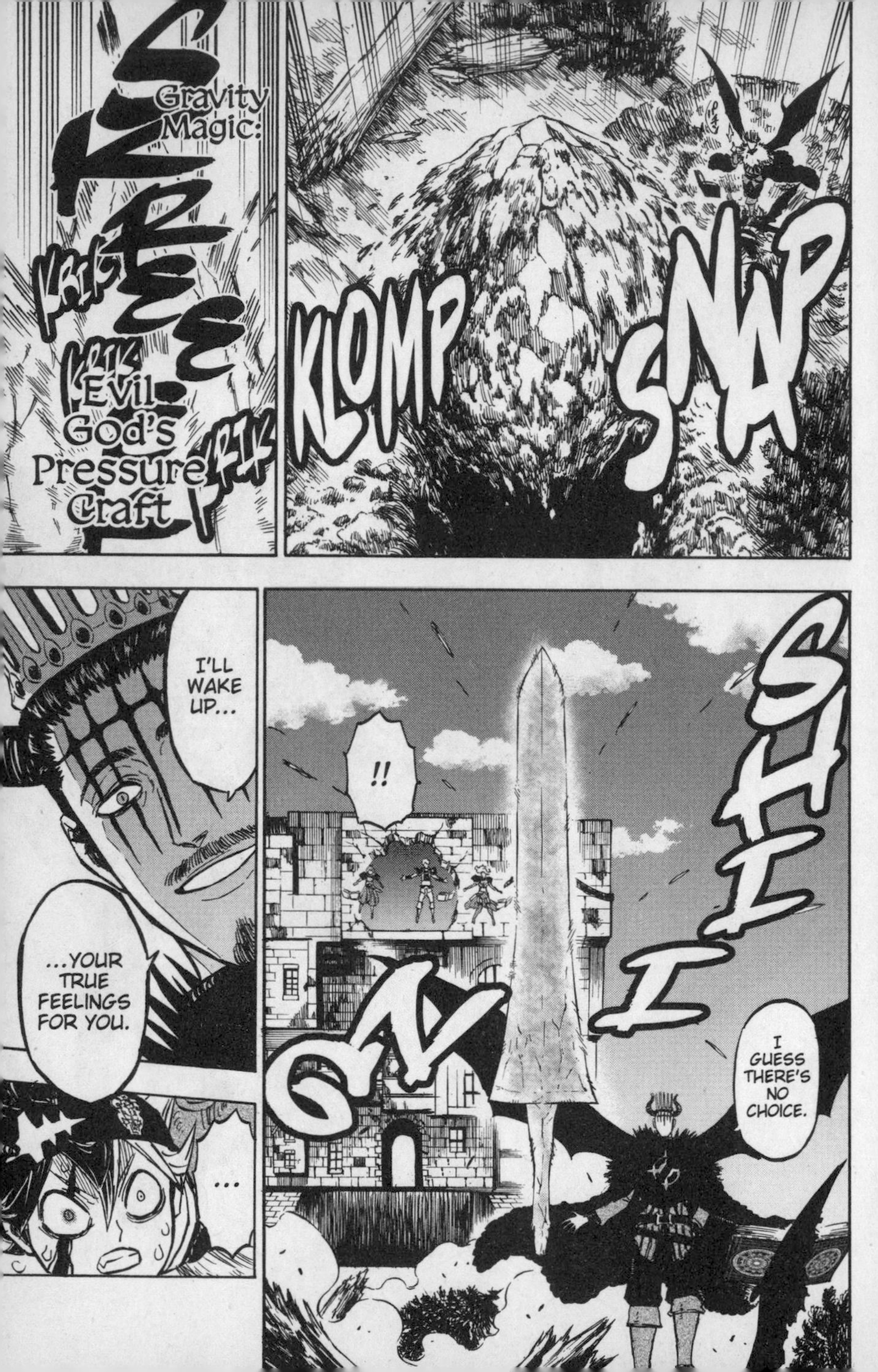
KLOMP
SNAP
Gravity Magic: Evil God's Pressure Craft
KRIK
KRIK
KRIK
SHIING
!!
I GUESS THERE'S NO CHOICE.
I'LL WAKE UP...
...YOUR TRUE FEELINGS FOR YOU.
...

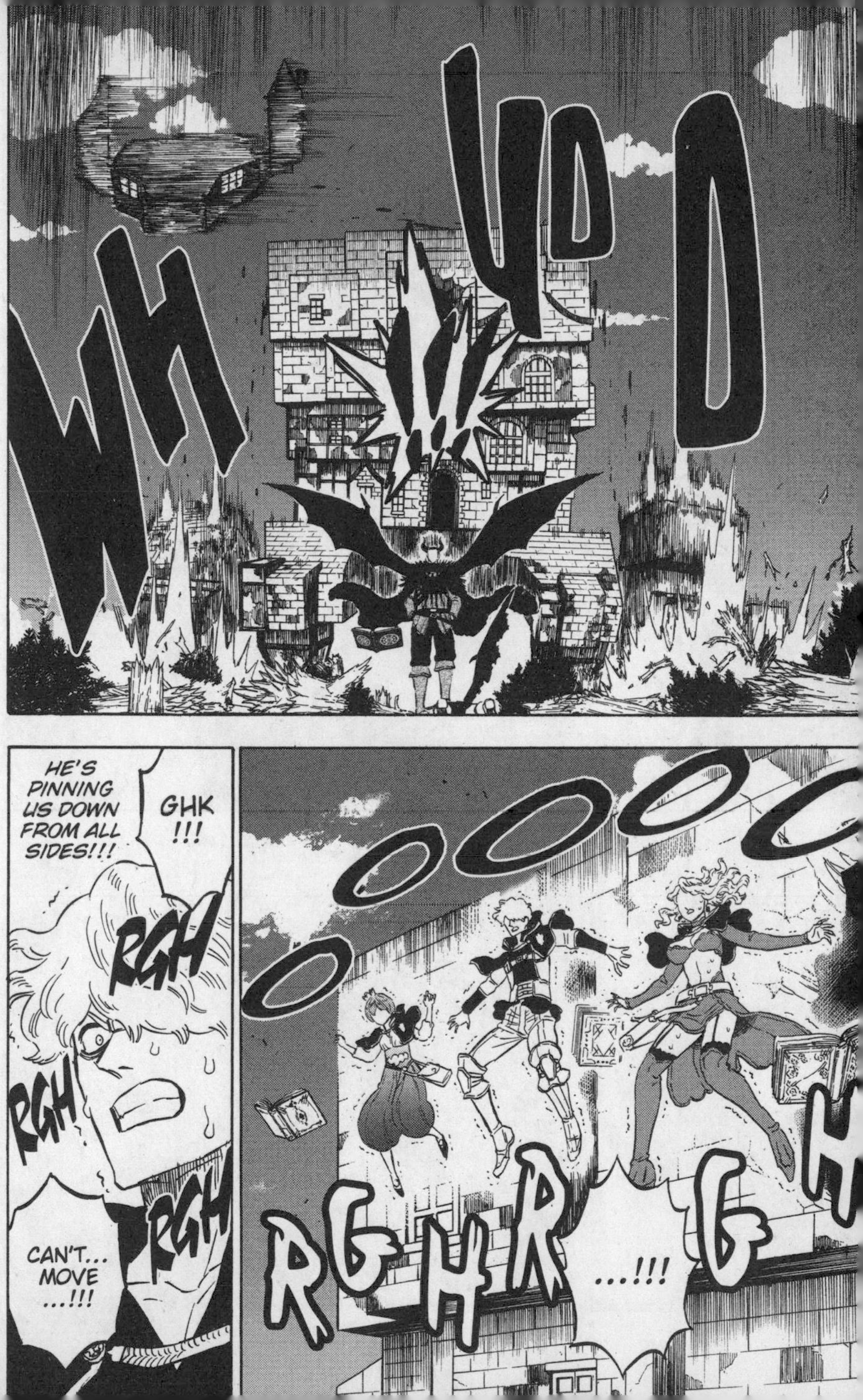
WHUDD
OOOOOO
RGHRGH
...!!!
GHK!!!
HE'S PINNING US DOWN FROM ALL SIDES!!!
RGH
RGH
RGH
CAN'T... MOVE ...!!!

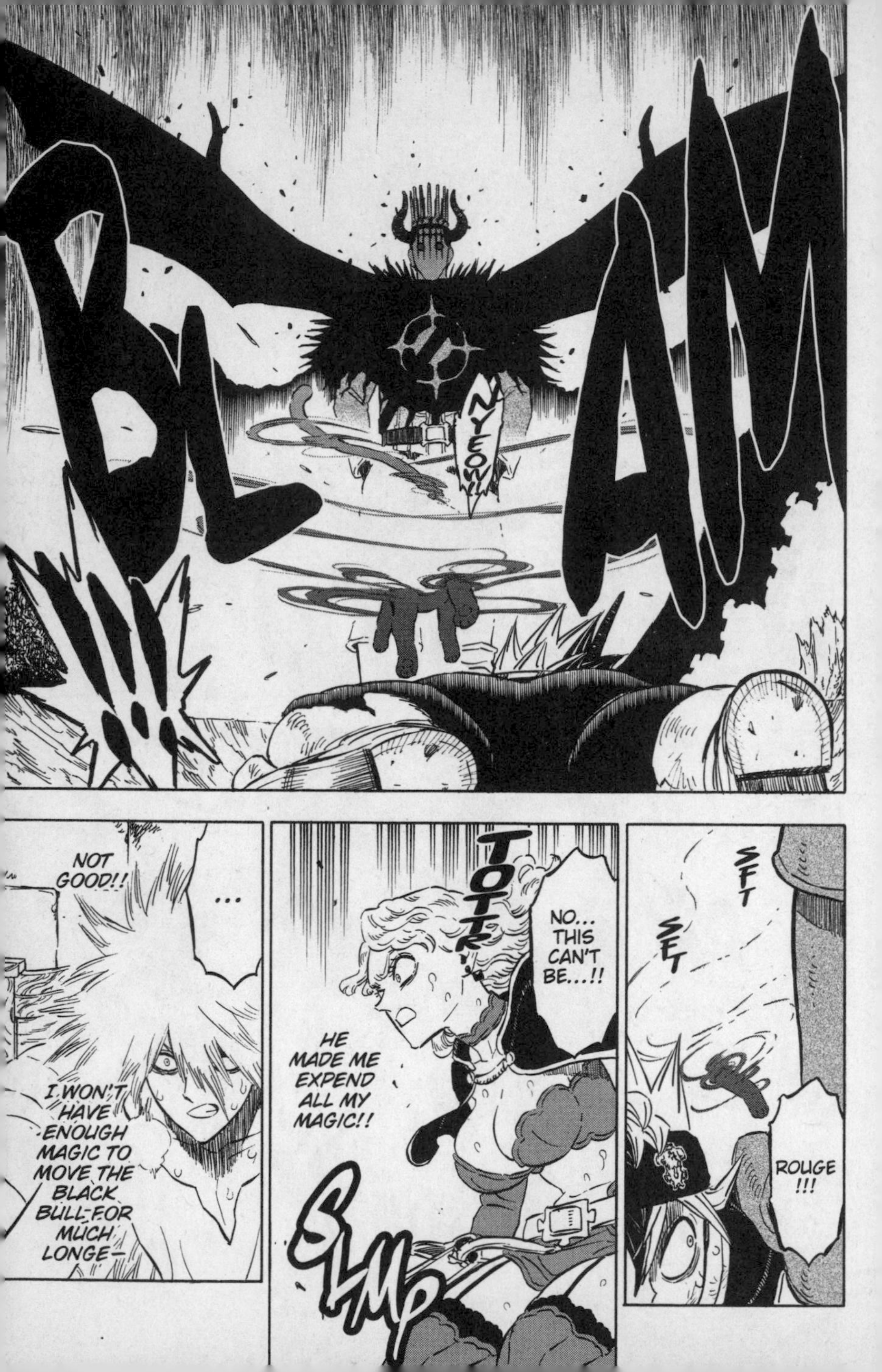
BLAM
NYEOWW!
SFT
SFT
ROUGE!!!
TOTTR
NO... THIS CAN'T BE...!!
HE MADE ME EXPEND ALL MY MAGIC!!
SLUMP
NOT GOOD!!
...
I WON'T HAVE ENOUGH MAGIC TO MOVE THE BLACK BULL FOR MUCH LONGE—

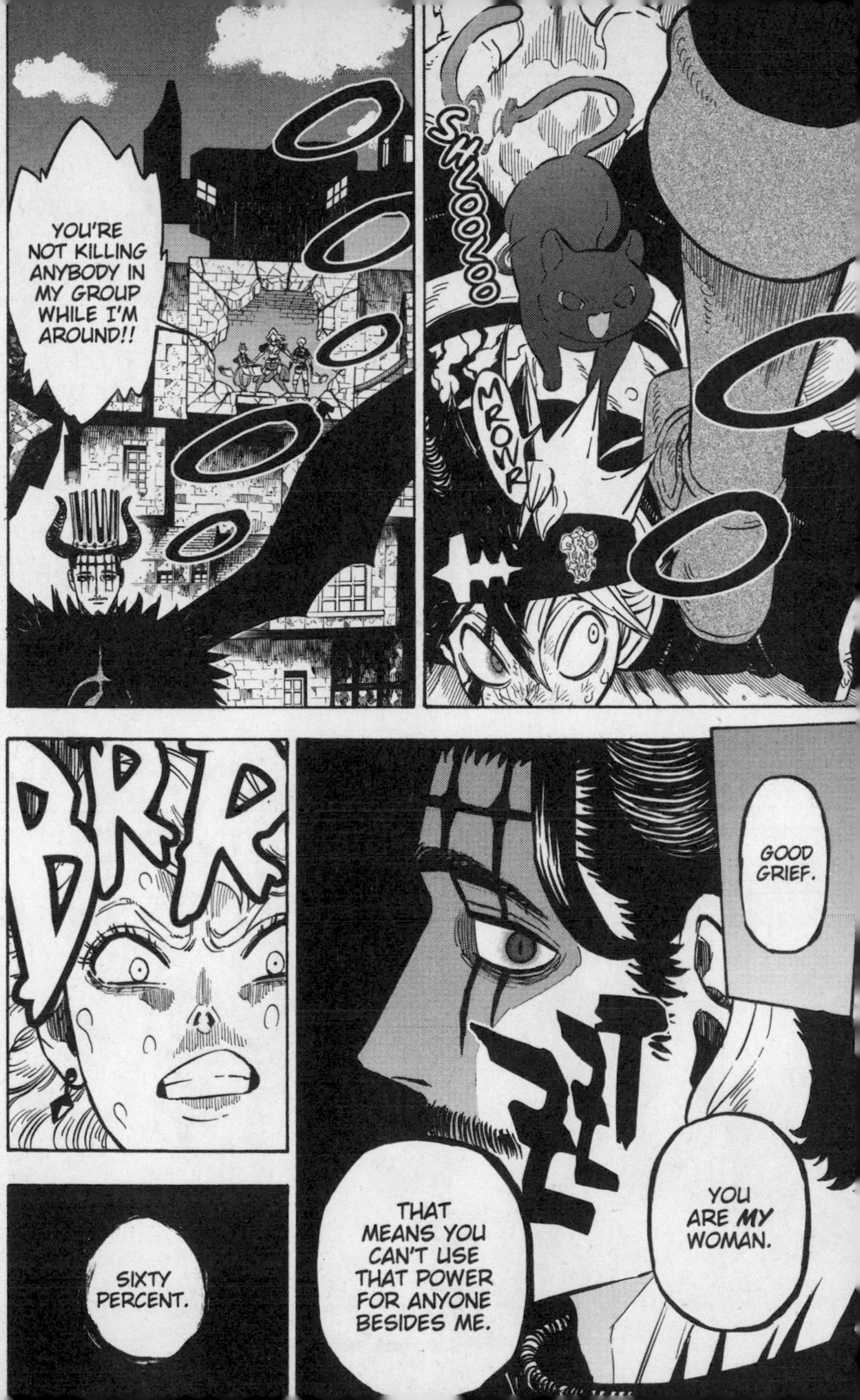
SHLOOLOO
MROWR
YOU'RE NOT KILLING ANYBODY IN MY GROUP WHILE I'M AROUND!!
GOOD GRIEF.
YOU ARE *MY* WOMAN.
THAT MEANS YOU CAN'T USE THAT POWER FOR ANYONE BESIDES ME.
SIXTY PERCENT.

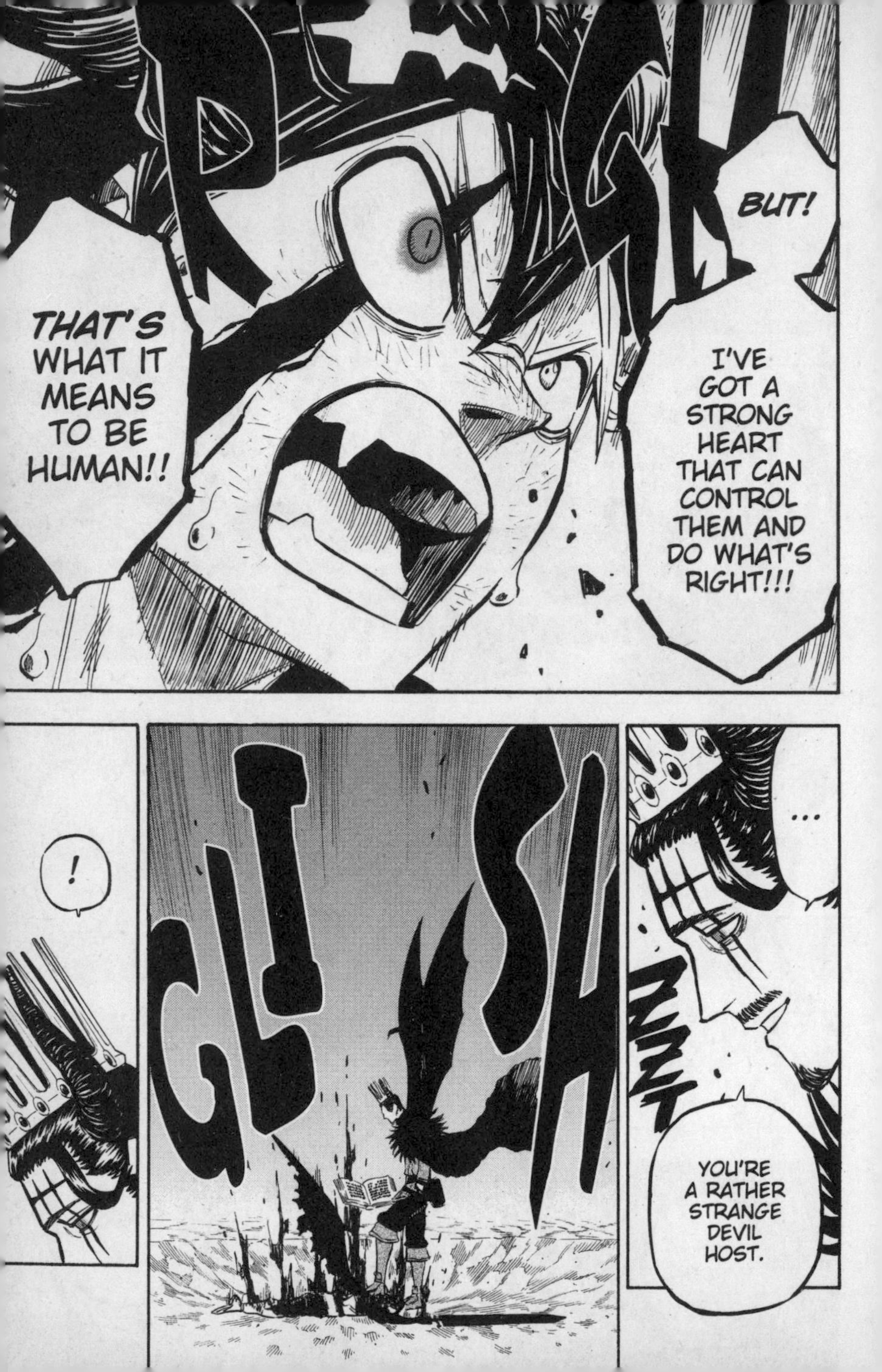
BUT!
I'VE GOT A STRONG HEART THAT CAN CONTROL THEM AND DO WHAT'S RIGHT!!!
THAT'S WHAT IT MEANS TO BE HUMAN!!
...
YOU'RE A RATHER STRANGE DEVIL HOST.
!

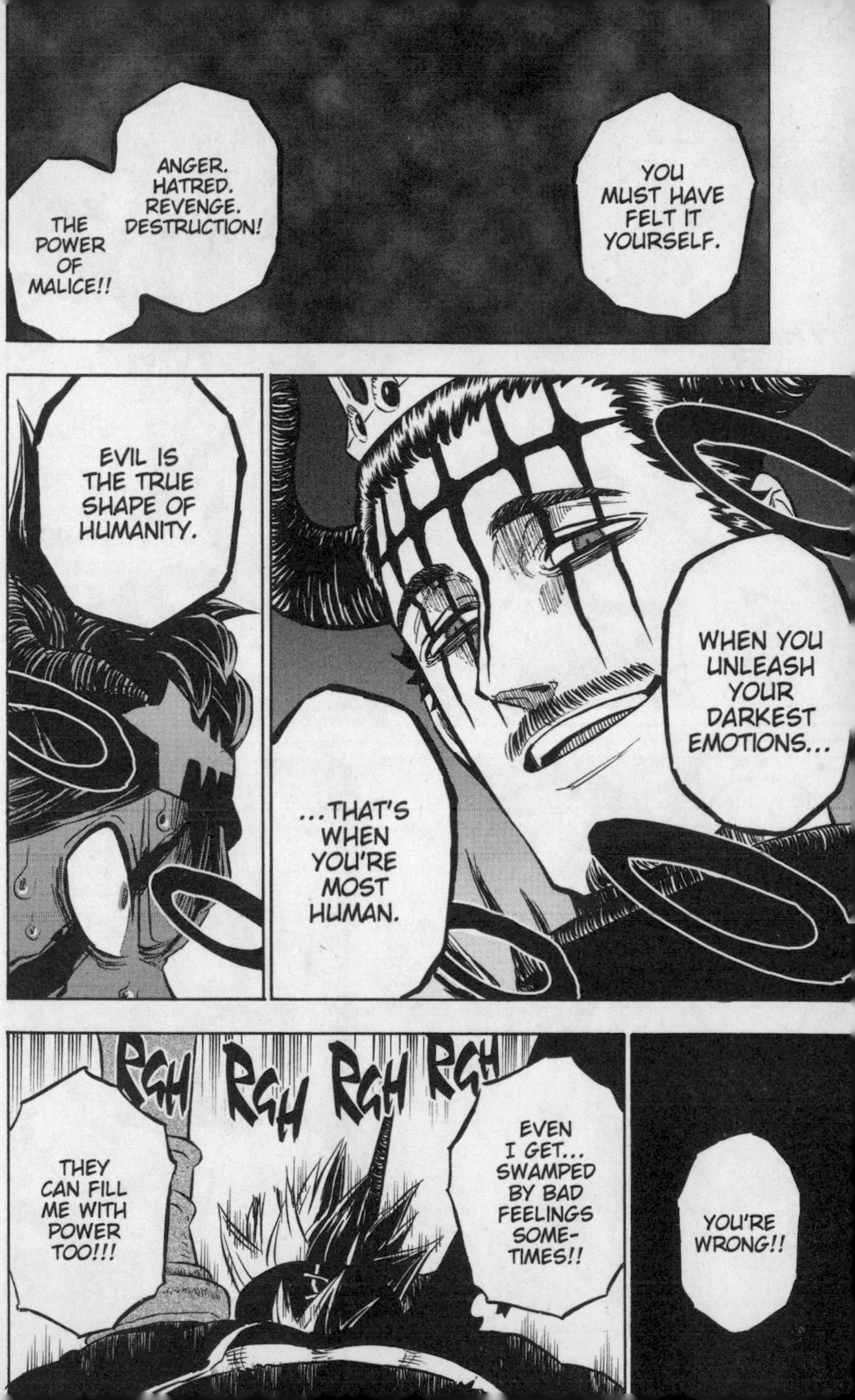
YOU MUST HAVE FELT IT YOURSELF.
ANGER. HATRED. REVENGE. DESTRUCTION!
THE POWER OF MALICE!!
WHEN YOU UNLEASH YOUR DARKEST EMOTIONS...
...THAT'S WHEN YOU'RE MOST HUMAN.
EVIL IS THE TRUE SHAPE OF HUMANITY.
YOU'RE WRONG!!
RGH RGH RGH RGH
EVEN I GET... SWAMPED BY BAD FEELINGS SOME-TIMES!!
THEY CAN FILL ME WITH POWER TOO!!!

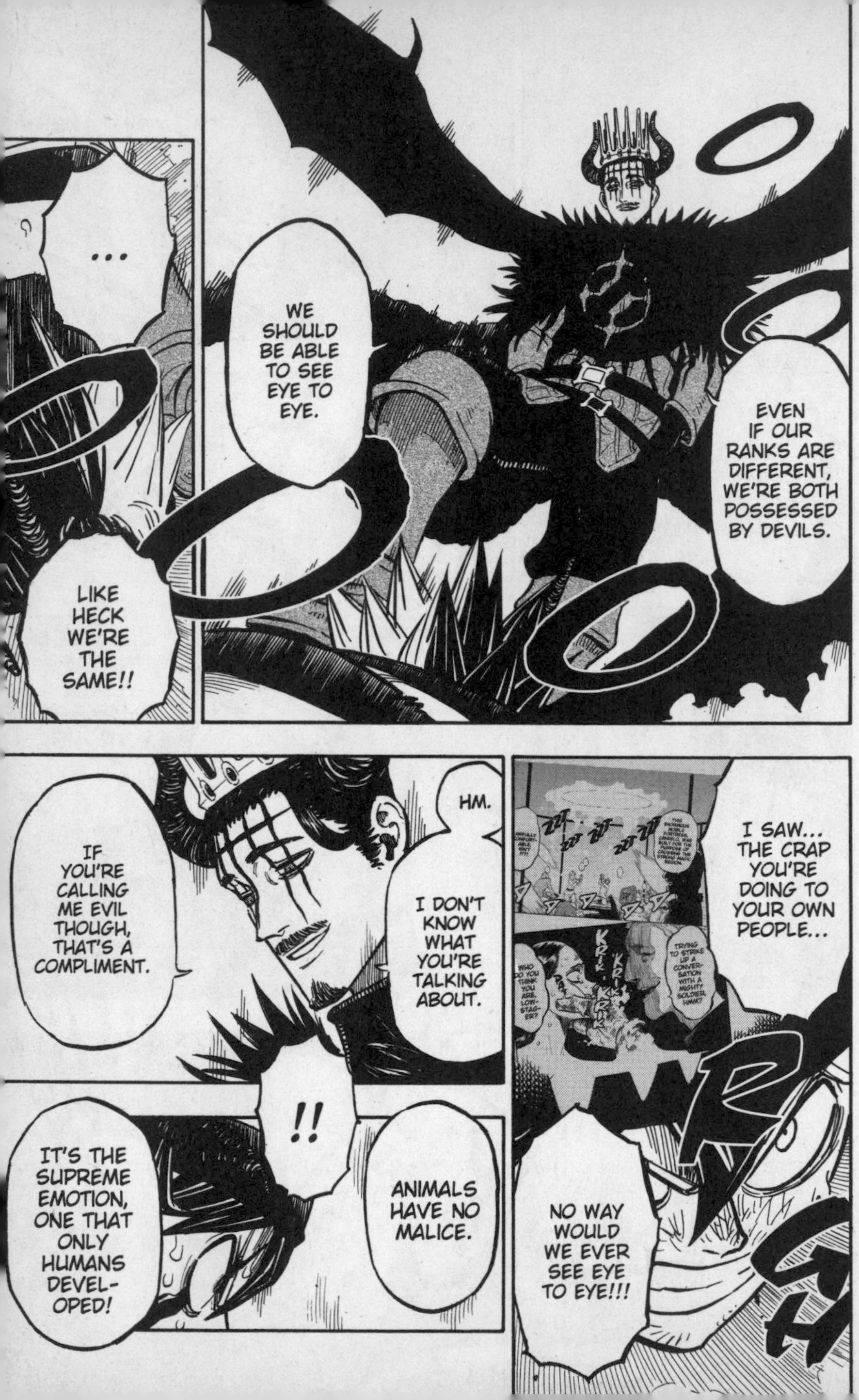
EVEN IF OUR RANKS ARE DIFFERENT, WE'RE BOTH POSSESSED BY DEVILS.
WE SHOULD BE ABLE TO SEE EYE TO EYE.
...
LIKE HECK WE'RE THE SAME!!
I SAW... THE CRAP YOU'RE DOING TO YOUR OWN PEOPLE...
TRYING TO STRIKE UP A CONVERSATION WITH A MIGHTY SOLDIER HMM?
WHO DO YOU THINK YOU ARE, LOW-STAGER?
NO WAY WOULD WE EVER SEE EYE TO EYE!!!
HM.
I DON'T KNOW WHAT YOU'RE TALKING ABOUT.
IF YOU'RE CALLING ME EVIL THOUGH, THAT'S A COMPLIMENT.
!!
ANIMALS HAVE NO MALICE.
IT'S THE SUPREME EMOTION, ONE THAT ONLY HUMANS DEVELOPED!

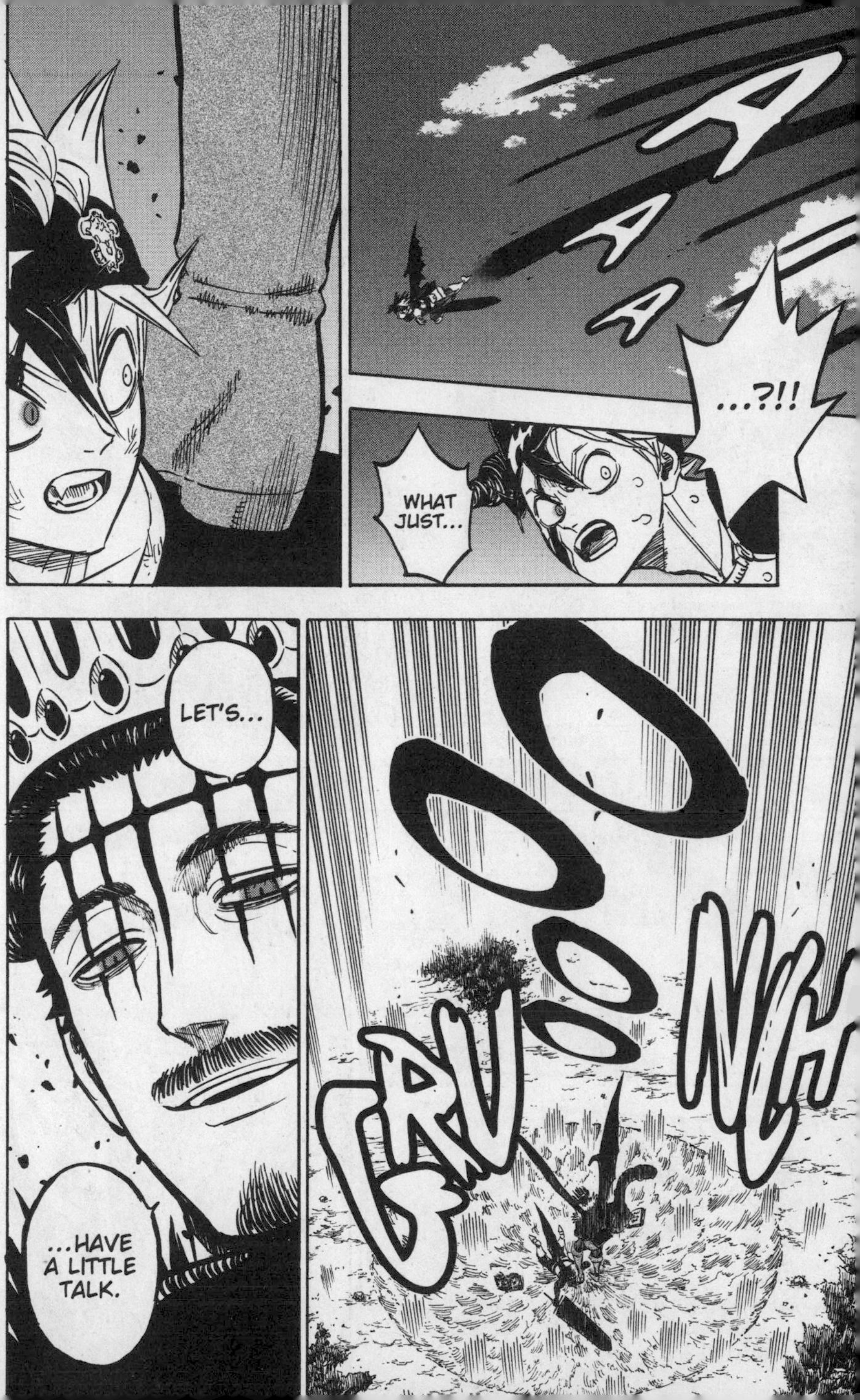
AAAA
...?!!
WHAT JUST...
LET'S...
...HAVE A LITTLE TALK.

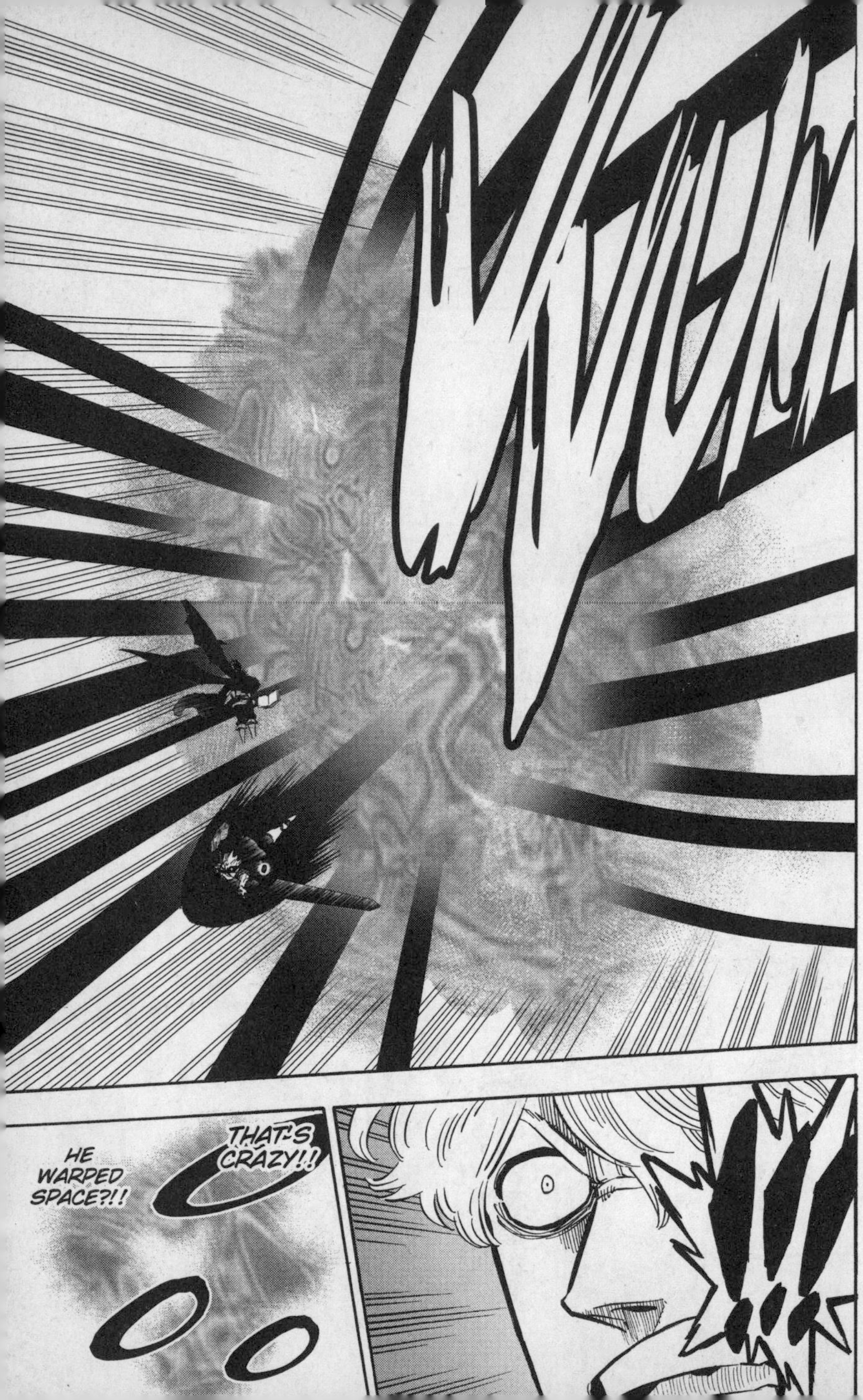
THAT'S CRAZY!!
HE WARPED SPACE?!!

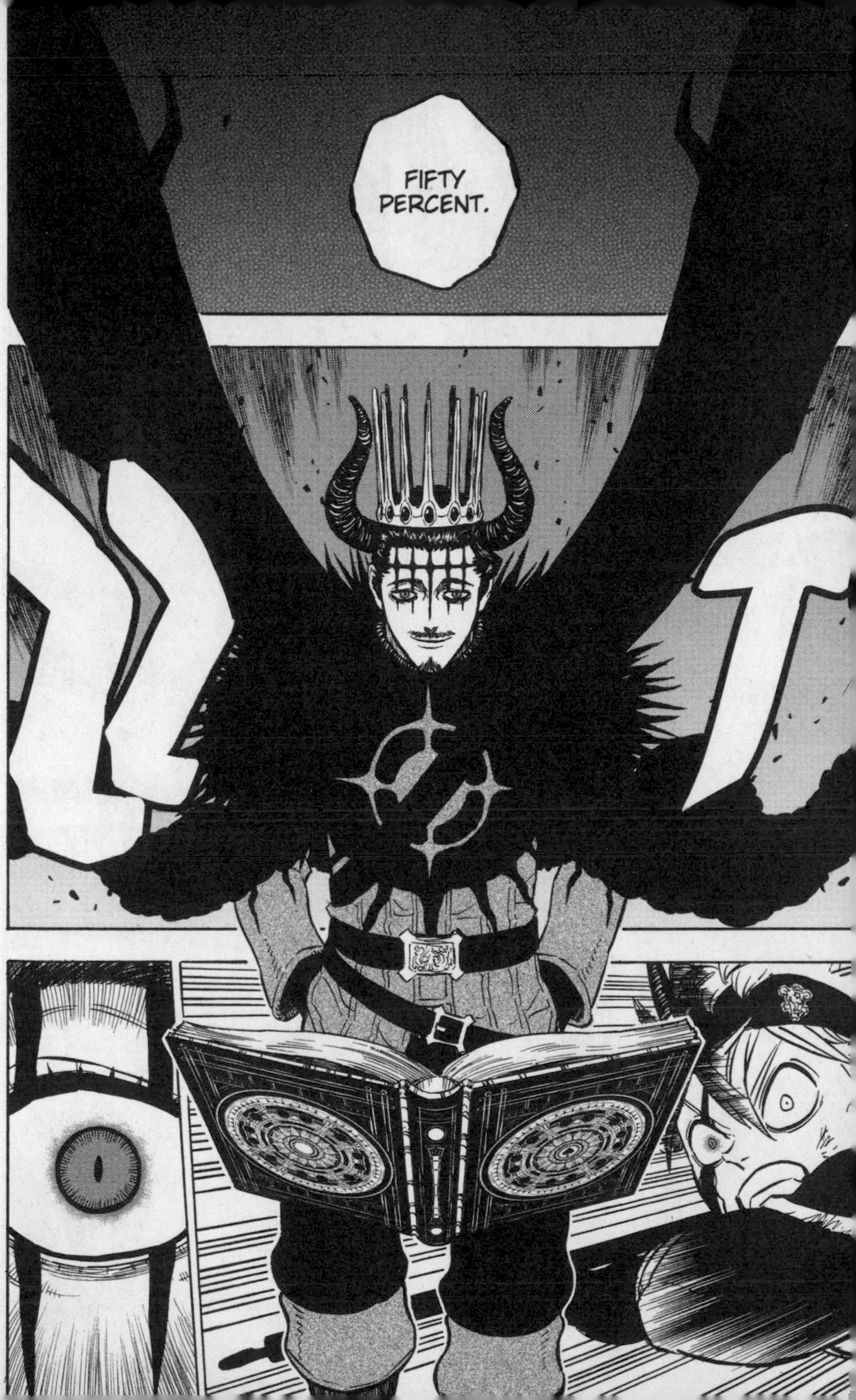
FIFTY PERCENT.

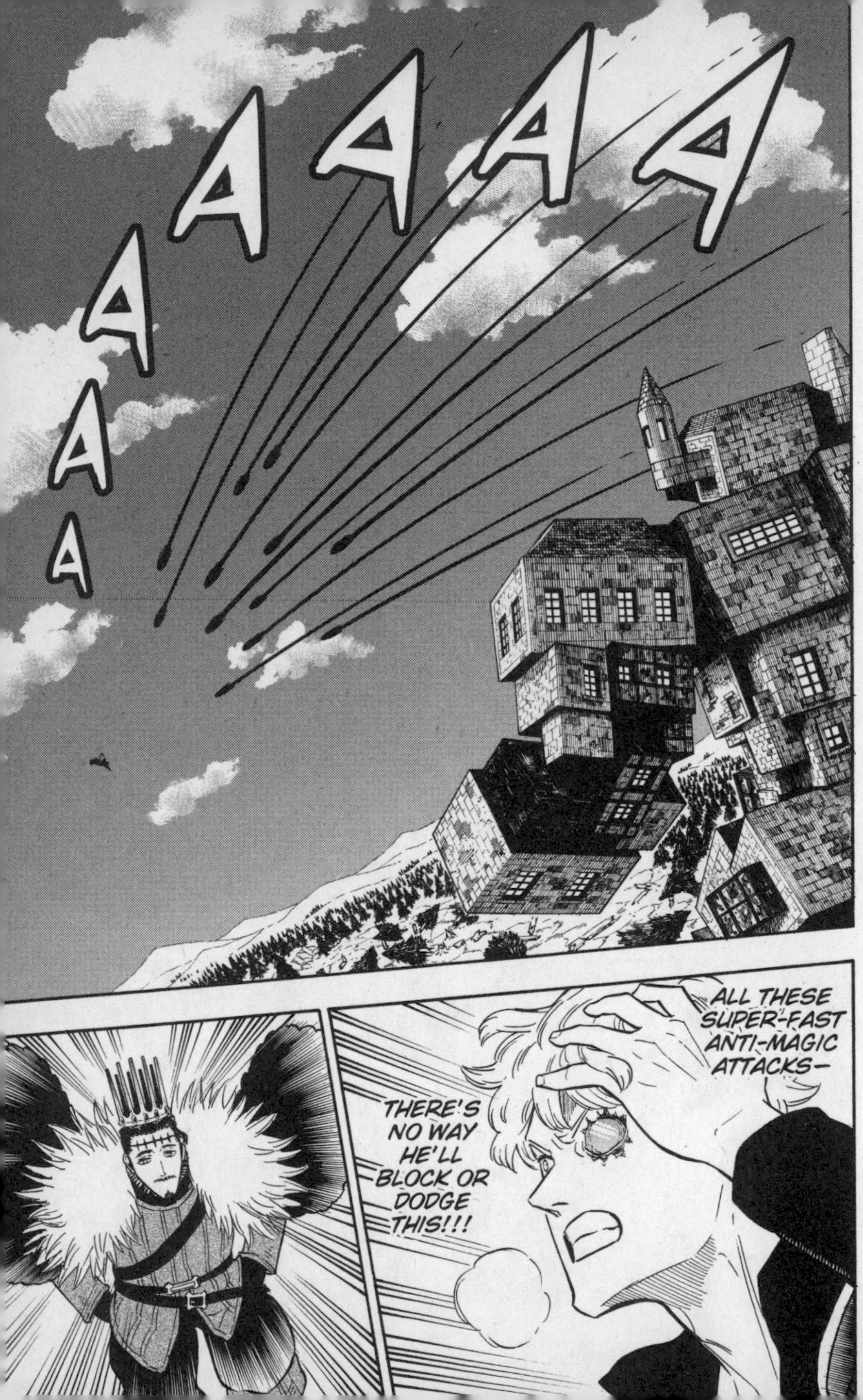
AAAAAAA
ALL THESE SUPER-FAST ANTI-MAGIC ATTACKS—
THERE'S NO WAY HE'LL BLOCK OR DODGE THIS!!!

BLACK ✤ CLOVER

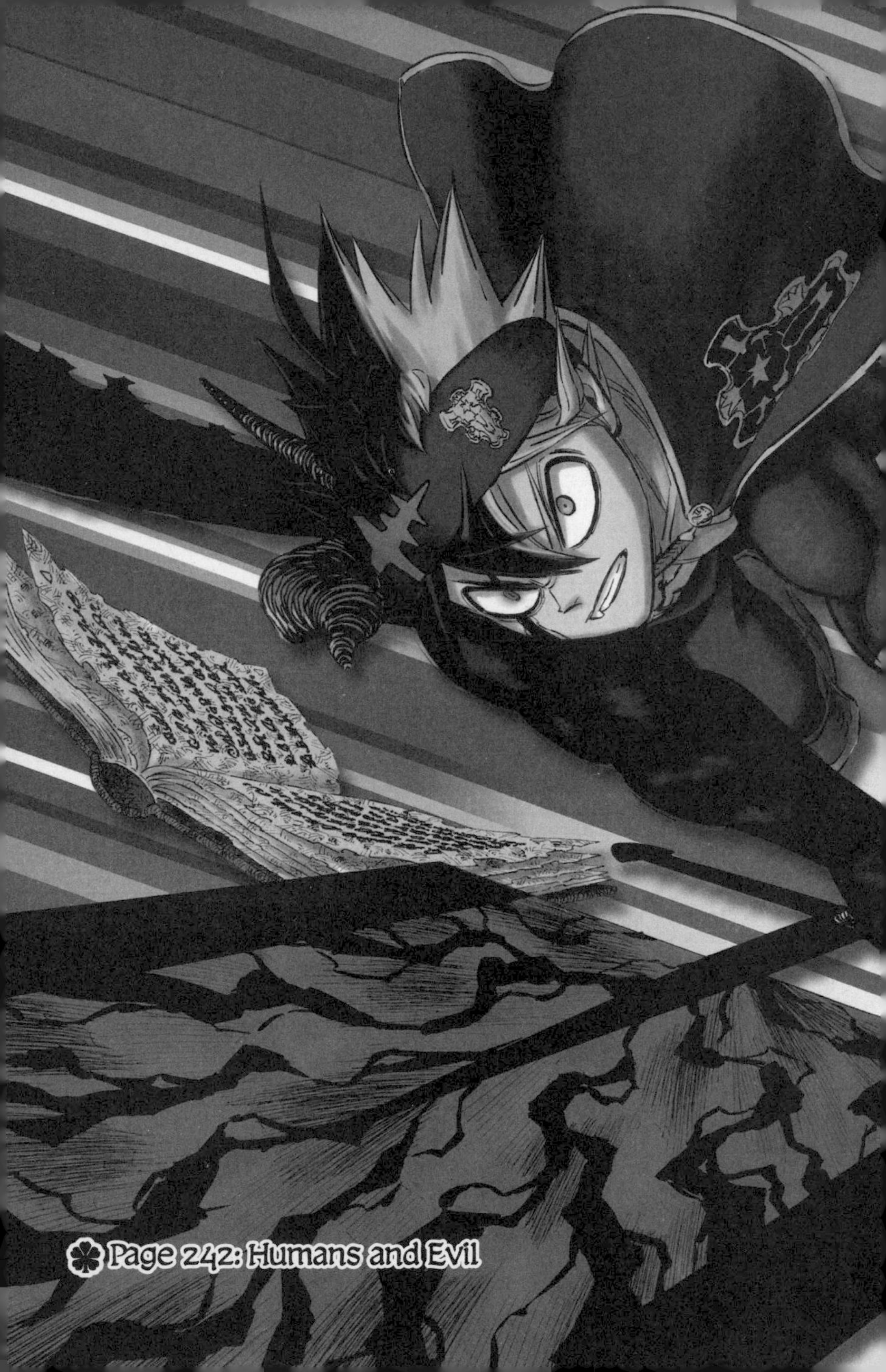
Page 242: Humans and Evil

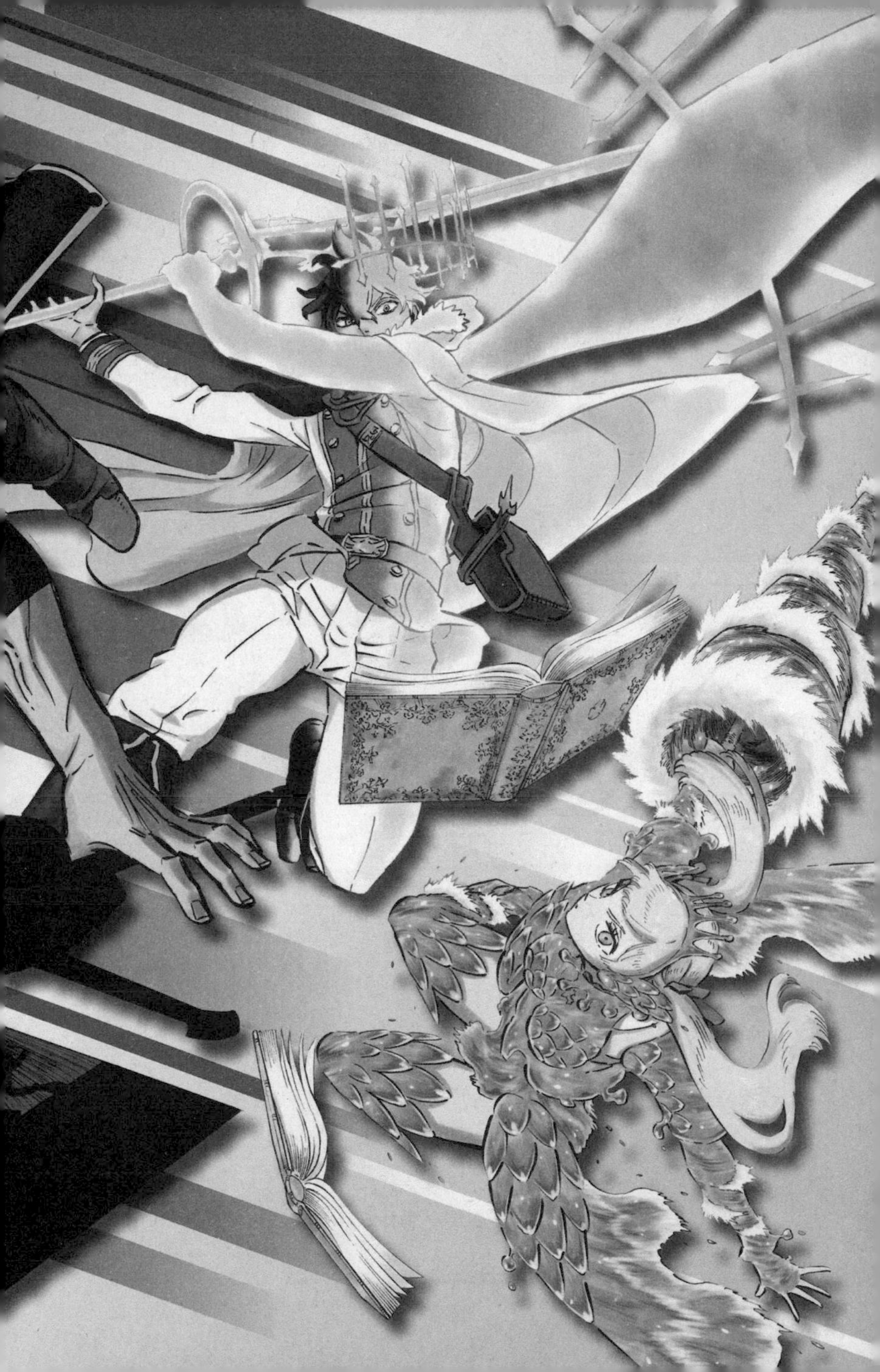

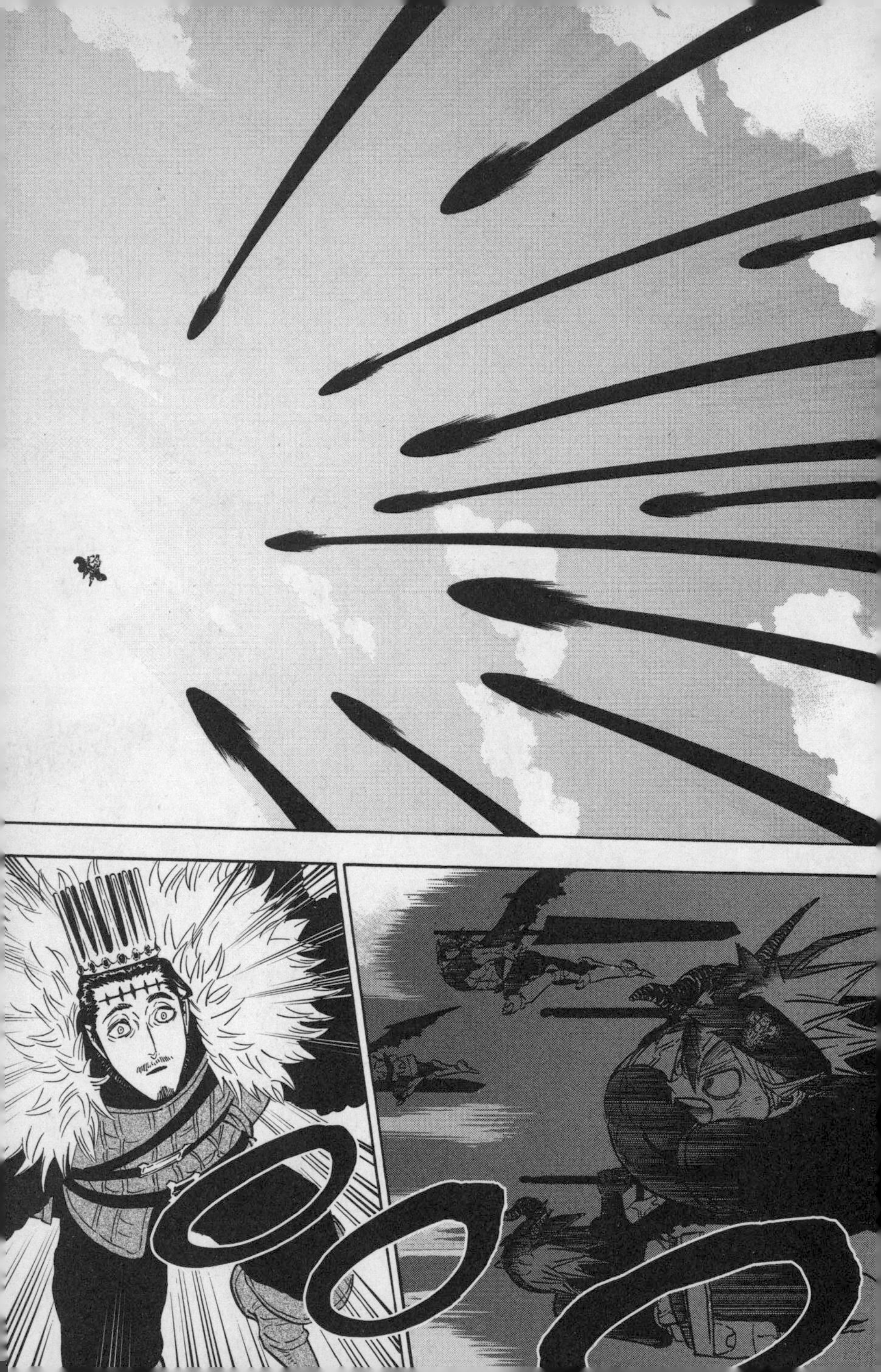

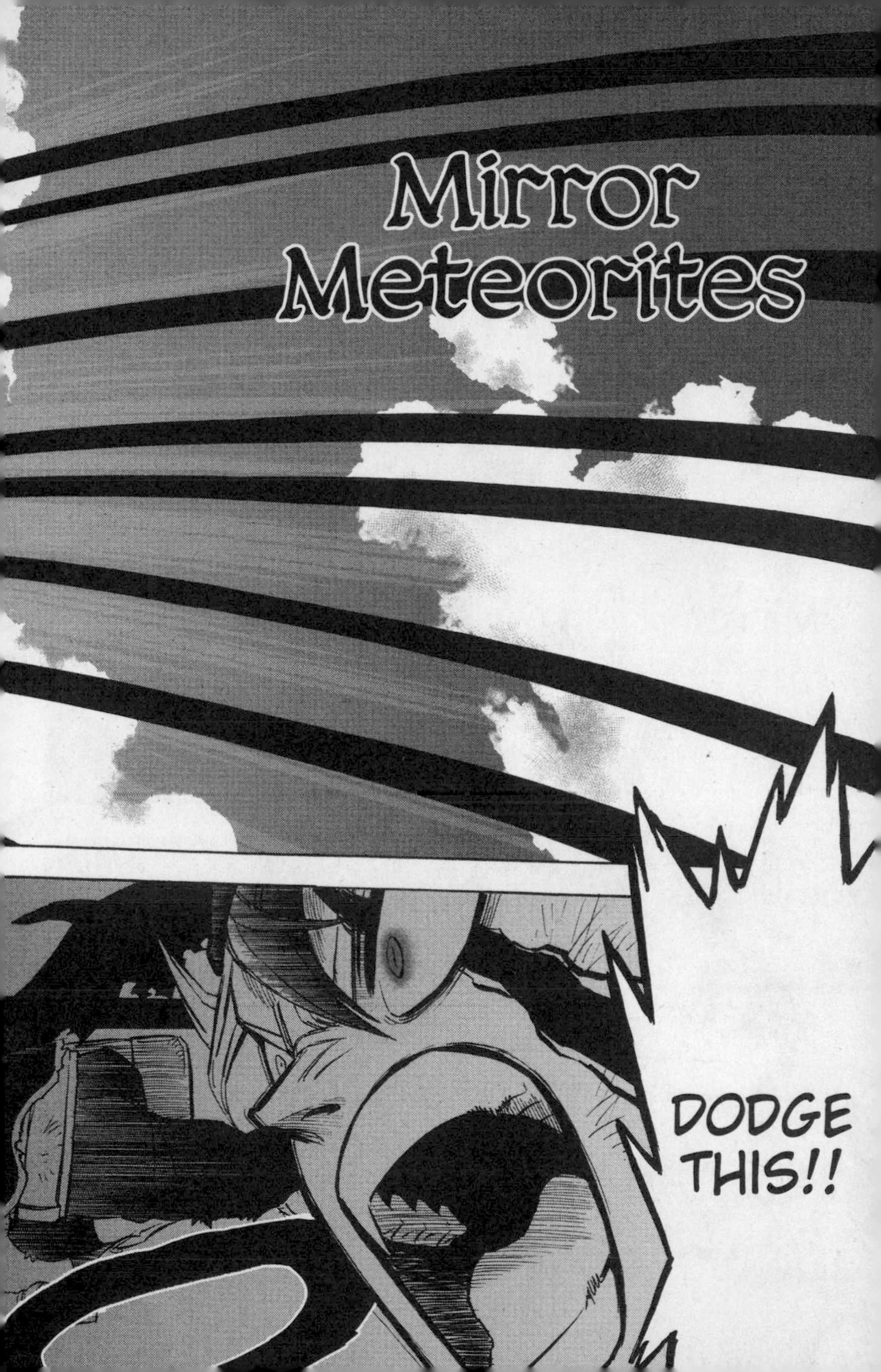
Mirror Meteorites
DODGE THIS!!

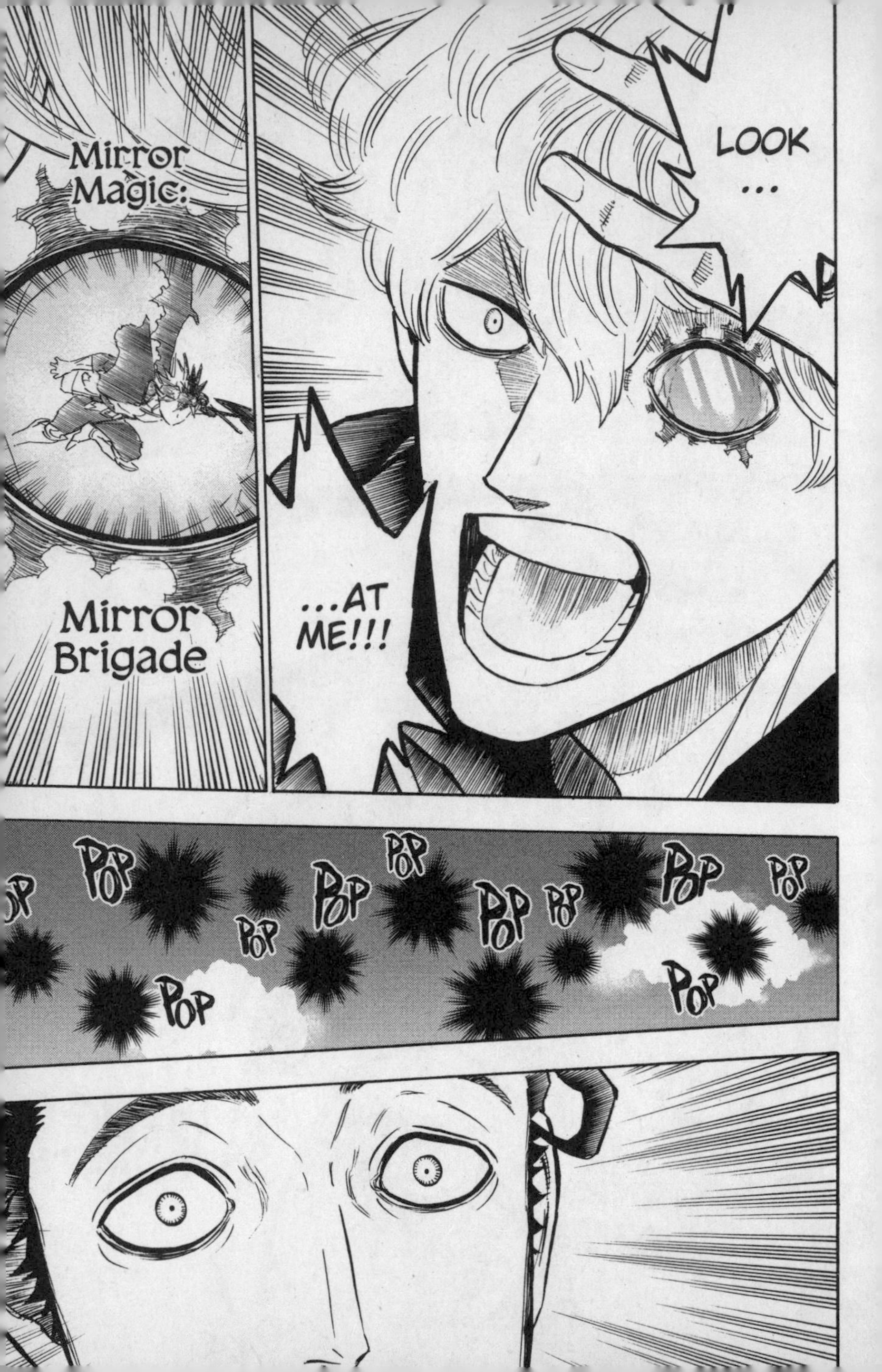
LOOK ...
...AT ME!!!
Mirror Magic:
Mirror Brigade
POP POP POP POP POP POP POP POP POP POP

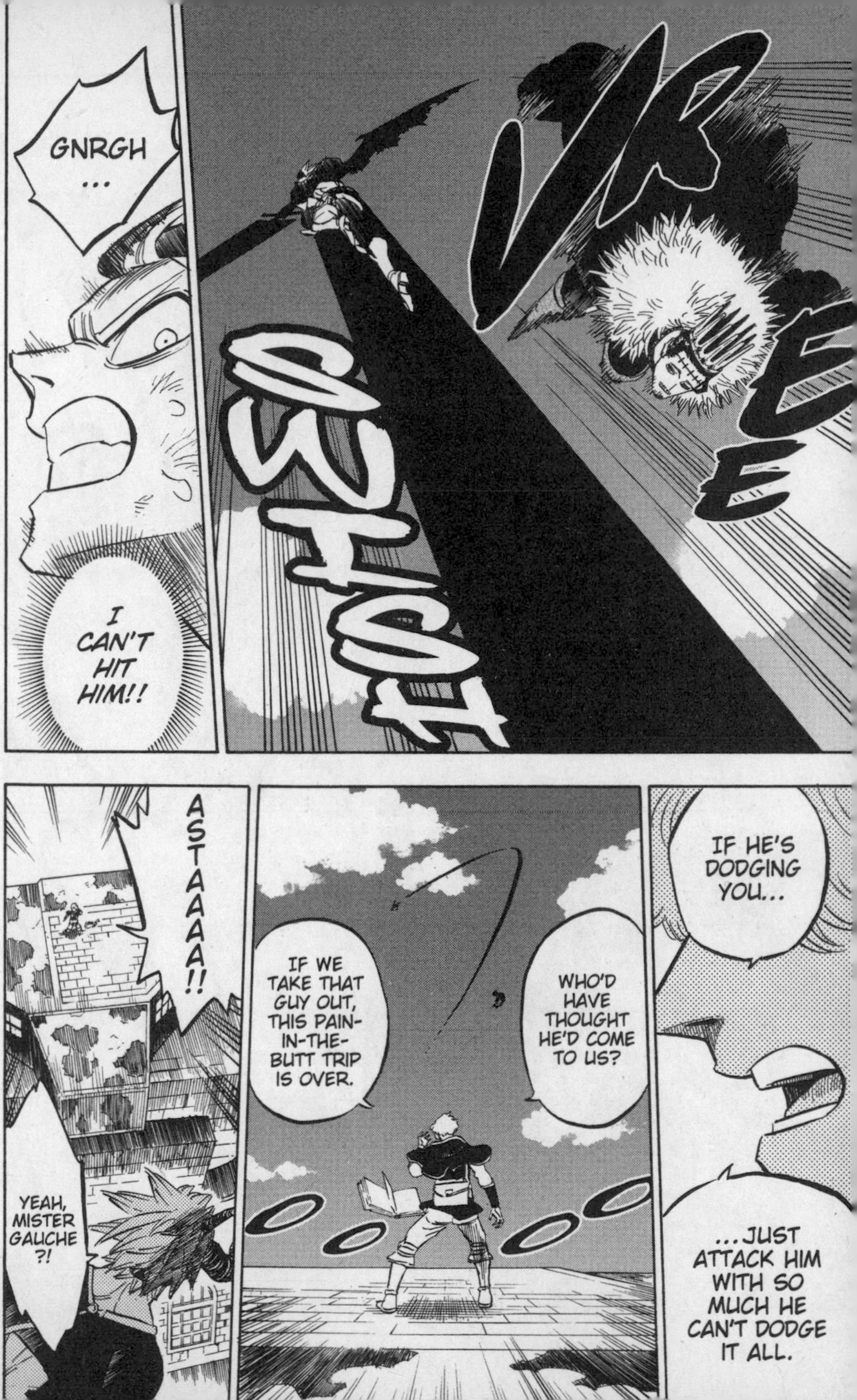
GNRGH ...
I CAN'T HIT HIM!!
IF HE'S DODGING YOU...
...JUST ATTACK HIM WITH SO MUCH HE CAN'T DODGE IT ALL.
WHO'D HAVE THOUGHT HE'D COME TO US?
IF WE TAKE THAT GUY OUT, THIS PAIN-IN-THE-BUTT TRIP IS OVER.
ASTAAAAA!!
YEAH, MISTER GAUCHE?!

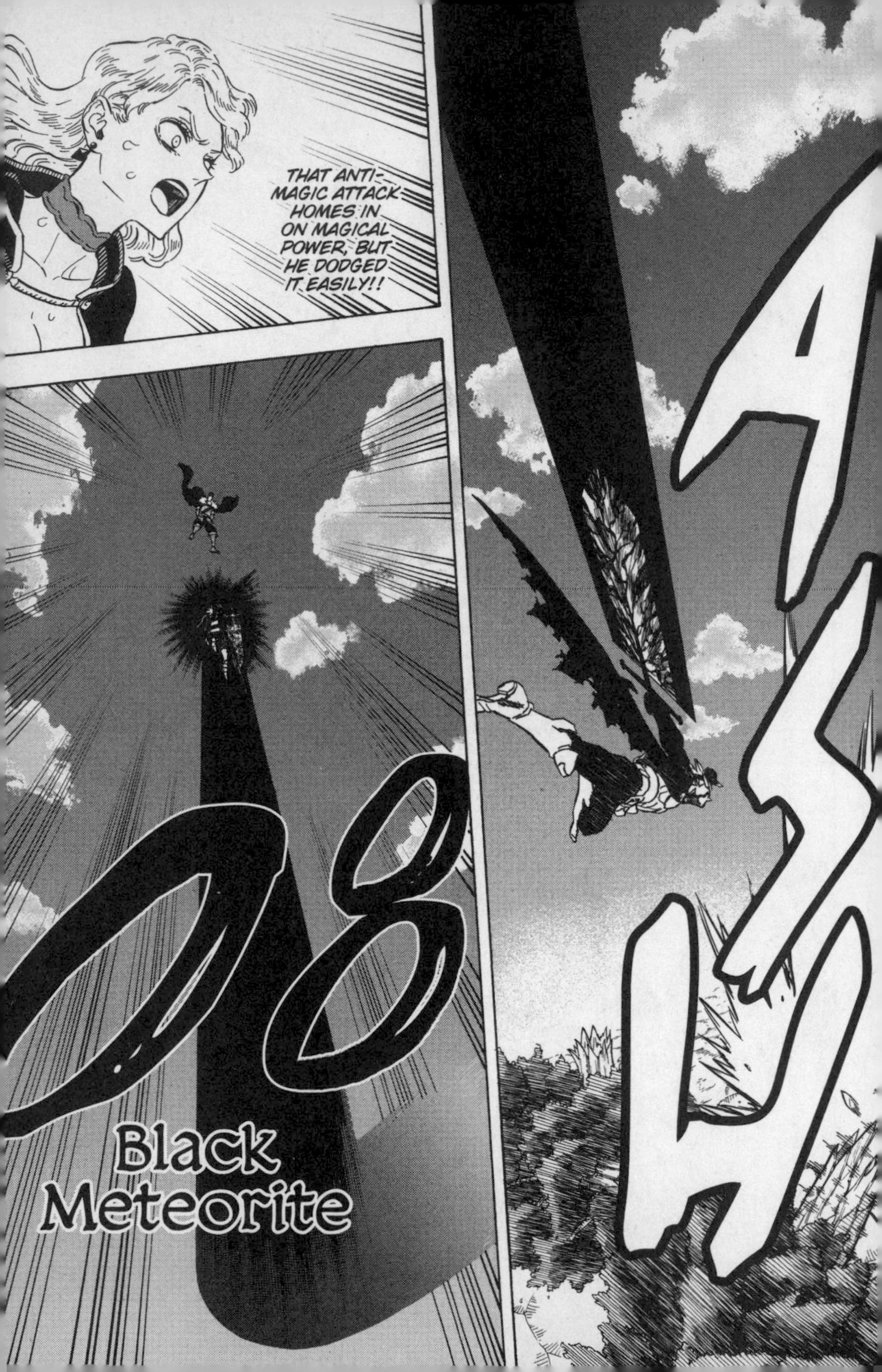
THAT ANTI-MAGIC ATTACK HOMES IN ON MAGICAL POWER, BUT HE DODGED IT EASILY!!
Black Meteorite

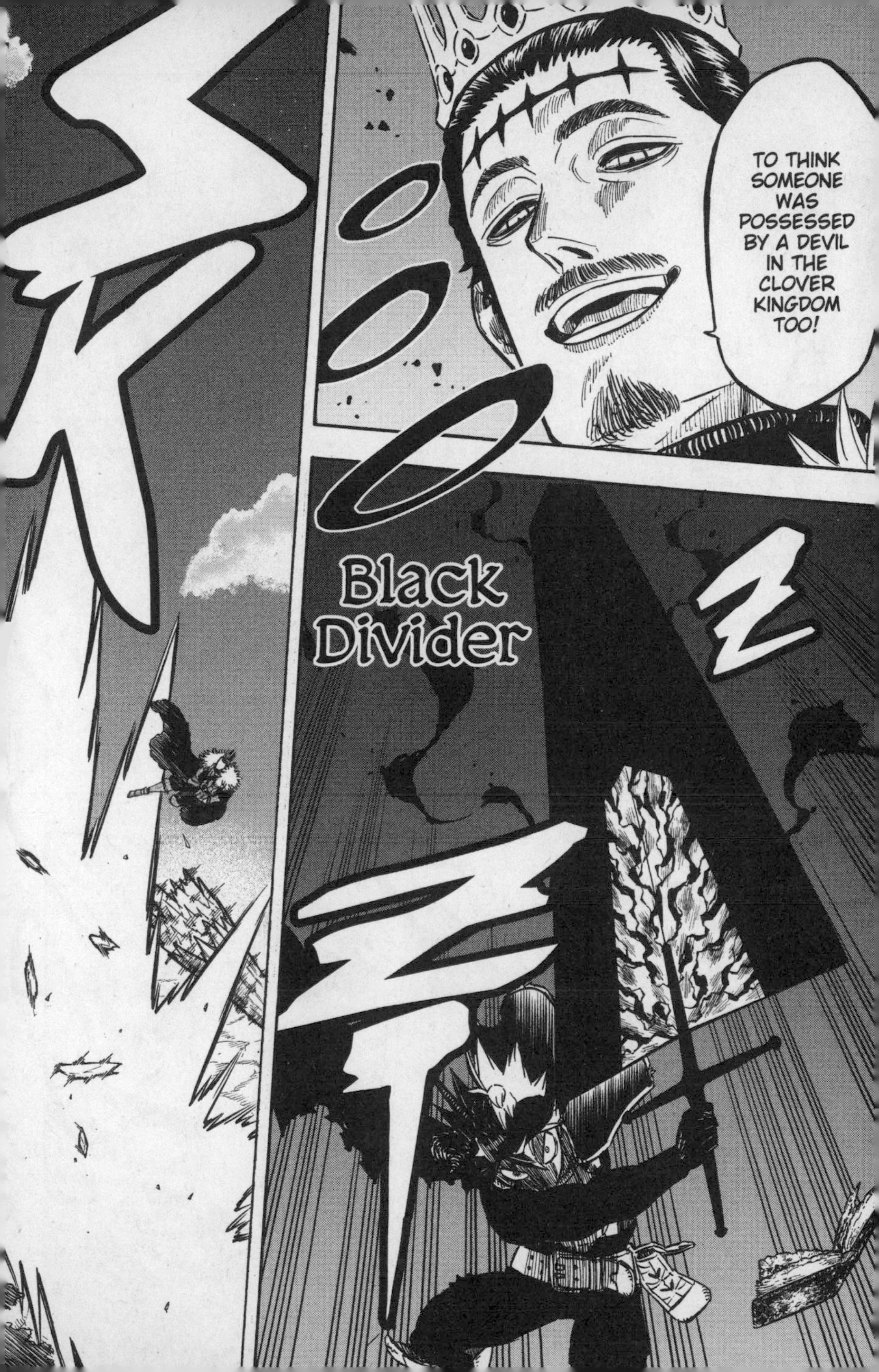
TO THINK SOMEONE WAS POSSESSED BY A DEVIL IN THE CLOVER KINGDOM TOO!
Black Divider

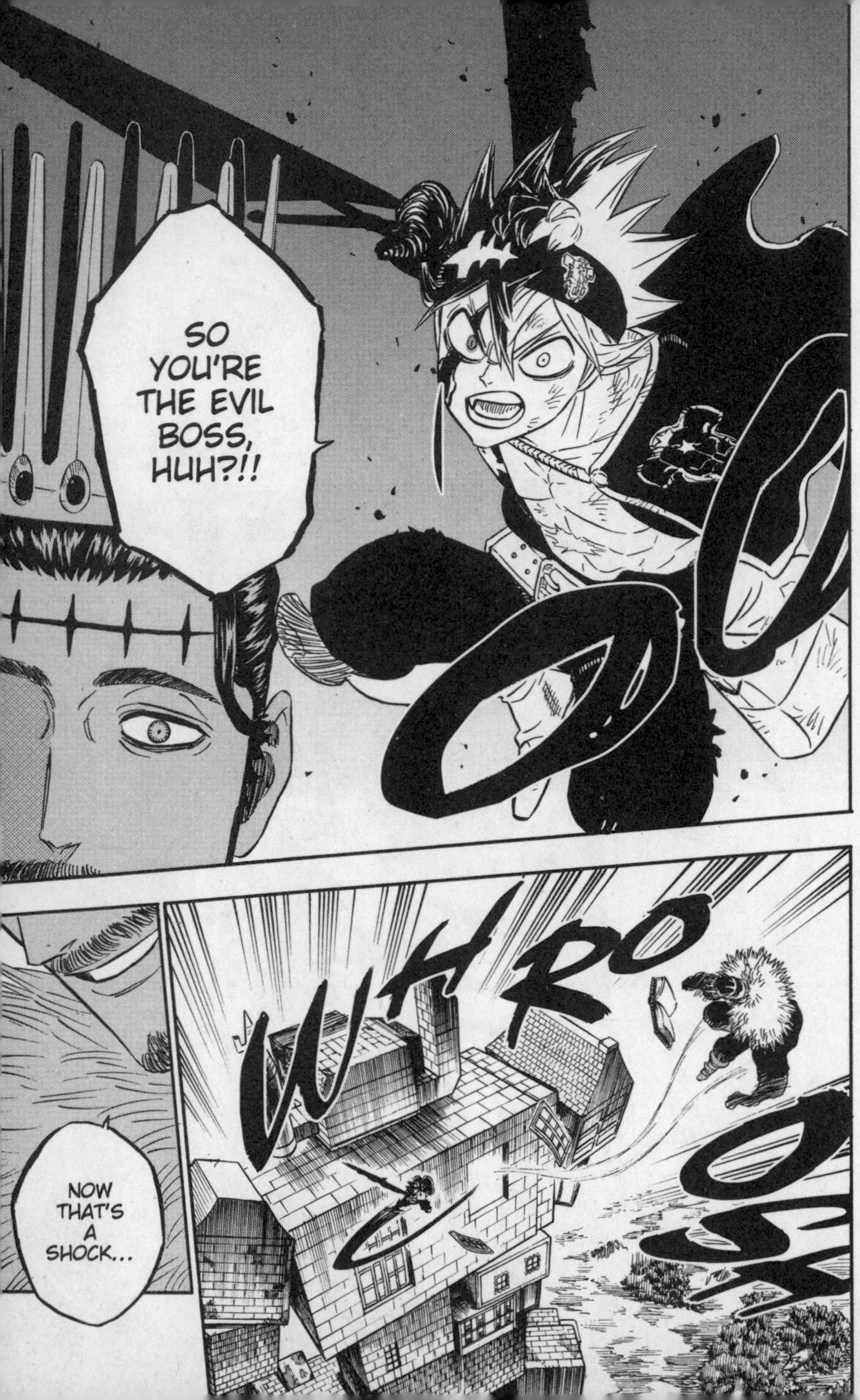
SO YOU'RE THE EVIL BOSS, HUH?!!
WHOOSH
NOW THAT'S A SHOCK...

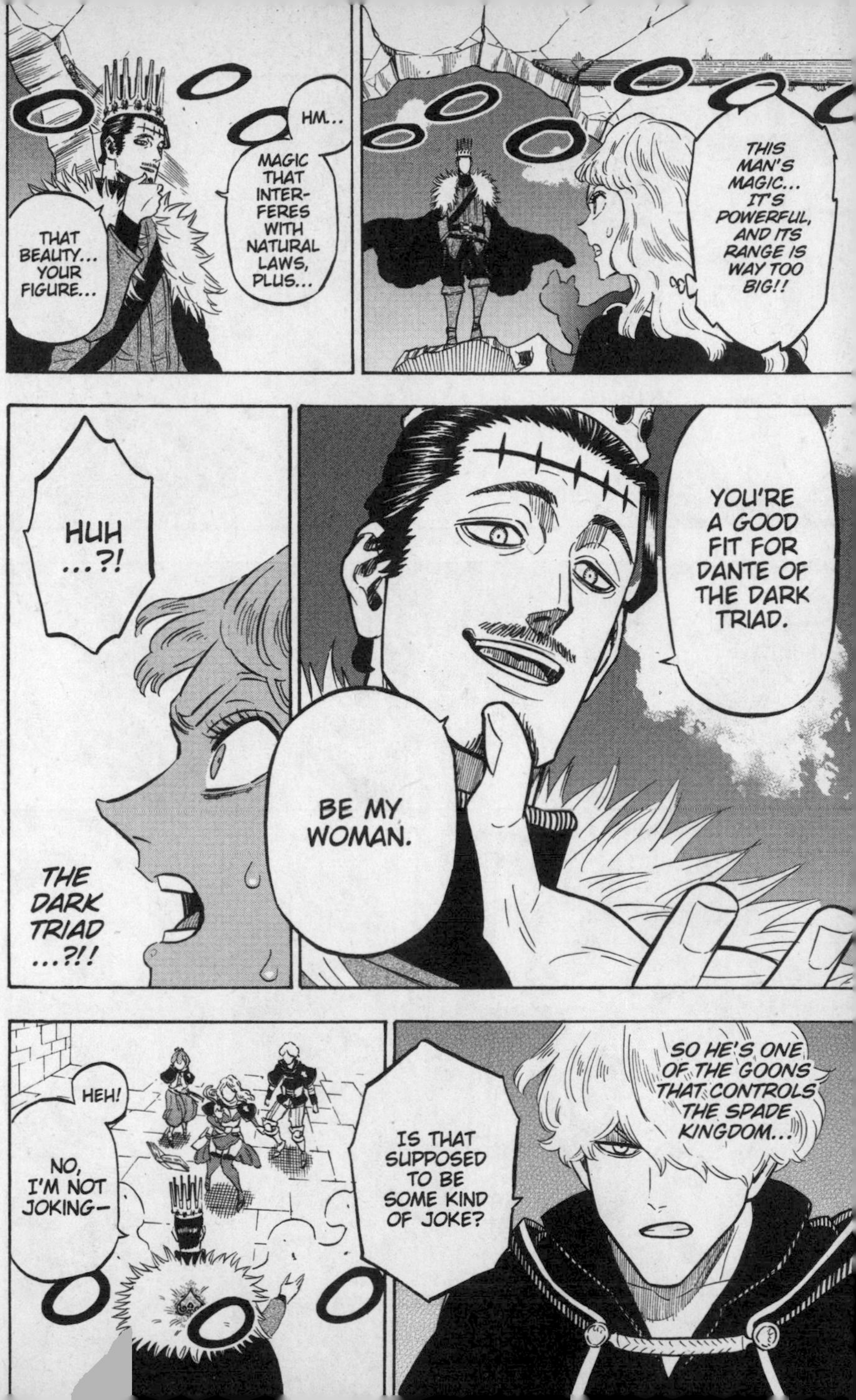
THIS MAN'S MAGIC... IT'S POWERFUL, AND ITS RANGE IS WAY TOO BIG!!
HM...
MAGIC THAT INTERFERES WITH NATURAL LAWS, PLUS...
THAT BEAUTY... YOUR FIGURE...
YOU'RE A GOOD FIT FOR DANTE OF THE DARK TRIAD.
BE MY WOMAN.
HUH ...?!
THE DARK TRIAD ...?!!
SO HE'S ONE OF THE GOONS THAT CONTROLS THE SPADE KINGDOM...
IS THAT SUPPOSED TO BE SOME KIND OF JOKE?
HEH!
NO, I'M NOT JOKING–

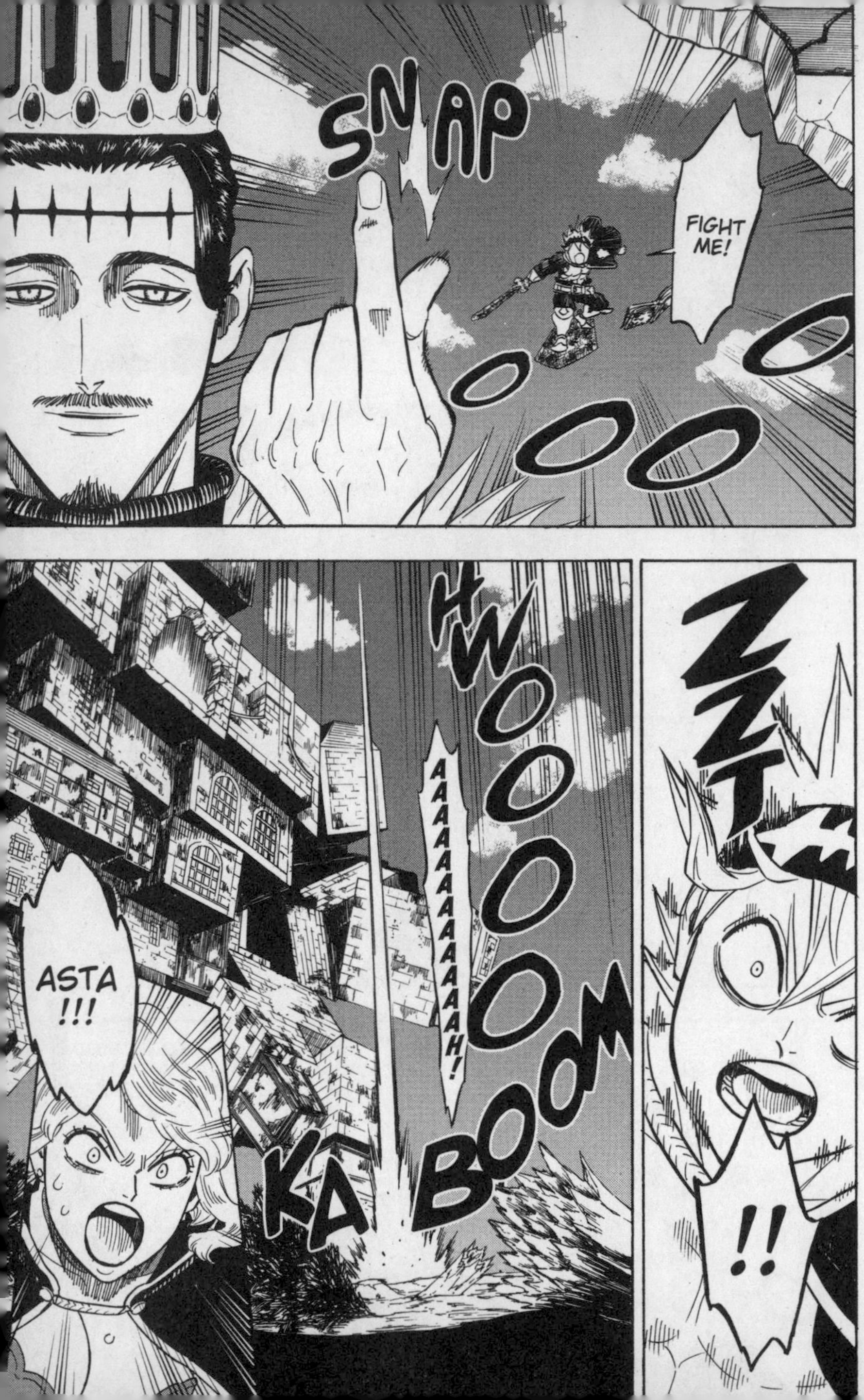
FIGHT ME!
OOOOO
SNAP
ZZT
!!
HWOOOOOO
AAAAAAAAAAAH!
KABOOM
ASTA !!!

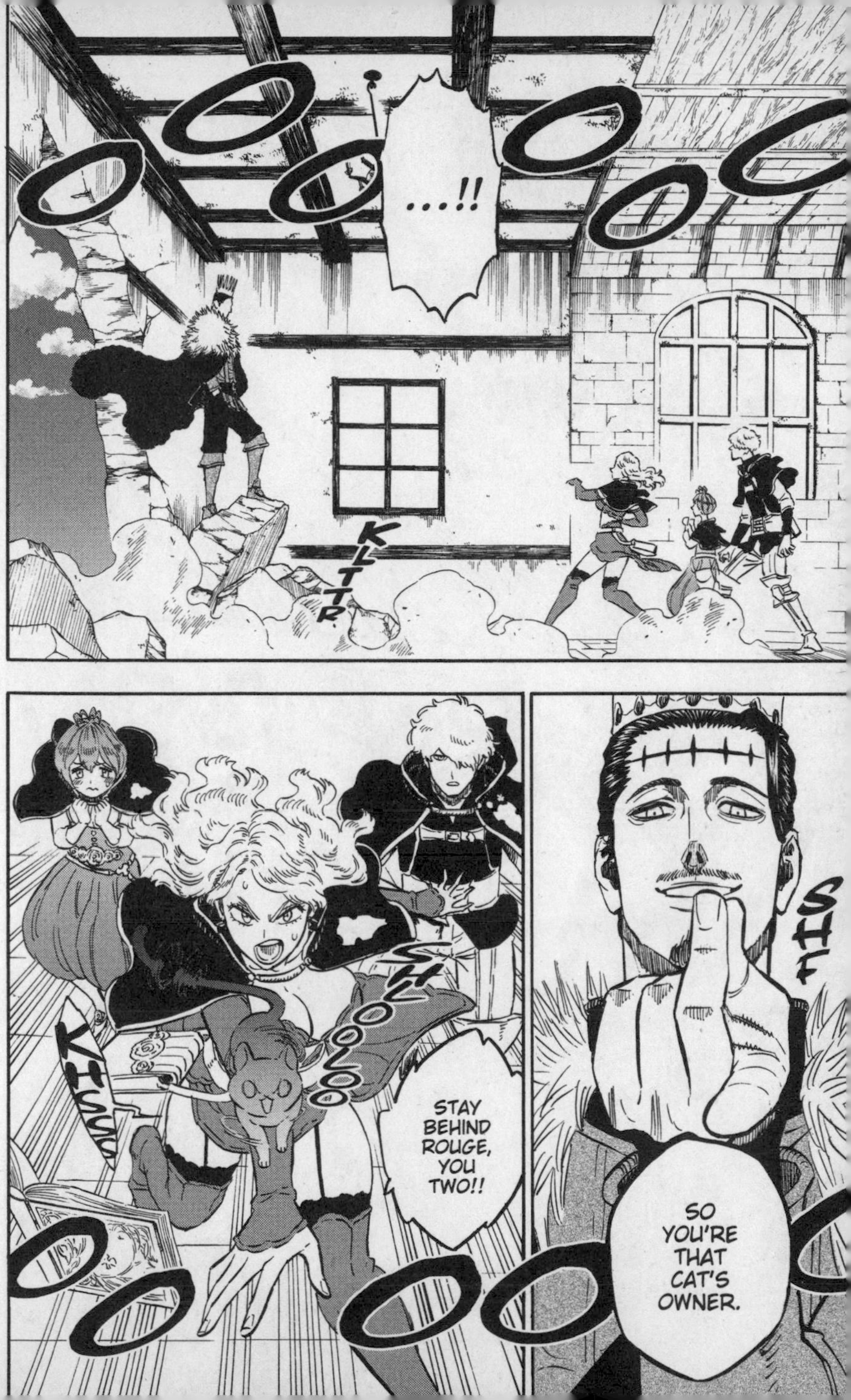
...!!
KLTTR
SHF
SO YOU'RE THAT CAT'S OWNER.
STAY BEHIND ROUGE, YOU TWO!!

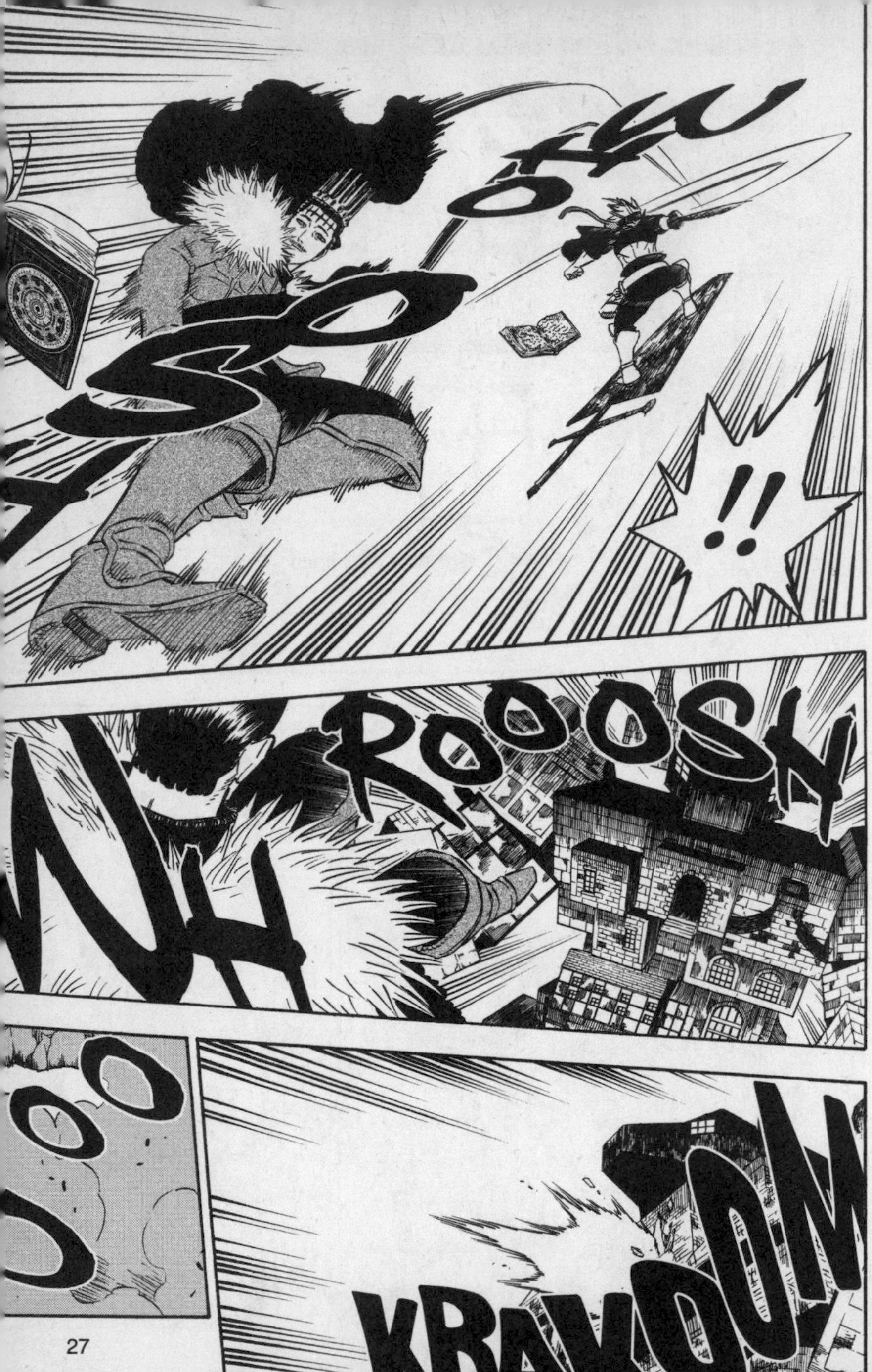
!!
WHROOOSH
KRAKOOOM

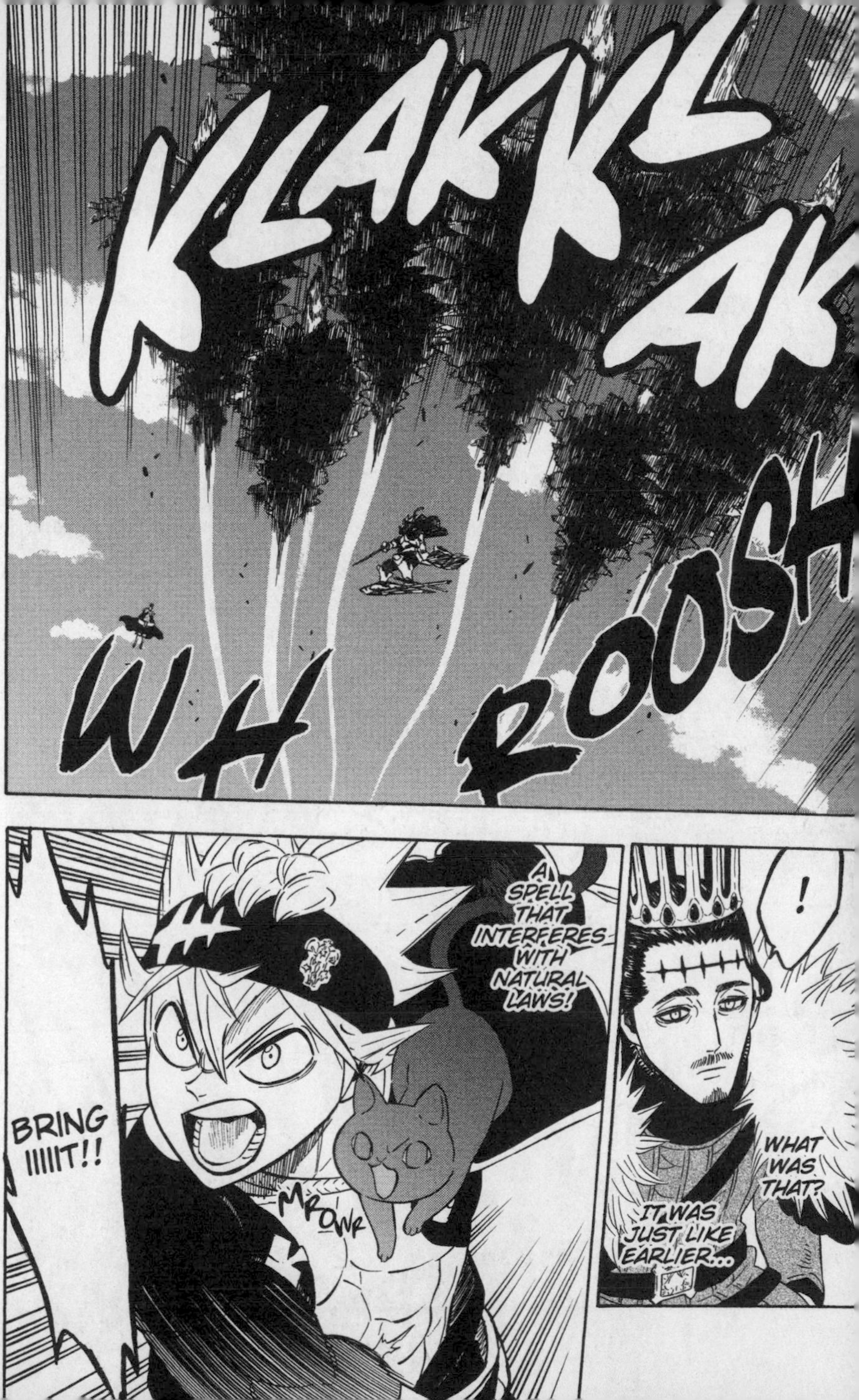
KLAKKLAK
WHROOSH
!
WHAT WAS THAT?
IT WAS JUST LIKE EARLIER...
A SPELL THAT INTERFERES WITH NATURAL LAWS!
BRING IIIIIT!!
MROWR

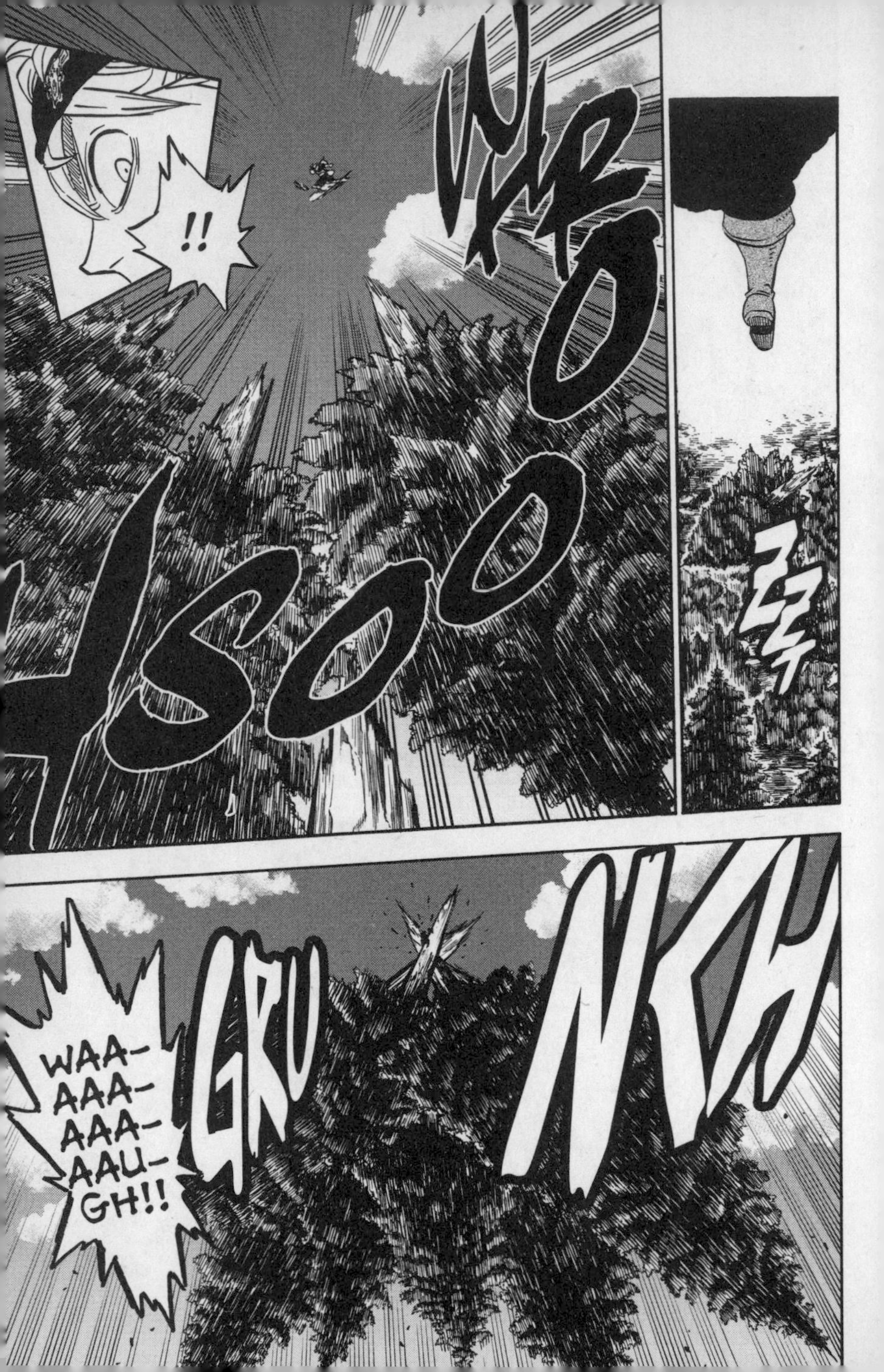
!!
GRUNCH
WAA-AAA-AAA-AAU-GH!!

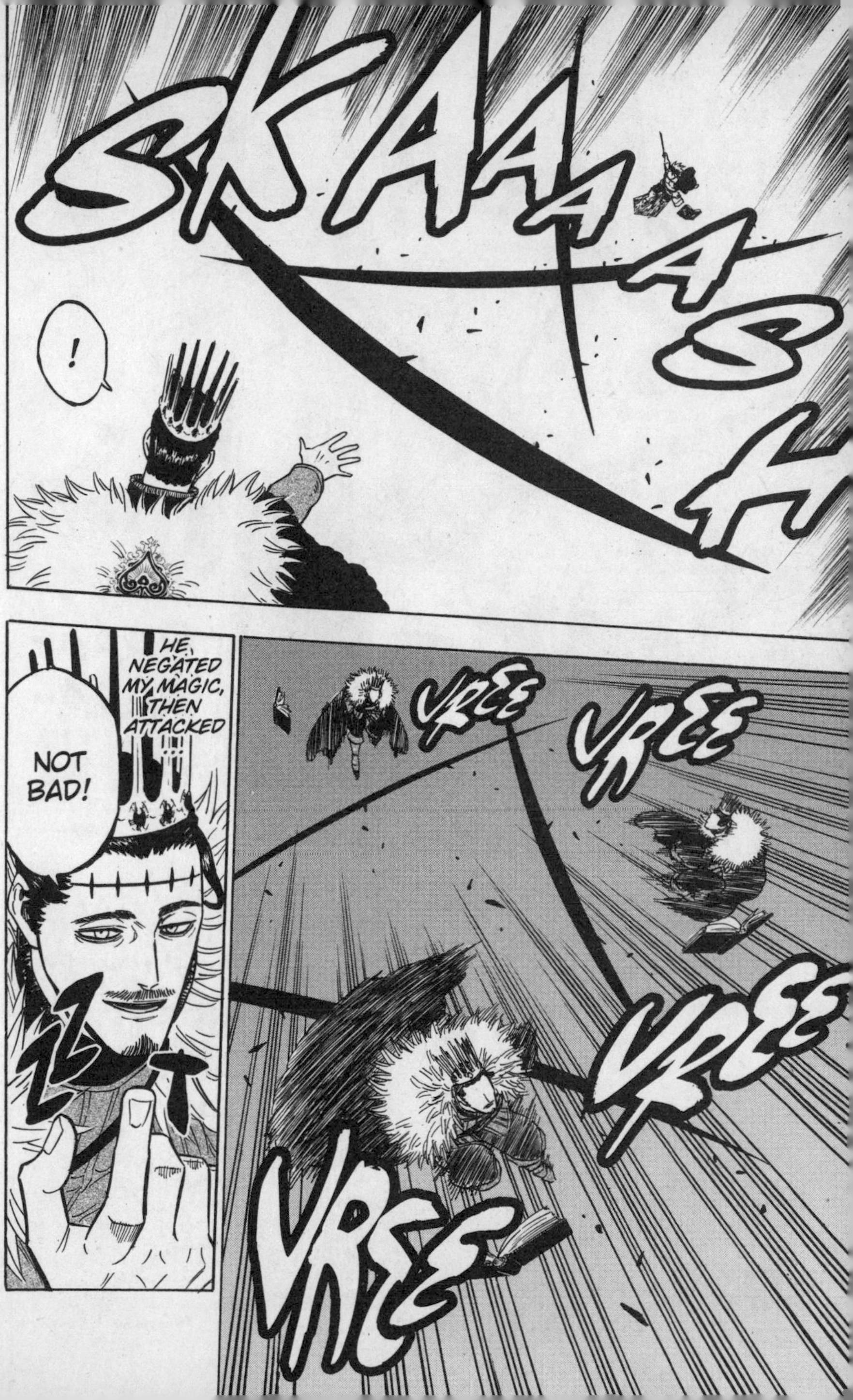
SKAAASH
!
VREE
VREE
VREE
VREE
HE NEGATED MY MAGIC, THEN ATTACKED...
NOT BAD!

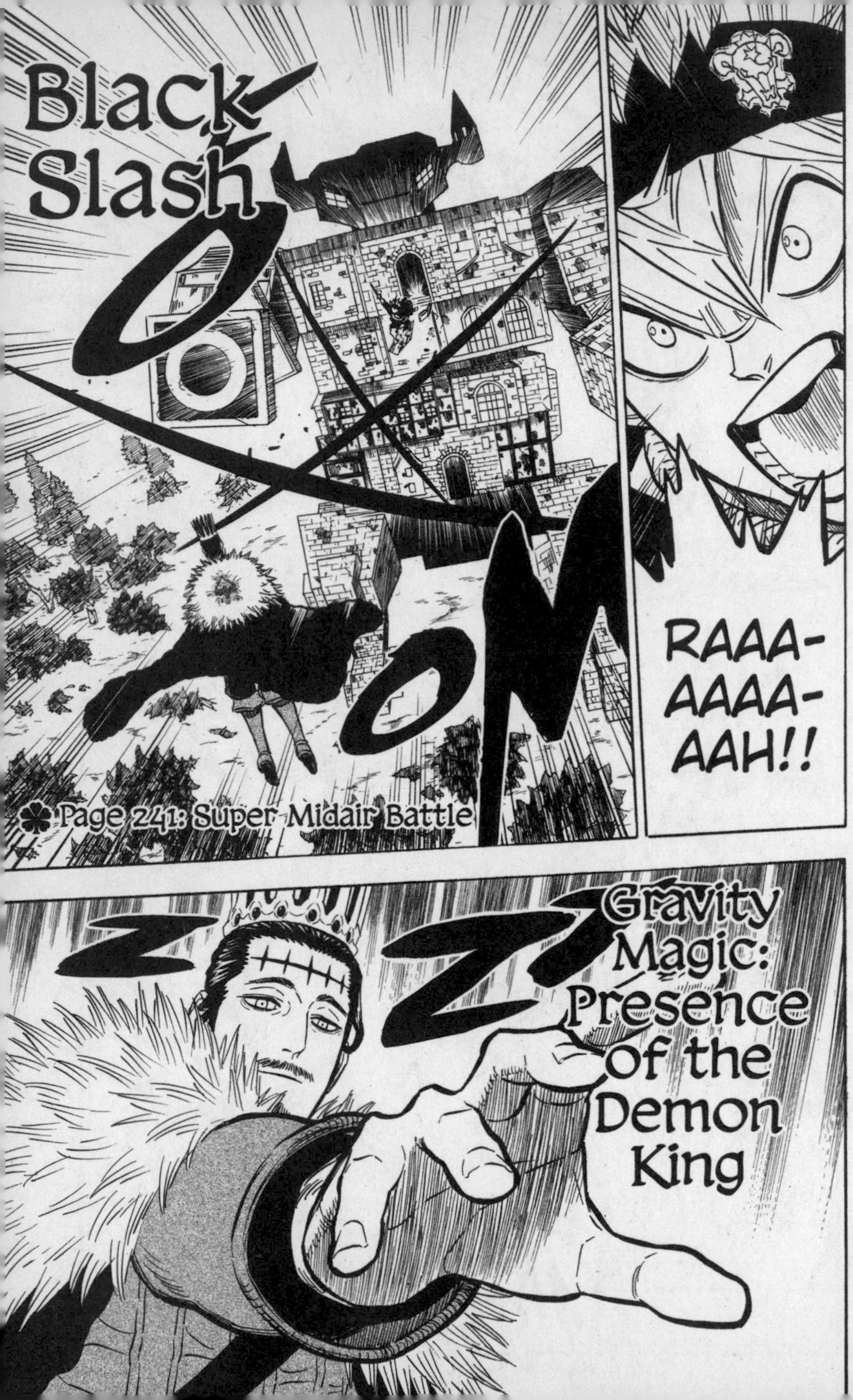
RAAA-AAAA-AAH!!
Black Slash
Page 241: Super Midair Battle
Gravity Magic: Presence of the Demon King

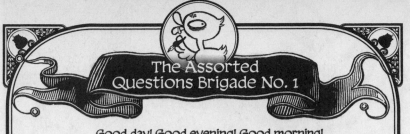

The Assorted Questions Brigade No. 1

Good day! Good evening! Good morning!
It's time for the letters corner.
We got a lot of sharp questions this time too!

Q: Please tell me which brigade members have the biggest fan clubs. (*Mio*, Chiba)

A: 1 Nozel 2 Fuegoleon 3 Charlotte (both guys and girls)

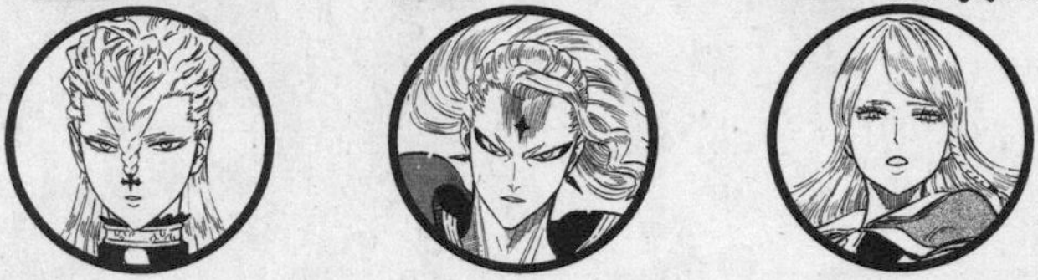

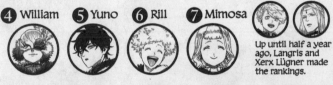

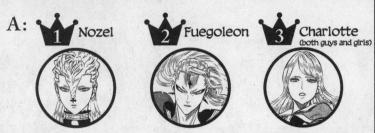

4 William 5 Yuno 6 Rill 7 Mimosa

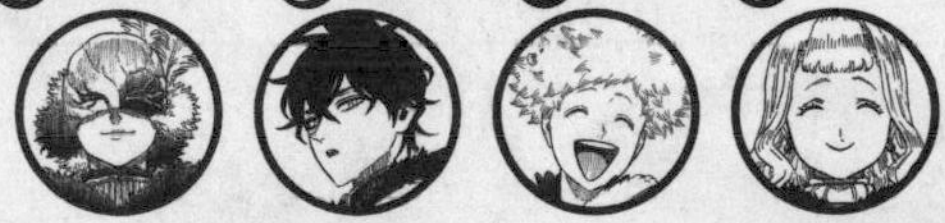

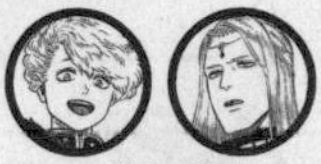

Up until half a year ago, Langris and Xerx Lügner made the rankings.

These guys have some wildly enthusiastic fans.

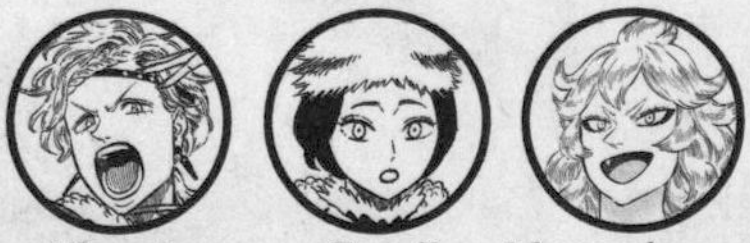

Kirsch Fragil Mereoleona

Q: In the era of Lumiere, the first Wizard King, Raia was apparently 25. At his first appearance (Page 51), how old was he? (*Cat-Nest*, Mie)

A: It hadn't been too long since his soul reincarnated, so he was probably about 25 or 26. The human Raia reincarnated into was a disgraced aristocrat about that age who was *this* close to committing suicide.

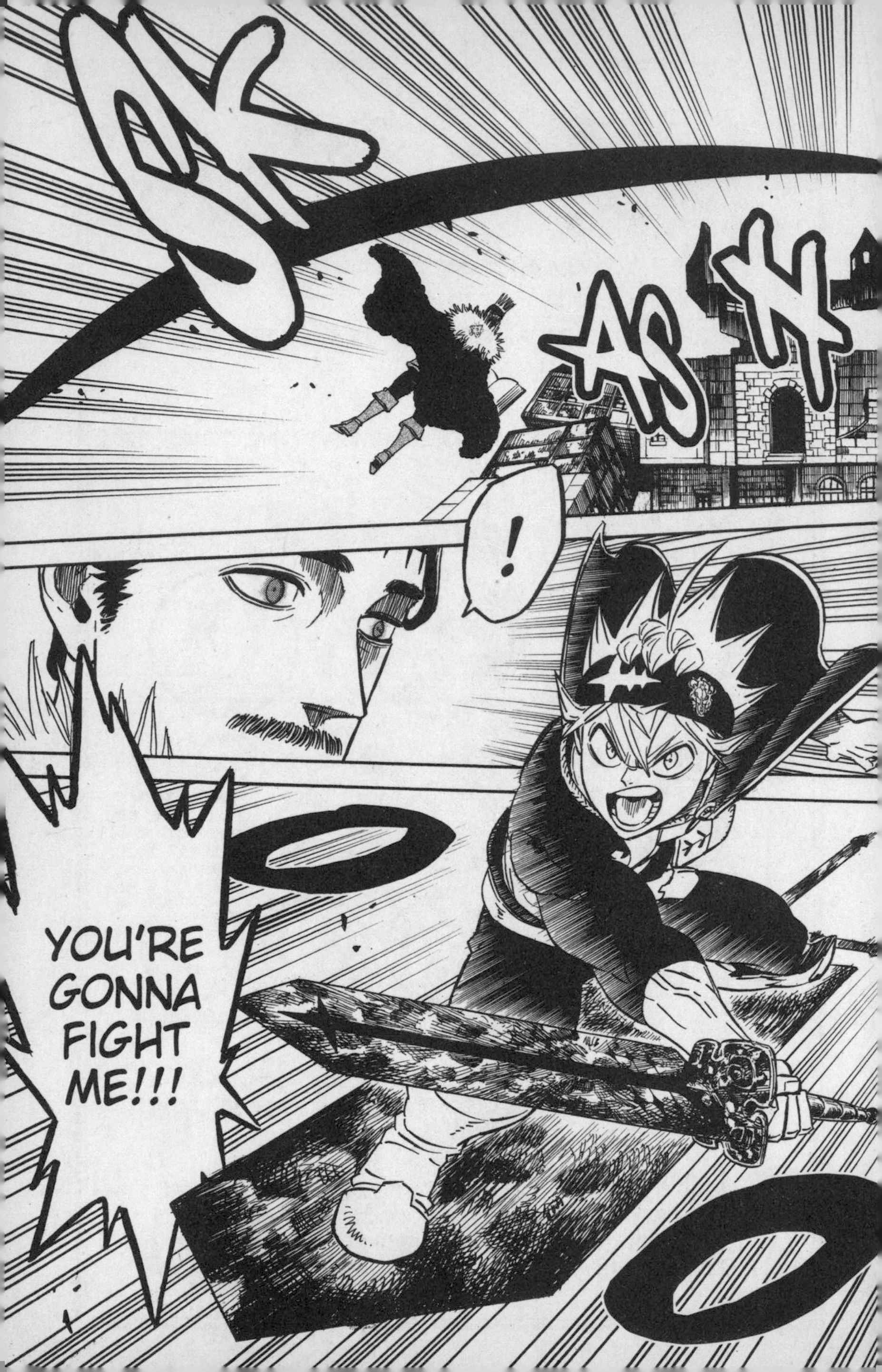
!
YOU'RE GONNA FIGHT ME!!!

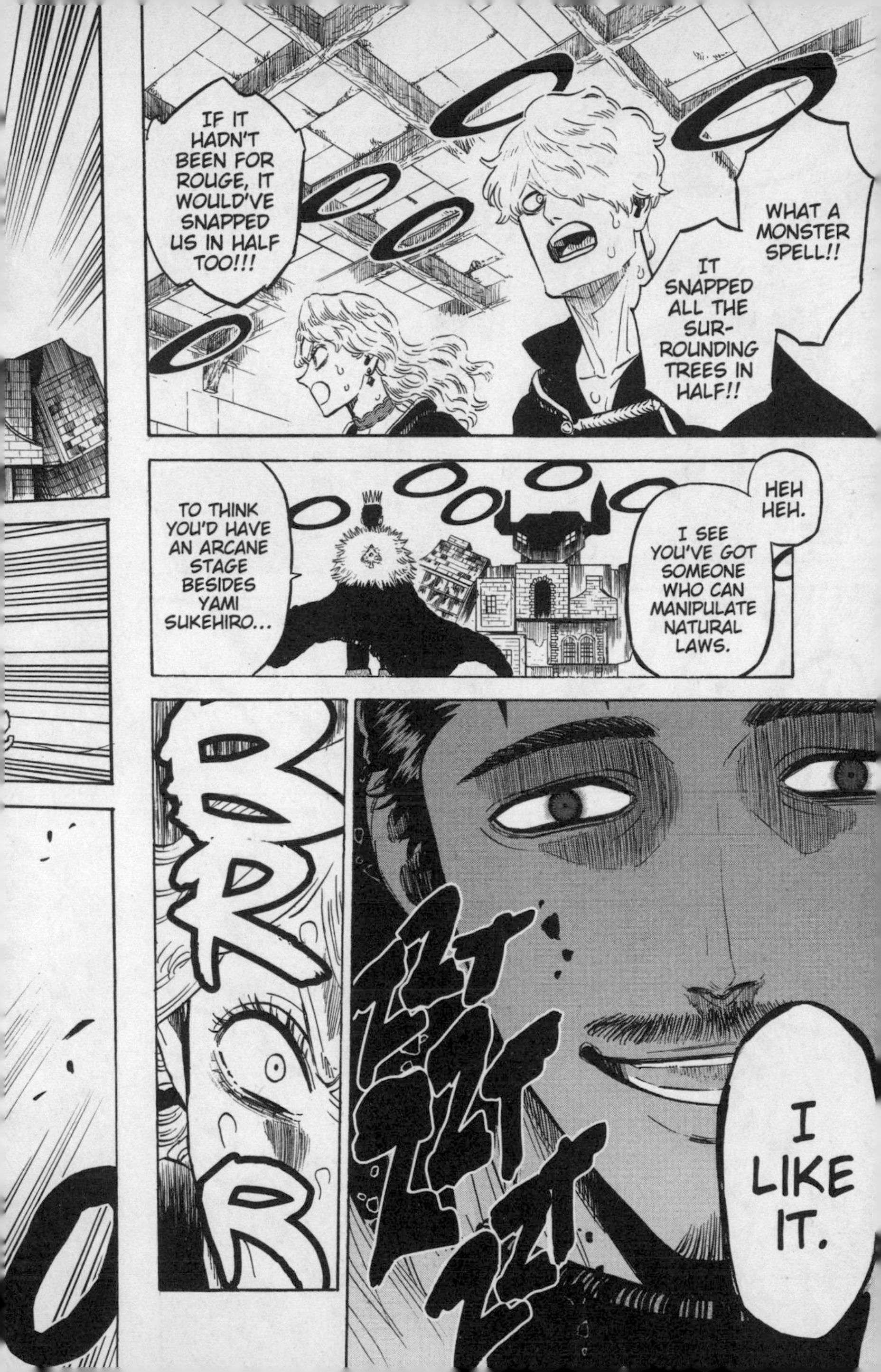
WHAT A MONSTER SPELL!!
IT SNAPPED ALL THE SUR-ROUNDING TREES IN HALF!!
IF IT HADN'T BEEN FOR ROUGE, IT WOULD'VE SNAPPED US IN HALF TOO!!!
HEH HEH.
I SEE YOU'VE GOT SOMEONE WHO CAN MANIPULATE NATURAL LAWS.
TO THINK YOU'D HAVE AN ARCANE STAGE BESIDES YAMI SUKEHIRO...
I LIKE IT.

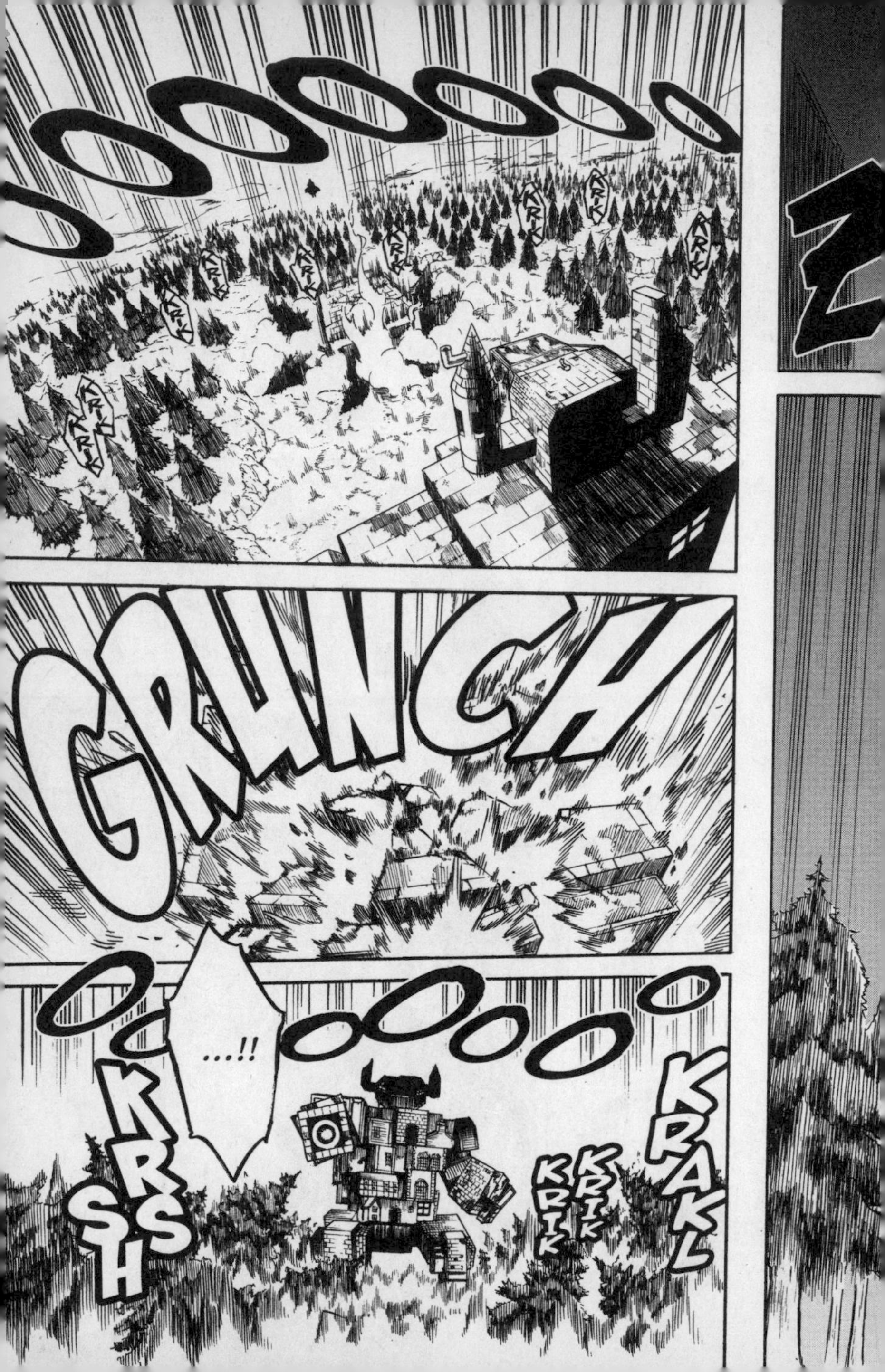
Z
OOOOOOO
KRIK
KRIK
KRIK
KRIK
KRIK
KRIK
KRIK
KRIK
KRIK
KRIK
GRUNCH!
OOOOOO
KRAKL
KRIK
KRIK
...!!
KRSSH

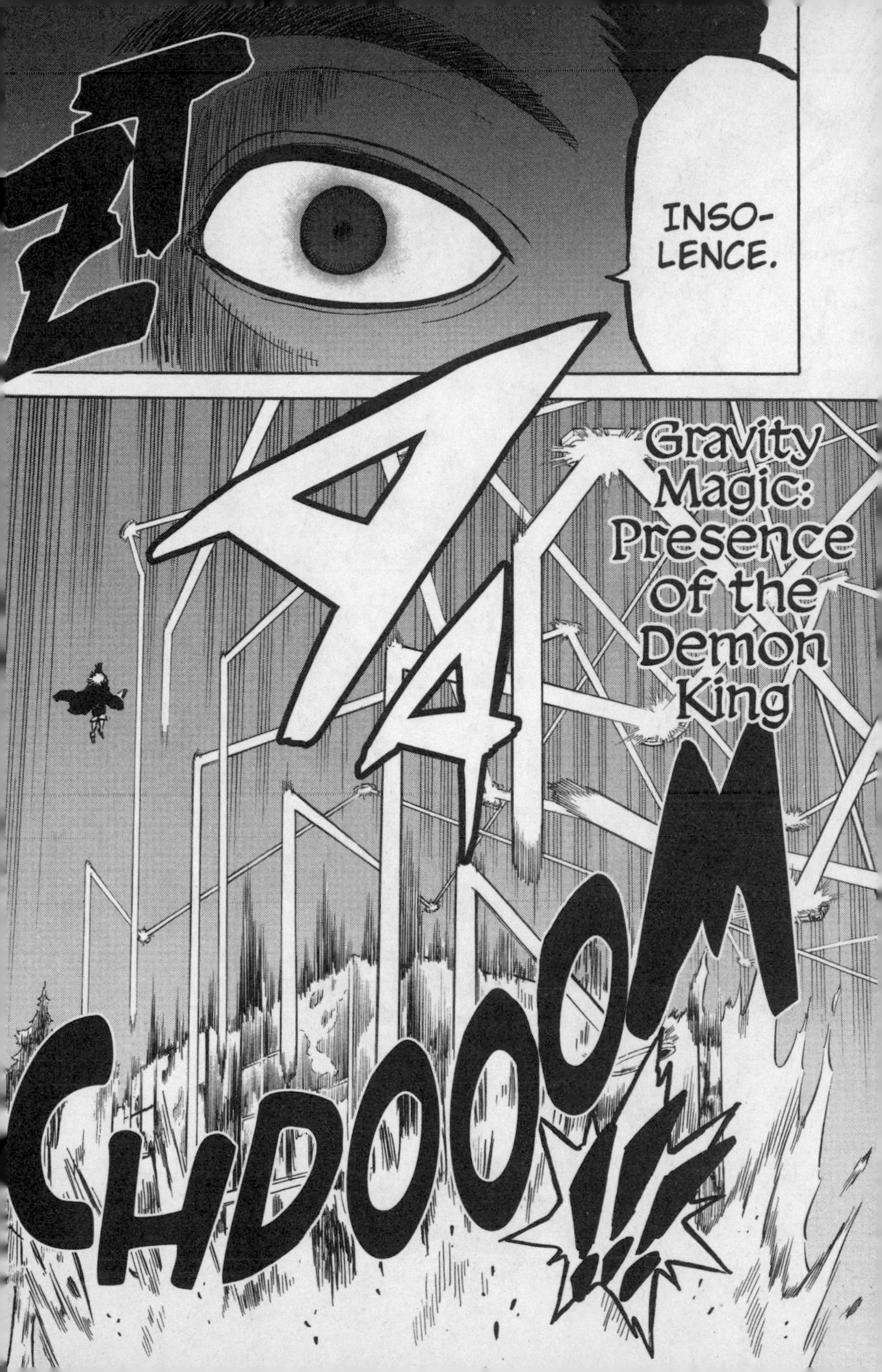
INSO-
LENCE.
Gravity Magic: Presence of the Demon King
CHDOOOOM!!

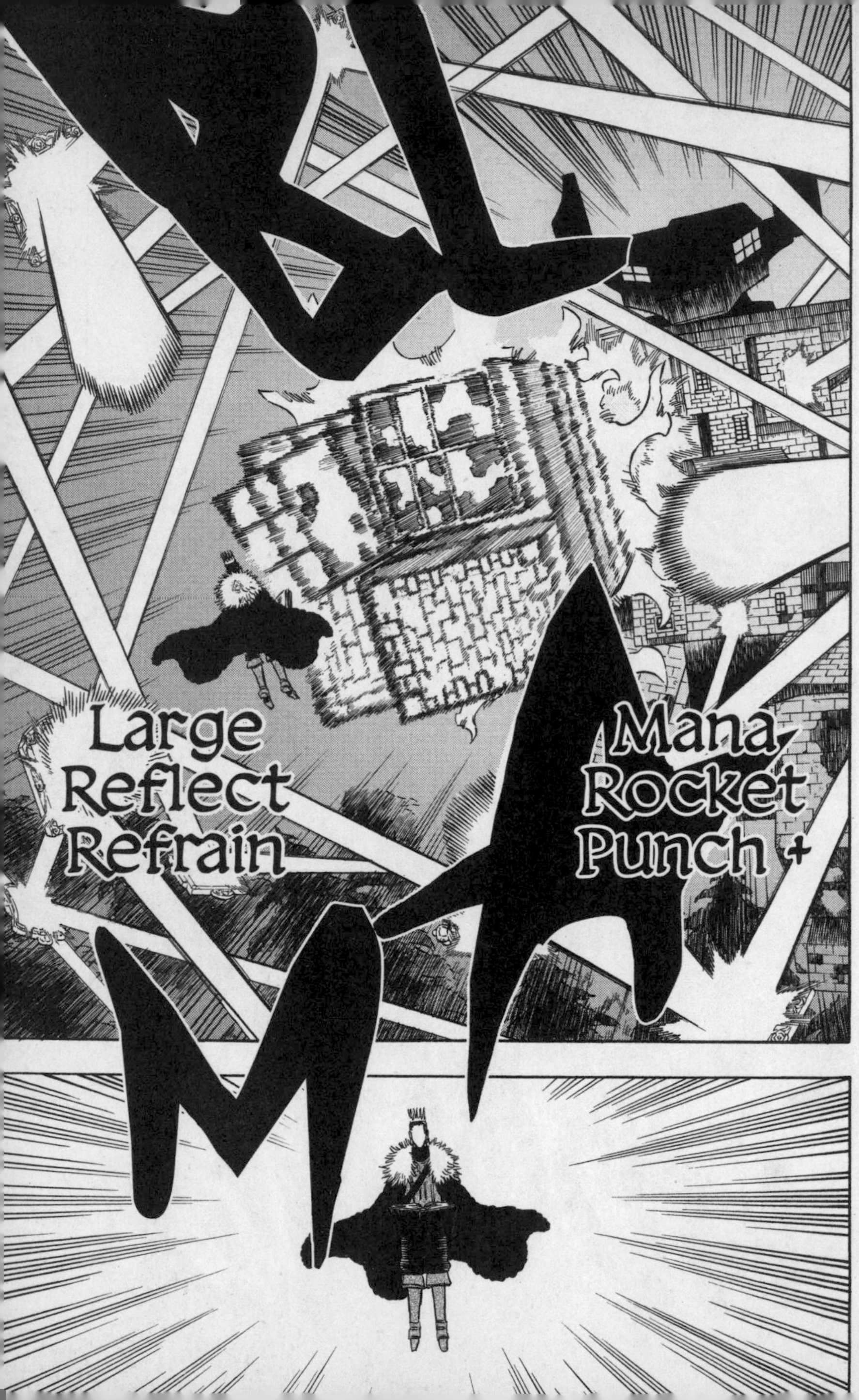
Mana Rocket Punch +
Large Reflect Refrain

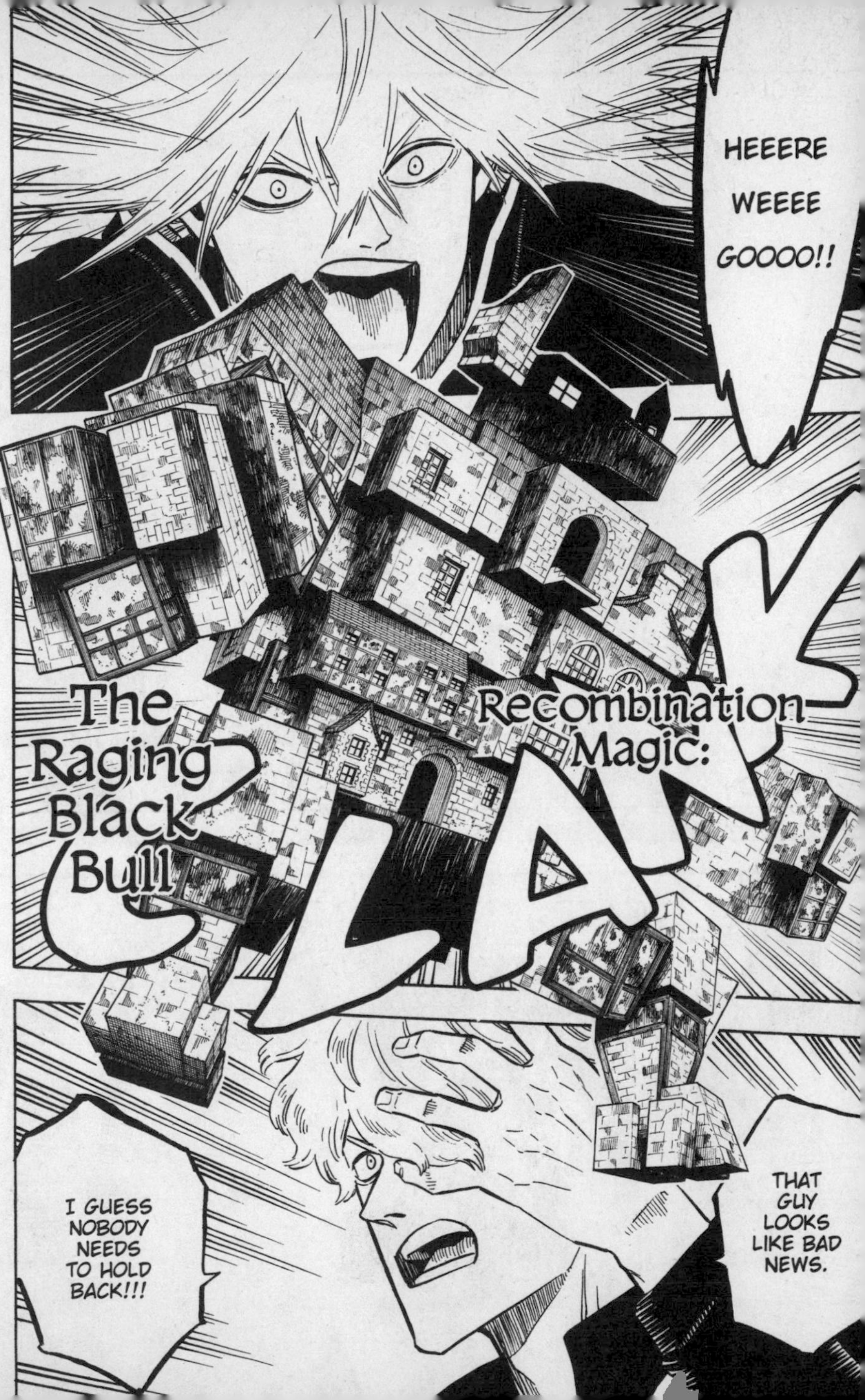
HEEERE WEEEE GOOOO!!
Recombination Magic:
The Raging Black Bull
THAT GUY LOOKS LIKE BAD NEWS.
I GUESS NOBODY NEEDS TO HOLD BACK!!!

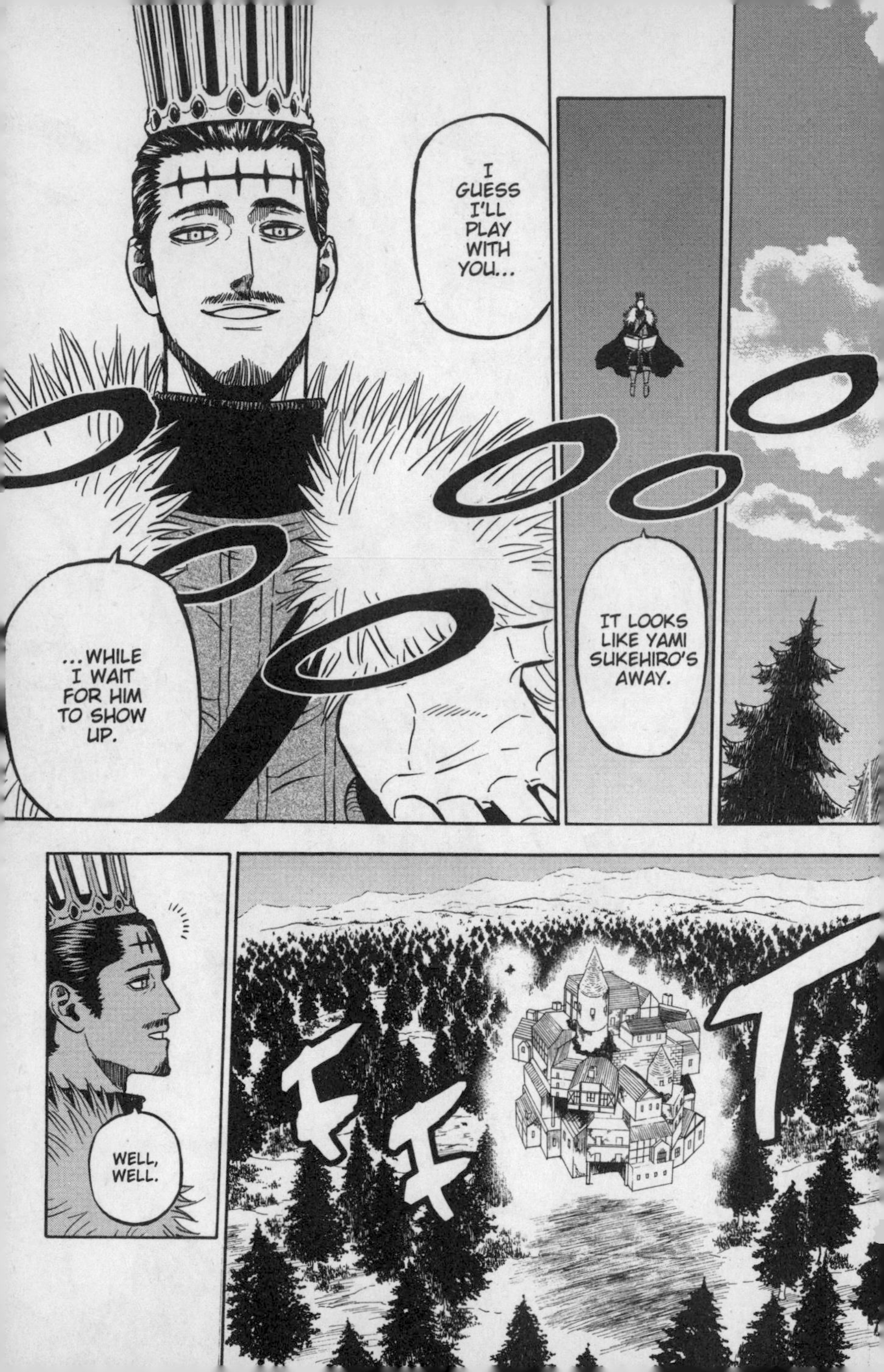
IT LOOKS LIKE YAMI SUKEHIRO'S AWAY.
I GUESS I'LL PLAY WITH YOU...
...WHILE I WAIT FOR HIM TO SHOW UP.
WELL, WELL.

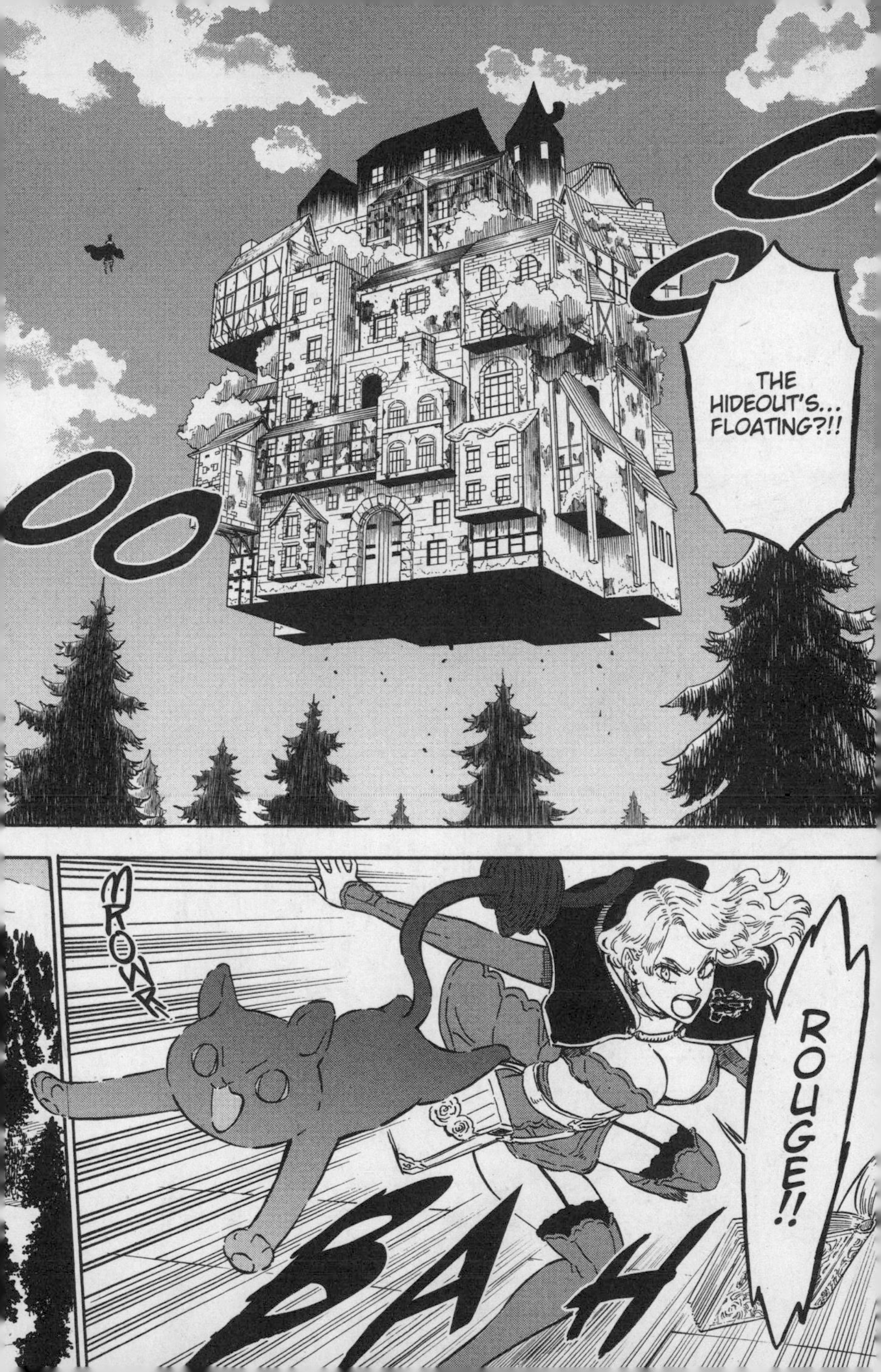
THE HIDEOUT'S... FLOATING?!!
ROUGE!!
MROWR
BAH

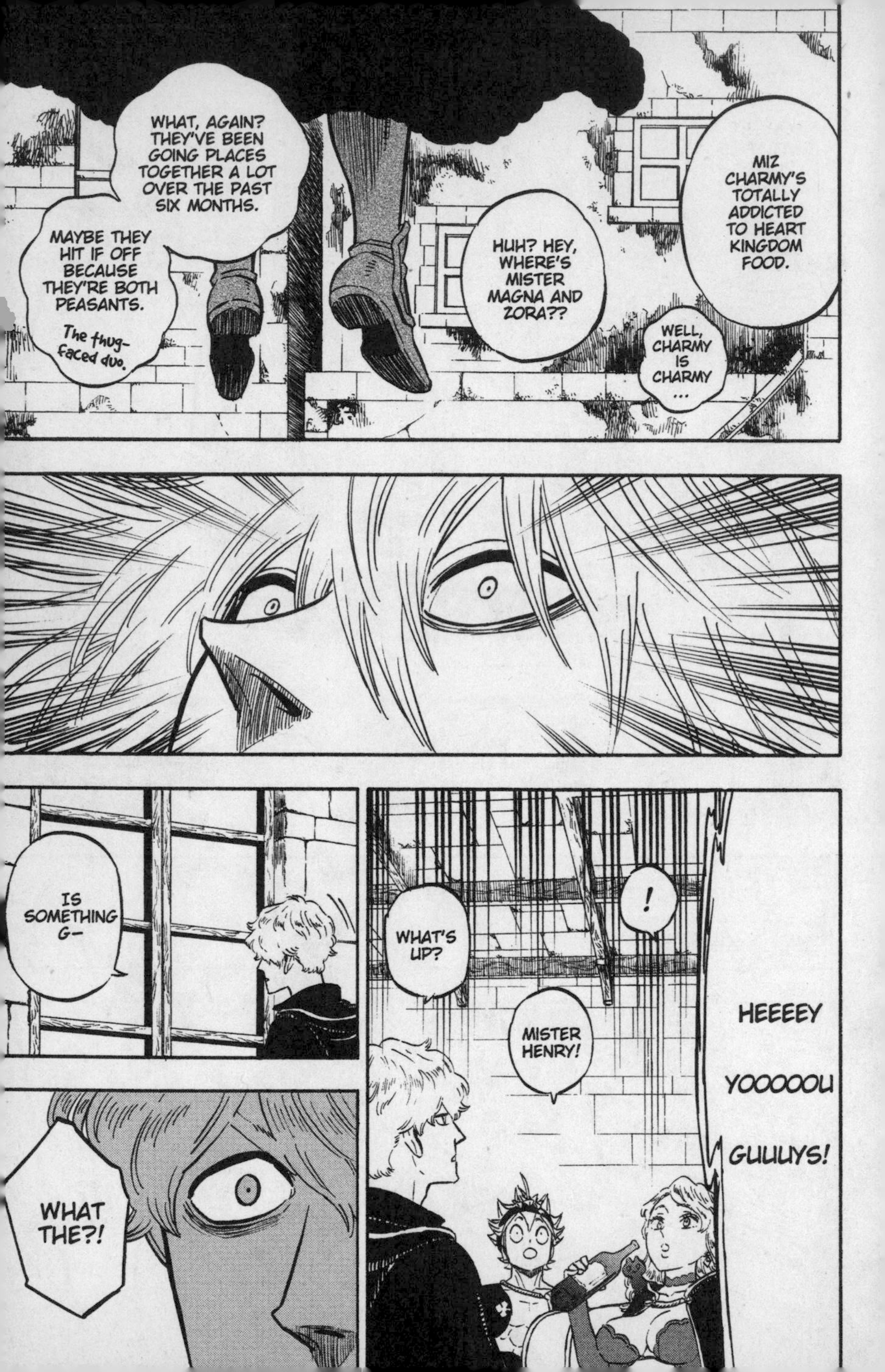
MIZ CHARMY'S TOTALLY ADDICTED TO HEART KINGDOM FOOD.
WELL, CHARMY IS CHARMY...
HUH? HEY, WHERE'S MISTER MAGNA AND ZORA??
WHAT, AGAIN? THEY'VE BEEN GOING PLACES TOGETHER A LOT OVER THE PAST SIX MONTHS.
MAYBE THEY HIT IF OFF BECAUSE THEY'RE BOTH PEASANTS.
The thug-faced duo.
!
HEEEEY YOOOOOU GUUUYS!
WHAT'S UP?
MISTER HENRY!
IS SOMETHING G-
WHAT THE?!

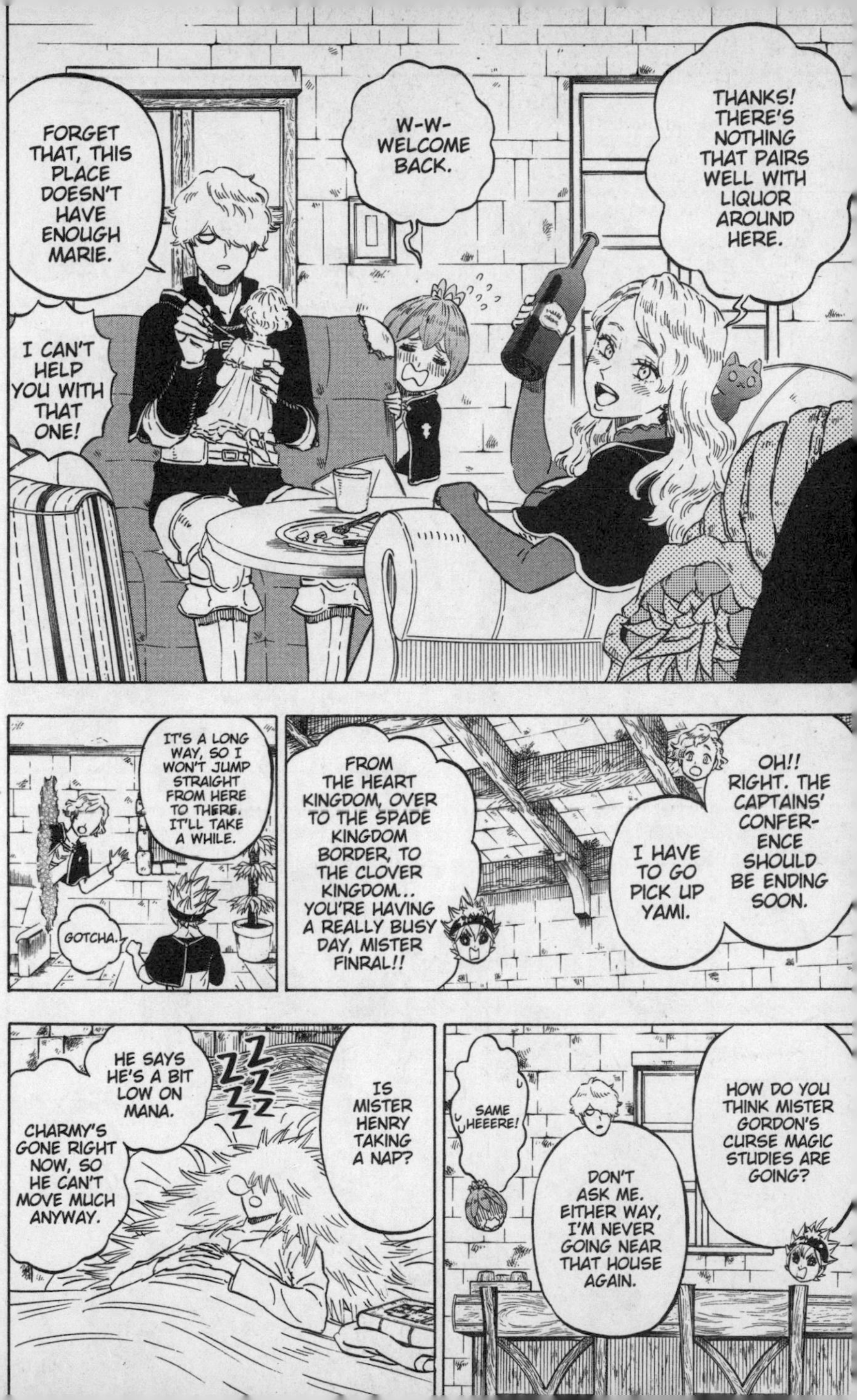
THANKS! THERE'S NOTHING THAT PAIRS WELL WITH LIQUOR AROUND HERE.
W-W-WELCOME BACK.
FORGET THAT, THIS PLACE DOESN'T HAVE ENOUGH MARIE.
I CAN'T HELP YOU WITH THAT ONE!
OH!! RIGHT. THE CAPTAINS' CONFERENCE SHOULD BE ENDING SOON.
I HAVE TO GO PICK UP YAMI.
FROM THE HEART KINGDOM, OVER TO THE SPADE KINGDOM BORDER, TO THE CLOVER KINGDOM... YOU'RE HAVING A REALLY BUSY DAY, MISTER FINRAL!!
IT'S A LONG WAY, SO I WON'T JUMP STRAIGHT FROM HERE TO THERE. IT'LL TAKE A WHILE.
GOTCHA.
HOW DO YOU THINK MISTER GORDON'S CURSE MAGIC STUDIES ARE GOING?
DON'T ASK ME. EITHER WAY, I'M NEVER GOING NEAR THAT HOUSE AGAIN.
SAME HEEEERE!
IS MISTER HENRY TAKING A NAP?
ZZZZZZ
HE SAYS HE'S A BIT LOW ON MANA.
CHARMY'S GONE RIGHT NOW, SO HE CAN'T MOVE MUCH ANYWAY.

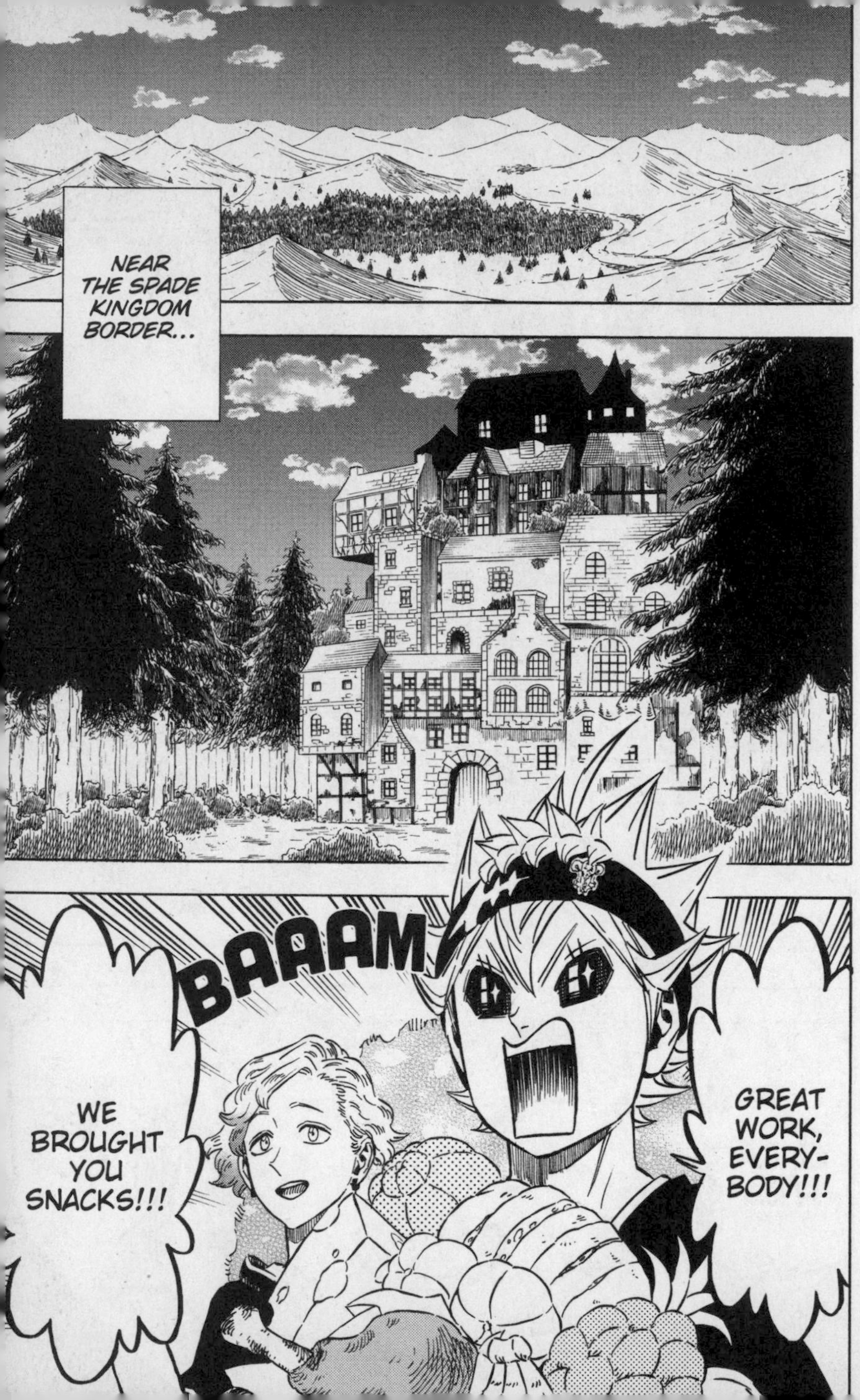
NEAR THE SPADE KINGDOM BORDER...
GREAT WORK, EVERY-BODY!!!
BAAAM
WE BROUGHT YOU SNACKS!!!

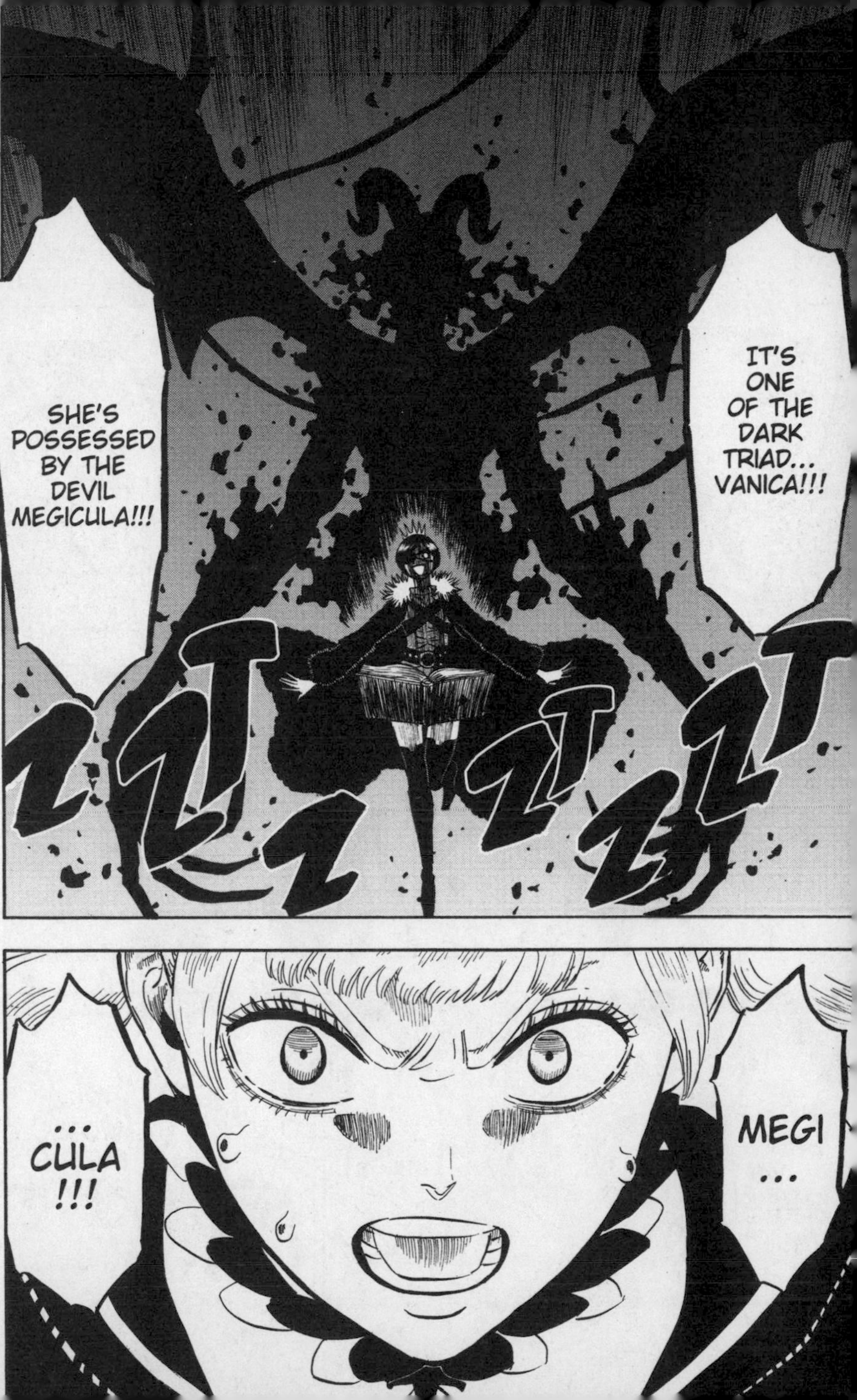
IT'S ONE OF THE DARK TRIAD... VANICA!!!
SHE'S POSSESSED BY THE DEVIL MEGICULA!!!
MEGI...
...CULA!!!

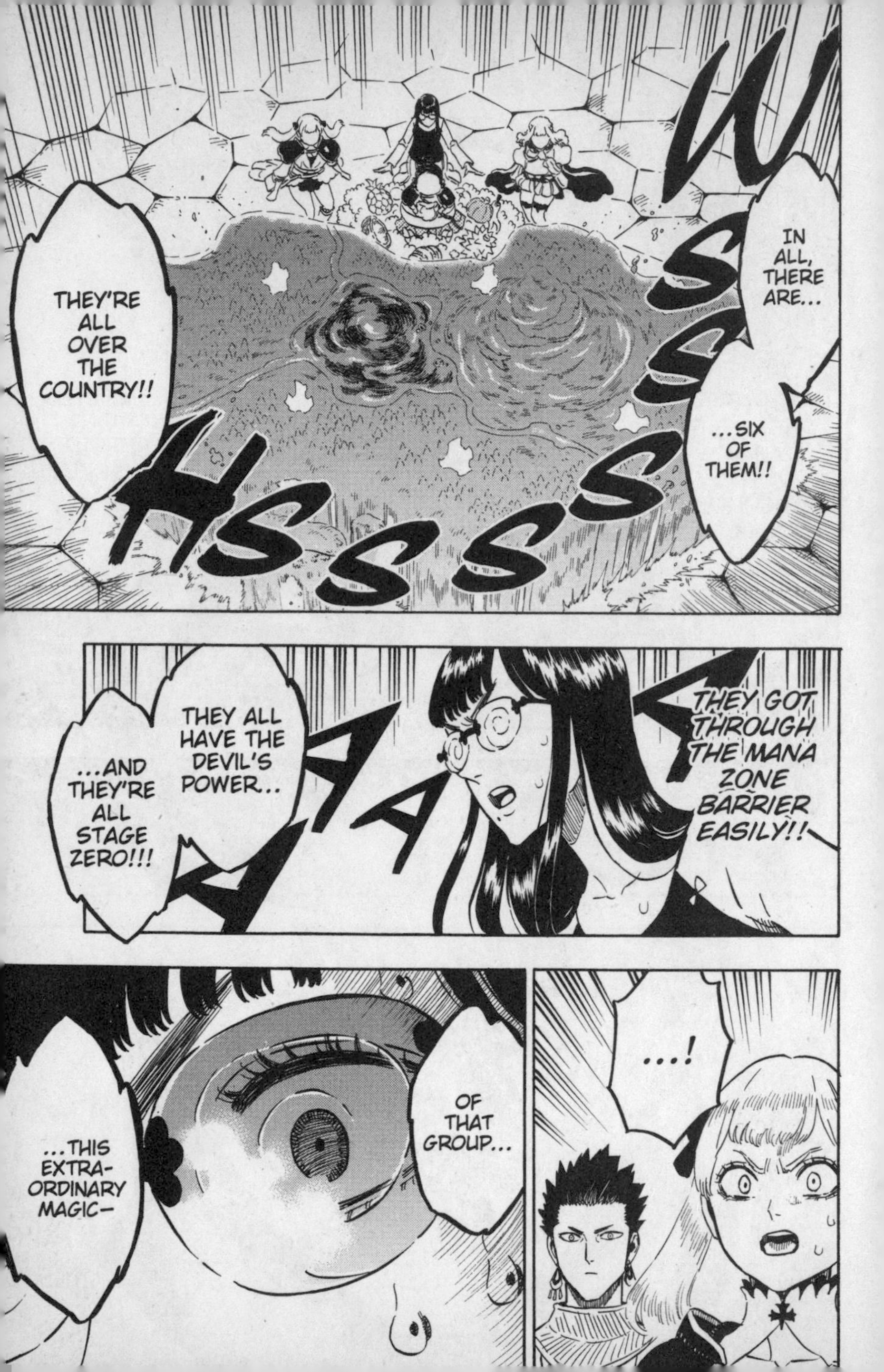
IN ALL, THERE ARE...
...SIX OF THEM!!
THEY'RE ALL OVER THE COUNTRY!!
HSSSS
THEY GOT THROUGH THE MANA ZONE BARRIER EASILY!!
THEY ALL HAVE THE DEVIL'S POWER...
...AND THEY'RE ALL STAGE ZERO!!!
...!
OF THAT GROUP...
...THIS EXTRA-ORDINARY MAGIC—

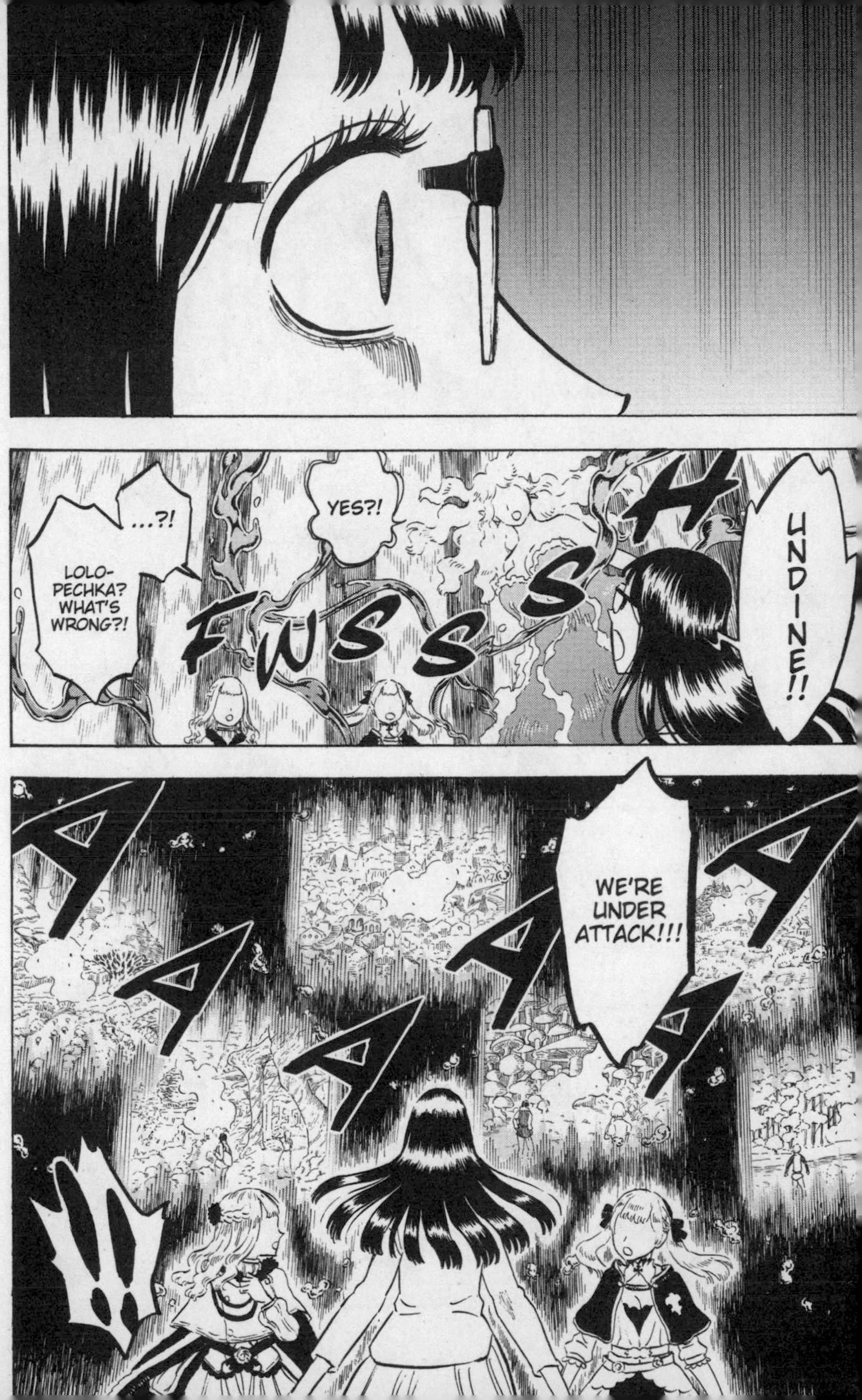
UNDINE!!
FWSSSH
YES?!
...?!
LOLO-PECHKA? WHAT'S WRONG?!
WE'RE UNDER ATTACK!!!
AAAAAAA
!!

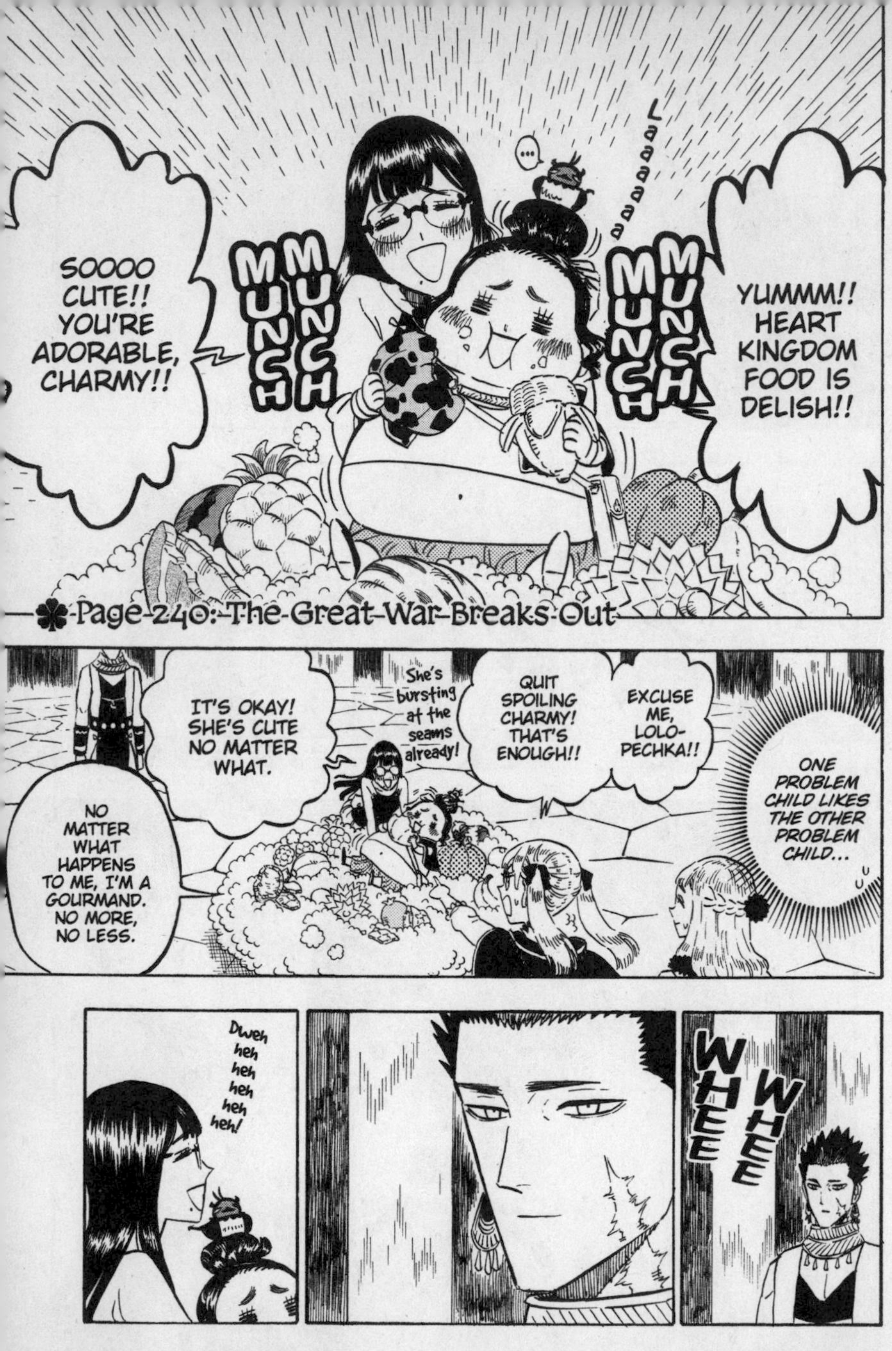
YUMMMM!! HEART KINGDOM FOOD IS DELISH!!
MUNCH MUNCH
Laaaaaaa
...
MUNCH MUNCH
SOOOO CUTE!! YOU'RE ADORABLE, CHARMY!!
Page 240: The Great War Breaks Out
ONE PROBLEM CHILD LIKES THE OTHER PROBLEM CHILD...
EXCUSE ME, LOLOPECHKA!!
QUIT SPOILING CHARMY! THAT'S ENOUGH!!
She's bursting at the seams already!
IT'S OKAY! SHE'S CUTE NO MATTER WHAT.
NO MATTER WHAT HAPPENS TO ME, I'M A GOURMAND. NO MORE, NO LESS.
WHEE WHEE
Dweh heh heh heh heh heh!

CONTENTS

BLACK 🍀 CLOVER

25

Grey

 Member of:
The Black Bulls
Magic: Transformation

She has a shy personality, and always acts timid. She can transform to look like whoever she's with.

Luck Voltia

 Member of:
The Black Bulls
Magic: Lightning

A battle maniac. Once he starts fighting, he gets totally absorbed in it. Smiles constantly.

Henry Legolant

 Member of:
The Black Bulls
Magic: Structure

His strange constitution absorbs magic from the people around him. He uses the vast amount of accumulated magic to pilot the hideout.

Vanessa Enoteca

 Member of:
The Black Bulls
Magic: Thread

She has an unparalleled love of liquor, but it sometimes gets the better of her. During battle, she uses her magic to manipulate fate, changing the future.

Gaja

Magic: Lightning

Lolopechka's close adviser. He has Zero Stage magic and is one of the Heart Kingdom's spirit guardians.

Lolopechka

Magic: Water

The princess of the Heart Kingdom. She's fundamentally klutzy and clueless. She's been cursed by the devil Megicula.

STORY

In a world where magic is everything, Asta and Yuno are both found abandoned on the same day at a church in the remote village of Hage. Both dream of becoming the Wizard King, the highest of all mages, and they spend their days working toward that dream.

The year they turn 15, both receive grimoires, magic books that amplify their bearer's magic. They take the entrance exam for the Magic Knights, nine groups of mages under the direct control of the Wizard King. Yuno, whose magic is strong, joins the Golden Dawn, an elite group, while Asta, who has no magic at all, joins the Black Bulls, a group of misfits. With this, the two finally take their first step toward becoming the Wizard King…

After half a year of training, Asta and the others have built up the power to resist the Spade Kingdom. Meanwhile, Yuno encounters someone who tells him he's a prince of the Spade Kingdom! But Zenon of the Dark Triad suddenly raids the Golden Dawn headquarters and devastates the brigade with his overwhelming power!

Yuno

Member of:
The Golden Dawn Magic: Wind

Asta's best friend, and a good rival who's also been working to become the Wizard King. He controls Sylph, the spirit of wind.

Asta

 Member of: The Black Bulls
Magic: None (Anti-Magic)

He has no magic, but he's working to become the Wizard King through sheer guts and his well-trained body. He fights with anti-magic swords.

Finral Roulacase

 Member of:
The Black Bulls
Magic: Spatial

A playboy who immediately chats up any woman he sees. He can't attack, but he has high-level abilities.

Yami Sukehiro

 Member of:
The Black Bulls
Magic: Dark

A captain who looks fierce, but is very popular with his brigade, which has a deep-rooted confidence in him. Heavy smoker.

Gauche Adlai

Member of:
The Black Bulls
Magic: Mirror

A former convict with a blind, pathological love for his little sister. He has a magic item in his left eye socket.

Noelle Silva

Member of:
The Black Bulls
Magic: Water

A royal. She feels inferior to her brilliant siblings. Her latent abilities are an unknown quantity.

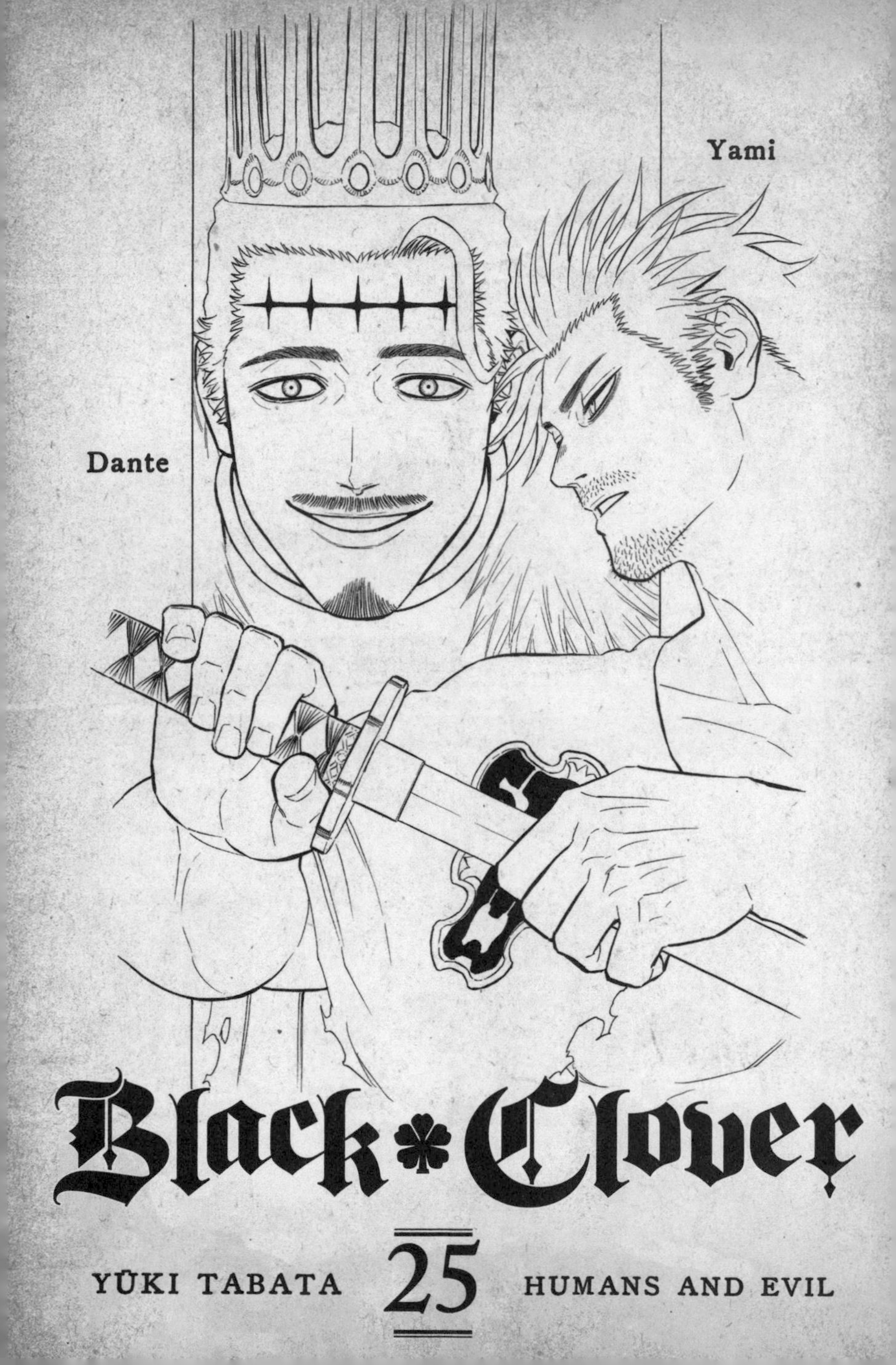
Yami
Dante

Black Clover

25

YŪKI TABATA

HUMANS AND EVIL

BLACK CLOVER
VOLUME 25
SHONEN JUMP Manga Edition

Story and Art by YŪKI TABATA

Translation ✹ TAYLOR ENGEL,
HC LANGUAGE SOLUTIONS, INC.

Touch-Up Art & Lettering ✹ ANNALIESE CHRISTMAN

Design ✹ KAM LI

Editor ✹ ALEXIS KIRSCH

BLACK CLOVER © 2015 by Yuki Tabata
All rights reserved.
First published in Japan in 2015 by SHUEISHA Inc., Tokyo.
English translation rights arranged by SHUEISHA Inc.

Printed in Canada

Published by VIZ Media, LLC
P.O. Box 77010
San Francisco, CA 94107

10 9 8 7 6 5 4 3 2 1
First printing, May 2021

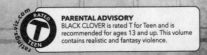

viz.com

COVID-19 has turned the world on its ear... My workplace has gone mostly remote as well, and many things are a lot harder. Being holed up in the house is normal for me, though, so not much has changed. And I think I'm actually pretty good with this type of stress. I'll do my very best, so all my readers can have as much fun as possible!!!

—*Yūki Tabata, 2020*

YŪKI TABATA was born in Fukuoka Prefecture and got his big break in the 2011 Shonen Jump Golden Future Cup with his winning entry, *Hungry Joker*. He started the magical fantasy series *Black Clover* in 2015.